# Contexts of Behavior

# Contexts of Behavior

## ANTHROPOLOGICAL DIMENSIONS

Robert J. Maxwell

## Nelson-Hall nh Chicago

Library of Congress Cataloging in Publication Data

Maxwell, Robert J.
   Contexts of behavior.

   Includes bibliographical references and index.
   1. Environmental psychology.   2. Interpersonal relations.   I. Title.
BF353.M38   1983        304.2       82-22428
ISBN 0-88229-715-5

Manufactured in the United States of America

10  9  8  7  6  5  4  3  2  1

The paper in this book is pH neutral (acid-free).

# Contents

# Prologue

At every moment of our lives we are experiencing and adapting to our environment, though we are usually unaware of doing so. The material that follows is designed to make explicit the interaction between ourselves and the things around us.

The first chapter introduces the concept of ecosystems, the structural focus of the book. Three major types of ecosystems are discussed: natural, interpersonal, and built. The first type of ecosystem is more or less "given," while the second and third are cultural constructs. The foundations of this view of the environment lie chiefly in ethology and the study of animal behavior in laboratories. I will review some of the more important works in this field and discuss the concepts emerging from them and the implications of those concepts for human welfare. The first chapter also deals with human physical adaptation to the natural ecosystem and examines the role of culture as an intervening variable in this process.

Chapter II simply sketches in the historical background of the rest of the book, presenting the most important traditional theories concerning our behavior within the three types of ecosystems. Its purpose is partly to establish the theoretical roots of our understanding of interactions between the environment and behavior, and partly to contrast these traditional notions with current views presented later in the book.

The third chapter deals with the first ecosystem mentioned: the natural. The environmental characteristics of this system are described, and a typology is presented, followed by a discussion of the principal means by which we adapt behaviorally to the natural environment. The chapter covers such traditional processes as wearing clothes, building shelters, and getting food, together with less obvious responses to the environment, such as genital mutilation. The final section examines natural disasters and our patterned reactions to them. I find this subject of particular interest because disasters occur irregularly, and our responses to them, though distinctly patterned, are largely latent. Disasters also represent extreme stressors of the natural environment and are an inexplicably neglected topic in anthropology.

The fourth and final chapter deals with the two constructed environments: the interpersonal and the built. They are constructed in the sense that they result from cultural conventions that may vary diachronically and pan-globally. The first part of the chapter describes certain characteristics of the interpersonal environment such as proxemic zones of distance and behavioral processes connected with the regulation of territoriality in people. The second section describes the mechanisms of interaction between the built environment and the people who use it.

The book thus moves from a description of the ethological, physiological, and historical backgrounds of the study of ecosystemic behavior to a delineation of the natural environment, interpersonal environment, and built environment, and our manipulations of and adaptations to each.

Analyzing behavior within these three kinds of environments is complicated, not only because the influence of our surroundings is all-pervasive, but because feedback mechanisms are involved: we live in an environment, we adapt to it, the adaptation changes it, and the change influences the way we behave. Further, the material to be reviewed is drawn from a multitude of disciplines and is of varying levels of complexity. I have tried to keep this discussion as simple as is consistent with its comprehension, relegating all necessary statistics, for instance, to footnotes, and providing a sufficient number of examples to clarify each of the points made. At the same time I have tried to avoid the disease of "amongitis" which so frequently afflicts cultural anthropologists (the Copper Eskimo do it this way, the Nama Hottentot do it that way, and so forth); so the studies that provide the examples are reviewed in some detail.

I would like to say that I have wielded no ideological axe, my sole touchstone being the fundamentals of the scientific method—axe enough, perhaps. I have also tried to keep the reader alert and to incidentally cover some usually disregarded topics by juxtaposing in an unlikely way discussions of related and sometimes exotic topics. Thus, for example, in chapter 3, under the general heading of Nourishment, the text moves from a treatment of subsistence patterns to cuisines, cannibalism, and the eating of dirt. Do not, therefore, look for unarguable continuity. This is not a book in which the prose marches with stupendous dullness from one predictable discussion to the next.

# Acknowledgments

I am grateful to Drs. Philip Silverman, Dean and Juliet MacCannell, Mona Takush, John Cronin, Richard Strand, and Pertti and Gretel Pelto for assistance in preparing this book. Much of whatever value is reflected in it is the result of my exposure to the analytical procedures of Professors John M. Roberts and Charles F. Hockett at Cornell several epochs ago. Finally, I am thoroughly indebted to my wife, Dr. Eleanor Krassen Maxwell, who suggested this report in the first place and who, quite literally, made it possible. It is dedicated to her.

Figures 5, 6, and 7 are reproduced by permission of the American Anthropological Association from the *American Anthropologist* 67 (1965): 186–214. Figures 8 through 11 are reproduced by permission of the American Anthropoligical Association from the *American Anthropologist* 65 (1963): 1003–26.

# CHAPTER ONE

# Ecosystems

An ecosystem may be thought of as a community of living things, both animals and plants, together with their shared physical environment. In this chapter I would like to deal first with certain well-recognized properties of ecosystems, and then describe briefly three types of ecosystems, defined largely in terms of their characteristic environments, which will receive detailed treatment later. Here I will also deal with adaptation to various sorts of environments, particularly physical adaptation both in infrahuman animals and in human beings.

## Properties of Ecosystems

Ecological biologists using arguments derived from field studies, laboratory experiments, and mathematical models concern themselves principally with three orders of dependency relationships.

The first is the dependence of organic forms upon other similar ones, or, more briefly, intraspecific relationships. Some of the most provocative work under this heading has been done on the effects of crowding under controlled conditions.

A second kind of relationship is that involving the dependence of several kinds of organisms upon at least some of the others in the interspecies community. Technically, the name for this set of relationships is biocoenosis. An example of biocoenosis is the relationship between the koala bear and the eucalyptus tree in certain parts of Australia, in which the former is dependent almost exclusively upon the latter for sustenance.

The third kind of relationship involves the dependence, direct or indirect, of all organisms on the inanimate environment, together with the reciprocal influence upon the environment of the organisms that live in it. This type of dependence is of course the most inclusive, and its description serves to introduce the concept of ecosystem.

Ecological relationships do not exist in a vacuum but take place in physical and chemical settings—sets of nonliving, or abiotic, environmental substances. These abiotic substances include basic inorganic elements, compounds such as water and carbon dioxide, and an array of organic compounds, the by-products of organismic activity or decay.

The abiotic environment also includes such features as moisture, winds, ocean currents, and solar radiation, which provides light and heat.

It is against this abiotic backdrop that the biotic compounds—plants, animals, and microorganisms—interact in an energy dependent way. The abiotic environment and the biotic assembly together form an ecological system, or ecosystem. Around this concept of the ecosystem, students of biological ecology have organized their data-collecting and interpretive efforts.

Ecosystems vary immensely in their dimensions. They may be as small as a culture of microorganisms, merely a dot to the unaided eye, or as large as the earth. They can be as terrestrial as deserts or as aquatic as streams. They can be constructed artificially in the laboratory or found naturally in the field. Despite all of these variations and despite the fact that each ecosystem is unique, certain general structural and functional attributes can be recognized in every one.

One universal feature of ecosystems is that they are all energy oriented. Radiant energy in the form of sunlight is the ultimate source of energy for any ecosystem. Sunlight is used in the photosynthetic process through which available carbon dioxide is changed into energy rich carbon compounds. The organisms that do these jobs in the ecosystem are termed producers, and they are typically chlorophyll-bearing plants—algae in ponds, grass in fields, trees in forests. Certain bacteria are also considered producers, but since they operate with compounds already formed through photosynthesis, they are not nearly as important as the chlorophyll-bearing plants. It is possible to think of the earth as one huge ecosystem partly covered with producers busily converting sunlight into the stored energy of carbon compounds.

The energy converted by photosynthesis in a producer is changed into other molecules that serve the nutritional needs of the producer itself. That is, the plant not only converts radiant energy into chemical energy, but it consumes some of the molecules in order to grow and maintain itself. Producers therefore are generally spoken of as being *autotrophic* (Greek: "self-feeding"). In the same way, organisms whose nutritional needs are met by feeding on other organisms are referred to as heterotrophic.

Some heterotrophs acquire their nutrition directly from plants. These primary consumers are generally herbivores such as sheep, cattle, goats, caterpillars, and so forth. Other heterotrophs get their nutrition indirectly from plants because they feed on primary consumers. These are the secondary consumers such as cats, vampire bats, and seals. And some ecosystems contain tertiary consumers; carnivores that feed on other carnivores, as polar bears eat seals. Animals, whatever their position in the chain, convert chemical energy into mechanical and heat forms in the course of metabolism. Mechanical energy is expressed when animals move.

A simple example of this autotroph-heterotroph relationship is provided by the Indians of the American Great Plains more than a century ago, whose existence was organized largely around the migration of the buffalo herds. The energy captured by the photosynthesizing prairie grass served as the food base for the buffalo, and the buffalo in turn for the Indian. In this chain, the prairie grass is the producer, an autotroph, and the buffalo and the Indian are heterotrophs: the buffalo a primary consumer or herbivore, the Indian a secondary consumer or carnivore. Other simple chains can be found among the Lapps in northern Europe, with their primary dependence on reindeer; the Cree of central Canada, who consume the foraging caribou; and the Ona of Tierra del Fuego, hunters of the guanaco.

In the relationships just described, the flow of energy through the ecosystem moves in only one direction and is noncyclic. In other words, animals may eat plants, but plants do not eat animals (except for unusual cases like the Venus's-flytrap and the pitcher plant). The key to understanding the noncyclic, unidirectional flow of energy is found in the energy losses that occur at each point of transfer along the chain. Part of the energy taken in by autotrophs is lost in the process of metabolism; thus a smaller portion of the original energy is available to the herbivore that eats plants. As a herbivore moves, it uses up much of the energy acquired from the plant. The carnivore that eats the herbivore receives even less of the energy that originally came from the sun.

The amount of energy transferred from one trophic level to the next is called the gross ecological efficiency of the food chain. Studies have shown that gross ecological efficiency in typical food chains is something on the order of 10 percent (Slobodkin, 1961), though the range of any given ecosystem may vary rather widely, with little consistency from one level to the next.

In any case, each time energy is transferred from one trophic level to another, some 90 percent of it is lost in the process. If there are several links in the chain, this means an enormous loss of energy. After a clump of grass worth 100 calories is ingested by a herbivore, its value has dropped to 10 calories. This leaves one calorie for the carnivore who eats the herbivore. This unidirectional flow of energy is one of the most important considerations in the study of ecosystems.

However, another kind of heterotroph is usually found in ecosystems. These are chiefly bacteria and fungi, referred to as decomposers. They do not consume food in the manner of a herbivore or a carnivore, but produce enzymes that they secrete into dead plant and animal matter. The decaying matter breaks down into simpler elements, some of these absorbed by the decomposers. But in the process of supplying their own metabolic needs, the decomposers do something essential for the survival of the ecosystem. In the course of breaking down protoplasm, they release some basic elements into the environment and thereby make these elements available for reuse by the producers.

Two processes have been going on in the food chain. One is the movement of energy, and the other is the flow of nutrient materials. The first of these is one-directional and noncyclic, but the flow of nutrients is cyclic and can be described in other terms.

A green plant converts radiant energy into chemical energy through photosynthesis, but at the same time it incorporates into its protoplasm many elements and compounds without which our life would be impossible—including carbon dioxide, water, nitrogen, phosphorus, sulfur, magnesium, and iron. As the plant is consumed by a herbivore, not only is chemical energy transferred but all of these materials as well. There is a comparable transfer of chemical energy and matter from herbivore to carnivore and so on, down to the decomposers. Although the energy is diminished at each step, the material component is not (a principle expressed in the law of the conservation of matter), even though some of it is lost to the ecosystem through respiration. Indeed, some sorts of matter may become concentrated at certain steps of the chain. One need only break open a rotten egg to discover how much sulfur is stored away in it. Figure 1 illustrates the idea that the flow of energy is noncyclic, while the flow of nutrient matter is not.

The two major flows of energy and matter through ecosystems are significant concerns in the contemporary scene, because we do not know enough about the details of specific ecosystems to predict what will happen to them as they are subject to more and more human modification. For example, radioactive materials and pesticides are frequently caught up in human-oriented food chains as a result of natural cycling processes, sometimes in unexpected ways and with unexpected results, as indicated by

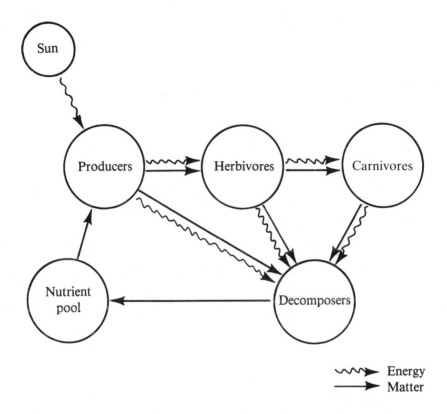

FIG. 1. MOVEMENT OF ENERGY AND MATTER IN AN ECOSYSTEM.

the contamination of swordfish with mercury and mother's milk with radioactive strontium.

In some ways, the contamination of nonhuman-oriented food chains has equally unfortunate consequences. The peregrine falcon, or duck hawk (*Falco peregrinus*) was abundant twenty years ago, found all over North America from its summer breeding grounds in Alaska to its winter range in the American Southeast. Its nests had been found on the ledges of skyscrapers in New York City. The peregrine falcon is strong, tough, slick and fast. (Speeds of up to 200 miles per hour during a dive on its prey have been attributed to it.) It is considered by many birds-of-prey fanciers to be the most independent, admirable, and attractive bird of prey found anywhere, and for centuries it was the bird most favored by falconers in Europe and elsewhere. Today, peregrine falcons have been reduced to a population of perhaps several hundred. They have not been systematically hunted by man or other animals. Their near extinction is a consequence of a more subtle but equally simple process. Farmers used DDT on their crops to keep the insect population down. The DDT ran off into streams where it was absorbed into plants. The plants were eaten by small animals, which were eaten by fish, which were eaten by ducks, and these ducks were in turn eaten by peregrine falcons. Thus the DDT was ingested by the falcon, and scientists have discovered that some of the compounds in DDT cause falcons to lay eggs with shells so thin that they break before they hatch. Twenty years ago, when falcon observers noted the increasing number of broken, unhatched eggs in the nests, they assumed that raccoons had been at work. They did not realize that technology could not change one element in a dynamic system without changing others, some of them inadvertently.

Ecological biologists study energy flows in ecosystems and the circulation of nutrients, minerals, and other substances. The circulation of these materials is usually given a specific name. The hydrologic cycle, for example, describes the circulation of water from the atmosphere to the earth, through plants and animals, back into the earth, into rivers, and finally into the sea and back into the atmosphere. Biologists like to break these cycles down into precise subdivisions, and in the process of studying the circulation of water within a particular ecosystem, they might specify how much of the water is returned through evaporation at each part of the cycle. The quantification of these processes in the field is difficult and subject to individual variations. Apart from the problem of actually measuring the water lost in a red maple through leaf fall and respiration, how does one find a "typical" red maple?

Ecological biologists are also interested in the structure and dynamics of ecological communities. How many herbivores do you need in a population in order to support one family of carnivores who prey on them? An early study showed that in California it takes about 360 deer to support one mountain lion in a way that will keep the population of both deer and mountain lions steady (Leopold, 1939: 234). Biologists also recognize that no ecosystem exists in isolation; they are not self-sufficient systems, nor can they be separated from other ecosystems. Every pond is surrounded by a swamp or field from which it extracts nutrients. Biologists recognize that, while some of these relationships can best be measured under controlled laboratory conditions, the ultimate test of laboratory-derived principles is in nature.

The concept of ecosystem emphasizes material interdependencies among the group of organisms that form a community (whether these dependencies are considered intraspecifically or interspecifically) and the relevant characteristics of the settings in which these organisms are found. The major task of the ecologist is studying the internal dynamics of these systems — insofar as possible, specifying exactly the material and behavioral trans-actions — and the ways in which these systems evolve. In other words, much of ecology is focused on the dynamics of ecosystems, rather than their static description. As one investigator has written: "When an ecologist enters a field or meadow, he sees not what is there but what is happening there."

What is happening there, among other things, is a patterned interchange of energy among the various parts of the system. Living things take in mat-ter as food from their surroundings and discharge matter back into these surroundings as waste products. They also use energy as these materials pass through the food chain.

Just as in internal physiology, system equilibrium (homeostasis) is one of the central organizing forces in ecology. Like other complex systems, all ecosystems strive towards a stable state (Buckley, 1968; Cannon, 1939), a condition of equilibrium. Clifford Geertz gives an example. A flock of sheep in a pasture appear to destroy the grass by chopping it off with their teeth and eating it. However, the sheep are also fertilizing the pasture with their manure. If the sheep were removed, the pasture would be "removed" too, given such other conditions as sufficient rain. Trees would seed and begin to grow, finally killing off the grass in the pasture, and woods would replace the field. The sheep and the pasture form an integrated, homeo-static system, one that is in a state of constant but balanced change. This is a simplified example, of course, though not the simplest conceivable (Geertz, 1963: 4).

People are, in principle, merely another element in the ecosystem, but at times human interference can become a distinctive feature of the system. Geertz draws another example from Clarke:

> Ranchers, . . . disturbed by losses of young sheep to coyotes, slaughtered, through collective effort, nearly all the coyotes in the immediate area. Following the removal of coyotes, the rabbits, field mice, and other small rodents, upon whom the coyotes had previously preyed, multiplied rapidly and made serious inroads on the grass of the pastures. When this was rea-lized, the sheep men ceased to kill coyotes and instituted an elaborate pro-gram for the poisoning of rodents. The coyotes filtered in from the surround-ing areas, but finding their natural rodent food now scarce, [were] forced to turn with even greater intensity to the young sheep as their only available source of food. [Clarke, 1954; cited in Geertz, 1963:4]

The ecological approach as developed in biology can be applied directly to the study of man, though not all of the ways in which this has been done are still considered respectable, as we shall see.

## Types of Ecosystems

Environments set the stage for behavior by providing a context that is antecedent to the behavior and exerts an influence on it. In this book I intend to deal at some length with three rather distinct types of ecosystems characterized by different environments. The first will be ecosystems defined by their naturally occurring backgrounds. Here I will discuss climate, climatic types, geophysical hazards, and the like, as arrays of stimuli that bring about various responses. The second type of ecosystems, characterized principally by artifacts, may be called the man-made or built environment. I will investigate the impact on human activities of such artifacts as buildings. Finally, I will treat ecosystems in which the chief feature of the environment consists of other people. Here I will make some observations concerning crowding, the management of interpersonal space, and so on.

In actuality, of course, all of us experience these three sorts of ecosystems as a single context for our thoughts and behavior, with our attention being directed at various times primarily to one or another of the three. Regardless of shifts in our attention, however, the three are dynamically bound up with one another. At this point, perhaps an example of the impact of a remote event will illustrate the dynamic nature of ecosystems.

If a pond, stream, or rose garden can be considered an ecosystem, so can the planet earth. With the easy transfer of people, goods, energy, and information, a change in the environment in one part of the world is likely to affect what happens elsewhere, in however small a measure.

Sometimes the measure is not so small. Krakatoa is the name of an island off the coast of Java. In 1883 it was an active volcano. Over a period of some weeks, it showed increasing activity. Finally one side of the volcanic mountain caved in, and seawater rushed into the opening. When water met molten lava, the resulting explosion produced probably the loudest sound that has been made on earth during man's history. People woke up in the middle of the night in central Australia, more than 1,000 miles away. The sound of the explosion could be heard more than 3,000 miles from the site of its origin. The sound was so loud, in other words, that if Krakatoa had been somewhere in the middle of Colorado, it could have been heard from Alaska to Florida.

The eruption also caused a tidal wave—or *tsunami* as professionals like to call them—that swamped islands around Java and on the Australian coast and finally rocked ships in South Africa, across the Indian Ocean. There was also a discernible rise in the water level of the English Channel.

Sound is a succession of waves of pressure in the air. Even when a sound is too far away to be heard, the change in air pressure may still be detected by instruments designed to measure changes in air pressure associated with the weather. In the case of Krakatoa, about fourteen hours after the eruption, violent movements were seen in instruments in England. The pressure waves had traveled northwestward, away from Krakatoa, across India and Europe. Some four hours later, the instruments moved again in England. These were the waves that had traveled the long way around the world, across the Pacific and the Americas and then the Atlantic. Hours later, the instruments moved again as the waves went around the world a second time. The last detectable jiggle showed up nine days after the explosion.

The most instructive effect of the explosion was on atmospheric stability, which directly affects the weather of the world. The explosion replaced an island containing fourteen cubic miles of rock with a flat plane on the ocean floor beneath about a thousand feet of water. The shattered rock, together with a cubic mile or so of superheated steam, was ejected into the atmosphere at a speed about three times that of sound. If anyone doubts that this was a great deal of matter, it has been estimated that the entire human population of the earth at that time could have been packed into the space.

Much of the rock became fine volcanic dust, which takes a long time to be cycled out of the atmosphere. The residue circled the planet, giving the moon a green tint and turning the sunsets blue, green, or gray for most of the following year. Another effect was a worldwide drop in temperature, since the sky was dark enough to prevent the usual amount of sunlight from getting through. At least six other recent volcanic events have caused a drop in temperature, and one of them, occurring in 1816, lowered the temperature around the world so much that it produced what was called "the year without a summer."

Such large-scale catastrophes illustrate the integral nature of the environment around us, an environment we often take for granted. It is worth looking in more detail at some of the characteristics of our planet and its environments, taking into account both its commonplace and its unusual properties. To understand people, we need to have some idea of the media within which they operate.

*Mechanisms of Adaptation to Environments*

Each of the major types of ecosystems — natural, man-made, and interpersonal — impose certain demands on the organisms that live in them, and these demands may be met in two major ways. The organisms may adapt by changing behaviorally. This mechanism may have merely short-term

effects (e.g., closing the window) or long-term ones (e.g., culturally patterned behavior such as manufacturing and wearing clothing). The second
major mechanism of adaptation is physical, consisting of changes in the
morphology and internal milieu of the body, largely by means of natural
selection.

At this point it may be helpful to examine a part of the body that links
both mechanisms of adaptation in a complex way: the human hand.

The upright posture adopted by human beings a few million years ago
freed their hands from locomotive tasks and made them available for more
sophisticated activities. The modern human hand has several features that
make it, in a manner of speaking, a most useful built-in tool. Among these
is a fully opposable thumb—that is, a thumb that can be brought around
the palm while, at the same time, rotating on its axis: this is the sort of
thing we do, for example, when forming a circle with thumb and fore-
finger to indicate, "All is well." Indeed, the importance for human adaptation of the palm and its fingers, particularly the thumb, is reflected in the
disproportionate amount of area given over to its control in the motor cortex, the portion of the brain that directs movement. Judging by the function of the motor cortex, a person would seem to be mostly hands and
speech organs (Penfield and Rasmussen, 1950).

Aside from such less coordinated movements as flailing or pounding,
the human hand has two fundamental prehensile working postures. The
first is the power grip. Here, the hand grasps an object between the palm
and the curled fingers, with the thumb pressing independently on the object or wrapped around the other fingers and reinforcing their pressure. It
is exemplified by a hand grasping a hammer. The second primary posture
is the "precision" grip, used whenever delicacy is more important than
strength in carrying out a task. In the precision grip, the object is held on
one side by the opposed thumb and, on the other, by the tips of one or
more fingers. It is exemplified by a hand holding a pencil, or a scalpel, or
chopsticks. The precision grip represents "the ultimate refinement in
prehensility" (Napier, 1962: 158). This does not mean, however, that less
complex functions of the hand have been somehow lost in the course of its
evolution. "The human hand remains capable of the postures and movements of the primate foot-hand and even of the paw of the fully quadru-
pedal mammal, and it retains many of the anatomical structures that go
with them" (Napier, 1962: 158).

It used to be accepted that the hand must have been more or less fully
developed in its human form, with such distinctively human features as a
fully opposable thumb, before culture, in the sense of tool making,
developed; that the modernization of the hand made culture possible.
Now, however, it is generally agreed that the occasional use of early tools

in itself influenced the development of certain anatomical features of the hand.

> The essence of the interpretation of evolution by selection is that selection causes change, and I believe that the form of the human hand *is the result* of the new selective pressures which came in with the use of tools. According to this theory, an ape's hand was pre-adapted to the use of tools. The hand was freed by the assumption of bipedal locomotion. Then new selection pressures coming with the use of tools changed the ape hand into the human hand.... The uniqueness of the human hand, those features which distinguish it from the hands of apes, is the result of culture. [Washburn, 1959: 24; italics in original]

This argument was anticipated in a little-known, ambiguous piece by Friedrich Engels, written in 1876. Though the language is loose, referring as it does to the inheritance of acquired skills, the point is clear enough.

> *The hand had become free* and could henceforth attain ever greater dexterity and skill, and the greater flexibility thus acquired was inherited and increased from generation to generation. Thus the hand is not only the organ of labor, *it is also the product of labor.* Only by labor, by adaptation to ever new operations, by inheritance of the thus acquired special development of muscles, ligaments, and, over longer periods of time, bones as well, and by the ever-renewed employment of this inherited finesse in new, more and more complicated operations, has the human hand attained the high degree of perfection that has enabled it to conjure into being the pictures of Raphael.... [Engels, 1950: 9; italics in original]

### Infrahuman Adaptation

Before we turn to human behavior, it may be useful to look at some of the work that has been done with animals other than humans. Most of these animal studies precede the work that has been done on behavioral adaptation in people. In fact, had these earlier field and experimental studies not been carried out, there might be less current interest in the behavioral adaptations of human beings. Many of them have implications for the adaptative behavior of people. The experimental work done on the effects of crowding in animal populations, for instance, shows rather convincingly that, beyond a certain threshold, the process is pathogenic. For ethical reasons, such experiments could never have been carried out with human subjects; with the current population explosion, the results of the studies are cause for concern. It should be noted that most of the studies carried out in the field deal with behavioral adaptation to the natural and "interpersonal" (or interanimal) environments, while most of the experimental studies superimpose a built environment upon the animals.

*Territoriality and Density.* Most of the ethological work we will consider here deals with the dynamic relationship between infrahuman territoriality and population density. Whether a population has too high a density depends partly upon the territorial requirements of a given animal, and these vary considerably from one species to another. The most popular works on the subject include Hediger's (1964) and Ardrey's (1966), and there exist a number of conceptual treatments and empirical studies varying in their levels of generality (e.g., Burt, 1943; von Uxküll, 1957; and Darling, 1937). Territoriality is a loose concept with several components, and we know more about territorial behavior in animals than in humans. Too frequently the term has been applied vaguely to human behavior that happens to resemble some of the things that animals do. Except at the most abstract and least useful level of analysis, it is one thing to talk about territoriality in animals that fight other animals of the same species in order to protect their nests from intrusion, and it is something else to talk about "object territoriality" in humans—in reference, say, to one's desire that a borrower return the object borrowed, whether it be a pencil or a car. Here, we will do what we can with the idea of territoriality in animals, reserving until later most applications of the concept to human behavior.

Altman (1970) has pointed out that most definitions of territoriality share certain features, such as antecedent, situational, organismic, and behavioral response elements. That is, most discussions of territoriality include references to antecedent events, such as invasion of the territory by another animal; situational contexts, such as a specified geographical place; one or another need of the organism, such as food, sex, or water; and different kinds of behaviors associated with the place, such as sleeping or refuge.

Among animals, territoriality seems most highly developed in birds and mammals—more developed among some kinds, such as carnivores, than others, such as hoofed animals. Territories are not simply spatial concepts. A territory is generally considered to be a fixed area inhabited by an individual animal or a larger unit such as a family, marked in some way as distinctive by the owners, and defended against intrusion from other animals or units of the same species. A range consists of the area in which the species is found. For example, the range of the red scaly lizard (*Sceloporus poinsettii*) is "southern New Mexico east to central Texas, and south in Mexico through Chichahua, Coahuila, and western Nuevo Leon to southern Durango" (Smith, 1946: 198).

Of course, the organism is not likely to be distributed evenly throughout all locations within the range of its species. It is found in pockets throughout its range, which are called biochores or, more generally, habitats. The red scaly lizard lives exclusively among rocks or boulders: "It may occur on rock fences as well as on natural piles of boulders and cliffs.

In Texas and New Mexico specimens are found in limestone bluffs in considerable numbers" (Smith, 1946: 200). Within the habitat, the territorial boundaries of each behavioral unit may be signalled in various ways — through sight, as in the giraffe; through hearing, as in insects, frogs, and alligators; or through smell, as in many of the carnivores. Farley Mowat, a biologist commissioned by the Canadian government to assess the effects of wolf predation upon the caribou herds, decided to mark his own territory when he occupied a cabin in the midst of the territory of a wolf pack. He followed the wolves' example by walking about the perimeters of his living area, urinating periodically to mark the boundaries of his territory. Unfortunately his supply of urine ran low and it was not until the wolves approached his cabin and dutifully marked out their territory that he learned that only a little urine sufficed to establish a marker, so that the whole boundary in question could have been covered easily (Mowat, 1963). A highly readable account of territorial behavior in animals can be found in Ardrey's *Territorial Imperative* (1966), but beware the extrapolations to human political behavior in the last chapters.

Home range indicates a geographical area that is ordinarily somewhat larger than a territory. In some animals, especially those that do not move about much, territory and home range may coincide, but home range is usually used to describe what we mean when we say an animal or person is "making his rounds." It denotes the complex of places that an organism routinely visits, and this may, of course, include several territories. The chipmunk, for example, has a home range of more than one hundred yards around his nest, while the defended territory has a radius of only fifty yards (Burt, 1943). Generally speaking, large animals have large home ranges and small animals have small ones. One important determinant of home range size is food requirements. Many herbivores do not need much space. A small herd of cattle or buffalo, for example, might minimally require a water hole and enough space around it so that, as they graze in a circular fashion, the grass they have cropped will be grown again when they next reach it. This is analagous to the man painting a fence that runs around a ranch: by the time he has painted it all the way around, it needs repainting. Predators, on the other hand, require much larger home ranges if they are to find enough food. They need to have a large number of prey animals under their "jurisdiction" if they are to feed on them without destroying the prey population. One study (Leopold, 1939) revealed that, in one square mile, there were many more prey animals than predators: 1 coyote, 2 horned owls, 2 redtail hawks, 10 blacktail jackrabbits, 15 skunks, 20 roadrunners, 25 cattle, 25 scaled quails, 25 cottontails, 45 Allen's jackrabbits, 75 gambel quails, 1,280 kangaroo rats, 6,400 wood rats, and 27,948 mice and other rodents. This sort of arrangement (sometimes called the pyramid of numbers) is made possible by the fact that smaller animals tend to have a higher rate of reproduction than larger ones.

It has also been observed that animals operate within their home ranges in terms of a space-time pattern; they do not move at random within the home range but usually follow set paths at certain times of the day or night. The regularly timed cyclical pattern of activities has been observed in many different kinds of animals, from house cats (Leyhausen, 1970) to spider monkeys (Carpenter, 1935: 175).

Hediger (1964:14) has observed that the home range used by an animal is differentiated into several areas with different functions. The home range is criss-crossed by trails leading from one area within the home range to another. The animal is familiar with these paths and may not use or be familiar with the areas between them. Prey may live and reproduce undisturbed in the unknown areas, occasionally venturing forth into the predator's path where they are caught. The home range also contains a home—some sort of nest or lair—where the animal hides, sleeps, and bears its young. Hediger designates this Home #1. It is frequently situated at the center of the home range and constitutes a territory that is defended. When an animal finds itself in danger elsewhere within its home range, too far away from Home #1 to reach it, it may seek out a secondary place of cover, Home #2, which may be one of several available refuges within the home range. Occasionally, the animal may make use of an emergency cover, Home #3. These home categories apparently apply to all vertebrates and many invertebrates. Home #1 may be surrounded by a protected zone in which, if the occupant is a predator, prey are spared; herbivorous occupants spare grass. It has been suggested that herbivores spare the vegetation in order to maintain a protective camouflage, or that the vegetation is so permeated with their body scents that it has lost food value. It has also been suggested that predators cannot "work up a proper frame of mind for hunting in the protected zone" (Hediger, 1964: 15). Outside the protected zone, of course, food is taken when it is available. It may be consumed on the spot or, in the case of carnivores, taken to a previously determined feeding place. It is not clear why certain spots are designated as places to eat. Certainly, the process has something to do with the animal's having found relative safety from disturbance there, but a preference for eating food in a familiar, rather than a strange, place may be quite widespread in animals, since it seems to be true of flatworms as well as tigers (Best and Rubenstein, 1962).

Home ranges sometimes overlap from one resident unit to another. Here the animals share paths and sometimes other resources. Where such overlaps are found, they are treated as neutral zones. When another animal of the same species is encountered here, it is not chased off or fought. Leyhausen systematically followed domestic cats around on their excursions through their respective home ranges and attempted to make continuous, uninterrupted recordings of their behavior, day and night. Leyhausen describes how these solitary animals regulate contact in neutral zones:

> Cats seem to regulate their traffic mainly by visual contact. It is often possible to observe one cat watching another moving along a path some distance away—say anything from thirty to one hundred yards—until it is out of sight. Some time afterwards, the watching cat can usually be seen using the same path. On occasion I have observed two cats approaching a kind of cat cross-roads from different directions. If they had gone on they would have met almost precisely at the crossing. Both sat down and stared at each other, looking deliberately away from time to time. The deadlock is eventually broken, either by one cat moving on towards the crossing while the other is looking away, hesitantly at first, then speeding up and trotting hastily away as soon as it has passed the point nearest to the other cat; or after a while both moving off almost simultaneously in the direction from which they originally came. [Leyhausen, 1970: 186]

The shapes of home ranges, and the location of homes within them, vary from one species to another in conformity with the pattern of environmental surroundings. Many are concentric or nearly so, while others take on irregular shapes. A hippopotamus's home range is usually pear-shaped, and the primary home is located at the narrow end of the area.

Home ranges are further differentiated into spots used for several other functions besides consuming prey. Areas may be selected for elimination, hunting, drinking, bathing, or storing food, and in addition, mineral springs or salt licks may be available for ungulates (hoofed mammals), rubbing posts for various animals, scratching posts for big cats, and so on. All of these spots are connected by familiar paths and visited periodically.

We have seen that a wide variety of animals, particularly fish, birds, and mammals, are territorial in that they routinely inhabit a given area which they mark as distinctive and defend against intrusion. Where a group of animals of the same species shares a given territory, the animals are likely to be arranged in a dominance hierarchy in which each animal knows which other animals it is subordinate or dominant to. The dominance hierarchy may be relatively stable, as among domestic cats (Leyhausen, 1971: 28) and baboons (Hall and Devore, 1965). It may vary situationally, as does the social structure of a free-ranging herd of grazing cows (Leyhausen, 1971: 24-25). Or it may be largely unilinear with an occasional quirk. In competitive barnyards, for example, chickens usually arrange themselves in a fairly durable pecking order in which A pecks B, B pecks C, C pecks D—but in some cases D pecks A.

What is the function of all this? What purpose is served by territoriality, or by integrating the animals who share a given territory into something resembling a single "social organism"? A phenomenon so widely spread throughout the animal kingdom must have some survival value. Some of the functions of territoriality are obvious. First, it facilitates match-making in some species. The male, having established a territory, attracts a female by making a loud noise or assuming an awkward pose. Often when a female commits herself to a male under these conditions, her movements thereafter are ignored by the other males, enabling the pair to get on with the business of reproduction. Thus we find that territoriality is often inten-sified during the mating season.

Territorial defense sometimes persists after mating, and some animals, such as herring gulls, pair up *before* establishing a territory. A second function of territoriality may be protecting the survival of the offspring. Raising young until they can fend for themselves may be a lengthy process dependent on the cooperation of the parents or the entire group. Later, it may involve parent-offspring cooperation. By confining the mating pair and the young to a limited territory, the entire enterprise is facilitated.

Territoriality may also limit aggression. In a group-shared territory with a dominance hierarchy, there may be little aggression, since each animal knows its social place. In addition, respect for territorial boundaries results in fewer acts of aggression between neighbors: a bit of fighting, sometimes sham, to demonstrate dominance, and the animals may get on with more important business such as self-maintenance and reproduction.

A final function of territoriality may be placing an upper limit on population size. When dominant animals establish a territory, less domi-nant ones need to seek theirs elsewhere. Usually, as the best territories are occupied, the remaining animals must seek out less fruitful places to live. If they are unable to adapt, they are less likely to reproduce and more likely to die. However, since these animals are the ones *least* able to get along in the original territory, some of them may be the ones *most* likely to adapt to new conditions. Where food supply is limited, the alternative to territoriality may be extinction. Most animals depend for their existence on a food source that requires a certain period of growth to replenish itself. Imagine, for instance, a situation in which a flock of crows depends for its livelihood on a cornfield of limited area. In the fall, a limited number of ears of corn will be available as food. If the population of crows is optimal in number, the crows will feed throughout the fall, winter, and spring, and by the following fall the cornfield will have renewed their supply of food.

Now imagine what would happen if this flock of crows increased in numbers beyond this critical threshold. The supply of food might be consumed by midwinter and, since there would be no more food until the following fall, many of the crows would starve, or perhaps *all* of them would starve. Whether the animals under consideration be crows, rodents, or some sort of predator, territoriality ensures that temporary surplus in an irregular food supply will carry the population through critical periods. To do otherwise—to live from hand to mouth, or from ground to beak—would mean operating like a trader on the stock exchange without a margin, or a general on the battlefield without reserves. To put it in game theory terms, the strategy would be a maximin one, "going for broke" as it were. The number of animals in the population would be maximized as long as the irregular food supply held out. The moment the food was exhausted, there would be an abrupt drop in the population. Natural selection, being an essentially conservative process, has a way of weeding out animals who behave in this fashion. In a sense, it is better to regularly sacrifice a certain number of surplus animals in order to ensure that a minimal breeding population will be left to carry the genes.

Wynne-Edwards (1962) has developed a controversial theory in which dispersal of the population is viewed as perhaps the primary function of territoriality. Many animals, he suggests, gather together periodically in demonstrative groups (peeping frogs in the spring, bellowing elephant seals, chirping birds in the evening, and the like), vast numbers of them in aggregation. These gatherings, which he terms epideictic displays, give the group an idea of the current size of the breeding population. What those peeping frogs are doing, in other words, is telling each other how many of them there are. When the group size increases beyond the optimum, aggression increases, and the more subordinate males are driven elsewhere.

*Population Crashes.* All animal populations except man seem to suffer periodic declines in their numbers, sometimes almost to the point of extinction. Biologists used to assume that these declines were the result of starvations, epidemics, changes in climate, increases in predation, and the like. The notion of an immutable inner expansive force held down by external checks on population growth dominated biological thinking until less than a generation ago.

Abrupt "crashes" of population were known for years, but in the early 1950s investigators began to realize that there was more at work than the imposition of simple external checks. Animals taken during a decline were as fat as those taken before the decline, and frequently the decline itself lasted long enough to reduce the population to the point of scarcity, so there was no question of a food shortage. Studies done on several kinds of animals, including muskrats (Errington, 1943), voles (Chitty, 1952), and

beach mice (Blair, 1951) suggested that territoriality, reflected in in-
tolerance for the presence of other animals, was an important consideration in some of these cases. A muskrat, for instance, is very much aware of
the number of other muskrats around him, and during the summer he
becomes especially sensitive to crowding and intolerant of the presence of
other animals. Competition for space leads to savage fights among the
muskrats, and the stronger and more determined animals drive away the
weaker ones. A defeated animal, forced to establish a new home range and
residence elsewhere, is more likely to be taken as prey than one that maintains its original home range. The ones that remain behind know their
home range well and are relatively safe from predation. These animals
constitute the breeding population, although even here the litters are
smaller when population density is high and larger when density is low.
Similarly, Chitty's (1952) study of voles (a variety of small rodent) on an
English farm revealed that offspring born during periods of high population density or during the subsequent periods of decline were likely to be
infertile and more likely to die from forces that usually caused voles to die.
And again, when density was high, voles fought more frequently and
fiercely among each other. Some evidence indicated that there had been
endocrinological changes among the animals. In a series of experiments
(Stricker and Emlen, 1953; Southwick, 1955a, 1955b), house mice were
penned together and permitted to increase in density without check and in
the presence of abundant food. As density increased, the number of young
mice who survived the period of weaning dropped drastically. For some
generations, the death rate among the young was almost 100 percent. Further, the number of young in each litter declined sharply after a long
period of crowding. A later field study by Southwick (1958) revealed that
fecundity decreased with crowding in natural populations of house mice in
England. As in other studies, the lowered rate of reproduction was the
result, not only of fewer pregnancies but of fewer surviving young.

In these and other studies, there was no question of starvation, predation, or epidemics. What mechanism could account for the sudden and
persistent drops in population density? The answer was forthcoming.

Early during World War II, Green and his colleagues (Green and Larson, 1938; Green and Evans, 1940) published the results of their study of
Canadian snowshoe hares, the natural population of which had been in a
five-year period of decline before the trend was reversed in 1938. When the
population was at its peak, occasional hares were found in the traps, dead
of what Green and the others called "shock disease." When the population
entered its period of rapid decline, the disease became widespread. J.J.
Christian (1950) later suggested that the condition was similar to that

described earlier by Hans Selye under the name of "the general adaptation syndrome."

Selye (1950) had noted that certain changes take place in the body both during intense emotional experiences and when the body is subjected to such stressors as severe cold or heat, injuries, or extreme fatigue. Emotion, like other stressors, causes the body to mobilize its resources and use them up at an increased rate. Selye proposed three stages in somatic reactions to stressors. The first is the alarm reaction, mediated by a subcortical structure called the hypothalamus that responds to perceived threat, in which various emergency mechanisms are activated, and the organism trembles, perspires, acts in an agitated manner or seems paralyzed with fear, and shows many other signs of being highly aroused. If the application of stressors continues, a second reactional stage emerges, the stage of resistance, in which the organism recovers from its initial alarm and seems to accommodate itself to a high level of arousal, doing what it can to function normally and showing a lowered resistance to any new stressors. If the stressful conditions are severe and prolonged, the organism finally enters the stage of exhaustion. Here the adaptive mechanisms of the body break down, signs of actual maladaption appear, and the organism weakens and may die.

The predominant mechanism underlying the general adaptation syndrome is an endocrinological one and involves the reciprocal relationship between the anterior part of the pituitary gland and the adrenal cortex. The pituitary gland is a pea-sized ductless organ situated at the base of the brain and connected to it by a tiny stalk. It is separated into two parts. The anterior part is most important for our purposes. It secretes six known hormones, most of which control the activity of other endocrine glands. Of these, three are gonadotrophic hormones, which promote the activity of the gonads, or reproductive organs, especially in females. Another regulates the activity of the thyroid gland, which in turn regulates metabolism, including all forms of energy expenditure in the body. Another hormone, the adrenocorticotrophic hormone, or ACTH, stimulates the cortex of the adrenal gland.

The adrenal glands, which sit atop the kidneys, also may be divided into two parts. The adrenal medulla at the core of the gland secretes two closely related hormones that prepare the body for emergency reactions, usually involving either fighting (rage) or running away (fear). The cortex, the outer part of the adrenal, secretes a number of hormones, one of the principal functions of which is to reduce the deposition of glycogen in the liver. This keeps energy rich carbohydrate compounds in the blood, available to supply any emergency requirements of the muscles.

When an organism experiences an intense emotion or is subjected to sudden stress, an emergency signal flashes throughout the body by way of the sympathetic nervous system. The immediate result of this sudden sympathetic arousal is activation of the mechanisms that prepare the body for a quick expenditure of energy. Most of these mechanisms, familiar to anyone who has been thoroughly frightened or angry, have an identifiable survival value. And that, in fact, is why we have them: they were favored by the process of natural selection during the course of our evolution. Increased muscle tension prepares the body to fight or run away at an instant's notice. Trembling is a sign of this tension. Blood is shunted to the muscles, away from the digestive system, which practically shuts down. Muscular effort means that heat will be generated and the body must be cooled, which is why we perspire when aroused. Goose pimples—pilomotor reaction, if you will—are residual mechanisms that used to raise the hair of our forebears, so that their bodies seemed larger and attackers were more likely to get a mouthful of fur than flesh. Pupils dilate, breathing and pulse rate quicken, and the body gives other evidence of diffuse arousal.

The sympathetic nervous system does not sustain this state of mobilization for long, however. One of its functions is activation of the adrenal medulla, which secretes epinephrine and norepinephrine directly into the bloodstream. The effects of these two hormones on the organs of the body are similar to those of the sympathetic system. The function of the adrenal medulla, in effect, is to support the action of the sympathetic system in emergency situations. First, the bodily changes associated with arousal occur through direct sympathetic activity. Later, the hormones from the adrenal medulla arrive via the bloodstream and maintain the mobilized state.

One of the requirements for sustained muscular effort, such as is likely to occur in a physical emergency, is a high level of blood sugar to provide part of the fuel for muscles. As already mentioned, blood sugar level is determined by the rate of activity of the adrenal cortex, since some of the hormones control the ratio of sugar stored in the liver or released into the bloodstream. Under conditions of stress, the anterior part of the pituitary secretes a hormone—the adrenocorticotrophic hormone (ACTH)—which influences the activity of the adrenal cortex in such a way that it releases sugar from the liver into the bloodstream. This means that more energy is immediately available to the muscles.

But when the stress is prolonged, the hormones from the adrenal cortex feed back to the pituitary. As a result, more ACTH is secreted, and this in turn raises the level of activity of the adrenal cortex and inhibits the secretion of gonadotrophin.

One effect of prolonged stress is that the adrenal cortex becomes larger in response to its increased activity. Another is that reproductive organs receive less hormonal stimulus than usual, and reproduction is interfered with. A third effect is depletion of the supply of sugar stored in the liver, leaving less energy available to combat new sources of stress.

The point of central interest in this somewhat oversimplified picture is that, under prolonged stress, the anterior pituitary and the adrenal cortex keep giving each other positive feedback. The adrenal cortex maintains the blood sugar level by secreting hormones that release energy-rich compounds from the liver. These hormones also activate the anterior pituitary, which responds by secreting ACTH, which has the effect of increasing the activity of the adrenal cortex. Thus the two endocrine glands are locked into the sort of system that used to be called a vicious circle, and this describes roughly the physiological mechanisms underlying the resistance stage of the general adaptation syndrome (see figure 2).

As the stage of exhaustion is reached, the gonads actually shrink in size, just as the adrenal cortex has grown larger, and the organism is less likely to reproduce itself. Moreover, since the organism's store of energy is depleted, it has little or no reserves to draw upon if a new emergency should arise, and so it is more likely to be caught and eaten if it is a prey animal, more likely to miss its target if it is a predator, and more likely to die from other causes in any case.

There is now considerable evidence that among some animals, particularly territorial ones, a high population density leads to increased aggression and this in turn initiates the general adaptation syndrome, which is likely to have a fatal effect on weak or submissive animals.

It is also possible that ACTH may directly inhibit reproduction without the mediation of the adrenals and in the absence of aggression, since an injection of ACTH inhibits maturation in female mice whose adrenals have been removed.

In other words, as crowding and perhaps aggression increase, certain endocrine feedback mechanisms may limit population growth. Such is the idea suggested in numerous publications by Christian and his colleagues.

But although the precise mechanisms involved may be a matter of dispute, most investigators would probably agree that crowding, increased competition among individuals, and aggression somehow play a part in the self-regulation of populations. There is, incidentally, increasing support for the proposition that these stress effects are generated, not so much by the amount of space available per animal in a crowd as by the absolute number of individuals, especially strange individuals, with which an animal must interact. That is, if crowded animals are kept singly in small

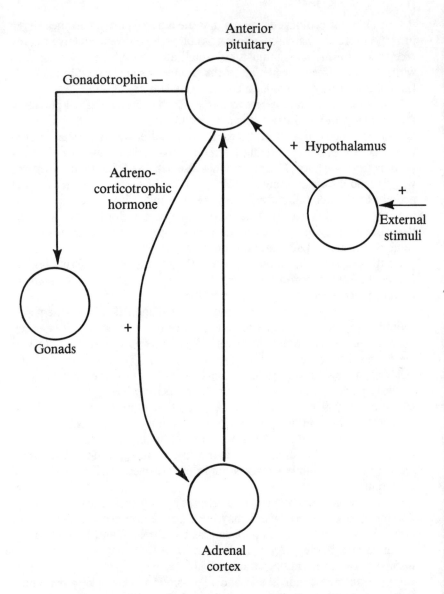

FIG. 2. RELATIONSHIPS AMONG SOME ORGANS INVOLVED IN THE GENERAL
ADAPTATION SYNDROME.

cages, the stress is less than if they were set loose to interact with each other freely. The culprit here is not simply crowding but competition for food, water, mates, or territory (Christian, 1950).

Field studies have demonstrated that, once high population density and the resulting competition trigger a population crash, the decline in the number of animals continues well beyond the point at which the geographical area could no longer be considered crowded. The decline may persist through several generations. This is understandable in the light of certain experiments indicating that stress on pregnant animals can produce, not only fewer offspring, but offspring that may be behaviorally or physically deficient. Pregnant rats, for example, produce young with congenital heart disease if they are revolved two hundred times in a wire drum. If the pregnant rats are revolved eight hundred times, they produce no live offspring at all (Sobin, 1954). Other experiments by Thompson and Sontag (1956) and Thompson (1957) have proved equally interesting. Thompson and Sontag exposed pregnant rats to the ringing of a bell, the sound being of such stressful intensity that the rats suffered convulsive seizures. The young, switched at birth to a control group of unshocked mother rats, proved significantly slower at learning mazes. Thompson's later experiment demonstrated that it was not the sound of the bell but the anxiety of anticipating it that affected the offspring. In this experiment, female rats were trained to expect an electric shock after they heard a buzzer. They could escape the shock by opening a door to another compartment in the cage. After mating, they were placed in the experimental cage. They were not shocked, but the escape door was locked so that when they heard the buzzer they were thrown into what, in humans, might be described as a panic. After birth, the young were transferred to control mothers, and again they developed into sluggish, dull, and timid animals. Even in coping with the normal problems of organismic existence, these offspring might be expected to suffer more stress than other animals, being more likely to lose out in the competition for territory, food, mates, and other resources and more likely to be bullied by other animals. It then seems possible that, if being outwitted, outbluffed, and outfought constitute strong stressors, additional malformations could be transmitted to the next generation.

Thus, it may be that initial conditions of overcrowding generate stressors that result in deficient offspring, and this deficiency in turn implies a more stressful existence, which results in deficient offspring in the next generation, even though the population is no longer overcrowded. Of course, a number of stressed or deficient animals in each generation do not live to produce viable young, through starvation, the lack of opportunity to mate, or increased susceptibility to predation, and so the population declines through several generations.

The many field and laboratory studies we have surveyed here indicate that, for a wide variety of higher animals, something seems to happen when the density of their population reaches a certain point. It does not matter much whether the process is called shock disease, the general adaptation syndrome, or adreno-pituitary exhaustion. The effects on the organism are debilitating and sometimes lethal, and they may be equally destructive to the animal society as a whole.

*The Behavioral Sink.* We must digress for a moment. Everyone has a right — indeed a duty — to be wary of extrapolating from animal studies to man. There are too many differences, most of them having to do with the incredible complexity of even the technologically simplest of human cultures, for most of us to enjoy, with Edward Chance Tolman, "sitting on the good old phylogenetic limb" (1945). However, fundamental similarities are obvious. We may not know how dogs think about things, but we know that their learning patterns are similar to those of humans.

Certain learning patterns of cockroaches are even more similar to those of people. Suppose an experimenter runs a hungry animal through a T-shaped maze, putting food at the end of the right-hand arm of the T 70 percent of the time, and putting food at the left-hand arm of the T only 30 percent of the time. Most animals will "figure out" the percentages and maximize their reward by turning to the right all of the time, but, human beings — and cockroaches — respond probabilistically, turning to the right approximately 70 percent of the time, and to the left approximately 30 percent of the time. They try to beat the system. There is clearly too much going on here for animal studies of the kind previously described to be dismissed as irrelevant.

Actually, the evidence from animal studies is likely to have implications for understanding human behavior insofar as (1) the animal subjects are more or less released from instinctive control over their behavior (for example, what porpoises do is probably more relevant than what ants do), and (2) the animal studies yield evidence that may have significance concerning human response to stressors.

The domestic albino strain of the Norway rat is a favorite experimental animal in America, as dogs are in the Soviet Union. This unfortunate creature has undergone every imaginable sort of treatment in the laboratory, from systematic vitamin deprivation to the implantation of electrodes in its pleasure center, until at this point we would seem to know considerably more about the domestic albino strain of the Norway rat than we do about people.

Some investigators have spun out futuristic fantasies based on the application of rat treatments to human beings. But others have argued against the extrapolation of these findings. Sometimes the intensity of the negative response seems associated with the personal inclinations of the respondent. Some findings published a few years ago concerned chromosomal damage found in offspring following the administration of relatively large amounts of LSD to pregnant rats. At the time of publication, I was involved in a large-scale study of illicit LSD use in the New York metropolitan area. Many female informants decided immediately to stop using the drug. When questioned about their feelings, some of the other respondents, particularly men, felt strongly that the experiments indicated little more than that massive dosages of LSD ought not to be administered to pregnant rats in a laboratory. They further could not understand how any investigation of drug effects in a few dozen animals could yield results that might be extrapolated to the thousands, perhaps millions of human beings using the drug at vastly smaller doses.

Extrapolation from animals to humans is precisely the point behind any study of drug effects on a few dozen animals. If, by administering massive dosages of the drug, one can produce ill effects among, say, half of the experimental animals, then one may reasonably suspect that if millions of human beings are using the drug, similar ill effects may show up in a few hundred people, or perhaps a few thousand. Because of the gravity of the potential danger to human welfare, experiments using a few dozen rats deserve our attention. The greater the number of potential users, the greater the significance of the animal results. In each case, the benefits of drug use must be balanced against the possible risk.

The several million users of LSD, then, have some cause for concern when the drug seems to cause chromosomal damage in Norway rats. It is appropriate to turn now to an experimental situation in which the "dosage" was not very much greater for the experimental rats than it is for many people currently, in which the damage caused by the treatment was unarguably profound, and in which the number of people subject to the experimental treatment may someday be, not a few million, or even many millions, but all of Homo sapiens. We will discuss the possible consequences of overpopulation.

Following the French Revolution of 1786, a number of writers were moved to produce visions of utopian societies in which men were ruled by reason and there was plenty for all. One of these was the *Esquisse d'un Tableau Historique des Progres de L'Esprit Humain*. Its author, the Marquis de Condorcet, contended that a natural order of civilization moved through ten stages, the ninth beginning with Descartes and the last beginning with the establishment of the French Republic and blossoming into a world of material abundance, without discrimination according to race or sex. (Ironically enough, the book was written while the author was hiding from revolutionary extremists who wanted him executed for advocating such counterrevolutionary causes as the abolition of the death penalty.)

An Englishman, William Godwin, who happened to be the father of Mary Godwin (author of *Frankenstein* and Percy Shelley's wife), was likewise inspired by the French Revolution to write *Enquiry Concerning Social Justice* in 1793. Godwin felt that the world was moving toward a society in which government would no longer be necessary and in which there would be no disease, misery, or anxiety.

Thomas Robert Malthus, then a curate at Cambridge, was more skeptical about the future of human civilization. In 1798 he published anonymously *An Essay on the Principle of Population as It Affects the Future Improvement of Society, with Remarks on the Speculations of Mr. Godwin, M. Condorcet, and Other Writers* (Malthus, 1970). In it, Malthus advanced what Kenneth Boulding (1959) has aptly called the Dismal Theorem. Like other animals, people would reproduce themselves at a geometric rate if permitted to do so, whereas cultivated land, on which we depend for food, can only increase at a faster rate than food production until certain checks on population growth come into play. These checks are "vice" and "misery." Malthus is a bit difficult to decipher in his discussion of the nature of these checks, partly because he seems never to have carefully thought them out, but also because of the delicacy of his language. "Improper arts to prevent the consequences of irregular connections" is interpreted by Anthony Flew as a reference to abortion (Flew, 1970: 24).

We may define "misery" as predation, disease, starvation, and other lethal effects of population growth. These forms of environmental resistance have most often engaged the attention of biologists. However, John B. Calhoun was more interested in "vice." "Setting aside the moral burden of this word, what are the effects of the social behavior of a species on population growth—and of population density on social behavior?" (1963: 33).

Calhoun is an animal psychologist at the National Institute of Mental Health's Unit for Research on Behavioral Systems in Bethesda, Maryland. His experiments with rats and mice explore directly the breakdown of patterns of social interaction under high-density conditions.

Calhoun's work on population dynamics, which began in 1947, can conveniently be divided into three parts: (1) the wild rat experiment, (2) the domestic rat experiments, and (3) the domestic mouse experiments. These classic studies, unfortunately, can be described only briefly here.

1. *The wild rat experiment.* In this initial study, Calhoun released a few pregnant wild rats into a quarter-acre outdoor pen. Since abundant food and nesting areas were supplied within the enclosure and the effects of

predation and disease were minimal, only the animals' social behavior could influence their population density. Systematic observation revealed that the birth rate was so high, and adult mortality so low, that 5,000 rats might have been expected at the end of twenty-seven months. Yet the population stabilized at 150 adults. The population never achieved its highest possible density because, even at 150 adults, social interaction was so stressful for the rats that females lost their ability to care for the young, and few offspring survived.

2. *The domestic rat experiments.* For his next investigations, Calhoun constructed a series of four indoor pens. The first pen was connected to the second by a ramp which bridged the wall between them. In the same way, the second pen was connected to the third, and the third to the fourth, but the fourth was in no way connected to the first. Each pen contained a drinking fountain, a food hopper, and an elevated burrow containing five nesting compartments. Each pen was large enough to comfortably accommodate twelve adult rats, which is the usual number for wild nesting groups. Theoretically, the overall structure of four pens should have supported forty-eight rats in reasonable comfort. The population was allowed to increase to eighty individuals, half male and half female, and then the infants that survived birth and weaning were removed in order to keep the population below the point at which a die-off might occur. Eighty is somewhat less than twice the number of animals that might be expected to occupy an area of such dimensions under wild conditions. This was by no means a "standing room only" arrangement. In addition, of course, the rats had an adequate supply of food and water and were not subject to predation.

The arrangement of ramps, as well as slight differences in the design of the pens, encouraged a somewhat higher use of the two middle pens. Groups as small as twenty-three might have been expected in the end pens, while groups as large as twenty-seven might have been found in one of the middle pens. It is instructive to look at the way the eighty rats actually distributed themselves through the four pens.

As time passed, the expected bias in favor of the middle pens increased beyond any reasonable expectation. The females were distributed fairly evenly across the pens, but eventually one or two dominant males established harems in the end pens, while all of the other males were concentrated in the central pens.

Calhoun describes the behavior of the dominant males in the end pens:

> Once a male had established his dominion over an end pen and the harem it contained, he was usually able to maintain it. Although he slept a good deal of the time, he made his sleeping quarters at the base of the ramp. He was, therefore, on perpetual guard. Awakening as soon as another male appeared

at the head of the ramp, he had only to open his eyes for the invader to wheel around and return to the adjoining pen. On the other hand, he would sleep calmly through all the comings and goings of his harem; seemingly he did not even hear their clatterings up and down the wire ramp. His conduct during his waking hours reflected his dominant status. He would move about in a casual and deliberate fashion, occasionally inspecting the burrow and nests of his harem. But he would rarely enter a burrow, as some other males did, merely to ferret out the females. [Calhoun, 1963: 37]

The dominant male also was likely to tolerate subordinate males in the end pens, but these were invariably timid animals, spending most of their time crouched in the burrows with the adult females and leaving their hiding places only long enough to obtain necessary food and water. They did not challenge the dominant male, nor did they initiate sexual activities with the adult females.

Since a dominant male maintained a harem of about eleven females, the size of the group approximated that found in the wild. The dominant male carried out normal mating procedures with his harem. When an adult female was in heat, the male chased her until she entered a burrow. She would then peer out of the burrow while the male paced around outside, eventually to emerge and permit him to mount her. The females showed normal patterns of maternal activity, making the proper cup-shaped nests in the compartments, and if any danger to the offspring became apparent, the mother picked them up and transported them, one by one, to a safer place. The mortality rate among infants and adult females was accordingly low; about half the infants in the end pens survived.

What of conditions in the two central pens? The females there became pregnant as frequently as those in the end pens, but far fewer live offspring were produced, and those were far less likely to survive to maturity. In this series of experiments, 96 percent of the offspring died before they could be weaned. The females of the central pens, in heat or not, were under continuous harassment from some of the males, and their patterns of maternal behavior were frequently disrupted. Instead of constructing the usual cup-shaped nests, females merely piled scraps of paper into a heap. As the experiment continued, they brought fewer and fewer bits of paper to the burrow and eventually bore their young on the sawdust floor, where they were abandoned and generally eaten by other adults. The stressors to which a female was subjected were especially severe during heat, when she would be pursued by a crowd of males who would enter the burrow after her, rather than wait outside. Mortality among females from disorders connected with reproduction was unusually high. Almost half of the first- and second-generation females had died from these causes before the seventeenth month of the experiment.

Of the adult males in the central pens, only 15 percent died, but those who lived showed striking behavioral aberrations. Somewhat fewer than half of the adult males in the central pens continued to compete in the dominance hierarchy, as wild rats do. Normally a fairly stable arrangement emerges from dominance fights, so that each male knows to which animals he is subordinate or dominant. In this case, no such stable hierarchy emerged, and periodic savage fights between competitive animals occurred, ending in the transfer of dominance from one individual to another. Despite the fact that these dominant rats were the most normal ones in the central pens, they occasionally went berserk, engaging in unprovoked attacks on lesser males, females, and juveniles.

But they were paragons of stability compared to the other males. Below these dominant animals on the status scale was another group who were frequently attacked by the dominant males but who were only moderately active and who did not usually fight for status. Their most noticeable problem was their pan-sexualtiy, since they did not seem able to discriminate between males and females, or juveniles and adults but made sexual overtures to all kinds of animals.

Two other classes of males developed in the central pens, both having dropped out of the struggle for dominance but having little else in common. The first were totally passive. They ignored all other animals, and all other animals ignored them. Frequently they moved about only when the others were asleep. They were healthy animals, fat, and without battle scars, but they were completely withdrawn from society.

The other kind of male was in some ways the most interesting. Calhoun calls them probers. Despite the fact that they took no part in fights for status, they were the most active males of all, constantly probing about, prodding and examining others, always moving, despite occasional attacks from the dominant males. They seemed only to fear the dominant males guarding the harems in the end pens. In addition, the males were sexually hyperactive and a female in heat in the central pens could depend on having a pack of them running after her, even entering the burrow, something none of the other males did. These were the animals who would live for long periods at the tops of the ramps leading down into the end pens, waiting for a fertile harem female to emerge. They might be frightened off by the dominant male but would return again. In the end, many of the hyperactive males became cannibalistic. Calhoun termed this disorganized social behavior of the central pens a "behavioral sink." In the case of these experiments, it seems to have resulted at least partly from the initial distributional skew, the result of differences in design, in favor of the two central pens.

Extracting food from the hoppers in each pen was a rather time-consuming process for the rats. Since, nearly from the beginning, more rats were found in the central pens, they more often found themselves eating from the hoppers in company with neighbors, and gradually, as the population increased, they apparently formed an association between eating and the presence of other animals. Rather than explore the gustatory possibilities of the low-density end pens, an increasing number of animals restricted their eating to the central pens. Finally, many of the subordinate end-pen males began patronizing the central pens, and since entrance to the end pens was restricted to a single ramp, the dominant male could easily prevent the return of the subordinate males. It was not so much that he kicked them out of the end pens as that he prevented their return. No such behavioral sinks were found in a second series of experiments conducted under largely similar conditions, but there were indications that the development of sinks was imminent.

It might be objected that the development of a behavioral sink represents a response to the unique conditions of the experimental arrangement used in this study—that such a sorry state of affairs could never be found in the field. However, there is no reason to believe that food sources are evenly distributed in nature. Suppose an animal belongs to a group of some sort, sharing a common territory, and makes an independent excursion away from the others.

> During such excursions an individual may encounter some locally abundant resource, which in fact may be found in only a few places of the...home range of the group. Even by chance, two individuals may find themselves simultaneously at the same such site, while responding to the resources available to it. Whenever this happens, there is the opportunity for each individual to become a secondary reinforcer for the other. As such secondary reinforcement becomes established, animals actively seek out places for satisfying such primary drives as hunger or thirst where others of their kind have already assembled.
>
> When several such sites are scattered over the range of a group, some will more likely be encountered than others. Gradually, all members of the group will assemble at the one place, where other factors affecting movement make it more likely to be encountered. Here each individual can be assured of the greatest likelihood of encountering others, of fulfilling its acquired secondary drive of needing to be near others. In time, all other sites within the group's range will be ignored. Each individual may pass by one or more sites where food and water can be obtained in order to reach the one site where it most likely will find others of its species. It is as if food is no longer food merely because it has the correct visual and olfactory characteristics—there must also be other members of the respondent's own species standing nearby.
>
> For the same reason that the ranges of individuals overlap, so do the ranges of neighboring groups. Thus, as the members of one group begin to spend an inordinate amount of time at one place, the several neighboring

groups nearest to it may likewise be attracted to this one place. I have called this process the development of a behavioral sink. In a state of nature it may cause at least seven times the optimum number of animals to assemble at one place, with a resulting accompanying array of abnormal behaviors developing. Prominent among these are nearly total dissolution of all maternal behavior, predominance of homosexuality, and marked social withdrawal to the point where many individuals appear to be unaware of their associates despite their close proximity. [Calhoun, 1966: 54]

If this sounds a little like Times Square, it may not be coincidental.

3. *The domestic mouse experiments.* Calhoun and his colleagues (1966; 1971) investigated social responses to high population density among mice. Here, the physical environment consisted of a series of four cells, each open to the others. The usual nesting facilities were provided along the walls, and a food hopper was placed on the wall of each cell in such a way that a mouse, in order to obtain food, would need to run across the outer surfaces of the nesting tunnels and hang onto the hopper while it gnawed at the exposed food pellets. The water supply was ample and access to it easy.

Groups of four different sizes were maintained in these four-cell universes, each group consisting only of males introduced at weaning. The groups of mice numbered four, eight, sixteen, and thirty-two. Calhoun suspects that the optimum size group for this sort of universe is between eight and sixteen. Above the optimum, a peculiar pattern of eating developed. When the group size was kept small, the mice used each of the four food hoppers about equally, but as group size increased above the optimum, a much higher percentage of food was consumed exclusively at one hopper. With a group size of thirty-two animals, as much as 52 percent of the food was obtained from one hopper, while the other three yielded only 32 percent, 12 percent, and 5 percent.

The explanation of this behavior is similar to that for domestic rats. When the size of the group is small, the chances are good that a given mouse will finish eating without encountering another hungry mouse at the same hopper. Above the optimum size, however, a hungry mouse at one of the hoppers is more likely to bump into other hungry mice who will act as secondary reinforcers, so that when the mouse is hungry again, he is more likely to return to the most crowded hopper. The dynamics are simple enough. In the end, this results in such an aggregate of mice at one of the hoppers that any individual mouse actually has difficulty reaching the food.

In a similar experiment, involving both male and female mice and a greater number of cells, the social pathology of the behavioral sink again became apparent as the population increased beyond the optimum. As the first generation of mice matured, they formed basic social units consisting of a dominant male, three competitive but subordinate males, and six reproducing females. The population increased rapidly. As the second generation of mice matured, the young males fought with the dominant males but, with few exceptions, were unable to beat them. With no vacant space to occupy as territory, the younger males became socially withdrawn. Some of them, referred to by Calhoun as "solitary withdrawns," cowered for most of their lives near the center of the floor space, making only those excursions necessary for obtaining food and water. The majority of displaced mice, however, became "pooled withdrawns," assembling in large aggregates. The pooled withdrawns carried a variety of scars and recent wounds. Few of these wounds were inflicted by dominant males. Rather, one or another of their own number would periodically become violently aggressive, attacking his associates indiscriminately. The animal who was attacked would ordinarily not defend himself or flee but simply crouch and suffer the insult.

At this point, reproductive capacity declined: frequency of conception was reduced, and young were no longer successfully raised. The population stopped increasing and became stable. An increasing number of mice became socially withdrawn. Even the capacity for violent outbursts of aggression disappeared. By the time all population increase had ceased, "there were, for practical purposes, no territorial males, no contesting males, and no reproducing females capable of caring for young; the genetic and learned templates for guiding effective adult behavior had been 'washed out' among all who had ever exhibited behavioral competence of a reproductive or aggressive nature" (Calhoun, 1971: 342).

This lack of competence was also found among the final class of mice, the "beautiful ones." The beautiful ones were adult mice who neither contested for territory nor were interested in sex. They carried no scars and, in fact, their coats were in excellent shape since they were given to frequent self-grooming. Essentially, they acted like juveniles who had aged without ever acquiring adult pattterns of social behavior. Since the beautiful ones were permitted to sleep in the nesting areas with juvenile mice, they may have been defined as juveniles by the other adults. Investigation of an enzyme associated with the adrenal glands yielded evidence that, unlike normal adult mice, the beautiful ones had never been stressed.

If Calhoun's earlier work was largely empirical, his recent concerns are increasingly with the theoretical implications of his experimental findings. It is difficult to outline his theoretical scheme in a short space, but such an effort must be made. Briefly, Calhoun feels that there is an optimal group number of socially effective adults for each species of animal. The number twelve crops up over rather a wide range of mammals, including mice, some other primates, and hunting-and-gathering humans. (Calhoun is especially interested in small mammals like mice and shrews since they represent roughly the sort of organismic form from which most higher mammals, man included, trace their ancestry.) The actual number of animals in the group will be greater than twelve, since it must include a varying number of infants and juveniles. This assemblage of animals will constitute a territorial group.

In a group of this size, an animal will comfortably handle the eleven other adults he encounters day after day. It should be noted that this is already a fairly complex group, since the animal will meet those eleven others in various combinations as well as individually, and under varying sets of circumstances. In a smaller group, environmental resources are not effectively exploited; in a much larger territorial group of free-ranging animals, the individual's capacity for managing social encounters is impaired.

Calhoun assumes that animals alternate between the need for social contact and the gratification of that need. He devised an interactional model called the "mythematical social pool game" and suggested that animals inhabiting a fixed area are something like pool balls on a table. A pool ball may be in need of social contact and, as it moves about the table, may encounter another ball in the same state and elicit an appropriate response. Each of them then enters a gratification state that lasts for some time after the period of contact. However, if a pool ball in need of social contact encounters another that is already in a state of gratification from a previous contact, the first ball will enter a state of frustration, in which it will remain for a period of time before returning to its original need state. The same thing happens when a needy ball encounters a frustrated ball. At all times, then, each ball will be in one of three possible states: need, gratification, or frustration. The proportion of balls in each state varies with the population density. Under optimal conditions, the number in each state will be in relative balance.

If the group is too small for the area it inhabits, a disproportionate number of balls will be in a need state. If the size of the group is too large, a disproportionate number will be in a state of frustration. As group size increases relative to area, all balls will essentially be frustrated since so few balls will be found in a need state, and few appropriate social responses will be elicited.

Thus, as the number of frustrating encounters increases as a result of the increasing size of the group, those balls most often frustrated will tend to leave the field or, since in this case the area is fixed, will withdraw from social intercourse — drop into the pockets as it were.

Of course, Calhoun is talking about more than pool games. "We call such balls by various names. Some are called mice, some rats, others man" (1966: 352). He then outlines the process by which an infinite number of evenly dispersed individuals may logically be assumed to draw themselves together into groups of twelve, with a range of seven to nineteen, assuring the effective exploitation of marginal territory.

Ordinarily, twelve adults will be in the process of caring for somewhat more than an equal number of offspring at any given time, and if the adaptation of the group is successful, these maturing individuals will enter the adult ranks, and the size of the group will gradually increase beyond the optimum number. At this point, the usual response is for the group to split. Half may remain in the original territory, while the other half migrates to a vacant area. In time, all available territories may be filled up.

What happens then? Calhoun suggests that, when physical space is totally occupied and population continues to increase, animals will develop behavioral pathology of the sort already described, which will reduce the numbers of the breeding population. However, man seems to be capable of replacing the minimum amount of physical space through an expansion of "conceptual area," by which term Calhoun appears to mean something akin to role differentiation and the values that facilitate it. He uses the Hutterites of the American Northwest as an example of this process. The optimum number of territorial Hutterites is about 75, including more than four children per family. When the group reaches 150 individuals, it splits and half of them establish a community elsewhere. "We must, therefore, conclude that role differentiation among the Hutterites is just sufficient on a cultural basis to make the overall group essentially two groups of twelve sharing the same area through restricting with whom it is appropriate to interact. Thus, insofar as any individual is concerned, the number of interactions per day will remain much as it was within a primitive hunter-gatherer group of twelve adults" (Calhoun, 1966: 357).

Calhoun limns in a fascinating historical speculation concerning the origin of conceptual space. As available space was filled and the human population continued to grow, more and more individuals were frustrated in their desires for social gratification. Individuals withdrew from society and entered creative fantasy space, "where the withdrawn individual generates objects for interaction out of his store of memory traces. These may be fantasied other people, but may just as well be any rearrangement of information which he finds pleasing" (Calhoun, 1966: 359). Social withdrawal is a prerequisite to intellectual creation, which forms the basis for the role differentiation that permits meaningful social contacts to continue at a rate that many of us find gratifying. As population continues to grow, then, the decreasing amount of physical space available to us is replaced by an expansion of conceptual area[1] and a restriction of social interactions. A man in New York City may structure his life in such a way that he has enduring social contact only with a few people at his job, a few others at home, a few outside friends, and (until 1981) Walter Cronkite, rather than 150,000 bakers, 1.5 million grocery store clerks, and so on. In other words, to the extent that a person's social behavior is unsatisfying, a person may daydream, watch media figures who seem always willing to talk to him, seek out a nondirective therapist, perhaps pray to an eternally interested god, or engage in some other form of fantasy.

There are two major problems, however. Because the storage capacity of the human brain is limited, conceptual area cannot expand infinitely. Moreover, as the human population continues to increase, the time it takes for the population to add more millions becomes correspondingly smaller, until eventually, a point is reached at which each million-person increase requires only an extremely short time.

In response to the first problem, Calhoun suggests that we may promote the efficient organization of society by supplementing conceptual areas through the use of electronic devices that enhance fantasy or creativity. Concerning the second problem, it would seem that there is some upper limit to population growth beyond which further increase would be physically impossible. Calhoun thinks that 9 billion is the upper limit to world population. With a total land surface of something less than 47 million livable square miles, a human population of 9 billion ought to leave almost 19 million square miles for mostly unperturbed habitation by other life forms. The real human population may overshoot this figure but not by very much and not for too long.

Assuming that people stabilized their numbers at about 9 billion, three scenarios would be possible. Two are dreary indeed, involving a pan-global human society of stunted individuals, whose lifeways are dictated by their concern for survival and whose cultural growth is nil. The third possibility is the reduction of the human population and the simultaneous expansion of conceptual area through the use of electronic prostheses — computerlike devices that would help people organize both society and their own individual problem solving. Ultimately, when most (or all) of the thinking on earth is done by these devices, it would no longer be suitable to call the remaining small number of people by their former name, *Homo sapiens.*

---

1. This may have been something like what Georg Simmel had in mind when he suggested that successful adjustment to the anonymity of city life required an expansion of inner life. "Intellectuality is thus seen to preserve subjective life against the overwhelming power of metropolitan life" (Simmel, 1964: 411). R.D. Laing might agree.

Though Calhoun presents a remarkable exploration of the relationship between space and the strategy of life, he seems largely to ignore the possibility of natural selection. The crowding and anxiety associated with encountering too many unpredictable strangers might, in fact, be so stressful that increasing numbers of people would be unable to reproduce, and this form of natural selection would lead to population stabilization or decline.

We have seen that anxiety in rats may produce behavioral aberrations in their offspring. Evidence exists that the same effect may be found in humans. We do know that the rate of malformations at birth seems to increase enormously during wars and periods of social upheaval, even in the absence of food shortage (Stott, 1962: 367-72), and some of these disorders may be associated with crowding (Anderson et al., 1958). It is not really inconceivable that individuals who are made particularly anxious by overcrowding may be selected out, in effect leaving the planet to intermittent schizophrenics with their nearly limitless conceptual area, or to anxiety-free, possibly psychopathic "operators"—perhaps both—as Humphry Osmond has suggested. In either case, the result would be a higher maximum human population than Calhoun envisages.

It may be argued that natural selection is too time-consuming a process to effectively alter the world's genetic pool before the critical point is reached in a few hundred years. However, there is no reason to believe that, if the stress is severe enough, natural selection cannot operate effectively over a few generations. There must have been a great deal of selection going on in the cities of medieval Europe, when families bore a large number of children and the majority of them died. In any case, not everyone would want to be around when the human population of the earth passed the 9 billion mark.

*Primates.* Turning from human behavior to animals again, we recall a previous statement that animal studies have significance for humans to the extent that the subject animals resemble humans in their release from instinctual control over their behavior. To put it simply, the justification for extrapolating from animal studies to human behavior decreases with increasing phylogenetic distance. Rats, mice, crows, and the like are really not very close to human beings after all.

Over the past ten years a series of important field studies of primates has revealed that some of our fellow order members display rather strong territorial inclinations. Comparing the great apes with humans, though, we find that the gibbons, who are *least* like us physically, maintain territories based on mating pairs, while the gorillas (Schaller, 1963, 1965) and the chimpanzees (Van Lawick-Goodall, 1965, 1971), who resemble us *most* in a physical sense, show very little territoriality. Both gorillas and chimpanzees seem to form open communities that blend and trade members with each other. New groups form and dissolve on a daily basis, depending partly on where food is available. Some animals dominate over others, but none defends any territory against conspecifics, nor do they defend their mates against overtures from subordinate animals.

Of course, the great apes have evolved a great deal since about 30 million years ago, and although they are more like us than is any other animal, they are still not very much like humans. It may be that in the course of their differentiation from humans, they lived under circumstances in which territoriality was for some reason maladaptive, or perhaps hominids evolved under conditions that favored a strong sense of territoriality. Or, finally, the territoriality of human beings may be a cultural response to particular human circumstances, having nothing to do with genotype.

## Human Physical Adaptation

This section will explore some studies of the connections between the physical characteristics of human beings and the environments inhabited by these people. We shall begin with a word on natural selection but otherwise avoid the kinds of material likely to be encountered in standard textbooks of physical anthropology. Some of these studies are particularly interesting because they reveal systematic differences, many of them genotypic, in physiological adaptations of living groups of people. Such topics tend to be neglected, partly because they seem to violate some of our most cherished sociopolitical values ("all men are created equal" and so forth). The differences exist however, whether we choose to recognize them or not.

*Survival and Natural Selection.* A particular environment demands certain things of the organisms that live in it. In order for a body to survive, it must "fit" the environment to a certain extent. Put another way, there is a lower threshold of fit, below which the organism dies. In this section we will examine some of the ways in which the body and the environment accommodate each other, with the understanding that most of the accommodation is done by the body.

A process of primary concern here is natural selection. Briefly stated, natural selection is the means by which populations change their physical characteristics in such a way as to enhance the likelihood of the survival of the group. This change comes about through the differential survival of offspring. A certain amount of variability exists in all natural populations. A change in environment may wipe out some of the individual members of the populations because they lack the capacity to adapt to the change. Those organisms that survive in the new environment will expand in numbers until the population is as large as it was before. Figure 3 presents this process in graphic form.

In figure 3a, the average environmental temperature (which, in this case, may stand for any critical environmental parameter) is fifty degrees Fahrenheit. Some organisms are best suited to survive at twenty degrees or eighty. However, since this is a stable, fully adapted population, the majority of organisms are best suited to function at the actual average temperature of fifty. Since these maximally adapted organisms will do better at competing for resources and reproducing themselves, their numbers will be greatest. No organisms can survive if they are adapted to temperatures beyond twenty or eighty, because the degree of their fit to the environment will be so low that they will be unable to compete successfully with better adapted individuals.

Now suppose there is an environmental change, and the average temperature drops to thirty-five degrees Fahrenheit instead of fifty. Such a drop would eliminate organisms that were best adapted to a temperature of sixty-five or greater and make most of the other organisms less fit than they had been. Immediately following such a change, the most ill-adapted organisms would die but most of the population would still consist of animals best suited to an average temperature of fifty, as in figure 3b.

With the passage of time, the organisms best adapted to the new average temperature of thirty-five will compete and reproduce more successfully than the others. We may also hypothesize that mutation—"spontaneous" genetic change—has filled in the lower end of the scale and some organisms in the population will be best suited to an average temperature of only five degrees.

The above model illustrates some important points about natural selection. In the original stable, adjusted population, there was a normal distribution of organisms in terms of their optimal temperatures. Some of the organisms were better suited to temperatures considerably higher or lower than the real average. However, it was precisely those deviant organisms that enabled the population to survive. Consider what would have happened had *all* the original organisms been maximally adapted—suited only to a temperature of fifty degrees—and none been deviant. Any change in the real temperature might have wiped out the population. Variety in the population allows its survival in times of change. This is a well-recognized generalization and has been variously referred to in different contexts as the "law of requisite variety" (Ashby, 1956) and the "law of evolutionary potential" (Sahlins and Service, 1960).

Changes in population characteristics as the result of natural selection can occur relatively rapidly when the selective pressure is great. Rats have

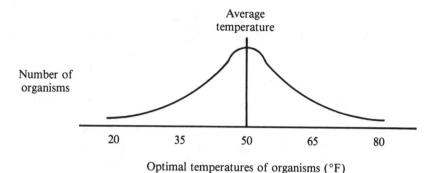

Average
temperature

Number of
organisms

20          35          50          65          80

Optimal temperatures of organisms (°F)

3A. ADAPTATIONS TO TEMPERATURE IN A STABLE POPULATION

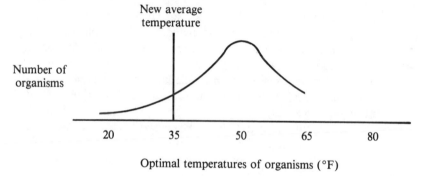

New average
temperature

Number of
organisms

20          35          50          65          80

Optimal temperatures of organisms (°F)

3B. ENVIRONMENTAL CHANGE

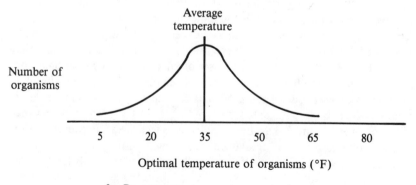

Average
temperature

Number of
organisms

5          20          35          50          65          80

Optimal temperature of organisms (°F)

3C. READJUSTMENT

FIG. 3. THE OPERATION OF NATURAL SELECTION.

39

been bred for their ability to learn mazes and, beginning with a single population, it has ordinarily taken only about eight generations to produce two strains of rats — "maze-bright" and "maze-dull" — whose maze-learning abilities differ to the extent that their scores are nonoverlapping.

Withal, there are limits to the adaptability of any given population, and when the limits are exceeded, the population will die off. As we have noted, the ability to survive gross environmental changes depends largely upon the amount of variety in a population. A breeding group in which all of the members are critically tuned to the prevailing environment has been called a specialized population; and a group whose members have characteristics not especially suited to any given environment but adequate for survival in several different environments is a generalized population.

There is something to be said for specialized populations. They can generally compete successfully against challengers and hold ecological niches for their own exclusive use, but they are extremely dependent on the particular environment in which they live. The Australian koala bears are good examples of specialized organisms. The koala bear is highly adapted to life in the ubiquitous eucalyptus tree and fills this niche to a fine extent. All other things being equal, as long as there are eucalyptus trees, there will be koala bears. But there may not always be eucalyptus trees in Australia. If the world should suddenly develop a craze for eucalyptus houses, the trees would probably go the way of the American bison — and so would the koala bear.

It would seem that one of the reasons for human survival so far — a few million years, not long in the paleontological scheme of things — is our relative generalization. We are outstandingly specialized in our upright posture and its consequences, such as distinctive feet, and in our unusually developed cerebral cortex, but these are not the sort of adaptations that link us irrevocably to any particular set of environmental conditions. For example, the human hand is a very generalized organ. The original amphibians who crawled out of the mud had five digits and the same general shape of the entire organ. Bats have five fingers and so do whales, but the form of their "hands" has been radically specialized. Because of the nonspecialization of the human hand, a wide range of locomotive behaviors is available to us. We can walk, hop, swim, climb trees, dive underwater, and so on. We cannot do all of these things equally well, but we can do them.

*Adaptation to Climatic Stress.* Nineteenth-century scholars of natural history tended to attribute much of the diversity of human behavior to underlying genetic differences. Some "instincts" were apparently universal, such as the tendency to seat oneself facing the center of a room rather than the walls (and *that* from William James [1962: 394]). It was further assumed that many of the differences between human breeding populations — races, religious groups, or social classes — were also attributable to inherited tendencies.

In the early part of this century, the scientific community began to challenge previous assumptions by distinguishing clearly between race and culture. By 1917, the idea of the "superorganic" had been built around the assumption that virtually all normative behavioral differences between human groups could be explained only by antecedent differences at the same cultural level. That is, only culture could explain culture. For example, if a Chinese infant were transported to America and brought up by an American family, he would learn to read and write English instead of Chinese, he would wear American clothes, get an American job, etc. His way of life, his culture, shaped his behavior. As A.L. Kroeber phrased it:

> Culture...is all those things about man that are more than just biological or organic, and are also more than merely psychological. It presupposes bodies and personalities, as it presupposes men associated in groups, and it rests upon them; but culture is something more than a sum of psychosomatic qualities and actions. It is more than these in that its phenomena cannot be wholly understood in terms of biology and psychology. Neither of these sciences claims to be able to explain why there are taxes and property laws and etiquettes and prayers in the world, why they function and perpetuate as they do, and least of all why these cultural things take the particular and highly variable forms or expressions under which they appear. [Kroeber, 1948: 8-9]

How about clothing? In any given geographic environment, any differences in the amount and style of clothing must be cultural in origin, as would hair styles, body ornamentation, taxes, and property laws. Since human biology is the same around the world, there would be no reason to expect that some people might be able to get along with fewer clothes in a cold climate than others could. If all manifest differences in patterned behavior are learned, and if resistance to cold weather cannot be learned, then all people must suffer equally when the temperature drops.

As usual, monolithic formulations that attribute all human differences in normative behavior to learning must be considered inadequate. Behavioral scientists are turning away from the conception of human nature as infinitely plastic, back to a concern with underlying biological differences, though today's interest in the biological underpinning is more sober than it was in the last century (Baker and Weiner, 1966).

New interest in empirical studies concerning physiological adaptations to climatic stress began during World War II, when armed forces personnel were stationed in exotic and sometimes climatically stressful places. Only a brief idea of the literature can be given here.

To date, these studies seem to deal primarily with adaptations to cold and to altitude, rather than to heat or dehydration. They are further limited by the understandable difficulty of finding representative samples of different societies. However, they do constitute an interesting beginning.

In Canada's Yukon, one team of investigators (Irving et al., 1960) studied the responses of Kutchin Indians and Caucasians to the arctic cold. They measured the temperatures (at several locations of the body) of eleven Kutchin and seven Caucasian men as they slept in light sleeping bags on two successive nights. The room temperature on the first night was 22 degrees Celsius and on the second 0 degrees. The Indians slept more, but all of the subjects were uncomfortably cold. It was revealed that the Indians generally had a slight metabolic advantage in response to cold, but it remained unclear whether this difference was due to biological adaptation or to the overall better physical fitness of the Indian subjects. Further experiments with the Kutchin, using Caucasians as controls, showed that, when subjects plunged their hands into very cold water, the Indians' hands remained somewhat warmer than the Caucasians', and moreover, the Indians' hands were more quickly rewarmed when withdrawn from the water, and with less pain (Elsner et al., 1960). Apparently the same is true of Eskimos' hands (Brown and Page, 1953). Similar work done with the Alakaluf at the southern tip of South America, another extreme climate, showed that these people too were somewhat better adapted to cold stress than were Caucasians (Hammel, 1960a, 1960b). Four groups of Mongoloids tested by the Japanese showed differences in the amount of blood flowing to the hand under exposure to cold, and the differential distribution of the hand's capacity to adapt to cold varied with the climates in which the four groups lived (Yoshimura and Iida, 1950-51). On the other hand, the reindeer-herding Lapp showed no such adaptation, nor did Norwegian fishermen or European controls (Krog et al., 1960; Hellström and Anderson, 1960). This sort of adaptation to cold works through an increase in metabolic rate, which burns up more calories, or an increase in blood flow to the extremities.

A rather different mode of cold adaptation is found in nomadic Lapps and in some Australian aborigines who live without clothing or substantial shelter in the desert, where night temperatures can be low. Insulation of the internal organs of the body allows the temperature of the extremities to drop but not that of the trunk (Scholander et al., 1958; Hammel et al.,

1959). The Kalahari Bushmen, however, living under conditions similar to those of the Australians, evidently show no cold adaptation, probably reflecting the fact that they arrived more recently in their current environment (Wyndham and Morrison, 1956; Ward et al., 1960).

Few studies have dealt with adaptation to heat, but there is some indication that American Blacks tolerate heat and humidity better than a group of white controls matched for age and economic background (Baker, 1958a; Adams and Covino, 1957), while whites seem to tolerate cold somewhat better (Baker, 1958b).

Work with Andean peoples indicates that populations that have lived for generations at altitudes exceeding 10,000 feet may become quite specialized in terms of adaptation to their hypoxic environment. The Indians who live high in the Andes have large chests, lungs, and hearts. Although their red blood corpuscles each carry less oxygen than ours, there are far more of them, and each person has more blood (up to two liters more) to carry the extra cells along. It is interesting to consider that, if these and associated features of Andean man were found in an individual at sea level, he might be diagnosed as having secondary polycythemia. However, such "disease" enables the Andean Indian to do strenuous manual labor in mines located near the mountaintops, at about sixteen thousand feet. It should be emphasized that the climate at this altitude is very stressful. Newcomers frequently fall ill from "mountain sickness," and their fertility is impaired (Monge, 1968).

It is sometimes impossible to know whether or not the physiological differences between hypothesized adapted populations and controls are genotypic. Perhaps physiological adaptation occurs on an individual basis, and no individual passes this acquired adaptation to his or her children. Or, as in the case of the Andean Indians, such a strong selective process may operate that the group itself is specialized.

Moreover, there would seem to be a distinct absence of investigations dealing with behavioral correlates of physiological and anatomical adaptation. It seems likely that if such gross and readily detectable differences separate adapted populations, associated differences in attitudes and temperament may also have their roots in human morphology. Perhaps so few studies exist because this is a taboo topic like the study of the differential destinies of beautiful and ugly people. We shall return to the subject later.

*Adaptation to Geographic Isolation.* A specific source of stress in the natural environment is geographic isolation, which has had some curious consequences in physical adaptation. One of the more controversial subjects in human taxonomy is the classification of the pygmies, the best-known populations of which live in the Congo forest in Africa, on the

Andaman Islands in the Indian Ocean, on the Malay Peninsula, and in the mountains of the Philippine Islands. Nobody knows where they evolved or, more important, how they got the way they are.

The usual explanations assume that a process of size reduction is involved and that the ancestors of the various pygmies were of normal size. Size reduction has been documented in the fossil records of other animals and this particular comparison between man and other animals might be enlightening. As Carleton Coon has pointed out (1962: 112-15), dwarf animals are rather common: deer in Japan and Cuba; elephants in the Philippines, Celebes, and Malta; mammoths and foxes on islands off the California coast; hippopotamuses in Liberia; chimpanzees in the Congo; ponies in the Shetlands, Iceland, Sardinia, Corsica, Cape Verde Islands, Timor, Bali, and Japan; buffalo in the Philippines and Celebes Islands; goats on Guadalupe Island, off Mexico; and a number of dwarf animals on the Ryukyu Islands south of Japan. It is extremely interesting to note that all of these animals are found either on islands or in areas of rainy forest surrounded by drier land. All of the islands are rather damp, with dense vegetation. Human pygmies too are found in rainy equatorial regions where vegetation makes travel difficult for larger people. Moreover, much of the food in rain forests is found in trees, and small people can climb trees better than larger people.

Other critical factors affect both human and animal populations living mostly in a limited geographic area. A critical population density must be maintained if breeding is to continue, but hunters and gatherers need a lot of room if they are to collect enough to feed themselves. In a limited area, a population of normal-sized people may find that there is not enough food around to support them at a density high enough to assure reproduction. On the other hand, small people eat less than big ones and consequently don't need to move around as much. Dwarfing is one way of keeping the population above the critical minimum density for successful reproduction. An island that could support sixty large people might support one hundred small ones, and that might make the difference between survival and extinction.

*Culture as an Intervening Variable in Human Evolution.* More attention has been directed recently to the interaction between the practices and artifacts of particular cultures and the evolution of the human body (e.g., Washburn, 1959). A study by Alice Brues (1968) expresses this trend. She begins by noting that some people are lanky and others are heavily muscled, with shorter limbs, and she relates these different body types to the use of different types of weapons. A long thin muscle, she suggests, can throw a projectile better than a short thick muscle, which can exert greater force over a short distance. Body form may thus be linked to differential efficiency in the use of weapons, a critical factor in human survival under primitive conditions. People whose bodies are better suited to the use of available weapons will tend to outlive others.

Before weapons, early humans followed the patterns of attack exemplified in the gorilla: with its large size and short limbs, it can smash or tear apart anything it can catch. But however terrifying a spectacle the gorilla may present, it must be a herbivore in the end because, as Brues puts it, "although he could kill anything he could catch, he cannot catch anything" (Brues, 1968: 191).

The first human weapons were probably blunt instruments that were seldom thrown since they were needed for repeated blows. No special body form was required, though the bigger the body, the better it could bludgeon. The situation changed with the development of projectile weapons like the spear, since the velocity of a thrown weapon is differentially associated with body form, a linear body build being most efficient. Since the spear is a more efficient weapon than the bludgeon, a selective advantage was conferred on people who were tall and lanky rather than short-muscled and stocky.

The next important development in weapons was the bow and arrow. The body form most capable of a powerful draw would display short limb segments and heavy muscles, at least in the upper part of the body — the opposite of the body form associated with the use of the spear.

During the Neolithic era, less than 10,000 years ago, the mode of human subsistence began to change from hunting to agriculture, which involved the use of the hoe. Since a hoe is more like a bludgeon than anything else, the best food-getter was no longer the lanky spearman or the laterally developed archer, but a sturdy peasant. Brues suggests that the lead taken by northern Europeans in mechanized agriculture may be related to the fact that they occupied a marginal cultural and geographic position during the spread of the spear and the bow. They closely resembled the old-fashioned bludgeoner, and their transition from ineffective hunters to effective farmers was easy.

As Brues sums up:

> It is interesting to speculate that even within our own species there has been some correlation between physique and habitual activity, resulting in a reciprocal influence between culture and body build. This influence may take several forms; a dominant weapon or tool may alter the average physique of a race using it over the course of time by giving a selective advantage to individuals of a body build best adapted to its use. It may also alter the numerical proportions of conflicting races of which one is physically better adapted to the use of a valuable implement.... And differences in physical

type between races may retard the transmission from one group to another of a new tool or weapon, and with it a whole new way of life. [Brues, 1968: 195]

*Summary Remarks on the Human Body.* It may be useful to summarize a few of the more important points suggested in this section. First, the human body is not infinitely malleable. Subject to enough stress, it dies, at whatever age. At the same time, human adaptability has led to a superordinate position among other animals. Under environmental stress, the first human response seems to be to adapt as an individual by altering either the internal or external milieu. For example, in low temperatures we may shiver (which warms the body), don more clothes, shut the windows, or build a fire. When the stress is more prolonged but less than lethal, adaptation may take place at a group level, by means of natural selection. The entire population may change in an adaptive way and may pass this change on to their offspring. There may be more residual differences between modern populations due to selective pressures in the past, and perhaps more selection going on today, than we realize.

The physical features commonly used in racial classifications today— hair texture, skin color, slight differences in the structure of the soft parts of the face—may not prove to be more significant than blood characteristics, the size of endocrine glands, and slight variations in certain neural tissues, which may currently be used to distinguish one population from another and which seem to cut across everyday concepts of race.

The old-fashioned classification of races—Mongoloids, Caucasoids, Negroids—and their constituent groups—Nordics, Alpines, Mediterraneans, and so on—may have been handy shortcuts in talking about vast, visibly different groups of people, especially as these are reflected in folk stereotypes. However, such classifications may soon be obsolete. In the future, I suspect that it will ultimately be realized that all men are not equal in every respect—not that some are better or worse than others, but that they are different—and human differences will likely show little correlation with the folk stereotypes of races.

In some instances there may be a greater difference in physiology and temperament between two white, middle-class Americans of Anglo-Saxon background, one of whose ancestors lived in cities and one of whose lived in the rural hinterland, than between them and a Bushman.

It is also worth noting that one of the more important influences on the characteristics of the human body—and one of the least studied—has been the contemporaneous evolution of disease microorganisms. The relationship between man and disease has probably always been significant in terms of natural selection, and it is likely to have grown more significant as people crowded together in cities and as they displaced other large animals. (A delightful and erudite description of the influence of typhus on human history can be found in *Rats, Lice, and History* [1971] by Hans Zinsser, a distinguished microbiologist who developed the typhus vaccine.) The rate of evolution of microorganisms has been increasing with the increasing use of antibiotics, which represents heavy selective pressure.

# CHAPTER TWO

# Traditional Theories of Environmental Influences on Perception and Behavior

Having established some of the ethological and evolutionary underpinnings of adaptations in natural, man-made, and interpersonal environments, we turn now to the work of some traditional theorists on the relationships between people and their surroundings. These theorists are traditional in the sense that their work is complete and they have themselves become historical figures in the development of human ecological theories. Most of these theorists tended to think in pan-global terms, and in this they differ from most living students of the subject. Few such macroecological minds seem to be around today. They also differ from modern theorists in that they deal almost exclusively with the naturally occurring environment, using a kind of natural history approach. I believe most of the major figures are represented here. I deal with them at such length because of their intrinsic interest, because I cannot imagine a book on human ecology that does not include them, and because they represent historical roots that tend to be neglected in current treatments of the topic.

As we shall see, people have always been interested in the influences of the environment upon the way people behave and think. Ancient Greeks and Romans, medieval Europeans, and postindustrial armchair theorists have expressed a variety of opinions, some of them well conceived but many of them just plain wrong.

## Hippocrates

The great physician Hippocrates was also a social theorist. One of his best works, *On Airs, Waters, and Places,* deals with influences of the climate, water, food, and regional topography upon the physical and mental life of the inhabitants. The second portion of the work provides the beginnings of a comparative ethnography based on environmental considerations. The treatise was held in high esteem as late as the eighteenth-century Age of Enlightenment.

Hippocrates suggested that areas with sharply defined climatic regions, such as the countries of Europe, produce a highly variegated human population. Places like Asia, where the climate varies little from one place to the next, witness a regularity of national character. Associated with the variable characteristics of most Europeans is an alertness, energy, and vigor, while Asians, he wrote, tend to be rather shiftless and unresponsive. Hippocrates also noted that the same correlations exist within any given geographical area. The Scythians, living north of the Black Sea in a climate characterized by only moderate changes, have a rather uniform temperament and are incapable of expending a great deal of energy, while the people living around the Sea of Azov, also north of the Black Sea but south of the Scythians, display the type of temperament expressed by most Europeans.

Like most of his contemporaries, Hippocrates expressed great interest in the relationship between environment and behavior, but his theories were bounded by the assumptions of his time. His use of the inductive method enabled him to see systematic differences between people living in different climes, but he borrowed from prevailing doctrines to explain these differences. He traced differences in health and temperament not only to climate (mediated by its effect on the humors of the body) but also to astrology. One's fate was to some extent connected with the movements of the heavenly bodies.

## Aristotle

A follower of Hippocrates, Aristotle was subject to many of the same limitations. The cold climate of northern Europe, Aristotle claimed, produced a people who were courageous and vigorous but who lacked the intelligence needed to achieve a high civilization. The Asians, on the other hand, were inquisitive and ingenious but lacked the spirit to rise above positions of slavery and serfdom. However, the Greeks (as Franklin Thomas interprets Aristotle), "being intermediate in position, were held to combine the advantages of both extremes without their shortcomings, and were therefore the best governed people in the world and by nature fitted to rule the earth" (Thomas, 1925: 33).

## Vitruvius

An architect named Vitruvius produced most of the writing that appeared in Rome on the relationship between climate and temperament. According to Vitruvius, the cold, moist climates of the north produce people who were tall and fair, with an abundance of blood in their bodies. Their blood gave them great courage in war but left them vulnerable to fevers and weak under conditions of high temperature. The dense, chill atmosphere tended to produce a sluggish intelligence in the same way that it produced torpor in snakes.

The dry heat of southern Europe produced dark, curly-haired people with little blood. They had very little courage in warfare but could endure great extremes of heat and fever. Because the atmosphere was so rare, the southern people developed a high intelligence.

Fortunately, explained Vitruvius, Rome happened to lie on a line midway between the chill, moist atmosphere of the north and the hot, dry atmosphere of the south. The Romans, therefore, lived in the climate most suitable for human habitation and most conducive to the best qualities of other climates without their disadvantages (a conclusion strikingly similar to Aristotle's if a few degrees different in latitude).

## Ibn Khaldun

Aside from a few original observations, interest in the relationship between physical environment and temperament slacked off greatly during the medieval period. Systematic relationships, to the extent that they existed, were not considered important since they were determined by God and no causal influence could link the two sets of conditions.

In this intellectual enterprise, as in so many others, further investigation was left to the Arabs. Ibn Khaldun (1332-1406), a historian and geographer, approached the two disciplines as sciences. He began by dividing the earth into several climatic zones, principally based on the work of an earlier geographer, Ibn Idrisi. Ibn Khaldun considered the southern hemisphere to be largely underwater and uninhabitable. After reviewing the earlier literature on the subject, Khaldun divided the earth into two zones representing the arctic limits of human habitation, three zones in temperate climes, and two, nearest the equator, of extreme heat. The people of the southern zones displayed ready passions and a tendency to seek out strong and pleasant stimuli, due to dilation of their animal spirits by the extreme heat; the people of the north were prudent, wise, and retiring, due to contraction of their animal spirits. Khaldun also suggested that wine produces internal heat and thus dilates the animal spirits, making one more passionate and pleasure seeking. The southern peoples, given their temperament, needed no such stimulation; but wine produced in northern people a behavior similar to that found normally in southerners. Comparing the two, "there is such an excess of heat from without that an inhabitant of a warm climate is like a dweller in a cold climate who is continually under the influence of wine" (Thomas, 1925: 44). This strangely foreshadows Immanuel Kant's later division of Europe into northern "Gothic" and southern "Romantic" temperaments, and, without the geographical trimmings, a modern school of individual psychology (best exemplified by Carl Jung and Hans Eysenck) built around the concepts of introversion and extroversion.

It goes without saying that Khaldun located a "middle ground," a temperate region whose inhabitants possessed the best qualities of northerners and southerners without any of their deficiencies. Where was this sterling temperament best expressed? The Arabian peninsula happened to be located in the torrid zone, but it was surrounded by large bodies of water which had a cooling effect. These two factors ensured that the climate of Arabia was actually temperate.

## Bodin

In the sixteenth century, French political philosopher Jean Bodin again called attention to the influence of climate and location upon the character of populations, claiming that a wise government should suit its constitution and laws to the nature of its residents. Bodin's theories were an outré blend of astrology and physiology, but he attempted to be precise and definite in his description of national temperaments. The people of the north were strong, not overly bright, inclined towards exhibitions of physical prowess, faithful, loyal, cruel, and not very interested in sexual activities. They valued liberty, were fickle in their religious life, and were intemperate (i.e., they drank a lot). The southern peoples were deceptive, canny, passionate, lecherous, jealous, long-lived, courteous, uninterested in politics, and extreme in their behavior. Fortunately, the people of the "middle ground" had the best qualities of both northerners and southerners without any of the disadvantages. They were truthful, reliable, and moderate. It was felicitous that France lay in the heart of this fortunate region.

## English Physicians

Richard Mead (1673-1754), whose most interesting work was his *Treatise Concerning the Influence of the Sun and Moon upon Human Bodies,* knew more about physics and other sciences than did earlier writers. Although his work is more limited in scope than theirs, dealing mainly with the effects of atmospheric phenomena upon physiological processes, he managed to drop the astrological and humoral burdens of earlier writers. Mead theorized that the position of the sun and moon affect the atmosphere. Since any serious deviation from the normal value of atmospheric pressure interferes with man's most efficient performance, solar and lunar changes or storms affect him adversely. Because all of these phenomena operate according to certain natural laws, people are indirectly subject to the same laws.

At about the same time, physician John Arbuthnot attempted to apply recent discoveries about the physical properties of gasses to problems of human nature that had originally been outlined by Hippocrates (cf. Arbuthnot [1751: 58]; quoted in Thomas [1925: 60]; Hippocrates [1957: 136-37]). Arbuthnot claimed that northern people were aggressive, vigorous, and hard-working. People of the south were generally languorous and given to contemplation rather than physical activity. There was a certain amount of individual flexibility in this arrangement, for on crisp days everyone tended to act in more energetic fashion, and on warm muggy days, everyone tended to slow down. Arbuthnot is thought to have greatly influenced the imagination of Montesquieu, and Arbuthnot's *Essay Concerning the Effects of the Air on Human Bodies* occupies an important position in the literature of human geography.

## Montesquieu

Baron de Montesquieu achieved what might now be called a breakthrough in his *The Spirit of Laws,* published in 1748, a lengthy and consistent exercise in the comparative method. Gone is the astrological and humoral baggage that so often vitiated earlier attempts at explanation, for by this time many ethnographic accounts were seeping back into Europe from missionaries and other explorers. As Mead and Arbuthnot used discoveries in physics to provide underpinning for their arguments, so Montesquieu used the recent and relatively accurate ethnographic reports. However, like Bodin, he was less concerned with formulating general principles relating environment to behavior than he was with applying rules of government and jurisprudence. These laws, Montesquieu argued, should be relative to the environmental context:

> They should be in relation to the climate of each country, to the quality of its soil, to its situation and exent, to the principal occupation of the natives, whether husbandmen, herdsmen or shepherds; they should have relation to the degree of liberty which their inclinations, riches, numbers, commerce, manners and customs permit. [Montesquieu, 1873, quoted in Thomas, 1925: 64]

Montesquieu held that people living in colder climates are "brave, vigorous, insensible to pain, devoid of sex passion and possessed of relatively strong physical frames and phlegmatic temperaments. The people of warm climates are weak, timid, apathetic toward physical exertion, vivacious, sensitive to pleasure or pain, inordinate in their sexual indulgences, and utterly lacking in mental ambition" (Thomas, 1925: 65). Montesquieu may sound a little harsh in comparison with modern theorists who tend to state probabilistic tendencies rather than immutable categories.

Montesquieu noted that people drink more alcoholic beverages in cold climates than in warm. Moreover, since women mature earlier in warmer climates, polygyny is common there, and in colder climates most marriages are monogamous. Thus climate influences culture, and therefore the rules of government must suit themselves to predetermined cultural patterns.

### Ratzel

In the middle part of the last century, Germany produced a school of investigators called anthropogeographers, perhaps given impetus by Karl Ritter, who with the naturalist Baron Alexander von Humboldt virtually founded the science of geography. It is difficult to summarize the work of Ratzel. He was a human geographer in the broadest sense, but he was extremely prolific, and little analytical consistency appears in his voluminous writings. He shared this remarkable prodigiousness with the other anthropogeographers and with German scholars of his time. "It is probable that every German who was not writing an *Allgemeine Kulturgeschichte* ["General History of Civilization"] in ten volumes was writing *Die Völkerkunde* ["History of Mankind"] in twenty" (Penniman, 1965: 93).

Ratzel's works are known to Americans through the writings of Ellen Churchill Semple. Perhaps his strongest influence in anthropology has been on Pater Schmidt and the other members of the *Kultur kreise*

("Culture circle") movement, mainly through his emphasis on the likelihood of the diffusion of cultural elements rather than their independent invention. Ratzel and the anthropogeographers have been described as geographical determinists who traced much of human behavior directly to the characteristics of its natural physical context, and Ratzel has drawn criticism for his supposed "reductionism." As Emile Durkheim put it:

> Thus we see how erroneous those theories are which, like the geographical materialism of Ratzel (see especially his *Politische Geographie*) seek to derive all social life from its material foundation (either economic or territorial). They commit an error precisely similar to the one committed by Maudsley in individual psychology. Just as this latter reduced all the psychical life of the individual to a mere epiphenomenon of his physiological basis, they seek to reduce the whole psychical life of the group to its physical basis. But they forget that ideas are realities and forces, and that collective representations are forces even more powerful and active than individual representations. [1965: 260 fn.]

In truth, Ratzel himself may not have been such a hard-nosed determinist (cf. Harris, 1968: 339-40). But he did, of course, posit a relationship between behavior and its natural context. According to Ratzel, lands with similar climates were likely to undergo parallel historical development. Climate affected man both directly and indirectly through the biotic environment, but human adaptability meant that climatic influences merely ruled out certain kinds of behavior and encouraged others. Warm climates tended to produce large populations whose members were easygoing and emotional; cold climates produced sparse populations whose members were energetic, somber, and frugal. Climate determined the limits of habitability and influenced the topography of a region, which in turn influenced the economic and political development of the inhabitants. It also influenced migration patterns, since immigrants tended to seek out — and function most efficiently in — the same sort of environments they came from. The influence of climate was profound enough to lend a certain "zonal stamp" to human activities. Residents of the middle, temperate zone were most favored by nature and were thus more advanced than residents of the frigid or hot zones. Even *within* the temperate zone, those living near the northern margins were superior to those living farther south. This was evidenced by the superiority of people living in the northern parts of the United States, Germany, Italy, and France over people living in the southern parts of the same countries. Winds played an important part in the development of civilization; intense storms encouraged progress by rendering the struggle for existence that much more severe.

## Determinism and Possibilism

Environmental determinism, or environmentalism, holds that geography is the most important factor determining the characteristics of socio-cultural systems. Therefore, learned behavior can best be explained by reference to contemporary environments. Few of the environmental determinists have gone so far as to say that every characteristic of a culture could be predicted from the surrounding environment. Such a proposition would be too easy to refute. As Hegel is reputed to have said: "Do not speak to me of geographical determinants. Where the Greeks once lived the Turks live now. That settles the question" (quoted in Bierstedt, 1970: 34). Or, to put it another way, look at Manhattan Island in 1492 and compare it to Manhattan Island in 1942, during which period the climate has probably changed only a little.

The most outstanding recent figure associated with environmental determinism is no doubt Ellsworth Huntington (1876-1947), a geographer and explorer who spent the last forty years of his life teaching at Yale and writing a series of tomes dealing with the relationships among geographic factors, culture, and psychology. Huntington is sometimes used as a bad example in introductory textbooks. References to Huntington are dutifully trotted out, his more excessive statements are quoted, and then his position is destroyed and dismissed by the author of the text, who points out that life on Manhattan today is different from what it was five hundred years ago.

Huntington, rabid geographer though he may have been, was not so poor a scholar. He knew several ways to handle embarrassing objections. One of his exits was race, which he called kith, and the other was culture. Each time he seemed to have worked himself into an extreme position, he pointed out the need to consider those other determinants of behavior. Once an investigator has left room for biological inheritance, culture, and environment, what else is left? If Huntington gave primary attention to environment, it is because he was a geographer and it was his business to examine the environment as a factor in shaping human behavior.

If most of the environmental determinists were geographers, most of the so-called possibilists were anthropologists. The possibilists argued that the environment had a limiting effect on behavior, rather than a determining one. The environment rendered some things impossible—coconut groves in Labrador, say—but as for what was possible *within* a given environment, there were always cultural alternatives. There was no guarantee that any particular possibility would be expressed in behavior. A classical example, given in many introductory texts, is that the Navaho and Hopi live in very similar environments, but the Navaho have turned largely to sheepherding and metalwork for a living, while the Hopi are largely agricultural, as they have been for a long time. Even in extremely demanding environments, there are always alternatives. The Eskimo of Alaska may build houses of snow blocks during the winter, but across the Bering Strait, the Chukchee live in tents made of hides.

Such a possibilist view has led some anthropologists to an emphasis on historical determinants of cultural phenomena. In the case of the Navaho and Hopi, for example, the Hopi have been agriculturalists for a thousand years or so, while the Navaho are recent arrivals in the Southwest and were previously just one more hunting and gathering group of Apaches.

If possibilism sometimes leads to an emphasis on historical particularism — the idea that culture is determined by what people have experienced in the past — then historical particularism can lead to a reification of culture. That is to say, if culture is determined by itself, then it evolves in accordance with certain internal dynamics to become a thing sui generis, isolated from everything except its own history. Kroeber's paper on the superorganic (1917) is usually cited as a landmark in the development of this approach, although certainly the idea goes back at least as far as Herbert Spencer's *Principles of Sociology* (1896). Kroeber's major point in the superorganic paper was a humanist one. At that time, people — and not only laymen — were inclined to write about such groups as the "Red" race and the "Jewish" race without paying a great deal of attention to the separation of learned behavior from physical appearance. Kroeber wanted to distinguish clearly between biology and culture and to emphasize the fact that such a distinction was vital in the behavioral sciences. However, in insisting on the independence of culture from other spheres of human experience, Kroeber managed to effectively isolate culture from environmental influences as well as biological ones.

Thus we have Leslie White and his students, for whom culture is truly a closed system, with an almost mystic quality, evolving and developing according to some scheme known only to God (White, 1949, 1959). White's theory cannot deal with particular cultures, only with culture as a whole; that is, culture considered as a pan-global phenomenon. His colleagues, Marshall Sahlins and Elman Service (1960), have tried to reconcile White's ideas about general evolution with Julian Steward's ideas about multilinear evolution.

## Mason

Around the turn of the century and before this tendency towards the reification of culture had begun, some interesting work was being done in ecological anthropology in America. Otis T. Mason wrote several papers (1894, 1895) in which he pointed out that there was a great deal of overlap between North American climatic zones and the areas occupied by the linguistic families of American Indians. (These languages had been classified in 1891 by John Wesley Powell, a one-armed explorer and geographer, later to become the hero of a Walt Disney movie.) Mason also noticed that Powell's linguistic areas showed a considerable internal similarity in other cultural traits as well. Not only were similar languages spoken in each climatic area, but baskets were made in similar ways, food-getting techniques were similar, and so on.

Mason classified North America into twelve "ethnic environments" according to each area's geological structure, vegetation, animals, climate, and potential for human exploitation. Mason proposed that the nonhuman environmental factors — climate, predominant animals, and so forth — determined cultural development, but he also made more specific observations that "sounded" more like possibilism. He noted, for example, that easy travel in dugout canoes along the northwest coast made possible the development of dispersed kin groups.

In his specific examples Mason was not committed to nonhuman environmental factors as the sole determinants of human events. Like most other American anthropologists of the time, he was probably influenced more heavily by the findings and concepts of archaeology than are most contemporary theorists in ethnology. He absorbed from archaeologists the importance of the ideas of trade and diffusion of cultural traits; so he was prompted to observe that very few impassable barriers separated the ethnic environments of North America. In fact, North America itself formed one whole ethnic environment, since there were few physical barriers separating the Indians who lived in any part of the continent. There were barriers, but they were more geological than climatic. The Mississippi is big, for example, but it is nothing compared to the Tsin Ling Mountains that separate North China from South China, providing a sharp boundary between the cold, arid, noodle-eating north, and the hot, wet, rice-eating south. The Rocky Mountains were effective barriers to migration but not to the movement of air masses moving north or south. The differences on each side of the Rockies were therefore less pronounced.

Mason should have written a book, but he never progressed beyond a few articles. He did not provide maps, and he discussed the distinctions between areas only in vague terms. The cultural inventories he listed for his ethnic environments were very short. At the same time, however, his ethnic environments were precursors of a more systematic classification to be made by Alfred Louis Kroeber, who is discussed below.

## Wissler

A somewhat different approach to human behavior took its motive force more directly from archaeology. Museum displays of tools, ornaments, and other artifacts are generally arranged according to the areas they came from, so that viewers can gain a more or less complete idea of what life was like in a particular place at a particular time. Using a similar system in 1917, Clark Wissler of the American Museum of Natural History distinguished nine North American culture areas. Wissler pointed out that the distribution of cultural traits in North America was similar to the distribution of types of vegetation and climate (Wissler, 1917, 1926); the correspondences were so close that Wissler wondered whether the occurrence of these cultural traits was in some way based upon ecology. He thought that merely demonstrating certain correspondences did not reveal much about the dynamics involved, but that such demonstrations might lead to the identification of relational principles. Some of Wissler's ideas were incorporated into an important introductory textbook—actually a compendium of seemingly unrelated bits of ethnographic information—written by Kroeber, who revised Wissler's classification and came up with ten culture areas (Kroeber, 1923).

### Kroeber and Ecology

One problem with this early approach to classifying culture areas was reliance on such limited ethnographic evidence. The trait lists were short, and the traits had little relationship to one another besides existing in the same area. Mason, Wissler, and Kroeber were throwing dozens of unrelated traits into the same bag and saying that these, together, defined the culture areas of North America. But really, on what empirical grounds could one divide the total continent up into nine or ten areas? The culture areas that these writers described were not really integrated units at all, so their usefulness in explaining relationships between the environment and cultural behavior was limited. (Marvin Harris's [1968] critique of the procedural bases underlying these classifications is exemplary.)

Kroeber continued his interest in regional surveys, publishing his *Handbook of the Indians of California* in 1925. In the 1930s he placed more and more emphasis on quantitative scrutinies of unrelated lists of culture elements. The 1930s were hard times. Many student anthropologists were simply unable to obtain the funds necessary for extended field work in exotic settings. But there was enough work to satisy all field workers if they visited an Indian reservation and collected long checklists indicating the presence or absence of one or another trait. There was added incentive in the knowledge that most American Indian societies were so quickly becoming disorganized or assimilated that if they were to be studied at all, it had better be soon. This collection of voluminous ethnographic materials—sometimes based on the testimony of only one or two informants for an Indian community—was especially prevalent at Berkeley, where Kroeber was both the chairman and the founding father of the department of anthropology. A series of papers in the *University of California Anthropological Records* demonstrates the limited usefulness of this bland empiricism. There are still reams of paper at Berkeley, waiting to be digested and analyzed by some scholar.

In 1939, Kroeber published his clearest statement of the relationship between ecology and culture. Here he discarded the trait lists and based his classification instead on subsistence patterns and population density, identifying nine major culture areas in North America. He suggested that subsistence modes and population were related to the possibilities of the natural biota for exploitation, but, still under the rather theoretically arid influence of Boas, he walked on tiptoes when faced with the possibility of setting up any scheme of causal influence. Franz Boas, his mentor at Columbia, was so thoroughly disenchanted with the wild speculations of the armchair evolutionists of the preceding generation that he had come to be overly cautious about making any sort of theoretical statement. Kroeber was not dramatically different from his teacher. Here is Kroeber in *Cultural and Natural Areas of Native North America:*

> On the one hand, culture can be understood primarily only in terms of cultural factors, but on the other hand no culture is wholly intelligible without reference to the noncultural or so-called environmental factors with which it is in relation and which condition it.... The interactions of culture and environment become exceedingly complex when followed out. And this complexity makes generalization unprofitable, on the whole. In each situation or area different natural factors are likely to be impinging on culture with different intensity. [Kroeber, 1939: 205]

Kroeber's emphasis was primarily on the *limiting* influence of the environment. It is difficult to discern any regularities in relationships when one gives up beforehand, saying that the relationships are so complex as to be unidentifiable. His possibilism is sometimes made explicit by means of the convention that was standard at the time:

> Six American states stretching in a belt from Ohio to Nebraska today produce nearly half the world's maize crop. This is a region in which the Indians

also farmed maize, but with less intensity than in many other regions; and their population remained scant. The difference is not in the plant, nor fundamentally in methods of farming it. It is factors extrinsic to the cultivation itself which have changed an area of below-average maize-growing into one of the most successful specialization. These factors are cultural: domesticated animals, economic demand and distribution facilities, methods of transportation, improved machinery. The natural environment remained the same. [Kroeber, 1939: 205]

Kroeber was engaged in important enterprises, mapping limits of natural zones of animal and plant life against the distribution of cultivated plants and attempting to estimate aboriginal human populations in each area. But he applied no consistent ecological approach to the problem of patterned behavior. The Eastern Woodlands area, for example, had a rather low density of population. One obvious step in trying to explain this is to examine food-getting techniques in the area in order to determine whether or not they would have permitted the development of high-density communities. Instead, Kroeber thought that the reason the Indians of the Eastern Woodlands lived in small and scattered clusters was that they had never developed the idea of the state — a sterile explanation. Kroeber would never go so far as to suggest that similar technologies, operating on similar environments, would produce similar social structures. At the same time, however, Kroeber acknowledged the importance of environmental influences; he wrote a long monograph in which areas of culture were organized partly in terms of environmental regularities, a book that no doubt influenced Julian Steward's work during the following decade.

After *Cultural and Natural Areas of Native North America,* Kroeber became fascinated with the growth of culture and particularly with the distinctive characteristics of so-called high civilizations, neglecting those processes that, from an ecological point of view, must be primary.

His basis for assessing cultures may best be called style.... He ascribed great importance to style in the much broader sense, which tended strongly to be aesthetically tinged. He variously characterized cultures by their principal manifestations, the Maya by their achievements in writing and calendrical systems, architectural forms, and decorative art; and by contrast the Inca by their accomplishments in vast irrigation works, roads, and bridges, and their organizing ability. In fact, Kroeber's major works were devoted to classification of cultures and civilizations on the basis of distinctive styles. [Steward, 1973: 49]

Kroeber's later work is of limited value because the procedures he used in describing societies were openly intuitive — no one could reliably duplicate them—and because the emphasis on style was misplaced, since distinctive features of culture are unique and in their own nature incomparable. Thus, *Configurations of Culture Growth* (1944), a long evaluation of high civilizations, is worthless because no true comparison of cultures is possible. Furthermore, Kroeber

> rarely wrote about the nature of subsistence, economics, or political and social structure, let alone their effects on other aspects of culture. That the dissimilar achievements of the Maya and the Inca were both built on dense, stable agricultural populations controlled by state structures was to Kroeber a matter for the social scientist, whom he distrusted. [Steward, 1973:51]

Kroeber was brilliant. In *Configurations of Culture Growth,* on which he worked for seven years, he discussed lucidly and in a charmingly offhand manner practically every endeavor known to man outside of anything related directly to environmental exploitation—philology, sculpture, painting, drama, literature, and music in Egypt, Mesopotamia, India, Japan, Greece, Rome, Europe, and China. Too bad that such intellect and energy should result in a work of which the author could write:

> In reviewing the ground covered, I wish to say at the outset that I see no evidence of any true law in the phenomena dealt with; nothing cyclical, repetitive, or necessary. [Kroeber, 1944: 761, quoted in Harris, 1968: 330]

## Social Ecologists

The term *social ecology* first described the efforts of a school of sociologists that blossomed in the early 1920s, mainly at the University of Chicago. Theirs was the first systematic attempt to employ concepts from biological ecology in analyzing the activities of human beings. The analogies at first tended to be rather raw, focusing on what was interpreted as the struggle for existence, cooperation and competition, territorial dominance, ecological succession, and demography. An example of this conceptual borrowing appears in Roderick McKenzie's essay, "The Ecological Approach to the Study of the Human Community," originally published in 1924.

> The structural growth of community takes place in successional sequence not unlike the successional stages in the development of plant formation. Certain specialized forms of utilities and uses do not appear in the human community until a certain stage of development has been attained, just as the beech or pine forest is preceded by successional dominance of other plant species. And just as, in plant communities, successions are the products of in-

vasion, so also in the human community the formation, segregations and associations that appear constitute the outcome of a series of invasions. [1968: 20]

In a sense, the social ecologists did for the American community, particularly the city of Chicago, what A.L. Kroeber was later to attempt for North American Indians. Two other names associated with social ecology are Robert E. Park and Ernest W. Burgess, who along with McKenzie were seminal figures in the theoretical development of the approach. Of course, many other sociologists were to study phenomena that could be interpreted in terms of ecological concepts (e.g., Zorbaugh, 1929). The list of students subsequently influenced by social ecology is practically endless, since after twenty years this discipline had become "one of the most definitive and influential schools in American sociology (Alihan, 1938: xi)." The bulk of the more important literature in the field is readily accessible (e.g., Burgess and Bogue, 1964; McKenzie, 1968; Theodorson, 1961). Probably the most important and concise historical summary is in Faris (1967).

Social ecologists were fond of examining spatial distributions and drawing up classificatory schemes on the basis of maps. One of the more famous models, and one of the earliest developed, was the concentric zone theory of the structure of cities, based on Chicago during the 1920s (Burgess, 1961, originally 1925). Burgess proposed that "the typical process of the expansion of the city can best be illustrated, perhaps, by a series of concentric circles, which may be numbered to designate both the successive zones of urban extension and the types of areas differentiated in the process of expansion" (Burgess, 1961: 38).

In this model, Zone I represents the central business district—"downtown" as it is called in most communities. Zone II contains businesses that engage in wholesale, light manufacturing, and the provision of services: small shops, garages, warehouses, and so on. Zone III is a lower-class residential area consisting mostly of workingmen's homes. Zone IV is also residential but the housing is in better shape, it is more expensive, and minority group members are likely to have restricted access. Zone V represents an area beyond the city limits where commuters live and from which they travel to work in the central business district. Complications may be introduced by rivers, railroads, coasts, and so on, so that no city fits the scheme perfectly, but overall, most communities are likely to exhibit structural features consistent with this model.

One consistency is the tendency of each zone to expand outward at the expense of the zone it is replacing, a process likened to that of ecological succession. Of greatest interest here is the interface between zones II and III. The theory suggested that as zones I and II expanded, the first residential zone was left to fall into disrepair because it would soon be converted into an area of light manufacturing. From the point of view of the owners, there was no reason to fix up the slums around the central city when they would soon be destroyed anyway to make room for businesses. This interface between the expanding business section and the residential areas was called the zone of transition, a term by now so classic that hardly any introductory sociology student can escape its reverberations. The zone of transition is characterized by the deterioration of physical structures, decreasing population, many transients, and a great deal of what was called vice in the 1920s.

The concentric zone theory came in for much criticism, chiefly the result of empirical studies of other cities in which these ideal zones did not appear (e.g., Davie, 1961, originally 1938). Other models of urban structure have been proposed, including the sector theory, which states that various districts and neighborhoods show a tendency to radiate outward from the central business area, and the multiple nuclei theory which states that whole geographical areas are added to the city in blocks, each area showing distinctive features, a process perhaps now finding expression in housing tracts and industrial areas at the urban fringe, built around shopping centers.

Probably, with the joint movement of people and services out of the cities, none of these models is in itself appropriate. It is difficult to determine whether the inner city residents, the supermarkets, or the industrial plants moved out first, but it is certain that the configuration of urban development has changed.

In any case, the concentric zone theory seems unsuitable for analyzing urban development outside the United States. An early study of the Mexican city of Merida showed that the pattern in and around Latin American centers diverges significantly from the concentric zone model. Here, there is a town square and downtown area, surrounded by fashionable upper-class housing. The poor areas are found not around the central zones but around the town limits. This is noticeable around Mexico City and, even more so, in smaller cities like Cuernavaca and resorts like Acapulco. In fact, an examination of the literature suggests that "a zone of transition might develop and the relationship of socioeconomic status to centralization reverse itself if...cities experienced rapid and uncontrolled industrialization and growth" (Theodorson, 1961: 327). In other words, where the growth of a city is slow, its most attractive and desirable areas are likely to be found near the downtown area. However, an immature, growing city like Chicago in the 1920s will exhibit structural characteristics more congruent with those of the concentric zone model. It is worth noting that the concentric zone theory of urban development fulfilled all the functions of a good case study: it articulated a problem, stimulated further research, led to a comparison of cases, and was subsequently modified in the light of later findings.

The entire approach known as social ecology came under some stringent criticism in the 1940s (e.g., Alihan, 1961, originally 1938; Hawley, 1944). Among the principal objections were (1) that there is nothing especially ecological in most of the studies, but "rather are these monographs general sociological studies in which territorial distribution is taken account of in reference to sociological data" (Alihan, 1961:94); (2) explanatory concepts such as competition are proposed as explanations for certain kinds of behavior, but the concepts themselves are post hoc interpretations, and their operation is not described in detail, so "consequently it is almost impossible to indicate what to look for in order to see competition in action" (Hawley, 1944: 401); (3) much of the actual research in social ecology consists of plotting the distribution of the characteristics of community life on maps, and leaving it at that, whereas mapping is usually considered only a first step in the analysis of things; (4) to the extent that social ecology adhered to its original biologically derived conception of community, it ignored communications and culture and thus artificially limited its own hermeneutic power.

Social ecology survived these criticisms, and modern examples of the approach still appear in the literature. Exemplary is Meyer's *Spatial Variation of Black Urban Households,* a comparative, statistical study of factors relating to black residential choice (Meyer, 1970). Some other interesting studies owing a debt to social ecology can be found in Alexander Spoehr's *Pacific Port Towns and Cities* (Spoehr, 1963), which represents one of the few attempts by anthropologists to examine the structure of cities. (John Gulick is another exception and one of the earliest [Gulick, 1953, 1963, 1967].) Urban anthropology, in practice, generally concerns itself less with the overall structure of cities than with selective aspects of the American urban life-style. Recently, too, a corresponding interest in urban environments has developed among psychologists, who seem to have adopted a mainly native point of view in searching out, for example, congruencies between the characteristics of cities and the cognitive maps of their inhabitants (e.g., Lynch, 1960; Downs and Stea, 1973), an approach that owes a great deal to economist Kenneth Boulding's *The Image* (1965) and which lends itself to quantitative analysis (e.g., Moore, 1975).

## The Cultural Core

Julian Steward has been responsible for the popularity and strength of the anthropological movement known as cultural ecology. Steward took a pan-global perspective to assert that environmental exploitation—subsistence patterns—form a stable, slowly changing set of acts—the "cultural core"—with a distinct and pervasive influence upon other sets of more or less distantly related acts, such as religion. This sounds more like Marxism than it really is; Steward felt that types of subsistence patterns are determined in a large part by the nature of the environment itself and that the level of technological development and the properties of the environment jointly tended to produce a particular kind of social organization. Steward applied this perspective to analyze the organization of Great Basin Shoshone Indians during his field work in the 1930s, where the demands imposed by a rigorous environment upon a people with minimal tools dictated an adaptive unit consisting of only a small number of individuals. Only a limited number of people could live and forage together because of the limited carrying capacity of their arid and unpredictable environment. Steward described seasonal changes in the composition of these nomadic groups. The family was the adaptive unit during the winter, when subsistence was particularly problematic, and families coalesced into larger interactional groups during the summers when, as one or another food source became plentiful in a given area, the carrying capacity of the environment increased.

Steward's general idea was not new, but the detailed and quite sensible attention he gave it was a refreshing change from the theoretical barrenness of the Boas years. Whether or not any of his individual propositions concerning the relationship between environment, subsistence patterns, and social organization hold up in the long run is less important than the fact that Steward provided ecologically oriented analyses with significant impetus. Similar analyses have since become common (e.g., Hallowell, 1949).

## The Hydraulic Society

Historian Karl Wittfogel has suggested that there is a direct link between certain parameters of the environment and forms of political organization. Essentially he has proposed that there are two basic kinds of agriculture, one that depends upon the amount of available rainfall and another in which rainfall is unpredictable and often heavy. The first set of circumstances imposes no particular hardship on people and has little impact upon the form of government. The second set of circumstances is best met by the construction of dams and irrigation and drainage systems and is likely to lead, through intermediary steps, to the development of strongly centralized, authoritarian states. Wittfogel applied his theory to historical materials, especially those dealing with China. "The analysis of the organization of the productive forces makes it possible to explain the stagnation of the oriental agricultural society from the particular, centralized structure of the system of production based on irrigation" (Wittfogel, 1959: 96).

Wittfogel also discussed the relevance of his theory, largely derived from Marx and Max Weber, to an understanding of non-Sinitic societies such as those of India, the Near East, and Egypt. In the 1920s, when Wittfogel was developing his ideas, his allegiance to Marxism was ideological as well as academic. His views, however, did not jibe with those of the orthodox interpreters of Marxism. Wittfogel's distinction between the development of European society, which had gone through a phase of feudalism, and of Oriental society, which had not, proved especially grating. Marx had proposed that capitalism developed out of the dispersed feudal estates of medieval Europe. If in Asia the means of production had directly produced a strongly centralized state, how could Asian societies develop capitalism? If they could not develop capitalism, how could they develop communism? In his discussion of Wittfogel's career, Marvin Harris observes that Wittfogel, in reaction to his critics, was led to abandon his materialistic notions and finally to view the "Oriental society" as something of an abstract idea divorced from its ecological foundation (Harris, 1968: 672-73).

This brief account of Wittfogel's theory has been unavoidably oversimple and incomplete in view of the range of historical and archaeological information under his control and his immense output. His theory has had considerable influence on anthropology and has generated a good deal of controversy. Some investigators have found evidence in its support (e.g., MacNeish, 1967) while others have discovered that in some societies such as Mesopotamia and Mesoamerica, while large-scale waterworks and despotic states are indeed associated with one another, the causality is the other way around, since the formation of the states seems to have preceded the development of irrigation systems (Adams, 1960, 1966). In places where irrigation systems were present but of limited economic importance, they seem to have had little influence on the polity. Mitchell has proposed that, in place of argument, the original hypothesis be altered

> to state that if there is centralized direction of irrigation activities in an arid or semiarid environment, then there will be a corresponding increase in centralized political power in other areas of social life. The extent of political power will vary directly with the extent of the irrigation system and its importance to the total economy. [Mitchell, 1973: 534]

## Huntington and Social Character

Ellsworth Huntington, the geographer and explorer, wrote a number of books about the influence of the environment upon human activities. Huntington felt that there were three main determinants of human behavior: (1) genetics, (2) climate, and (3) culture. The following account is taken primarily from his mature work, especially *Mainsprings of Civilization* (1959).

Huntington's ideas about genetic influences on human behavior were based on a unit he called a *kith*. The kith is not a powerful concept. It is based on the simple assumption that children tend to inherit certain things from their parents, including features that are anatomical, physiological, and temperamental. By temperament, Huntington meant emotional and motivational elements of personality. There is some evidence from psychology and psychiatry that we may inherit not only mental disorders like schizophrenia but also other components of personality, such as emotional stability and introversion-extraversion. Some studies show that we inherit these components of personality to about the same extent that we inherit our intelligence, namely about 80 percent (Shields and Slater, 1961).

In any case, Huntington's kith is a group of people who share personality characteristics because of their common ancestry. Generally speaking, these characteristics result from natural selection having taken place earlier in their history. Huntington says:

> If a considerable group of men and women are selected because of strongly marked innate traits, such as the power of self-control, their children as a group will show a high degree of the same traits, although not so high as the parents. If such a group is completely isolated, either physically or socially, and there is no further selection, future generations will continue indefinitely to differ from the unselected ancestral stock. [Huntington, 1959: 224]

Kiths, as Huntington defines them, are smaller than races and often derived from a "mixture" of races (whatever that means), and they usually cross national boundaries or else form only part of a single nation. Members of a kith usually have a common language and similar cultures, and they marry freely within the group. Kiths vary in size and durability. Outstanding examples of small kiths (microkiths) include the royal families of Europe, the patricians of old Rome, and the ancient self-contained aristocracy of Athens which, for many generations, was virtually endogamous. Other kiths are larger, like the Rumanians, Prussians,

English, early Puritans, or Hakka-speaking Chinese, and Huntington calls these macrokiths.

As kiths become larger, the innate qualities that distinguish them from other kiths become less evident. Almost every nation includes many microkiths and often many kiths. Also, a nation may exert such a variety of selective demands that no traits appear in common among its inhabitants. Above the level of nations are the traditional races, each made up of so many kiths and nations that it is scarcely possible to demonstrate hereditary psychological characteristics. Huntington suggests, then, that genetically determined differences decrease in importance from individuals to microkiths and then to kiths, nations, and finally races. As the importance of the inheritance of character decreases, the importance of physical environment and culture *increases.*

Huntington writes about temperature influences on human behavior in a simple manner. Members of all kiths tested seem to react to temperature in much the same way (the research dealing with the adaptation of human beings to extreme temperatures had not yet been carried out). Regardless of one's genetic ancestry and place of origin, an individual feels comfortable under essentially the same conditions as other individuals.

The systematic and nearly uniform relationship between temperature and human comfort depends upon the fact that the internal temperature of the body is a human universal: 98.6 degrees Fahrenheit. A clothed human body functions best under an outside temperature of 60 to 70 degrees. At these temperatures, one can do ordinary work without raising the body temperature much above normal. When work is done at somewhat higher temperatures, the body must activate homeostatic mechanisms in order to maintain the normal internal temperature. At still higher external temperatures, or if the work becomes very vigorous, maintenance of normal temperatures becomes problematic, a temporary fever is induced, and toxins accumulate in the bloodstream and are not eliminated quickly enough. All of this results in a general sense of fatigue.

Machines that reduce this discomfort are mostly of recent invention, and Huntington suggests that throughout human existence people have found that the easiest way to adjust to temperatures above the optimum is to do as little as possible.

Outside temperatures below the optimum produce different behavioral effects. Of course, if it gets too cold, purposeful activity can be reduced just as much as it is in extremely hot weather. Someone who is constantly shivering and numb with cold is not much more effective than someone prostrate with heat. But between the optimum and very low temperatures, there is a considerable range within which it is fairly easy to find ways to keep warm (clothing, shelter, fire, and foods high in carbohydrates). Not only is it a challenge to find ways to keep warm in cold weather, but physical work itself, in achieving these solutions, constitutes an adaptive response.

> In other words, although both high temperature and low challenge man's ingenuity, the usual response is to get the better of heat by doing as little as possible and of cold by using the body and mind as effectively as possible. This contrast between protection from hot weather by passivity and from cold weather by activity is one of the most vital factors in the history of civilization. [Huntington, 1959: 278]

This simple fact is reflected in the distribution of what used to be called "high cultures," or the "birthplaces of civilization," including parts of Egypt, China, India, the near East, Mesoamerica, and Peru. Some of these societies developed outside the tropics, as Huntington would have predicted. Others developed within 25 degrees of the equator but, as Huntington points out, most of them are located in arid areas like Egypt where low humidity makes relatively high temperatures endurable. (It's not only the heat, it's the humidity.) In Cairo, the mean temperatures in October and May are about 75, but they seem no hotter than Philadelphia in June, with a mean of about 70, because of the difference in available water vapor.

Other high cultures have developed near the equator on temperate plateaus or mountains (the Aztecs and the Incas) or on abnormally cool seacoasts, where the temperature stays close to the optimum throughout the year (the early Mayans). Still other cultures, such as that of the people of the Indus Valley in India, seem to have been developed by people who had recently migrated from cooler climates and who may have been subjected to vigorous selective pressure for exceptional energy and endurance.

The reasons behind the existence of virtually universal optimum human temperature of about 65 degrees Fahrenheit for day or night are not determinable. Why should our tissues not be organized around a normal internal temperature of 10 or 15 degrees higher or lower than 98.6? Huntington speculates that monkeys in equatorial lowlands function best at external temperatures of about 80 degrees, and polar bears may have an optimum external temperature of about 40. However, in man, the optimum temperature may be related to an annual cycle of reproduction—an *annual* cycle, mind you. It pleases us to think that we are free to breed at all times, but Huntington examines the statistics and discovers an annual cycle of reproduction similar to that of some other animals, with a maximum number of births in early spring. Other conditions readily modify this pattern but it seems generally to hold up.

The meaning of this annual maximum [of human births] seems to be that primitive man, like the animals around him, was best able to survive if the young were born in the late winter or early spring. Young animals are born in the spring because both the weather and the food are then favorable to survival. The same was doubtless true of primitive man. Our species presumably acquired its primary climatic adaptations in an intermediate type of moderately warm, but by no means equatorial, climate. From February to April, in such a climate, vegetation bursts forth, the birds lay eggs, and young mammals are born. [Huntington, 1959: 283]

In other words, mothers who give birth at such a time are better able to find food for themselves and their offspring than mothers who give birth at any other season. Huntington infers that natural selection was taking place among our earliest hominid ancestors. Those whose powers of reproduction were most stimulated at a definite temperature were those whose children were most likely to survive. The desire and ability to reproduce should reach its maximum nine months before the maximum number of births, at which time the external temperature may have approximated that which has now become the human optimum, namely about 65 degrees.

Climate seems to affect certain social conditions as well as the human body. Huntington takes a simple illustration.

A hot climate, especially if it is humid, makes people feel disinclined to work. This encourages the more clever people to get a living with as little physical exertion as possible. Their example fosters the growth of a social system in which hard work is regarded as plebeian...By encouraging one type of social organization and discouraging another, climate has great influence upon the development of civilization. [Huntington, 1959: 285]

The sort of contrast that Huntington had in mind was illustrated by two women he knew, both of whom lived in a hot city in northern Australia.

One was comely, dark-haired, fairly plump and of a merry, easy-going temperament...a delightful hostess....Kindness of heart was one of her dominating characteristics....In a sudden emergency she would work desperately to help even her enemies. Nevertheless, her idea of doing good was to feed the hungry and clothe the naked without asking them why they became so. "Make them happy and let them go. It's too much work to go digging into their past lives to find out what's the matter with them." That was her attitude toward everything, including the climate. "Oh, yes, it's hot sometimes, but I love it. If it's too hot, don't work so hard. Why wear yourself out for nothing?" The other woman, equally charming, was fair, slender, blue-eyed, and more nervous than her friend — an intense, eager sort of person. Her house would always look more spick and span than that of the other, but her guests would find her absorbed in other things. She would have to run off to a meeting of her welfare board over in the poorer quarter. A community containing many people of her sort could scarcely fail to make rapid progress. This was her opinion of the climate: "Oh, I hate it. The winter is well enough, but in summer you can't do what you want to do, and it makes the people lazy and makes them careless about sanitation and food and all sorts of things. I want to get back to the South where it's cool." [Huntington, 1959: 285-86]

Huntington suggests that people of the first type are more likely than those of the second type to settle in a tropical or semitropical setting. Thus a process of selection through migration concentrates easygoing people in warmer climates, and the same process may have been at work in the past. The less active type has a better chance of survival in warm regions, and the more active type in cool ones. Thus, the differences between cultures located in warm regions and those located in cooler ones is partly due to biology and partly to cultural adaptation. With respect to biology, a warm climate (and its accompanying diseases) does tend to make people less active. With respect to cultural adaptation, under any given geographical conditions the organization of society tends gradually to assume the form most nearly adapted to the surrounding habitat. This process is likely to promote a certain sort of ideology. For example, if one needs to prepare housing, clothing, and fuel for the fire as a means of combatting the winter cold, then the resulting society is likely to place a high value on foresight and thrift. (Huntington does not speculate that the absolute necessity of having a minimum of food and shelter for oneself and one's family might also lead to selfishness and a lack of hospitality.) In cold climates, virtues like thrift and industry are more necessary than in warm climates, and so we should expect that, even in the absence of biological differences, cool climates and warm ones would evolve different sorts of social systems and different ideologies.

Religious imagery varies greatly in different cultures, and Huntington observed an interesting effect of physical environment on descriptions of God's relation to man. Such descriptions need to be expressed in language, and the language of hunters, gatherers, pastoralists, and horticulturalists is full of natural imagery. In Palestine, it was natural that

people should speak of God's protecting care as "the shadow of a great rock in a weary land." This simile means a great deal to people who live close to the hot, treeless desert, but nothing at all to those in a Siberian forest. One appreciates such a rock at noonday in Transcaspia when one tries to take a siesta in the burning sun with a temperature of 120° and no shade except that of a restless horse. The ground is hot to the touch, a breath of air feels as if a furnace door had been opened, the horse will not stand still, and the sun smites one continually.... To reindeer herders in Lapland, however, a God who provides a place where "the sun shall not smite thee by day" seems positively cruel. To sit in the warm sunshine is bliss. [Huntington, 1959: 290-91]

Huntington uses the Japanese and the New Zealanders to show a striking contrast in religious imagery. Most of Japan is heavily forested and is made up of rough mountains. When the trees are cleared they are replaced by a tough grass, too coarse for good grazing. Moreover, the hot, humid summers typical of most of Japan are poor ones for raising woolly animals such as sheep. So Japan ends up understandably with only one sheep for every two thousand humans. In such a land there is little meaning in the Twenty-third Psalm: "The Lord is my shepherd. I shall not want. He maketh me to lie down in green pastures." The Japanese psalm, Huntington suggests, should read: "The Lord is my guide among sweet cherry blossoms. He showeth me still waters that reflect the glory of nature." (No one is perfect.) However, the imagery of the Old Testament is admirably suited to New Zealand, an area of green pastures and many sheep, twenty for each human inhabitant.

Elsewhere in the world, religious images are influenced by climate. In northern India, spring and summer are very hot. At a city close to the birthplace of Buddha, the average temperature for day and night is about 93 degrees Fahrenheit; the maximum is about 105 or 110. Small wonder, says Huntington, that Buddhists envision a hot hell, with six levels based on torture by heat. In the highest level, people are burned and then allowed to recover before the next burning. In the second level, they are cut up as well as burned, but they still have a breathing space for recovery. In the lowest level of hell, burning goes on continuously. When Buddhism diffused a few hundred miles northward to Tibet, a hot hell did not seem like such a bad idea to shepherds who lived in a climate where the warmest month is about the same temperature as the coldest month in northern India. Hell was suitably changed. There are still six levels of hell in Tibet, but torture by cold is the chief form of punishment. In the lowest level, the awful pain of fingers being thawed after having been frozen is spread to all parts of the body (enough to turn one towards Islam!) Such low-level correspondences may be rather general. Some Eskimo groups, too, have a cold hell. These apparent relationships led Huntington to consider related problems of a more general nature. Gods, for instance.

Animism is usually defined as a belief in supernatural spirits. Though such a definition seems broad enough to include almost all religions, empirically, animists tend to share certain beliefs. They look on spirits with fear, and the spirits themselves are whimsical, interfering in the affairs of men and women for other than moral reasons. The mediators between society and the supernatural (sometimes generically called shamans) may be the best or the worst people in the community. People become shamans not because they have spent their lives in contemplation or worked hard for the welfare of their neighbors but because they control the supernatural to some extent.

Animism today tends to be found in regions where it is difficult to practice modern agriculture: in tropical rain forests like those of the Amazon basin in South America, in rugged mountain areas like the interior of the Philippines, or in extremely cold and barren areas like the arctic tundra. Huntington says that there are many reasons for this peculiar distribution of animism, but one of the most important is the topography and climate.

> One of the chief elements in animism is fear of the unknown. Such fear is encouraged by life in a tropical jungle. An ignorant savage, let us say, is walking in the jungle, when a stick falls on his head. He can detect no cause. No leaves stir in the branches above him; no monkey or bird moves away. It seems as if someone had deliberately thrown the stick, but no one is visible. The easiest supposition is that some creature like a man, but more ill-tempered and quite invisible, must have done it. The same line of reasoning suggests that an invisible spirit is at work when the man stumbles on a hidden root, hears a frightening sound in the dark, or is afflicted with some strange illness. A walk through the jungle in the dark becomes a painful ordeal because of the fear that evil spirits may be lurking almost anywhere. [Huntington, 1959: 295]

Of course, one need not be an "ignorant savage" to feel uneasy in the forest (though nowadays a much more sophisticated attitude is fear directed towards our urban landscapes), as evidenced by a Western writer's description of a solitary stroll through the glades of a remote forest.

> So little do you see that the feeling comes over you that you are alone in the midst of mysterious hidden things. The feeling that immediately follows this is that these mysterious things are not merely hidden, but are specially hidden from you. The circle that moves with you is the veil built up against you. You could imagine that you were a trespasser, or at all events are regarded as such. Then you have the horrible feeling that from behind the tree-trunks watching eyes are looking upon you. It is bad enough at any time if you are alone and all is quiet; it is worse as the sun sinks and the light fades; it is worst if by any ill chance you happen to know that you have lost not only your way, but your sense of direction. At all times you may see things happen of

which the reason is hard to divine. [Maxwell, 1911; quoted in Porteous, 1928: 15]

Huntington hypothesizes that, all things being equal (a condition that never prevails), animism thrives better in a forest than in open grasslands or deserts. The heavy vegetation provides innumerable niches and hiding places for the various spirits that come to abound there.

Aside from the simplemindedness of some of his prose, what Huntington is talking about may be real enough. In open land, one can see what is around him. But in a dense forest, especially at night, one could be ambushed at any moment by any agent—human, beast, or supernatural—that decided to do so. We can smile at this because we generally walk around in well-lit streets or sit at home in houses where lighting is both reliable and as bright as we care to make it. If we found ourselves in a sparsely populated forest at night, I am certain that, for most of us, the experience would be unsettling. Most of the island of Tutuila, in American Samoa, is densely forested. One night, as I was walking along a path through the bush—having been repeatedly warned to watch out for ghosts—an owl screeched at my elbow before flapping away into the darkness. My immediate reaction was too embarrassing to recount.

This fear of spirits and ghosts is still very real in Samoa. One informant of mine, a Samoan who had spent two years in college in the United States and more than a year in the Marine Corps, was hitchhiking through the desert in southern Arizona and found himself stranded at night on a lonely highway. He was frankly frightened to be there alone and in the dark because he might be approached by ghosts at any time. As a matter of fact, he was not worried about Samoan ghosts, because they were still back in Samoa, of course. He wasn't overly worried about the ghosts of white men, because he could at least speak their language. What he truly feared were *Indian* ghosts, since he would have been at a loss in any encounter with them.

In any case, Huntington's most obvious problem is that, although his argument has a certain validity on its face, he ignores the overwhelming likelihood that animism persists where it does because such marginal areas as rain forests, tundra, and so on are least likely to be colonized and industrialized by Europeans. Animism was probably a worldwide belief until fairly recently; and animists exist where they do because they were, in a sense, wiped out everywhere else. Furthermore (never mind the backward areas of the globe, inhabited by Huntington's "ignorant savage") some Jews believe in *dybbuk* and some Irish people believe in leprechauns; until a few hundred years ago, most of them probably did. There is an unfortunate ethnocentric tendency in Huntington, which perhaps was not unusual among lay people of 1925, when Huntington was working out his ideas, but is surprising in a man of his experience and erudition. At one point, he discusses the "unintelligent ritual" of Hinduism.

Hinduism, he suggests, developed in an area where hard work was made difficult by the climate, but where conditions of life were so poor that it was arduous work to support all of the people. The Hindus (we may presume he means most of the inhabitants of tropical and subtropical India) had not succeeded to any great extent in providing for themselves. The country was ravaged by disease and overpopulation; the general level of health, vigor, and economic development was poor. Under these conditions, it was easier to practice nonresistance with Gandhi than to wage a long, hard fight against the oppression of the English. Not enough energy was available to counteract the effects of British peace, British famine relief, and British medical services, which had permitted the population of India to expand without enlarging the available amount of agricultural land. (Huntington published this opinion in 1945; the situation in India has not changed, unless it has changed for the worse, despite continued famine relief, improved medical services, occasional armed conflict, and India's entry into the nuclear club — at dues of an estimated $3 billion over the next decade.)

The same influences of torrid climate and poor physical health appear in religion. Among people who lack energy, religious merit tends to take the form of passive suffering rather than active work for others. It is easier, in a sense, to lie on a bed of spikes or sit in contemplation than run around working for reform all day.

A similar effect surfaces in the nature of Hindu and Buddhist gods (if one can call what Buddhists have, a god). They are passive and inactive. Huntington then turns his attention to Judaism, Christianity, and Islam. Animistic and Hindu belief in many gods and innumerable minor spirits may be the natural result of life in the tropical jungle, whereas the monotheism of these latter religions is an equally natural product of deserts.

Tropical jungle, with its dense foliage, short field of vision, and damp darkness at night encourages faith in a vast number of spirits. The effects of a desert are quite different. The contrast between the high God of the deserts and grasslands and the implike spirits of the jungle has been recognized for some time and is controversial. Huntington says that he holds neither to possibilism nor to environmental determinism. There is, of course, absolute determinism in one respect: a walk through the jungle and a walk through the desert generate different kinds of experiences in individuals. At the same time, it is quite possible for anyone, anywhere, to fix his mind on whatever God he or she chooses.

Let us look more closely at that walk through the desert or open grasslands. A nighttime stroll gives one clear, dry air, bright starlight or moonlight, practically no vegetation, safe footing on relatively stable ground, little danger of beasts and little annoyance from insects, and safety to sleep or rest practically anywhere. On the other hand, the desert dweller has to contend with a blazing sun, sandstorms, drought, and an absence of readily available food. Where the desert nomads dwell, the things that man principally fears are "big things" rather than "little things," as in the bush. They are wind, sun, cold, heat, and lack of water. They have little of the intimate quality of the dangers of tropical rain forests. The person who lives in the desert is as free as the person who lives in the jungle to believe in local, intimate spirits, inhabiting bushes, stones, lizards, and so on, but there is not much incentive to do so. It is therefore natural for desert religions such as Judaism, Christianity, and Islam to pin faith on one or a few powerful gods who rule large areas. (Huntington must have been unfamiliar with the ethnographic material of desert-dwelling societies of central Australia where stones, bushes, lizards, and so on acquire just such mythic properties.)

Some of Huntington's basic assumptions are sound enough. It is difficult to deny that many of his suggestions may be true. Of course it is harder to do manual labor in a very hot climate than in a temperate one. And it is reasonable to expect that physical environment has some kind of effect on religious beliefs and practices. Unfortunately, he falls into the trap of making large-scale evaluations of religions, instead of merely trying to describe the interaction of religious practices and environments. Instead of focusing his attention on these interactive processes in any systematic way, he begins to develop a hierarchy of religious beliefs, with animism at the bottom and Christianity at the top. In other words, he concentrates on religious form to the exclusion of the subsistence and economic practices underlying the form.

So Huntington, in a sense, appears to us in the guise of a nineteenth-century cultural Darwinist, placing the ignoramuses at the bottom of the ladder and the aristocrats in England and the English colonies at the top. If the ignorant savages were wiped out in the course of the diffusion of religions, well, he accepts such situations with aplomb and with hardly a nod in the direction of their occurrence. (See Sopher [1968] for a more reasonable view.)

Huntington lacked a touch of humility and an understanding of some of the fundamental ideas behind the theoretical framework provided by functionalism, or more generally, systems theory, within the last forty years. When things survive for a long time in a society, they usually do so for a good reason: they do something to help that society maintain itself. The sacred cows of India might seem like "unintelligent ritual" to Huntington, but, in fact, those tough stringy animals don't have much meat on them to begin with. Moreover, they eat a coarse, bunchy grass that human beings don't use anyway, and they perform several very useful services for people: they plow agricultural land, and they provide fuel in the form of cow chips (Harris, 1966).

# CHAPTER THREE

# The Natural Background of Human Activity

In this chapter I would like to make some observations concerning features of the naturally occurring environment and our responses to them. First I will discuss climate and the resulting differences in the biota—the animals and plants that characterize a particular climate. Then I will explore some of the means by which we adapt culturally to our natural environments, including the use of buffering mechanisms such as clothing and shelter; different types of food-getting techniques; and some aspects of sexual behavior. I will also discuss the reflection of the natural environment in speech and cognition. I will then turn to a discussion of geophysical hazards as examples of particular environmental stressors, and my conclusion will cover some of the means by which we cope with such temporary but extreme sources of stress. The chapter is thus organized broadly into two parts: a description of natural environments and our adaptations to them, and a description of certain environmental stressors and our reactions to them.

## Climate and Physical Background

Weather conditions are affected by air masses that pass through an area. An air mass is defined by meteorologists as a large body of air with uniform characteristics with regard to moisture and temperature. It has stayed at a specific place on the earth's surface long enough to acquire characteristics associated with the surface on which it has rested. An air mass then moves out in the form of wind, carrying the characteristics of the place where it originated to other areas.

The classification of air masses is based on where they originated—their source regions. Source regions are classified as polar or tropical and subdivided into maritime and continental areas.

Polar continental air masses come from a cold continental source region. They ordinarily consist of frigid, heavy, dry air, and as they move equatorward from their place of origin, they may become a polar outburst, an unexpected intrusion of frigid air into areas that are usually characterized by warm, moist air. Polar continental air masses are often associated with clear, sunny weather.

A tropical maritime air mass originates over warm ocean water and usually moves towards a polar region. It consists of warm, light, unstable air and usually carries large amounts of moisture. As one of these air masses moves over land in summer, the air may be further heated, resulting in hot, humid weather. Source regions for tropical maritime air masses are any of the equatorial portions of the oceans.

Polar maritime air masses carry cool, moist air, generally not as cold as that in polar continental air masses because the circulation of ocean waters prevents the sea from becoming superheated or supercooled. Frequently these air masses bring fog to the land. They are commonly found off the northwest coast of America and over the northwest coast of Europe, particularly Ireland, Britain, and Scandinavia.

Tropical continental air is hot and dry. The source regions are large continental areas around the equator. These air masses are not common, since land around the equator generally tends to be low-lying and well watered and the land masses themselves are not large.

Tropical weather is controlled almost entirely by tropical air masses and there is not much change in temperature from one day to the next or from one season to the next. Polar weather, similarly, is controlled by polar air masses, and although there is some seasonal variation in temperature, it is usually minor, changing from cool to cold and back again. In the mid-latitudes, the movement of air masses becomes particularly important. Here, weather is dominated by polar air in winter and by tropical air in summer, but the weather can change in any season if one type of air mass replaces another.

When two unlike air masses meet, as they regularly do in mid-latitude regions, they cause the atmospheric disturbances popularly called storms. The area where the two air masses meet is called a front. This zone of contact has different weather conditions on either side, and the entire storm moves from west to east with the prevailing winds at an average speed of about twenty-five miles per hour.

Where warm air replaces cold, the disturbance is called a warm front. With the passage of a warm front, warm air rises gradually over a retreating wedge of cold air, and the resulting zone of contact is a smoothly inclined plane. The precipitation in a warm front, whether rain or snow, tends not to be very heavy, but it lasts for some time and is accompanied by a long period of cloudiness and overcast skies. The kind of gloomy drizzle that lasts for days is usually associated with the passage of a warm front.

When a cold front passes over an area, the weather change is more abrupt. The polar air mass bulges up against the warm air and pushes it upward rapidly, causing a great deal of turbulence, sometimes gale winds, thunder, and lightning, and on occasion, tornadoes. The precipitation that accompanies a cold front is heavy but relatively brief. In the summer, the precipitation may be in the form of hail.

The foregoing, it should be pointed out, presents a simplified picture of some complicated goings-on. Some of the complications of North American weather involve the jet stream, a sort of tube of fast-flowing air, moving at about 200 miles per hour, 6 miles above the earth's surface. The jet stream generally moves air from west to east across the United States at about forty degrees of latitude, but for unknown reasons it may snake southward or northward or break up into several sections. It is fairly certain that changes in the characteristics of the jet stream influence the nature of storms occurring in the United States, but no one knows exactly how or why.

Again, regional topography may play a part in determining the weather at any given place. It takes longer for sunlight to heat water than land, and it takes longer for water to give up its heat to the atmosphere. Thus, air temperatures in the vicinity of large bodies of water are likely to be more equable—experience fewer extreme high and low values—than inland areas. Around the world, coastlines generally have fewer extreme temperatures than continental locations. Mountains, too, influence the local weather. A moisture-laden wind, forced to climb over a high mountain barrier, disgorges its moisture on the windward side, leaving the leeward side dry. No one who has traveled between Reno and Sacramento can be unaware of this rain shadow effect.

Atmospheric phenomena can be described and analyzed in terms of four climatic elements: (1) temperature, (2) precipitation, (3) air pressure, and (4) winds. The properties of these climatic elements differ widely from one place to another, but they show up in consistent patterns in given places. When climatic elements form such regular patterns, one may speak in terms of climatic types. Areas with similar climates are scattered about the globe, but they occupy broadly similar positions with respect to continental location and distance from the equator. This is the direct result of the circulation of air set in motion by solar heating at the equator and the rotation of the earth about its axis. Each climatic type is associated with a particular set of soils, vegetation types, and animal life, and so influences human behavior in two ways: directly, through the impact of weather conditions, and indirectly, through the mediation of the biota.

The earliest recorded scheme for the classification of climates was that of the Greek philosophers, who distinguished three types: torrid (between the tropics of Capricorn and Cancer); frigid (within the arctic and antarctic circles); and temperate (between the tropics and the polar circles). This classificatory scheme, based on arbitrary events, was commonly used in Europe until the last century. Later schemes, put forward primarily by German climatologists around the end of the last century and the beginning of this, were based not on arbitrary criteria but rather on features of climate associated with biological responses. The later schemes included rainfall, as well as temperature, as criteria of climatic type. The most popular and widely used is probably that proposed by Wladimir Köppen (1918). It is in some respects not very sensitive: following the rules of one version, New Orleans and New York share the same climatic type. (Other classificatory schemes, such as that of A.A. Miller, do not suffer from this particular defect; see Monkhousen, 1970: 453-55.) The Köppen criteria themselves have been modified a number of times over the years, but the system as a whole has proved most durable and popular. The Köppen climatic types are designated by a series of letters representing important climatic features. The first letter (always capitalized) indicates a primary category; the lowercase letters that follow indicate major subdivisions, second lowercase letters minor subdivisions. Disregarding numerical values, we may collapse some of the categories and characterize each type and its major subdivisions in plain language as follows:

Af:        Hot and wet year round.

Am:        Hot year round; short dry season in winter; heavy precipitation the remainder of the year.

Aw:        Hot weather summer; hot dry winter.

BSh:       Hot year round; unreliable precipitation.

BWh:       Hot and dry year round

BSk:       Hot summer; cool to cold winter; unreliable precipitation.

BWk:       Hot summer; cool to cold winter; dry year round.

Cs:        Hot dry summer, cool wet winter.

Cf:        Warm to hot wet summer; cool wet winter.

Cw:     Warm to hot wet summer; cool dry winter.

Cb:     Cool wet summer; cool wet winter.

Dfa:    Hot wet summer; cool to cold wet winter.

Dfb:    Warm wet summer; cold wet winter.

Dfc:    Warm to cool summer; very cold winter; some precipitation all
        year round.

Dwc:    Warm to cool wet summer; very cold dry winter.

ET:     Cool summer; cool winter; little precipitation.

H:      Undifferentiated highlands.

The taxonomy of climates commonly found in textbooks and atlases generally involves further condensation of categories and, in fact, the weather patterns of the world can probably be adequately described in only twelve categories. The classification that follows is a rather typical one, in this case derived from Pearson (1968).

*Rainy Tropical Climates (Af, Am)*

These climates are hot and rainy during all months of the year. Temperature readings may be incredibly uniform from one season to another, especially near the sea. Ocean Island, for example, has a mean range of about 1 degree Celsius from month to month during the year. The greatest areas of rainy tropical climates, sometimes called tropical rain forests, are across the widest part of South America, the Amazon basin, and in the central Congo basin and the Guinea coastlands of Africa. Monsoonal variations of this climatic type, indicating particularly intense rainfall during the summer months, are found in southern India and Indonesia. These places are hot but, more accurately, they are muggy. The maximum temperatures may not rise much above 95 degrees Fahrenheit or fall much below 65 degrees, but they are the rainiest places on earth. New York receives about 40 inches of precipitation during the year, and Seattle gets about 80 inches, but Pontianak, in Borneo, has about 126 inches per year. The greatest amount of precipitation recorded during a twelve-month period was 1,041.78 inches, in Cherrapunja, Assam, India, located in a rainy tropical region, in 1861.

Rainy tropical climates promote certain kinds of soil and vegetation that make them fairly unattractive for human habitation. Plants grow rapidly and continuously because there is neither a winter nor a dry season, producing a dense forest of broadleaf trees that are green the year round. The trees tend to be large, and the interlocking top branches form a canopy, blocking out sunlight and preventing very much shrubbery growth. The constant daytime darkness and the clear forest floor, broken only by the huge pillars of tree trunks, create a sort of natural cathedral. Towards the margins of the tropical rain forests, where rainfall may tend to be heavier during some months of the year and lighter in others, the trees are farther apart and sunlight can reach the ground, so that an almost impenetrable growth of bushes, shrubs, and vines covers the forest floor. This is the kind of vegetation that is sometimes referred to as *jungle,* a word derived from Hindi *jangal* and ultimately from Sanskrit *jangala,* which meant any kind of wasteland, including desert.

Animal life tends to be both abundant and varied, oriented towards life in the trees or in streams. Large animals are actually rather rare, but there are numerous reptiles and amphibians, primates, birds, bats, and fish (some of which are flesh eaters). There are also more than enough insects to bother both humans and animals since, in the absence of a cool season, insects breed continuously and not only irritate one's body in various direct ways but also carry disease and destroy buildings. The climate also seems ideally suited to the reproduction of certain kinds of microorganisms, and putrefaction is rapid.

One might expect soils to be fertile in tropical rain forests, but this is not the case. Warm water soaks into the ground or moves across the surface quickly, carrying away nutrients and fine particles and leaving behind a coarse dirt, high in such minerals as aluminum and titanium. There is little chance for organic material to accumulate in the ground because putrefaction is so rapid. Deep-rooted plants like trees may reach far enough into the soil to find the necessary nutrients, but more shallow-rooted crops produce a low yield.

### Savanna Climates (Aw)

These climates are transition zones, found on the poleward margins of the tropics, between the equatorial rain forests and the deserts. Temperatures are relatively high all year, between about 50 and 100 degrees Fahrenheit. There is a period of summer rain and a dry winter. As the distance from the equator increases, the amount of summer precipitation drops. Most of the rainfall is in the form of torrential downpours and may be highly irregular from one year to the next, both of which features render the climate poor for farming. Generally speaking, savanna climates have weather resembling that of the tropical rain forests during the summer and that of deserts during the winter. Savanna climates are found on all continents, including Australia, and are usually called by some local name, such as the Sudan north of the equator in Africa and the veld south of the equator in that continent.

Huge trees are found on the equatorial margins of savanna climates but, moving poleward, these gradually give way to areas of both forest and grass, producing a parklike, almost manicured appearance. These areas are then replaced by grasses dotted with only a few scattered trees. Near the desert the grass is shorter and scattered over the bare sand, with occasional thorny bushes between. Sometimes these bushes coalesce into thorn forests, most inhospitable places. All of this, of course, reflects the fact that rainfall decreases with distance from the rainy tropics.

Savanna climates support a wide variety of animal life which differs widely in form but, from one continent to another, tends to have a characteristic look. There are many reptiles and insects, but large mammals are also common. The open grassland provides an abundance of food for herbivores like zebras, antelopes, and kangaroos. The herbivores in turn provide food for many carnivores, especially big cats like lions and leopards. Finally, there are usually a host of such scavengers as hyenas and vultures to eat the leftovers.

The soils are relatively poor because summer downpours wash away much of the organic material. In the dry seasons, the soil tends to be compact, hard, and cracked.

*Arid Climates (BWh, BWk)*

Arid climates are divisible into several subtypes according to the Köppen scheme, but they all share one common characteristic: evaporation exceeds annual precipitation, so they are all extremely dry. They are found mostly on the western sides of continents between about twenty and thirty degrees of latitude, and they extend inland from there, bulging away from the equator and towards the poles. Like savanna climates, they are found on all continents.

Since they extend from the tropics well into the middle latitudes, deserts show considerable differences in both average and extreme temperatures. Tropical deserts are hot the year round, but middle-latitude deserts, like the Gobi or the American Great Basin, have hot summers and cold winters. One might roast in Utah in the summer, but one can also ski near Salt Lake City in the winter.

One other feature that deserts have in common, aside from their extreme aridity, is a great difference between the temperatures of night and day. In other climates, atmospheric moisture acts as a sort of blanket, slowing down the incoming rays of the sun during the day and preventing the rapid heat loss at night. Because deserts have little moisture, the land receives the full blast of the sun during the day and heats up rapidly. At the surface of the ground, temperatures reach 180 degrees Fahrenheit. At night the same lack of moisture permits the heat to dissipate into space, and the temperature drops quickly.

Precipitation in deserts is highly irregular. Annual rainfall figures mean little for desert locations because a community may go for several years with no rainfall at all and then suffer a thundershower which dumps several inches of rainfall all at once. The downpour causes flash floods, runs off rapidly, and does the vegetation little good.

The desert biota is generally adapted to the lack of water, and surprisingly little land area is completely barren of life. Some plants have very short growth periods, allowing them to take advantage of the brief rains. Others have thorns, small leaves, tough bark, or deep and extensive root systems which enable them to conserve water. Animal life in the desert tends not to be obvious because many of the organisms are nocturnal or live underground. Protective coloration is common and so is adaptation for speed, since there is little impediment to locomotion. As on the poleward margins of the savanna, there are plenty of reptiles and insects but few birds, and the larger mammals are generally absent because of the scarcity of grazing area. (One exception is the highly adapted camel.)

The soils of the desert are poor, caked with minerals and salts. All in all, deserts tend to be difficult places to make a living, for humans, beasts, and plants.

### Semiarid Climates (BSh, BSk)

These climates are broad transitional zones between deserts and areas with more precipitation. They are characterized by grasslands on long, rolling hills that may be so low as to be barely visible. The grass tends to be tufted and bunched on the desert margins, taller and thicker away from the deserts. These areas are most commonly found in the interiors of large continents and generally go under one or another local name, such as prairies (with tall grass), plains (with short grass), steppes, *pusztas* (Hungary), or downs (Australia). Semiarid climates cover a great deal of ground, from the margins of the tropics to the mid-latitudes, so they show as much variation in annual temperature as true deserts do. In the higher latitudes, again, there may be a marked difference between summer and winter temperatures, as in Denver. The daily range of temperature is not so extreme as in the deserts.

Annual precipitation is higher than in deserts but still quite low. As one travels from the desert margins across the grasslands to the boundaries of the humid climates, precipitation increases but is still unpredictable from one year to the next. In some ways, this great irregularity can be more catastrophic to human welfare than the near absence of rainfall in the desert. The yield of any crop cultivated in a semiarid climate depends largely on the amount of water available. Because the rainfall varies a great deal from one year to another, the crop yield will also be irregular. A succession of years with heavy rainfall can, in a manner of speaking, lure a group of farmers deeper and deeper into the grasslands, closer to the desert margins. Finally, when rainfall reverts to normal, or lower than normal, the farming communities are wiped out. An interesting article by Peter Gould (1969) examines the game theory aspects of banking on wet years or dry years in a variable climate. Rainfall differs from that of savannas because it occurs all year round rather than in a distinct summer rainy season.

The true grassland forms a continuous cover of tufted grass with occasional bulbous plants. Frequently rainfall is concentrated in early spring, and the grass may be blue or green, turning yellow during the drier summer and brown during the winter. Hardy trees may line the riverbanks. Towards the desert, grasses become sparser and coarser and are replaced by types of vegetation characteristic of more arid regions, like sagebrush and cactus.

Reptiles, rodents and insects are numerous here, and the grasslands once supported an abundance of herbivores such as wild horses in Asia, bison in North America, and guanaco in South America. The larger carnivores are lacking but were formerly widely distributed, particularly the lion in Asia and the mountain lion in North America. Currently, the most common carnivores of the grasslands are smaller animals such as coyotes and foxes.

The soils that develop under semiarid conditions are gray or brown, fertile but difficult to farm. Agriculture in steppe climates is a rather tricky proposition. Not only is precipitation light and variable, but the ground tends to be matted with grass, and the shallow roots of these grasses interlock under the surface, producing a soil difficult to till without a plow. Moreover, in the absence of irrigation, the soils tend to dry out when the grass cover is broken, and they are subject to wind erosion, turning into a powdery sort of dust that blows about and piles up in drifts like snow. This happened in parts of the Great Plains during the 1930s, when much of Oklahoma, Kansas, and neighboring states turned into what was called a dustbowl. In any case, human interference has changed the nature of the grassland. Many of the trees of the humid margins have been removed and the native grasses replaced with domesticated ones. The more adequately watered areas have been plowed up or converted to ranches. It has been proposed that a small area of relatively unchanged steppe in the Great Plains be designated Grasslands National Park, but no decision has yet been made.

## Mediterranean Climates (Cs)

Areas with a Mediterranean climate experience warm or hot summers, cool rainy winters, and a great deal of sunshine all year round. They are referred to as Mediterranean climates since one such region is found surrounding that body of water. Generally they are located on the poleward margins of dry regions. They only infrequently extend far inland because in most cases the inland margins are rather precisely defined by mountains. Aside from the Mediterranean itself, they are found in four other areas of considerable size including parts of California, Chile, South Africa, and southern Australia.

Temperatures are never very extreme because winds are ordinarily light and air moving in from cold waters off the coast is likely to be cool in comparison to the land. This results in equable temperatures the year round, although seasonal differences increase away from the coast. San Francisco's warmest months, for example, average about 59 degrees Fahrenheit and its coolest about 54 degrees. The cool water also produces a great deal of fog.

Mediterranean climates are transitional between semiarid regions on their equatorward margins and humid climates on their poleward margins, so that precipitation, which is confined largely to the winter season in the true Mediterranean climate, increases towards the poles and decreases towards the equator. Los Angeles, for example, is drier than San Francisco, which in turn is drier than Bodega Bay.

Typical vegetation consists of an evergreen forest of small trees or bushes that are adapted in one way or another to the harsh summer drought. Plants have waxy leaves or thick bark and some are so succulent that water can be squeezed from them by hand. During the rainy winter, the land is green and flowers abound; in the summer, the land is dry and somewhat parched, except that in coastal locations fog may be frequent enough to nourish some of the vegetation throughout the year, including the California redwoods, which are never found far from foggy areas (see Gilliam, 1970).

Mediterranean climates have been popular with people and most of the land has been occupied by humans for so long that much of the distinctive animal life has been wiped out. The soils also have few distinctive characteristics because the areas tend to be hilly and the kind of soil under one's feet depends very much on local topography. However, it may generally be said that the soils are thin, as they are in most mountainous areas, and the dry summers make cultivation difficult.

*Humid Subtropical Climates (Cf, Cw)*

These climates cover the east coasts of all continents along the lower middle latitudes and usually extend some distance inland. They are characterized by hot summers, mild winters, and much precipitation, particularly during the summer. In the United States, the band runs from southern Florida almost to New York City. Brisbane, Australia, is located in such a climate, and so is much of the North Island of New Zealand,

Buenos Aires, southeastern China, southern Japan, and northern India. (In the case of China, the climate is dominated by monsoonal conditions, which make for a somewhat drier and colder winter.)

The summers are long and hot. Temperatures on the coast average about 80 degrees Fahrenheit, but inland extremes of more than 100 degrees might not be considered unusual. Although this is no hotter than the tropical deserts, the higher humidity makes it seem so. In the winter, temperatures average between 35 and 50 degrees, but frosts are not rare, and occasional outbursts of polar air may cause winter temperatures to become very low. This is not likely to happen in Asia, where an east-west chain of mountains seals off some of the southeastern portion of the continent from the colder north, but the United States lacks such a natural barrier, and New Orleans has experienced winter temperatures as low as 8 degrees Fahrenheit.

Precipitation is abundant all year round, but with a tendency to be especially heavy in the summer due to frequent thunderstorms. In fact, the southeastern coast is the most thunderstorm-ridden area one can find in the United States. San Jose, California, has about 1.4 thunderstorm days per year and New York City has about 25, but Tampa, Florida, has more than 90.

Humid subtropical climates are located between areas that have sharply defined winters and those that are hot the year round; so they support a wide range of animal and plant types. Broadleaf forests are the most widespread type of vegetation. In many areas these are mixed with conifers such as white and yellow pine. Toward the poles, deciduous trees such as dogwood, maple, and walnut predominate; toward the equator, one finds an extraordinary variety of trees, including camellia, camphor, palmetto, and bamboo. Moving westward, away from the coast, the vegetation changes to grassland as the precipitation falls off.

Southeast China no longer has much native wild life, but the American southeast still has a wide variety of native animals, none of them particularly distinctive except in the swamps, which are common and support a kind of vegetation and animal life all their own. Animals are more limited in kind and number in humid subtropics elsewhere. Soils of the region are rich in nutrients and particularly good for agriculture, especially towards the west.

## West Coast Marine Climates (Cb)

These climates have cool wet summers and cool wet winters. They are located along the upper-latitude west coasts of all continents, including a small part of southern Africa, some parts of southern Australia (around Melbourne), the southern tip of South America, most of northwestern

Europe including Great Britain and Scandinavia, and in North America between northern California and well up along the Alaskan coast. Because the winds are mostly onshore and the sea is nearby, these climates are controlled by relatively mild, humid air masses, which tend to make them unusually temperate, considering how far from the equator they are. The sea offshore is usually warm. The Gulf Stream, or North Atlantic Drift, a great oceanic river of tropical origin, brings high enough temperatures to the western portions of Ireland and Scotland (situated at more northerly latitudes than Moscow) to make possible the outdoor cultivation of decidedly tropical-looking plants. There are few heat waves in summer and few cold spells in winter. But overall, with their nearly continuous cloud cover, they tend to be rather dreary.

The constant rain supports an abundant growth of vegetation, most of it in the form of forests, either broadleaf or evergreen. The denuded moors, heaths, and highlands of Great Britain and Ireland are the result of deliberate clearing of the forest followed by sheep grazing, a business for which the area seems not especially suitable (Darling, 1956: 781). Where forest growth is not interfered with, these humid climates can produce the sort of dense, cool-weather rain forests to be found in Olympia National Park in Washington State, where trees and shrubbery are festooned with moss.

Animal life is not highly adapted to the climatic conditions, and most animals in west coast marine areas represent types that are found elsewhere as well, such as deer, bear, and rabbit. Neither are the animals abundant, particularly in the southern hemisphere.

As in Mediterranean climates, soils depend very much upon local conditions, since most of these areas happen to be hilly. Generally speaking, where the forest is deciduous, as in some parts of northwestern Europe, soils have a reasonably high organic content and may be productive. Where forests are predominantly evergreen, the forest floor is covered with a thick layer of needles and the soils are highly acidic and poor for cultivation.

### Humid Continental Climates, Hot Summer Phase (Dfa)

Humid continental climates tend to be divided into hot and warm summer subtypes. The hot summer phase (Dfa) is found on the eastern sides of continents and extends far into the interiors in the middle and upper latitudes. The areas covered are far more extensive in the northern hemisphere than in the southern because the continents in the south have less land mass in the appropriate latitudes. Relatively isolated from the effects of maritime air masses, these areas tend to have extreme seasonal variations in temperature.

The largest area having a hot summer phase of humid continental climate is the east-central United States, an area encompassing such places as St. Louis, New York State, Iowa, Chicago, and so forth; similar areas exist on the other northern continents as well. Berlin is located in such a climate, and so is Beijing (Peking).

Precipitation is adequate but not excessive. In North America, much of the precipitation tends to be affected by low pressure centers that form over the continent. Since there is no barrier extending east and west, polar continental air masses from Canada regularly meet tropical maritime air masses from the Gulf of Mexico, and there are periodic changes in the local character of the weather. Further, along the east coast, a depression approaching from the west, with its counterclockwise circulation of air, draws up southeasterly moving winds, bringing rain at all seasons. Farther into the interior of the continent, rainfall is somewhat heavier during the summer, associated with convectional thunderstorms, and is lighter year round because this climatic type borders on the semi-arid grasslands.

Other environmental features show considerable variation, since winters become more marked and severe in a poleward direction and precipitation falls off in the western margins. The vegetation is mixed, as it is in the humid subtropical areas on the equatorward margins, but generally speaking, the forest is broadleaf and deciduous on the flat lowlands, where the soil is good, and coniferous in mountains, where the soil is poor.

Animals are plentiful in these areas, and the types resemble those found in the humid subtropics. The sharpest division of animal types is found in the west, where forest changes to grassland.

Soils are generally fertile and productive except that, where rainfall is particularly heavy, some sort of fertilization is required if they are to stand up well under continued use.

## Humid Continental Climates, Warm Summer Phase (Dfb)

This climate closely resembles the hot-summer subtype; the differences are the result of latitude. These areas are found exclusively in the northern hemisphere and in two areas: (1) a rather narrow strip along the eastern and central American-Canadian border and (2) in a more extensive Eurasian belt running between Poland and northern Japan, through Russia and central Siberia. The winters are longer and more severe than in the hot-summer phase, and temperatures range from 10 to 15 degrees Fahrenheit in winter and from 65 to 70 degrees in summer. Minneapolis and Moscow share this climatic type. Changeable weather can be expected at any season, but generally winters are dominated by cold, dry polar continental air masses and summers by warmer air masses from the south. Weather conditions in spring and fall are especially erratic.

Precipitation is similar to that of the hot summer subtype, decreasing toward the westward margins. Deciduous forests are still the predominant type of vegetation, but there are more needle-leaf trees like spruce and pine, and these predominate in the north.

Wildlife is mixed. Some of the animals, such as deer and bear, are likely to be found to the south as well, but others, such as moose, reindeer, and caribou, are associated with subpolar regions.

Soils resemble those of the hot-summer subtype to the south, but the shorter growing season imposes some limits on the sort of crops that can be cultivated.

### Subarctic Climates (Dfc, Dwc)

The subarctic climates are sometimes called polar continental climates. Winters are long and severe, summers are brief, and warm only during the day. Subarctic climates extend across North America between the gulf of the St. Lawrence River and Alaska and across Eurasia between the Baltic and the Pacific and through the heart of Siberia, dropping more to the south on the eastern sides of the continents.

This is an area of great seasonal temperature range, especially in Asia, where the greater land mass causes intense cold in winter. Some of these places are the coldest on earth, colder even than the polar ice caps. In Siberia, one location varied from a high temperature of 98 degrees Fahrenheit in the summer to -94 degrees in the winter, an annual range of 192 degrees! One Siberian village stands as the coldest inhabited place in the world. Such winter temperatures reportedly can freeze birds in flight or wine in casks and even make it difficult to strike a match.

Precipitation may be adequate along the eastern coasts, especially in summer, but decreases towards the interior of the continent. As a whole, subarctic climates are not areas of heavy precipitation. The ground may be covered with snow for much of the year, but it does not lie in any great depth.

The short summers, long cold winters, and low precipitation produce mostly hardy forests of a few types of coniferous trees which occur in vast uniform stands with an occasional birch or larch interspersed among them. The predominant trees are pine and spruce. Undergrowth is sparse, as it is in all needle-leaf forests, but in the clearings one may find a few shrubs or stunted bushes such as cloudberry. Mosses and lichens are common.

Animal life is rather varied, and all of it is adapted to the extreme cold of the subarctic winter: polar bear, reindeer, mink, and other fur-bearing animals are plentiful, as are fish. Soils, however, are poor, partly because of the infertility of the floor in needle-leaf forests, and partly because of the permanently frozen subsoil. But in any case, the growing season is so short that agriculture is unimportant.

## Polar Climates (ET)

Polar climates are found on the extreme north of the North American continent, of Greenland, the interiors of the larger islands within the Arctic Circle, and the northern coast of Asia. The type is represented in the southern hemisphere by Antarctica. These climates are sometimes divided into three subtypes, all of which have low temperatures all year round, as well as several months of almost constant daylight and an equal period of almost constant darkness. The tundra subtype is found along the equatorward margins of the area away from the sea. There is a brief summer, usually clear and sunny, during which the temperature rises somewhat above the freezing point. This relatively warm period permits the development of characteristic tundra vegetation, crowded growths of usually berry-bearing shrubs in between rocky outcrops covered with moss or lichens. Only an occasional dwarf tree may be observed. Winters in the tundra area are very cold, though not as cold as those in the Siberian heartland. Precipitation is light, usually in the form of snow. The true polar climate is similar to the tundra type except that the ground is permanently frozen and in most places covered with snow. The last subtype is the marine arctic, found on the numerous islands within both the Arctic and Antarctic Circles. Temperatures are not so extreme as in the other subtypes and precipitation is considerably greater.

A variety of animals may be found in polar climates, both on land and in the sea, such as polar bear, whale, seal, penguin, and a number of coastal birds like skua. They are all adapted in one way or another to the constant cold of the region. No soil types exist. What ground appears is rocky or covered with gravel and unsuitable for farming.

## Highland Climates (H)

It is difficult to generalize about highland climates (H) because they are so varied. Climatic conditions may differ significantly for places which are separated by no more than a few feet. In general, the conditions in any given place are governed by altitude and local topography. As altitude increases, the climate becomes colder. Conditions at the foot of a mountain may be identical to those of the surrounding climatic type. Higher up the mountain, conditions begin to approach those of polar climates, and the more poleward the mountain is located to begin with, the lower the altitude at which polar conditions are achieved. With respect to topography, the equatorward side of the mountain is warmer than the poleward side because it receives more sunshine, so the types of vegetation and animals may be different. Further, if moisture-bearing air masses typically reach the mountain more often from one side than the other, they will discharge their moisture before they get over the top of the mountain, leaving the leeward side dry. One of the few generalizations to be made about mountain climates is that they tend to be cooler than the surrounding area, but even this is not invariably true.

In a sense, the presence of mountains in the United States gives us a chance to experience a greater number of climatic types, if we are curious about such things, than might otherwise be the case. One may, for example, climb Mt. Whitney for a taste of true polar climate or hike around the higher reaches of Yosemite National Park to gain some understanding of what tundra is like.

### Adaptation to Natural Environments

Samoa is technically considered to have a tropical rain forest climate. However, the almost constant trade winds provide relief from the heat and high humidity. Further, since the Samoan islands are located far from any sizable land mass, the biota that has managed to reach them is limited. Many bothersome insects are absent, and there are no large animals that might be dangerous. During my two years of field work in Samoa it frequently occurred to me that, if the islands were uninhabited, a human being could be dropped there, naked, and still survive with ease because of the equable climate and the abundance of easily obtained food in the natural evironment. Indeed, it could be argued that one would be safer there than in the South Bronx. Most people on earth are not so lucky as the Samoans, finding themselves in less abundant natural environments where survival—or at least a reasonable degree of comfort—depends upon their own effort and ingenuity. Human activities are therefore intricately intertwined with the features of the natural environment, and the purpose of the first half of this chapter will be to explore some of those causal strands.

*Buffering Mechanisms*

Buffering mechanisms may be defined as things that people put between themselves and their natural environments for protection from extremes of weather and other dangers. The two chief types of buffering mechanisms to be discussed here are shelter and clothing.

*Shelter.* I will approach the discussion of shelter first from an archeological perspective, reviewing a study that yields some insight into what we may gather of prehistoric life-styles from information about a society's characteristic architecture. Then I will describe the rather remarkable adjustment of native Tierra del Fuegans to their unkind environment, to illustrate the relativity of needs for shelter. I will describe a recent work that purports to explain the determinants of house form, then examine the housing that typifies three societies—the Japanese, the Hungarians, and the Iroquois—and discuss the links between houses and the life-styles of their occupants.

There are enough correspondences between house form and life-style to render it unfortunate that so few examples of prehistoric housing have survived. Still, if there are few intact houses from the preliterate past, there are indications of the general layout of such shelters. Any ground area walked on by enough people for a long period of time tends to be more compressed and hardened than the surrounding ground, and the floor plans of shelters no longer in existence can sometimes be reconstructed. One interesting question one might ask is, What can the floor plan of a building tell us about the life-styles of its inhabitants?

Michael C. Robbins has proposed that there is an important link between life-style and floor plan, namely the relative permanence of the settlement pattern. "If a regular difference in the type of ground plans for the dwellings of peoples with mobile and sedentary community patterns can be discerned, then on the basis of the assumption that archeological cultures are comparable to living cultures known to ethnology we should be able to determine the relative permanence of archeological settlement patterns from the evidence of the ground plans of their dwellings" (Robbins, 1966a: 3).

From a survey of the ethnographic evidence, Robbins concludes that "the most suitable and predominant dwelling of mobile or semi-mobile peoples is a form of dwelling with a circular ground plan" (Robbins, 1966a: 5). Domes, or forms similar to domes, lend themselves readily to transport, offer the most resistance and the least obstruction to high winds, and provide the greatest volume with the smallest outside area. Of course, the same effects could be achieved with floor plans of another shape, but more effort would be required.

In contrast, settled populations seem to turn the dome into a quadrangle and raise it on walls, which increases the volume of usable living space. The extra work required to do this may not be very much, but it is enough that, for the most part, only sedentary people do it. It is also easier to add sections to a square or rectangular house than to a circular dwelling. All of this permits a greater number of people to live inside the same dwelling.

There are instances in which the shift from a subsistence pattern based primarily on hunting and gathering to farming has been accompanied by a gradual change from circular houses to quadrangular housing, as in the eastern United States and near the "four corners" area of the Southwest.

Robbins explores the relationship between ground plan and permanence of settlement in a cross-cultural study of a carefully selected sample of fifty societies, based on data provided in early issues of the "Ethnographic Atlas." His conclusions, all of which are statistically significant, are that, first, impermanent settlements are associated with circular floor plans and permanent settlements with rectangular, square, or quadrangular ones; next, that circular floor plans are associated with smaller settlements; finally, that circular floor plans are associated with the absence or casual practice of agriculture, while rectangular grounds plans are associated with more intensive agriculture.

The implications of this study are many because, when one discusses the shift to intensive agriculture and large local communities, one is also likely to be discussing movement on a scale of societal complexity about which we already have some rather good information. In other words, if we know nothing more about a vanished society than the characteristic floor plan of its houses, we might already know quite a lot.

Not everyone lives in a house, not even some people we would most expect to do so. The southern tip of South America, beginning at about the fortieth parallel, is exposed to the chill winds, rain and sleet, and icy waters of the so-called roaring forties. Because there are few land masses in these latitudes to break up the eastward flow of air around the globe, humidity is high and winds are strong. Storms are frequent, and they are notorious among sailors. Here Sir Francis Chittendon's sailboat, on which he alone circumnavigated the globe a few years ago, turned over and came right side up again; and here near Cape Horn, H.M.S. *Bounty* under Capt. William Bligh was turned back by fierce storms in her initial attempt to reach Tahiti. Great amounts of precipitation—nowhere under fifty inches a year, and considerably more on the western slopes—result in a dense and chiefly evergreen temperate forest interspersed with deciduous trees. The land is hilly and sometimes mountainous, broken up into numerous islands, and penetrated by fjords that twist between the steep mountainsides. Overall, the land looks much like that of the northwest coast of North America—not surprising since both areas are characterized by west coast marine climates.

Culturally, however, there are great differences between the northwest coast Indians and the people of Tierra del Fuego, who are generally known as the Ona. The Indians of the northwest—the Kwakiutl, Haida, Nootka, Bella Coola, and others—lived together in sizable villages strung out along the littoral, one of the few areas in which hunters and gatherers found the yield of food reliable and predictable enough to settle down. Since they lived largely off the fruits of the sea and rivers—that is, mobile animals such as seals and fish—they did not need to move around from one harvest to the next, like most hunters and gatherers, but could sit still and let the harvest come to them. Their material culture was relatively complex, particularly their woodworking, and they lived in large slab-timbered houses and carved what are now known as totem poles from trees in the forests that ringed their villages.

The Ona were not so ingenious or, let us say, so lucky. When relatively permanent contact was established between the Ona and the Europeans, the Ona occupied all of Tierra del Fuego except the southern coast, which was heavily forested and offered fewer of the game animals needed for food, especially small rodents and guanacos (an animal related to the llama but more graceful and somewhat larger). The Ona who lived in the plains of the northern and central part of Tierra del Fuego built flimsy shelters of guanaco skins fixed to upright poles, necessarily light and temporary for a population of nomadic bands but poor shelter against the raw wind. There were originally perhaps two thousand Ona occupying an area of some twenty thousand square miles. But their land was occupied by Europeans, alien pathogens were introduced, and a rather systematic program of genocide was carried out. Today there are only a handful, perhaps fifty people, who identify themselves as Ona (Gusinde, 1931, 1937, 1939; Steward and Faron, 1959: 406).

Nearby, the Alakaluf of the southern archipelago of Chile, fared no better. They had an even drearier climate—rainier, more densely forested, and more mountainous. Crop cultivation was virtually impossible because of the combination of landform, climate, and available technology. They hunted land animals and gathered wild plant food, but most of their food was obtained by gathering shellfish and hunting sea mammals and birds. Apparently one of the reasons for this difference in development between the Northwest Coast Indians and the Alakaluf and their neighbors was the abundance of fish along the coast of Canada and Alaska, compared to their scarcity in the waters of the Chilean archipelago, where archaeological evidence suggests that fish were always relatively unimportant (Steward and Faron, 1959: 399). Shellfish provide a more meager subsistence base and prevent the establishment of permanent settlements and the development of craft specialists and other evidence of increasing societal complexity. When food became abundant—when a herd of seals was slaughtered or a whale killed—the surplus was temporary and could in no way have been predicted. Since the Alakaluf depended upon the gathering of shellfish along the shores, they were perforce broken up into small groups traveling at frequent intervals from one location to the next, limited in their technological development by the fact that everything they owned needed to be carried with them in small canoes. The men were chiefly occupied with the hunting of sea mammals and the spearing of shellfish in shallow waters, but the women dived for shellfish in deeper waters, bringing them up in baskets held between their teeth. Adults and children collected shellfish by wading along the shore. This took considerable fortitude in such dismal weather, characterized by snow and sleet, and in icy waters whose temperatures ranged between 40 and 50 degrees Fahrenheit. There is evidence that part of their ability to withstand such stress was attributable to biological adaptation.

The Alakaluf seem to have walked about outside in heavy winds and sleet with no clothing at all, or perhaps only a skin cape, and to have survived by burning more calories than most people do (Hammel, 1960a). The Alakaluf lived in small huts like the Ona's, frameworks of poles around which hides or sometimes bark could be wrapped—the sort of shelter we might think suitable only for protection from the sun. Currently, as a result of disease, assimilation, and the other ordinary results of exposure to Europeans, the Alakaluf, having survived long enough in this hostile environment to have become adapted to it, are reduced to a few settlements along the coast, mostly housed in A-frame huts of corrugated tin, still spearing shellfish along the shore and sometimes selling model canoes carved out of wood to the tourists who pass through the more populated straits on passenger ships.

Just as remarkable were the aboriginal Tasmanians, who lived in scattered bands of about fifty people and who were among the most technologically simple people ever recorded. They too inhabited a heavily forested mountainous land situated in a west coast marine climate, with weather stormy and raw the year round. But their shelters were even cruder than those of the South Americans, rough windbreaks of upright sticks against which brush or tree branches might be piled; the shelter was roofless and three of its sides were open to the elements. There were never very many Tasmanians, but those who were around came into conflict with the European sheepherders who moved onto the island in the early part of the last century. They were shortly rounded up by a missionary and removed to Flinders Island, closer to the Australian mainland, an experience none of them survived.

Shelter refers to whatever inanimate objects people interpose between themselves and their environment for protection from external conditions and to satisfy other, less strictly technological, desires, such as the need for privacy or the need to display the social rank of one's family. Like clothing, shelter may perform both instrumental and expressive functions, permitting the body to maintain physiological equilibrium and also reflecting the social identity of the inhabitants.

The range of variation in the forms and materials of housing is enormous. Generally speaking (and without citing innumerable cross-cultural illustrations at this point), we may find societies in which shelter may be only a simple windscreen, and other societies where shelters appear so durable that their destruction can scarcely be foreseen.

It is unfortunate that the subject of shelter happens to be one of those ethnographic and archaeological areas to have received a great deal of attention (every orthodox ethnography seems to contain some description of housing and other buildings) while the ratio of available information to theoretical comprehension has remained inordinately low. Would that housing had been the subject of as much analytical effort as, say, kinship!

As it stands, shelter has been discussed largely in terms of low-level generalizations, among the lowest-level of which is the position assumed by environmental "possibilists," namely that within any given set of environmental circumstances, several alternatives exist in patterns of shelter, and no single alternative is dictated by the environment. Here, the particular housing strategy selected seems to depend upon historical chance, or perhaps cannot be accounted for at all.

A step above this is the idea that the forms of shelter are indeed determined, although the determinants are so varied and complex that they can never be understood except in relation to one another. Of course this is true in the most simple sense. In a more literal sense, it depends upon what we mean by "understood," because certainly if we need to wait until we are in a position to grasp *all* of the determinants of housing form (or anything else) we will wait forever.

Rapoport's book *House Form and Culture* is a useful beginning in understanding the interaction between some of these forces. He describes and illustrates the influence on architecture of climate, building materials, methods of construction, the building site, the need for defense, subsistence patterns, geographic mobility, religion, storage facilities, the need for social control, cosmography, the reflection of status differences among the inhabitants of a house, the provision of ritual space, features of family structure such as polygyny and caste differences, the need for privacy, the relationship of the house to neighboring houses, and so on.

Again, however, we are confronted with repeated denials that any causality is to be attributed to any given feature of nature or of human sociality, as if there were something basically wrong with causality. The position is essentially a possibilist one, and the tactics Rapoport uses are well-established ones: exceptions to each generalization are brought out, as if they somehow disproved the statement, and instances are given in which, under similar sets of circumstances, differing and alternative tacks have been taken. Thus: "materials, construction, and technology are best treated as modifying factors, rather than form determinants, because they decide neither *what* is to be built nor its form" (Rapoport, 1969: 25).

"Change of materials does not necessarily change the form of the house" (Rapoport, 1969: 26). "Site makes some things *impossible*—one cannot have a floating house where there is no water—but all the forms have been used and all have variants" (Rapoport, 1969: 29). "The communal dwelling has been linked by some to the need to form a survival unit. Even if this explanation is accepted, we find that this form is not an inevitable result of the need for defense" (Rapoport, 1969: 32). "Generally, since people with similar economies may have different moral systems and world views, and since the house is an expression of the world view, economic life has no determining effect on house form" (Rapoport, 1969: 34).

It must be said, however, that Rapoport's problem, one he shares with many others who have dealt with the subject, is a misunderstanding of what "determinism" means. Certain properties of nature and of human beings are frequently described as having some "impact" or "influence" on house form, but any suggestions of "determinism" are played down or rejected. The difficulty of course is that "impact" and "influence" can mean nothing unless some element of determinism is incorporated into the definition. I believe that Rapoport may be proposing that the most suitable method of comprehending the vast number of influences on house form is some form of multivariate analysis, and that it may be unfruitful to tease out any single determinant in an attempt to establish a causal thread, because any given determinant is likely to account for too small a proportion of the great variation found cross-culturally in house form.

This is rather a more reasonable position, although I disagree with it and Rapoport is actually responsible for some generalizations that are verifiable. For example, concerning the interplay between sociocultural and physical factors: "The more forceful the physical constraints, and the more limited the technology and command of means, the less are nonmaterial aspects able to act" (Rapoport, 1969: 58). One might argue that this is not a very profound hypothesis, but it is a step upward from no hypothesis at all. Rapoport further provides a worthwhile bibliography on the subject of influences upon patterns of shelter.

We might hope to see more investigations like Jacques May's description of the relationship between the environment of the Red River delta in Viet Nam, the lifeways of its inhabitants, and disease patterns. Houses in the hills are made of wood and stand on high pilings or stilts. The ubiquitous pigsties are under the houses, and cooking is done inside the house. Mosquitoes that transmit malaria therefore feed on animals instead of people, and they tend to avoid the house because of the smoke and fumes generated by cooking. But on the flatland of the delta itself, houses are built of mud and straw, materials that do not readily permit construction at any distance above the ground, so that the pigsties and the kitchens are both at some distance from the house itself and provide no protection from disease-carrying insects (May, 1957: 96). We might also be referred to a historical account of housing that will cause you to be glad even of the hovel you live in today (Gauldie, 1974).

Finally, perhaps, I should also mention the possibility that the shape of a shelter may influence more than people's behavior. It seems that the shape of pyramids may cause cosmic waves to resonate inside them, and it has seriously been suggested that this resonation has widespread effects upon objects placed inside the pyramid and may even slow the decomposition of corpses. Even more *outré* is the possibility that these same forces may promote the growth of crystalline structures. For example, the crystals on the edge of a blunted razor blade may reproduce themselves in a pyramid and thus restore the original sharp edge of the razor. One investigator

> tried putting [a razor blade] under his model pyramid, but nothing happened, so he went on shaving with it until it was blunt, and then put it back in the pyramid. It became sharp again. Getting a good razor blade is still difficult in many Eastern European countries, so Drbal tried to patent and market his discovery. The patent office in Prague refused to consider it until their chief scientist had tried building a model himself and found that it worked. So the Cheops Pyramid Razor Blade Sharpener was registered in 1959 under the Czechoslovakian Republic Patent No. 91304, and a factory soon began to turn out miniature cardboard pyramids. Today they make them in Styrofoam. [Watson, 1973: 88]

Watson gives instructions for the building of such a pyramid and suggests that the reader may try to generate the effect for himself.

It might be worthwhile at this point to describe the organization of two kinds of households, one in its relationship to external factors, and one in terms of its internal domains. These descriptions should be helpful as illustrations of the sorts of things anthropologists might fruitfully investigate.

In the rural Japanese village of Niiike, one does not simply build a house according to personal desires. Rather, the dwelling is sited and oriented according to a template of demands imposed upon the builder by history. These demands determine the arrangement of the house and outbuildings and the plan of rooms within the house. They derive from a system of directional rules, called *hōgaku,* which are astrological in origin. The house itself is laid out on a zodiacal grid and forms the center of a circle, around the periphery of which lie the domains of the various animals of the zodiac. Outbuildings and such facilities as water pumps are then placed in relationship to the dominant animals. Furthermore, despite some vacillations, certain directions have more or less consistent good or bad qualities. Northeast and southwest are poor directions, but southeast is always good. Income flows from southeast to northwest, so strong rooms are located in the northwestern part of the house to collect income. Wells are never dug on the southern or sunny side of the house because they may dry up. And since bad luck travels from northeast to southwest, openings are left in each of these directions in order not to impede the flow of ill fortune.

*Hōgaku* is not as influential in Niiike as it is in other Japanese villages, but the system is still important, the measure of its importance being the inconvenience people will suffer in order to act in accord with it.

> The system deeply affects those who choose to observe it. One looks for a bride who lives in an auspicious direction with relation to his house. One postpones a trip if the day is inauspicious for travel in that direction or else goes first in a different direction, then turns towards his destination. [Beardsley et al., 1969: 80]

Even if one does not hold to such beliefs, to ignore the rules risks the criticism of the neighbors. Sometimes a significant amount of inconvenience is involved in their observance. When one man was about to marry and set up a house, the rules caused him considerable difficulty.

> His family owned a good site in the midst of the community, but it lay in an inauspicious direction from his father's house. So Takeshi set up a branch house in the low paddy field in front of the village. Though in a fortunate direction from his original home, the site had to be raised with a gravel fill to keep the house from being perpetually damp. Even then it was not above danger from flood, and the well water was unusable. He and his wife felt lonely and estranged living even fifty yards away from the community. [Beardsley et al., 1969: 30]

Five years later, a new auspicious site was calculated, and the old home was torn down and reconstructed on the new site. As far as the cost of all this was concerned, not counting family labor,

> about two-thirds of a full year's declared income, was an investment in the imponderable, in *hōgaku*, the art of calculating lucky and unlucky directions. [Beardsley et al., 1969:81]

And as Robert J. Smith has remarked:

> The whole issue of geomancy is critical. The Japanese house was as it was through careful attention to the "good" and "bad" directions. The association of its parts is similarly dictated. The Japanese no more understand the idea of

combining the bath and the toilet than we understand hara-kiri. The separation of such functions, of such interest to the psychoanalytic school, is real. Automatic washing machines are not as popular as you might think because they require the mixing of underwear and dish towels, for which the traditional house kept two separate basins in the laundry. [1963]

Of course, many dwellings are arranged internally so that separate functions are carried out in separate places. Often these functions are simply different — we cook in the kitchen and eat in the dining room — but in some dwellings the separate areas might best be comprehended under the terms *sacred* and *profane*. This seems to be the case in the household of the Hungarian peasant, for example, reported in Silverman (1963) and shown in Figure 4.

Most of the interaction in the home occurs in Room I. The dashed line that diagonally intersects Room I divides it into the profane area (A') and the sacred area (A). The profane area is that part of the room in which the women work and in which the old people and the children spend their leisure time. The area immediately in front of the door is not considered a part of the room itself, but rather belongs to the hallway. Visitors may stand here and explain who they are and why they have come. Some visitors, particularly those who bear good news and who have respectable occupations, such as shepherds, may be invited in and asked to enjoy a glass of brandy while standing by the table. However, visitors whose position in the community is low, such as beggars and gypsies, will not be asked to step into the room. If they are offered food, they eat it while standing at the threshold. On the other hand, if they are obviously tired and in need of rest, they may be asked to use the bench by the oven, with the clear understanding that they will shortly be on their way. Family members may insult one another by telling them that their place is on the oven bench, where the beggars sit. Honored guests and close friends, of course, are permitted to sit at one end of the bench in the sacred area, but only after having been invited to do so.

Women dominate the region around the oven, which in a sense serves as the focal point of the household. This is where most of the household activity occurs and where it is warmest during the cold winters. The benches near the oven serve as resting places for nonproductive household members, such as old people, as well as for beggars and gypsies.

The sacred area is strikingly different from the profane area, in appearance and in function. Instead of cooking utensils, religious objects and a variety of ornate cups and plates hang on the wall. Important religious ceremonies are performed here. For example, on Thursday evenings, food is placed under the corner bench as an offering to a snake that is presumed to live there and that is also presumed to bring the family good

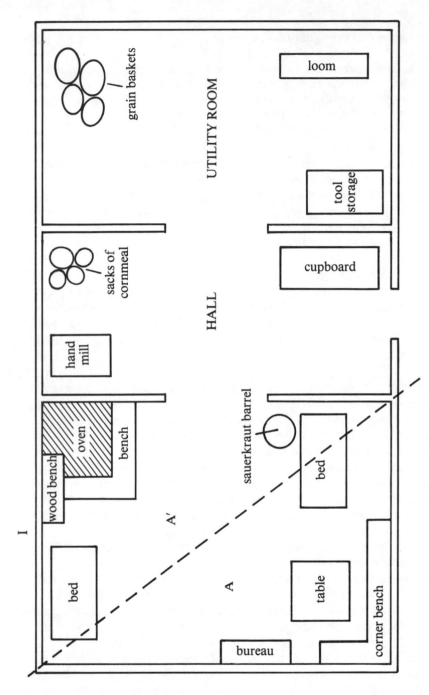

FIG. 4. FLOOR PLAN OF A HUNGARIAN PEASANT HOUSEHOLD (AFTER GUNDA-DEBRECEN, 1962).

luck if it is periodically propitiated. The table itself is invested with spiritual power; ill people are placed upon it in order to take advantage of its healing properties. Unmarried women avoid sitting on the bench around the sacred table because unfortunate consequences, especially sexual and reproductive, would follow.

The behavior of individuals at mealtimes reflects both the ecological layout of the household and the position of its members. The male head of the household always sits at the corner of the bench where both walls meet, and the working men sit on either side of him. Children under the age of eighteen eat sitting on the floor. Married women eat while standing near the table. However, the wife of the household head, and any nursing mothers, may be seated while they eat.

Whatever food is left over is put into a bowl and given to old grandmothers, to be eaten in some unobtrusive part of the profane area. It may be said that we come away from the Hungarian household with an impression that, although it is not divided into numerous tiny rooms, it manages nevertheless to be clearly differentiated by behavioral means, so much so that there might as well be walls between the regions. (See also Canter and Canter, 1971.) The point is well illustrated in Morgan's study of Iroquois households, dated though the report is.

Lewis Henry Morgan, it will be recalled, was a rich lawyer and businessman from Rochester, New York, who, in the course of helping to found a secret society, a fraternal organization something like that of the Freemasons, became interested in the Indians who had provided him with a model. The resulting book, *Houses and House-Life of the American Aborigine,* is largely of historical interest. It appears to have had virtually no impact on American anthropology or on those behavioral scientists who have shown an interest in architecture.

In truth, the book, published in 1881, is not very useful. Morgan's local Indian models were Iroquois, a matrilineal people who lived in multifamily longhouses. Morgan proposed five major connections between social life and the multiple-family house, including: (1) the law of hospitality, (2) communism in living, (3) ownership of land in common, (4) the practice of having one meal each day, and (5) separation at mealtimes — men first, women and children later. Morgan then ran through his list showing how these activities were linked with the structure of the house. The "law of hospitality," for example, was linked with the longhouse in that strangers were always fed upon first entering the village — there being no such things as cafeterias or restaurants — and, in multiple-family dwellings like the longhouse, there was ordinarily a considerable surplus of food and someone around to serve it to the strangers in the communal space. In addition, the great number of people living in the house tended to promote feelings of psychological security, so that no one need feel concerned about physical safety when admitting a stranger into the home. (Contrast this situation with that of the lone housewife in a contemporary setting, faced with the necessity of deciding whether or not to permit a stranger claiming to be a salesman into her home.) In these and other ways, the longhouse was conducive to hospitality.

Morgan went on from such apparent truisms to draw conclusions that may have seemed defensible in the light of what knowledge was available to him (some of these conclusions having to do with the universality of primitive communism), but that are now clearly unjustified.

*Clothing.* Clothing and shelter are designed to provide, among other things, protection from surrounding conditions. They are buffering mechanisms that reduce differences between the external milieu, the surroundings of the human body, and the internal milieu, the bodily organs. In principle, clothing and shelter perform similar functions. They differ in that clothing is a more portable and generally less efficient protective mechanism than shelter, which is ordinarily stationary and capable of accommodating energy sources in addition to those provided by the human body. In other words, the inside of a suit of clothes can be heated only by the body itself, whereas one may build a fire inside a dwelling. The difference is academic in some tropical and subtropical areas where neither clothing nor shelter are necessities, but the more hostile the climate, the more apparent are these differences, which in fact hold true whether we are discussing Eskimo igloos and parkas, or moon-landing vehicles and extravehicular life-support systems.

In warmer climatic areas, such as tropical rain forests, clothing can be a positive hindrance, and even outside of tropical areas, the human body can show a surprising resilience in the face of environmental stress. The Indians of Tierra del Fuego and the Chilean archipelago have provided examples of people living in particularly dismal climates whose use of clothing is minimal: a coating of grease on the body, a skin cloak, and not much else.

Three basic classes of garments are in common use around the world. One is the loincloth and its variant forms, usually found in the warmer parts of the world. The material from which it is made varies from deerskin in North America to grass leaves in Melanesia and beaten bark among the Mbuti pygmies of the Congo. Sometimes, instead of a loincloth, men will wear a penis sheath, which serves more to call attention to the groin than to cover it, as did the codpiece, fashionable among European men four hundred years ago.

In some parts of the world, such as modern Polynesia and much of Southeast Asia, the loincloth hangs below the knees. This permits walking but interferes with activities which require more vigorous movements, such as swimming. In Polynesia, people cope with the problem simply by lifting the hem up, all the way around, and tucking it into the waist of the garment. Knee-length loincloths are in everyday use in Samoa, where they are sometimes wrapped around the waist and secured merely by tucking in one end, and sometimes worn with a belt. Younger men and women are inclined towards bright prints; older people are more likely to wear loincloths of darker, solid colors. It is now possible to buy manufactured loincloths with adjustable waists, secured by buttons, and featuring pockets on the sides. A well-dressed gentleman might be seen returning from church of a Sunday morning, dressed in sports jacket, white shirt and tie, loincloth and sandals.

Rather more extensive covering is provided by another basic garment, the robe, the variant forms of which include the cape, the cloak, the Arab burnoose, and the toga. Robes have been commonly used by hunters and gatherers of temperate climates on most continents, excluding Australia. In most instances these were simple sheets of animal skin—buffalo among the Plains Indians of North America, for example—but since they were visible from a greater distance than were loincloths, and since they were on the whole more impressive garments, they sometimes served to signal the wearer's status in ways that loin coverings did not, as in much of ancient Polynesia, where cloaks woven for royalty out of brilliant feathers constituted truly resplendent garb.

In tropical and subtropical deserts, where humidity is low and cloud cover generally lacking, robes may provide protection against the very high daytime temperatures and the uncomfortably low nighttime ones, as does the Arab burnoose, which consists of a robe of variable thickness to which a small hood is attached. Huntington relates an illustrative anecdote:

> Once when I was exploring ruins in the midsummer heat of the Trans-caspian desert, my companion, a Turkoman, wore a thinly quilted robe that fell below his knees. The second day out he said, "If I'd known it was going to be so hot, I'd have worn a thicker robe." He wanted fuller protection against the sun. [Huntington, 1959: 303-4]

The most efficient means of protecting the body from low temperatures is to provide it with tailored clothing, the third major type of garment. Tailored clothing consists of close-fitting vests and loin coverings to which tubes of material for arms and legs are attached, the ideal type being perhaps a suit of long winter underwear or the "wet suit" worn by some scuba divers.

Among many of the North American Indians, these tubes were detachable, but in most instances tailored clothes involve permanently attached sleeves and legs, although of course other garments may be wrapped around the body over the tailored clothes. Frequently, tailored clothing is worn by the men of a community while women wear robes or clothing whose tailoring is confined to the upper torso. Presumably this had to do with differences in the ease with which urination is effected; the likelihood that men, spending more time out of doors, needed greater protection; and differences in the symbolizing of social status.

Some societies do not conform to these generalizations concerning dress. Traditional garb of the Highland clans of Scotland a few hundred years ago—that is, MacKenzies, Grants, Frazers, and so on—was the kilt, which was in essence a loincloth. And for added protection against particularly strenuous circumstances, they carried wrapped around their torsos a plaid, which was in essence a woolen blanket that served as a robe. This mode of dress, incidentally, appeared at the beginning of the seventeenth century and evolved out of a garment consisting of a loose, full shirt on top of which was worn a thick woolen knee-length sweater with a wide neck and short sleeves.

This manner of dress was never adopted by the so-called Lowland clans, many of whom were located near the border with England, including the Bothwell, Home, and Johnston clans, for example, not to mention the renowned Maxwells. The Lowland people adopted the tailored pantaloon. However, both the Highlanders and the Lowlanders developed tartans: traditional patterns of color woven into the cloth, identifying the clan of the wearer (*The Scottish Clans and Their Tartans,* 1968).

The kilt, of course, along with other loose and drafty sorts of clothing, would seem more suited to warmer climes than that found in the Scottish Highlands, and in fact resembles more closely the genre of clothing traditionally associated with the Mediterranean area of Europe than that of the Gothic northern areas. Historically, these two contrasting clothing traditions have been in a kind of stylistic clash for several thousand years. The Phoenician merchants traded with people along the coast of Cornwall, in southwestern England, at about the time of Homer. The area was described by Strabo as "inhabited by a people wearing black garments, or cloaks, reaching down to their heels, and bound round their breasts" (quoted in Fairholt and Dillon, 1885). This original resemblance to Mediterranean dress was later reinforced by the Romans who conquered much of Britain and who introduced the toga. With the expansion of the tribes of northern Europe—the Goths, Franks, Longobards, and the like—the tendency was reversed and tailored clothing became predominant, even in Rome.

It is curious to note, however, a seasonal alteration on American campuses between Mediterranean features of dress and Gothic styles, an idea suggested in Roberts et al. (1971: 264). During the warmer months, tailored clothing tends to be replaced by looser, more flowing garb. Shorts appear in place of trousers or pants, and the shorter they are, the more they resemble wrap-around loincloths. Hosiery and leotards, and their lineal descendants, pantyhose, are replaced by the bare legs of the Mediterranean; shirts are no longer tucked into the waistband but are left to hang freely down the torso. The tailored boots and shoes of northern Europe disappear to some extent and are replaced by Mediterranean sandals. Even the material from which the clothing is made tends towards a seasonal alteration, from animal products like furs, skins, and hair in the winter, to the vegetable fibers of the Mediterranean in the warmer months.

The kilt, as noted, is an exception to the proposition that tailored clothing predominates in poleward areas, but its exceptional quality applies only to its instrumental value, which is to say its value as a buffer, and not to its expressive value as a mechanism for signaling the status of the wearer, in which respect its purposes are highly codified. This is a feature it has in common with many other buffers in European society, such as fisherman's sweaters (Thompson, 1969), medieval armor (Ashdown, 1970), and shields (Franklyn, 1968: 13 – 18) around whose pictorially eloquent faces the illiterate ranks of soldiers rallied in battle.

The expressive value of clothing cannot be ignored. There is a tendency, where clothing is minimal, for body ornamentation to assume this function. In some cases, the ornamentation may be permanent — as in tattooing — or, where the color of the skin is too dark for tattooing to be readily visible, scarification. It may be that these permanent alterations in the appearance of the body tend to be common to the extent that statuses are ascribed rather than achieved — that they signal relatively unchanging aspects of identity, such as maturity or sex. Presumably then, more ephemeral characteristics of the individual, such as membership in temporary organizations, are more likely to be signaled by more readily changed conditions of appearance, such as wearing the hair in a specified style of wearing garments of a certain color. Funeral customs frequently illustrate the variation, close kinsmen of the deceased permanently altering their appearance, as through lopping off a finger, and more remote kinsmen using temporary signals, such as donning garments of a particular color, black in Europe and America, for example, and white muslin in China.

Of course the application of materials directly to the body, in which the expressive function is usually predominant, can have instrumental value as well. Coating the body with an adherent such as grease or paint provides some protection from noxious temperatures. The Fuegans knew that, and so do long-distance swimmers. But ordinarily, body decorations have much more to do with public appearance than with survival.

Mick Jagger of the Rolling Stones is said to be a striking presence on stage. Here are some of the reasons why: makeup base (8N Max Factor Pan-stick), spread over the chest and face and set with powder; technicolor rouge; "very heavy" purple eye makeup; dark brown eyeliner pencil; brown mascara "to give more sparkle, more definition to the eyes"; Leichner eye shadow from Germany, usually purple or green, and coordinated with his costume; color-coordinated face sparkles affixed to his eyes and cheekbones using a tube of Duo Surgical Adhesive; gold glitter affixed to his chest; gold glitter sprinkled on his hair just before a performance so that, as he prances around, it flies off and is picked up by the spotlights. "Mick, according to [his makeup man] is unrecognizable without makeup. His face is completely plain, lined, washed out. Now that Mick is aging, [his makeup man] has taught him...certain Hollywood makeup tricks to 'enhance' his image" (Elman, 1972: 45).

It might be worth adding the apparently truistic observation that, aside from certain strictures imposed on dress by the environment, styles of clothing are culturally determined and subject to what seems at times to be arbitrary variation. However, Kroeber has convincingly demonstrated that in fact many such changes, aside from such fleeting developments as the Nehru jacket for men, conform to regular cycles, imposed upon an underlying and relatively inflexible basic pattern.

As for the basic pattern of women's clothing, over the past few hundred years considerable change in fashion has occurred, but the basic pattern "aims at amplitude from the hips down but slenderness above; the silhouette extremes would be: full or wide skirt, long or low skirt, narrow waist, and therefore waistline just at the waist proper" (Kroeber, 1948: 333).

Variations from this norm occur in particular features of dress (e.g., the fullness of the bust or the altitude of the hem) in regular swings that take fifty years or more to reach one extreme, only to begin moving back towards the other. Further, Kroeber and Jane Richardson (1940) have shown that the more extreme deviations from the normal pattern tend to occur during periods of social upheaval such as wars, revolutions, or great political or economic changes.

Underneath all of this pulsating, however, there remains the basic pattern — the theme upon which these variations are made — and the basic pattern differs from one society to another.

> It is remarkable how virtually all changes of fashion, alike in Classical, Western, and East Asiatic costume, have consistently operated each within the basic dress pattern of its own civilization. Fashion decrees a thousand bizarre forms and extravagances; but it never has produced, among Occiden-

tals, a man's type of dress based on the toga instead of trousers, nor a woman's with a Japanese silhouette. [Kroeber, 1948: 332—33]

Roberts et al. (1971) report that detectable differences in attitudes towards certain elements of tailored clothing—shirts and shoes—still exist between informants from France and the United States, on the one hand, and informants from Turkey, India, Chile, Cameroun, and Egypt, on the other. Their argument is that tailored clothing constitutes a pattern, or system, somewhat like the alphabet, in which things are recognized as somehow going together, and that the pattern tends to diffuse from one area to another as a whole. France and the United States, whose basic pattern of dress is derived from northwestern Europe, represent areas in which tailored clothing has been the standard for a longer period of time than in the other areas mentioned. (Their Cameroun informant had himself worn robes.) Roberts et al. subjected their data concerning preferences for various combinations of shirts and shoes to an elaborate statistical analysis. It is enough to say here that informants from France and the United States had their minds made up. Their attitudes towards these elements of tailored clothing were firm. In contrast, informants from other areas were significantly less likely to show consistent attitudes towards tailored clothing.

Finally, with reference to the fleeting details of dress, we may remind ourselves of Margaret Mead's work suggesting that there is a great deal of cross-cultural variation in the differential attention paid to dress and grooming by men, on the one hand, and women, on the other, and that in some societies women may be the basic providers, while men spend a greater proportion of their time polishing their appearance (Mead, 1935). Whether or not, in Mead's study, the reversal of roles (by our standards) was the temporary result of disorganization developing out of the imposition of British colonial rule is beside the point. Margaret Mead can be taken as a reliable observer and her statements were true in time and space.

Similar situations have occurred in Euroamerican history as well. A few hundred years ago, our European forebears, if they were gentlemen, wore wide and dashing hats, wigs, face powder, handmade lace on shirts and underwear, embroidered coats, silk stockings, garters, and shoes with high heels and silver buckles, and they splashed scented water on themselves. Here are some comments by John Gay concerning the wigs worn by fashionable males during the early years of the eighteenth century:

> Others who lay the stress of beauty in their face, exert all their extravagance in the periwig, which is a kind of index of the mind; the full bottom formally combed all before, denotes the lawyer and the politician; the

smart tye-wig with the black ribbon shows a man of fierceness of temper; and he that burdens himself with a superfluity of white hair which flows down the back, and mantles in waving curles over the shoulders, is generally observed to be less curious in the furniture of the inward recesses of the scull. [Quoted in Brooke, 1954: 73]

From a letter written in 1753:

The Duke went, and was very fine; his coat dark mouse-colored velvet, embroidered with silver; Jenny Glegg's work, and the finest I ever saw; the waistcoat Isabella satin, embroidered the same as the coat; there was a great deal of finery. [Brooke, 1954: 93]

And twenty years later:

The chief topick of conversation yesterday was Lord Villier's appearance in the morning at Court in a pale purple velvet coat, turned up with lemon-color, and embroidered all over with S.S.'s of pearl as big as pease, and in all the spaces little medallions in beaten gold, *real solid*, in various figures of Cupids and the like. [Brooke, 1954: 93]

If insulted, these perfumed popinjays would challenge you to a duel and punch you full of holes with a rapier, with true macho readiness.

Adequate discussions of dress style for men and women during these periods, though theoretically barren as usual, can be found in Brooke (1954) and Squire (1974), and a brief reference to the recent history of undergarments, for the more esoteric-minded, in Kybelova et al. (1968: 449-67) as well as in the last few generations of Sears, Roebuck catalogues. One of the better summary statements, which treats the adaptive value of decorations in a comparative context, is in Roach and Eicher (1973).

*Nourishment*

A person who has worked hard all day building shelter against the onslaughts of the natural environment, is a hungry person. In a moment I will describe several types of food-getting techniques recognized by anthropologists, but I will not dwell on them at any length since this is the sort of material that is easily retrieved from any introductory anthropology text. I will devote more space to subjects I find interesting because they are surprising, exotic, or neglected. I will then review three studies that illustrate different aspects of the dynamics of the search for nourishment: the passive adaptation to the differential distribution of wells in India, the active attempt to acquire more and more of the all-important camels among the Arabs, and the drastic change in reindeer herding among the Lapps brought about by the introduction of the snowmobile. In each case, the impact of the search for nourishment on social life will be examined.

*Subsistence Patterns.* Subsistence patterns refer to the ways in which people get food. There are several major types, none of them "pure"; the vast majority of people are omnivorous and have always been so. Even a modern urbanite may find the time and opportunity to add a bit of freshly bagged game or fish to the larder.

In hunting societies, of course, great importance is attached to the killing of wild animals, either stalked singly or caught in a net or some other sort of trap. A primary dependence upon fish occurs chiefly in the higher latitudes where winters are severe (R.B. Lee, 1968: 43). The precise ecological situation of fishing societies is not clear. Some of them, such as the Alacaluf, whom we have already mentioned, have not been very successful. How much of their present circumstances can be traced to contact with Europeans is impossible to guess; no doubt quite a lot. Other societies chiefly dependent upon fish, shellfish, and marine mammals, have met with considerable success. All along the northwest coast of North America, from northern California to the vicinity of present Skagway, such societies as the Yurok, Kwakiutl, Haida, Tlingit, and Eyak maintained stable populations in permanent settlements along the littoral. Some of these societies have become "classics," both in the ethnographic literature and in popular mythology, partly because of their seagoing canoes and totem poles and an art style that pleases Western eyes.

Hunting and fishing correspond to predation in the animal world. Gathering, the third primary method of subsistence, involves searching about for wild plant foods. The searching need not be aimless, since gatherers generally are familiar with their own territories and have a fairly good idea of where given plants are located and when the edible material tends to be most abundant. Hunting and gathering are almost always combined in some proportion. Generally, the proportion of food obtained through gathering is higher near the equator, lower towards the arctic. In fact, in the case of the Kalahari Bushmen, most of the caloric content of their diet is derived from gathered foods, of which the Bushmen observed by Lee identified eighty-five edible species. Of the average number of calories per person per day—2,140—only 690 were derived from meat. The other 1,350 calories were derived from gathered vegetable foods, 1,260 of these calories from a single source, namely mongongo nuts. There was, in fact, such a surfeit of mongongo nuts that millions of them rotted on the ground because no one bothered to pick them (Lee, 1969). And these Bushmen are classed as hunters!

Pastoralism refers to the herding of relatively large domestic animals. Pastoral societies occur in many parts of the world, most notably in grasslands and savannas in large parts of Africa, the Middle East, and the Asian steppes. The particular animals involved vary from camels to reindeer. The degree of domestication of the animals also varies. In some cases, they are more or less completely dependent on human beings, herded about under constant surveillance from one grazing area to the next, branded, ear-clipped, or otherwise identified as belonging to one or another herder, and are relatively docile. In other instances, the resemblance is more to human beings following a herd of wild animals, occasionally killing some of them. Large domestic animals have a great many potential uses: they can be eaten, ridden, milked, burdened, exchanged for other goods, skinned, petted, sacrificed, and so on. Probably no society takes full advantage of its domestic animals; the use to which such animals are put is selective. The Chinese, for example, eat beef but do not milk their cows and therefore use no dairy products. We ride horses but seldom eat them. A final characteristic of pastoral societies is their enforced nomadism, sometimes alternating between seasonal pastures, in which case the movement is referred to as transhumance. Hyams (1972) gives a general overview of the uses to which animals may be put and sketches some relevant history; Zeuner (1963) is another important source; Leeds and Vayda (1965) are equally interesting and more relevant for anthropologists.

Horticultural societies practice the planting, cultivation, and harvesting of domesticated food plants. Associated tools are usually simple, sometimes little more than a digging stick or hoe. A few domestic animals are ordinarily kept, such as pigs and fowl. Little or no surplus food is produced. Since the yield is just enough to feed the community members themselves, such societies can afford few full-time craft specialists. At the same time, however, horticulturalists remain in permanent settlements and so can build shelters and accumulate material goods unthinkable to people forced to move after short periods of time. It may be that, like some hunters, some horticulturists need not work for very long to acquire sustenance. The men of the Kuikuru of central Brazil take care of the crops, and they only spend about two hours daily gardening, and another one and one half hours fishing. The other ten or twelve waking hours are spent in recreation (Carneiro, 1961, cited in Hoebel, 1966: 247). Since the Kuikuru cultivate only about 95 of the 13,500 acres available to them, we can assume that they could work harder and accumulate much more food, but since there is little trade and little population pressure, there would be nothing to do with the surplus.

Finally, agriculture is a very general term used to encompass a variety of planting, cultivating, and harvesting techniques that produce a surplus and exchange or sell it to some agency outside the community. In addition to simple mixed farming, in which a variety of crops and domestic animals are raised on small farms (the sort of arrangement common in parts of New England today) a number of rather specialized forms of agriculture have developed with the increasing ease of transportation and thus trade.

Mixed farming may become a specialized enterprise when vegetables and fruit are grown near densely populated areas and the large urban population provides a ready market for certain kinds of fresh food. This is called "truck farming" and is found, for example, in the Imperial Valley near Los Angeles, where melons and lettuce are grown, and in New Jersey, where tomatoes and corn are among the chief truck crops for the New York metropolitan area.

Dairying is another example of specialized mixed farming and is commonly practiced in areas where sufficient rainfall provides good pasturage, including much of northwestern Europe, from which the once-abundant forests disappeared long ago (Darby, 1956). The names of many of our important dairy cows reflect this limited distribution: Jersey, Guernsey, and Holstein are all areas located within the belt of west coast marine climate that covers northwestern Europe.

Another major subtype of agriculture is cereal agriculture, characterized by vast fields of wheat or other grains, the reduction of human labor by means of technology, and the production of a yield that is *entirely* surplus. These areas are sometimes referred to as the "grain belts" of the world.

Commercial grazing, or ranching, differs from pastoralism in that the human population is settled, rather than mobile, and the entire yield is sold as surplus rather than consumed by the producers themselves. If the immense, lightly settled grain belts provide the densely populated industrial centers with the necessary staple grains, the equally wide grasslands committed to commercial grazing provide the industrial population with meat and other animal products.

In many parts of east and southeast Asia, an intensive form of agriculture depends primarily on wet-rice irrigation. These areas tend to be densely populated and the land is carefully tended, with a number of crops being cultivated at the same time. The work is arduous, and little of it lends itself to mechanization. Land is in very short supply, and every bit of it tends to be used for some purpose. One gains some understanding of intensive agricultural techniques from the ethnography of the Japanese village of Niiike.

> Footpaths laced geometrically across the flat valley floor as divisions between paddy fields serve as short cuts....Here the passersby must walk in single file or in pairs to avoid slipping off into the rich mud of the rice field that lie two or three feet below the paths and roads.

Literally at the back door of the shops lined along the main street...neat fields of vegetables and irrigated rice plots begin....Above the fields, the hard, sandy surface of the side roads is banked with solid stone walls. The grassy edge of each road, like the grass along the paths, ditches, and high dikes beside the river, is cropped to a stubble the whole year. Weeds that escape the tethered plow-oxen and goats are cut off with short sickles and added to the compost heap in each farmyard. Farmers use the narrow ditch banks to plant a patch of vetch or a row or two of soybeans. [Beardsley et al., 1959: 73]

The ethnographers described the landscape as one "which long ago surrendered to human control" (Beardsley et al., 1959: 73). Clifford Geertz has contrasted wet-rice cultivation and its ecological consequences with the diversified horticultural system it is gradually replacing in some parts of Java (Geertz, 1963). At the same time, there are indications that wet-rice agriculture is giving way to a more diversified farming pattern, as a greater number of cultivators are willing to risk planting less dependable crops than rice, but crops which yield a higher profit when sold (Jay, 1969: 9).

A final subtype we might mention is plantation agriculture, born at about the same time as many of the European colonial empires which in fact generated them, although they now persist even though the empires have vanished. Plantations are found largely in the tropics or subtropics; they emphasize a limited number of crops, such as tea, cocoa, sugar, spices, coffee, bananas, rubber, and tobacco; and they produce a commercial crop that is mostly exported.

It has been stated a number of times that the field of human ecology is a vast one, but our space here is limited. The problem is particularly acute with reference to subsistence patterns and the section on economics that follows. It could be argued with some justification that the relationship of people to their natural environments, mediated by the means they use to extract plant and animal products, constitutes almost the whole of what we might call traditional ecological anthropology. Certainly, subsistence practices are one of the prime areas of anthropological interest. An extensive literature has developed around the subject, including a number of exemplary case studies (e.g., Meggers, 1957; Linton, 1939; Reina, 1967; Fox and Cumberland, 1962; and others), some rather more general statements (e.g., Geertz 1963; Rappaport, 1968; Wagner, 1960), collections of important articles (e.g., Vayda, 1969), and introductory and review articles (e.g., Vayda and Rappaport, 1968; Anderson, 1974). One of the reasons for the depth of this interest is the assumption that subsistence practices exert a considerable causal influence on other aspects of social structure. That the interest has been expressed largely in treatments of premodern subsistence practices is partly due to the fact that until relatively recently, they were the only means of subsistence available. After all, plants and animals were domesticated probably not more than 12,000 years ago. We will review more closely some important and representative works shortly. However, for fuller discussions and examples, the reader is referred to the works mentioned above.

The !Kung Bushmen of Botswana live in the inhospitable Kalahari Desert. Rainfall is between six and nine inches per year, most of it occurring between November and April. Landscape is rough and sandy, characterized by scattered growths of low trees, shrubs, and thorn bushes or acacia. This marginal environment has kept the !Kung relatively isolated until quite recently.

Between 1963 and 1965, the !Kung living in the Dobe area were studied by R.B. Lee and several others. Lee's primary focus was ecological, mostly treating the relationships among group structure, demography, and nutrition. The !Kung of the Dobe area are hunters and gatherers of a sort that is now becoming increasingly rare. They have no livestock, firearms, or agriculture. They subsist entirely on whatever game they can bag with bow and (poisoned) arrow, small animals and eggs they may find, and wild plant foods they may gather. Hunting is largely men's work; gathering is women's work.

The !Kung follow a seasonal cycle in their movements, governed by the availability of water. During the rainy summer, small pools appear everywhere, and the !Kung are split up into smaller camps, formed around one or another source of water. When the dry months arrive, many of the smaller pools disappear and the population comes together at the larger remaining pools. By the end of the dry winter, the population is restricted to the eight permanent water holes found in the area.

Although there is seasonal variation in some of the types of food available—berries during the summer, roots during the winter, and so on—there is an overall similarity among the actual methods employed in getting food. The men hunt and the women gather whatever food is available within hiking distance of the water hole where they are camped. For the most part, food is readily available within easy walking distance of the camp. It is only at the end of the dry season, before the summer rains begin, that large groups of people find themselves drawn together at one of the eight water holes, the food supply in the vicinity of the camp is played out, and longer hikes must be planned.

In an intensive analysis of !Kung Bushman subsistence, Lee and his colleagues found that, despite the fact that Bushman technology is simple and the environment harsh, about 40 percent of the population studied were nonproductive young and old people. The working adults of both sexes engaged in active hunting and gathering only a few days per week; in fact, the Bushmen led a relatively easy life (R.B. Lee, 1968, 1969, 1972; Lee and DeVore, 1976). Lee tried to develop quantitative measures of a number of ecologically primary variables, including "abundance and variety of resources, diet selectivity, range size and population density, the composition of the work force, the ratio of work to leisure time, and the caloric and protein levels in the diet" (Lee, 1968: 33). The results contradict commonsense notions about the subsistence status of hunters and gatherers, and even the statements of some professionals, one of whom reported:

> It is vividly apparent that among the !Kung Bushmen, ethos, or "the spirit which actuates manners and customs," is survival. Their time and energies are almost wholly given to this task, for life in their environment requires that they spend their days mainly in procuring food. [Marshall, 1965: 247, quoted in R.B. Lee, 1968: 36]

Lee recorded the daily activities of the Bushmen living at one of the winter water holes and calculated the number of man-days of work as compared to the number of man-days of consumption. On the average, the adults of the camp worked at food-getting about two and a half days per week, at an average of six hours per workday, or, in other words, somewhere between twelve and nineteen hours per week. The hardest-working man in the camp, who hunted on sixteen out of the twenty-eight days during which records were kept, put in about thirty-two hours per week. At the beginning of the recording period, when food was readily available in the immediate vicinity of the camp, twelve hours was the average; by the end of the recording period, immediate food sources were depleted and longer hikes were necessary, raising the average to nineteen hours.

But is such a modest amount of effort sufficient to supply the !Kung with an adequate diet? Are they hungry, ridden with the effects of malnutrition, dying at an early age? Apparently not. Eight percent of the population were older than sixty. There was no overt evidence of any of the more common nutritional diseases such as kwashiorkor. During the recording period, 410 pounds of meat were brought into the camp, and about 700 pounds of vegetable foods, mostly the ubiquitous mongongo nuts. Analysis of these victuals yields a total output of 2,140 calories and 93.1 grams of protein per person per day. The recommended daily allowances for small persons leading active lives is 1,975 calories and 60 grams of protein; so it is evident that caloric intake exceeded the requirement by a comfortable margin. Furthermore, the !Kung usually preferred certain kinds of foods over others, and they exercised this preference in foodstuffs. Of about eighty-five species of food plants available to them, the Bushmen derived only 10 percent of their food value from seventy-five of them. Nor did they eat just any kind of animal they encountered; here too they exercised choice. Two hundred and twenty-three local animals were recognized and named, but only fifty-four were considered edible and only seventeen were regularly hunted. The !Kung regarded such potential food animals as rodents, snakes, lizards, and termites with distaste.

If the !Kung did not need to spend very much time actively engaged in the food quest, then what did they do? A woman could gather enough food in one day to support her family for three days. The rest of the time she spent resting, embroidering, chatting with visitors or neighbors; at home there were a number of chores to be performed, including gathering firewood and preparing food. The men hunted for longer periods, but they hunted unevenly. A man might hunt vigorously for a week or so, then do nothing for the next two. In the camp, men mostly chatted with visitors, danced, or gambled.

One may question whether or not the Bushmen are typical hunters and gatherers. Certainly, the availability of food plants drops off in higher latitudes until, in the arctic itself, there are virtually no vegetable food sources. Here the dependence on hunting, which is the least reliable means of getting food among the !Kung, is complete. That is to say, if the Bushmen are doing rather well, we might expect the Eskimos to have a more precarious adjustment to their environment. Lee advises, however, that we should not exaggerate the admittedly difficult position of the northern hunters, "since most of the Eskimos in historic times have lived south of the Arctic Circle ... and many of the Eskimos at all latitudes have depended primarily on fishing, which is a much more reliable source of food than is the hunting of land and sea mammals" (R.B. Lee, 1968: 41). Nevertheless, Balikci (1968) has reconstructed the subsistence status of the Netsilik Eskimo for the 1920s and 1930s, and the picture that emerges indicates that by no means can one take for granted the truth of the proposition that hunters represent "the original affluent society." Despite a great deal of ingenuity and flexibility in subsistence-related activities, and despite adaptive demographic controls such as the killing of unproductive old persons, female infants, and invalids, the Netsilik did not have much leisure time, and during 1921 and 1922, about 10 percent of the population died from starvation.

Studies of nutritional input and effort output are becoming more popular as alternatives to the more usual descriptive study couched in generalities. Investigations aimed at one or another end of the input-output equation, sometimes considering both ends, include Haswell (1953) on a village in Gambia; McCarthy and McArthur on the work load of aborigines in Arnhem Land (1960); Odend'hal on Indian cattle as an energy system (1972); Rappaport's (1968; 1971) well-known study of the ecological structure of the Tsembaga, a population of shifting agriculturalists in New Guinea; and Clarke's (1971) study of a New Guinea highlands community. Harris's original comparison of some of these energy systems is refreshing and unusual in an introductory text (Harris, 1971: 202 – 18). Pelto and Pelto's text also gives extensive consideration to diet (Pelto and Pelto, 1976; also see Poggie et al., 1976). Heider has cautioned that quantitative studies of nutritional input and effort output involve field techniques that are sometimes difficult to execute. In the case of his own fieldwork among the Dani of New Guinea, Heider found that "planting and weeding are done by women in time segments ranging from ten minutes to an hour or two, and often when the women are casually stopping off at one garden on their way elsewhere. Harvesting takes place equally casually...I could conceive of obtaining accurate data only by spending an immense amount of time personally watching individual gardens" (Heider, 1972: 222). Heider is uncertain of the degree of confidence that can be given quantitative studies of energy systems.

*Cuisines.* Most nutritional studies have dealt with diet – the actual chemical makeup of food, including fats, proteins, carbohydrates, vitamins, and minerals. Considerably less attention has been given to cuisines, which are the customary ways of preparing and presenting food.

Of course the actual extraction of food materials from the environment is primary in the sense that one must have food before one can eat it, whereas the method of its preparation may seem to be secondary, something that can be perfunctorily performed or indeed dispensed with entirely.

There are a number of instances, however, when the preparation of food is as important as acquiring it. With surprising frequency, anthropologists have found staple foods that in their raw state are completely inedible or even poisonous. Manioc, a sweet tuber grown mostly in the tropical rain forests of Central and South America, is an extremely important crop in some societies. We ultimately get our tapioca from it. In its unprocessed form, however, the root contains dangerous quantities of prussic acid. Before the root can be used, it is generally soaked in water to free some of the poison, then grated and heated to liberate the rest.

The staple food of most of the California Indians was acorns, which littered the ground under the oak trees that abounded in this Mediterranean climate. Before they could be eaten, the acorns needed to be ground, then leached in water for several days to free them of the tannic acid they contained. In some parts of Polynesia and Southeast Asia, taro root is one of the staple foods (taro is the decorative plant we call elephant ears). In its raw form, taro contains enough oxalic acid to render it inedible.

I once interviewed the director of the Hospital of American Samoa in the village of Utulei concerning the frequency and methods of suicides in the Samoan population. He explained that the traditional method for killing oneself was to gather a seaweed called matamala from the coral reefs, eat it, and die of cyanide poisoning. A few weeks later, during Sunday dinner with my Samoan host, I inquired after the identity of what appeared to be a particularly tasty boiled green, flavored with coconut cream. My host replied that this was a kind of seaweed they called matamala. Noticing my response, he hastily assured me that matamala was not only edible but was considered a fine food after it had been properly prepared. (I have often wondered about the first person to discover this.)

Most Americans are familiar with a somewhat diluted version of the classic cuisine of Western Europe: appetizer, soup, salad, entree, and dessert. Certain conventions may be reversed regionally; melon, usually a dessert here, is more often an appetizer in Europe; the customary Basque meal has two main courses, and the salad immediately precedes the dessert. Americans are also likely to have had some exposure to Eastern cuisines, in which much of the food is chopped into bite-sized pieces before it is cooked and served, since table utensils consist of chopsticks alone. We may also have noticed that in a multicourse East Asian meal, the delicacies tend to come at the beginning, just after the appetizers, the rationale being that no eater wants to fill up on soup and rice when he knows some special dishes will follow.

Some of the traditions associated with the commercial preparation of foods are likely to be dropped in household cooking, which tends to be more opportunistic and pragmatic. Hunters and gatherers generally eat whatever food they define as edible whenever they get it. Many traditional agrarian societies use meat more for flavoring than for anything like a main course, except on festive occasions, and one gets the impression that, whatever ancillary comestibles are used, ordinary meals consist of some bland, starchy substance—spaghetti, rice, taro, maize, noodles, potatoes—flavored with some more or less spicy sauce. With industrialization, the changing nature of cuisines has had both fortunate and unfortunate consequences. The tendency for cuisines to become more elaborate and to be subject to more demanding critical standards is of interest primarily to those who can afford to worry about meeting such standards at home or about the ability of commercial establishments to satisfy them. Many people in the postindustrial world probably have suffered to some extent from a deterioration of the nutritional quality of their diet. The dental damage caused by prepared soft drinks and other sugar-laden substances would be enough to give one pause.

Historically and geographically, cuisines share some general tendencies. The cooking process serves several purposes. Aside from rendering certain poisonous foods edible, cooking softens certain tough or fibrous foods and retards spoilage, a particularly important consideration in the absence of refrigerators or ice, especially during the summer, or all year round in the tropics. The need to think about putrefaction may in fact be intimately linked to the strength of bonding in preindustrial societies. While it is possible for a nuclear family under such conditions to kill and eat a chicken before it spoils, it is impossible for them to do so with, say, a cow. Cooking slows down the process of putrefaction but it does not by itself stop it. The meat from a large animal is generally distributed along certain predetermined paths, sometimes with the majority of the meat going to families other than the immediate owner's. The system works because one's kinsmen or neighbors are in turn bound to give one certain portions of whatever large animals they kill. In effect, it is as if kinsmen and neighbors acted as deep freezes for one another.

It should be recognized, though, that tolerance for spoilage varies greatly from one society to another. A taste for fermented foods is, in fact, fairly common. The Chinese make considerable use of a fermented bean sauce; and in our own society we use beer, wine, and vinegar regularly. This taste sometimes extends to dairy products as well as vegetable ones, including sour cream and Gorgonzola.

In addition to this tolerance, there are several means of preserving foods besides canning and freezing, such as smoking, pickling, drying, and salting. The use of herbs, which are made from the leaves or stalks of plants (e.g., parsley, bay leaf), and especially spices, which are made from fruits (e.g., pepper), bark (e.g., cinnamon), seeds (mustard), or roots (e.g., horseradish), not only slows down decomposition but helps to disguise any disagreeable taste resulting from whatever spoilage has occurred. They have also served as medicines, aphrodisiacs, and aromatics (in which form they have often accompanied or provided the focal points for ritual, as they continue to do in the Catholic mass). We, who tend to take herbs, spices, and other seasonings for granted, might find it difficult to appreciate the importance of such condiments to the Europeans of five hundred years ago. The search for these substances was one of the principal inspirations behind what is now known as the Age of Exploration. Wars have followed competition over access to spices.

Little work of theoretical import has been done with cuisines, although the need has been noted (Freedman, 1968). However, Levi-Strauss has suggested that "like language, it seems to me, the cuisine of a society may be analyzed into constituent elements, which in this case we might call 'gustemes,' and which may be organized according to certain structures of opposition and correlation" (Levi-Strauss, 1967: 85).

He tries programmatically to distinguish English from French cuisines by comparing them in terms of three oppositions. The first, endogenous/exogenous, has to do with whether the traditional main dishes of a meal are prepared from ingredients likely to be at hand or from exotic, imported materials. Central/peripheral contrasts the staple food with its accompaniments. And the marked/not marked opposition refers to the savory or bland quality of the food. As he describes it:

> In English cuisine the main dishes of a meal are made from endogenous ingredients, prepared in a relatively bland fashion, and surrounded with more exotic accompaniments, in which all the differential values are strongly marked (for example, tea, fruitcake, orange marmalade, port wine). Conversely, in French cuisine the opposition endogenous/exogenous becomes very weak or disappears, and equally marked gustemes are combined together in a central as well as a peripheral position. [Levi-Strauss, 1967: 85]

He claims that other oppositions may be introduced in the analysis of other cuisines, such as sweet/sour, which are not mutually exclusive in Chinese or German cooking. Still other oppositions must be taken into account in order to understand, for instance "the opposition between roast and stew, which plays such an important role in the native cooking of the interior of Brazil (roasting being the sensual way, and boiling the nutritive way — and they are mutually exclusive — of preparing meats" [Levi-Strauss, 1967: 86]).

I admit to a certain degree of difficulty in following some parts of Levi-Strauss's argument here.[2] However, he has elsewhere presented a more

---

2. I tremble, realizing that I am making the admission in so many words that I don't understand the man who is probably the most influential anthropologist alive today. Part of this difficulty is doubtless due to some deficiency of my own. Some other part may be due to Levi-Strauss's sometimes wanton way with language, expressed in shifting semantics, anfractuous reasoning, paradox, and general stylistic pyrotechnics. I would not, for example, know how to recognize a sensual way of preparing meats if I saw one, nor have I ever regarded boiling as an especially nutritive way of preparing meats. As for his expository style, at its best it is a delight and a challenge to follow, but there is another extreme as well. In any case, he has given us such classics as the following: "I therefore claim to show, not how men think in myths, but how myths operate in men's minds without their being aware of the fact" (Levi-Strauss 1969: 12). "As the myths themselves are based on secondary codes (the primary codes being those that provide the substance of language), the present work is put forward as a tentative draft of a tertiary code, which is intended to ensure the reciprocal translatability of several myths. This is why it would not be wrong to consider this book itself as a myth: it is, as it were, the myth of mythology" (Levi-Strauss 1969: 12). "It is in the last resort immaterial whether in this book the thought processes of the South American Indians take shape through the medium of my thought, or whether mine take place through the medium of theirs" (Levi-Strauss 1969: 13). "The intention of the composer, ambiguous while still in score...becomes actual, like that of myth, through and by the listener. In both instances, the same reversal of the relation between transmitter and

elaborate discussion of the opposition between boiling and roasting in connection with his remarks on cannibalism, and we will turn to this shortly.

*Cannibalism.* The eating of human flesh by human beings would seem
to belong to a set of acts so "unnatural" that it must surely inspire universal
repugnance — one of those topics, like incest, personal dissolution, and the
dentist, that we shy away from thinking about. But on the contrary, tales
of cannibalism have had an enduring popularity over the millennia. Sometimes these tales have a moral in tow; sometimes they are related simply for
the intrinsic interest of the narrative.

Among the Salteaux and their neighbors, the Windigo monster was a
cannibal, and in Homer's Odyssey, Odysseus feeds the cannibal giant wine
after his awful repast, until "drunk, hiccuping, he dribbled streams of li-
quor and bits of men" (Homer, 1963: 156). Adult fare, true, but what
about Hansel and Gretel? Legend aside, the story of the Donner party
seems of perennial interest, and several best-selling books have described
the ordeal of the survivors of an airplane crash in the Andes, treating the
cannibalistic details without discretion, not to say with relish.

Historically, Europeans seemed fascinated with the tales of early explorers who encountered cannibals on some of the islands of Polynesia and
Melanesia and among Caribbean peoples such as the Callinago, from
whom, ultimately, we may derive our word for the person who performs
such an act.

Until recently, it might be said, the chief question asked by anthropologists concerning cannibalism as nourishment was not "Why?", but
rather "Why not?" Why don't people of all societies take advantage of
what is presumed to be a rich source of protein? Certainly there were
enough societies, dependent on one or two cereal staples, in which malnutrition was a constant problem and such a dietary supplement would be
useful. Garn and Block attempted to calculate the nutritional value of
human flesh: "A 50 kg man might yield 30 kg edible muscle mass if well
and skillfully butchered, and 30 kg edible muscle would yield about 4.5 kg
(4500 gm) protein, or 4.0 kg protein assuming 90 percent digestibility"

---

receiver can be observed, since in the last resort the latter discovers its own meaning
through the message from the former: music has its being in me, and I listen to myself
through it" (Levi-Strauss 1969: 17). "Castes decree women to be naturally heterogeneous;
totemic groups decree them to be culturally heterogeneous. And the final reason for this
difference between the two systems is that castes exploit cultural heterogeneity in earnest
while totemic groups only create the illusion of exploiting cultural heterogeneity" (Levi-
Strauss 1966b: 124). "Simplifying a great deal, it may be said that castes picture themselves
as natural species while totemic groups picture natural species as castes. And this must be
refined: castes naturalize a true culture falsely, totemic groups culturalize a false nature
truly" (Levi-Strauss 1966b: 127).

(Garn and Block, 1970: 106). This amount, they estimate, would feed sixty adults, but the portions would be skimpy. On a ration of one man per week, this amount would be reduced to nine kg per day, which would be worthwhile only as a supplement to a diet that was particularly protein-deprived. They conclude: "while human flesh may serve as an emergency source of both protein and calories, it is doubtful that regular people-eating ever had much nutritional meaning" (Garn and Block, 1970: 106).

Randall (1971) objected that it is possible that human flesh is not comparable to the flesh of other animals in nutritional terms; we need comparative data on the issue. Walens and Wagner (1971) argued that the Garn-Block hypothesis was oversimple. First, there was no reason why people should eat only the muscles of other people; there were numerous instances of other tissues being regularly consumed, including the liver, brain, and genitalia. Next, Garn and Block had set up a hypothetical population relying entirely on human flesh for its protein. No such population had ever existed. However, there were many people of the world now suffering from kwashiorkor and other diet-linked diseases who could profit from the addition of a handful of meat per day to their diet. Walens and Wagner also pointed out that the usefulness of cannibalism as nourishment had to be measured against its "cost," which was a social question. In many areas of the world a balance is maintained between a high birth rate and a high rate of mortality. "Such circumstances yield a regular supply of human corpses as a natural by-product of the life cycle" (Walens and Wagner, 1971: 270). It is no more costly for the undernourished to consume this flesh than to let it decompose.

Dornstreich and Morren (1974) have proposed a model cannibalistic population that more closely approximates the empirical situation. They discuss cannibalism among the Miyanmin, a New Guinea people, who describe human flesh as a most savory food, comparing it to pork, and who eat it not out of nutritional deprivation but simply because it tastes good, and who did so until 1956. Instead of Garn and Block's sixty adults weighing sixty kilograms apiece, they generate a population that has the same biomass but is more realistically distributed in terms of age and sex, and that is similar in size to many cannibalistic New Guinea populations. One victim, assuming a 60 percent dressing-out proportion, yields about 6,156 grams of protein. Considering the amount of protein available to various New Guinea populations from alternative sources, Dornstreich and Morren find that the most prominent alternative source, the wild or domestic pig, contributes between 1 and 7 percent of the human requirement for protein. "A local New Guinea group of 100 people (46 of whom are adults) which obtains and eats some five to ten adult victims per year would get as much meat from eating people as it does from eating pork.

Far from being supplementary or nutritionally insignificant, this amount of protein would provide as great a contribution to dietary protein as any other single source of animal food" (Dornstreich and Morren, 1974: 9). This additional meat would solve the protein problem of a population whose diet would otherwise be marginal. Judging from these data, it seems reasonable to conclude that when Garn and Block suggested that "Less than one man per week for a group of 60 would not appear to be nutritionally worthwhile, even as a protein supplement" (Garn and Block, 1970: 106), they were incorrect. Cannibalism as nutrition can "pay off" in certain protein-insufficient populations.

Turning from the biological value of cannibalism to a consideration of its social meaning, we find that Levi-Strauss (1965, translated into English in 1966a) has suggested an analogy between certain properties of speech and various methods of preparing food. Let me try to summarize his rather complicated argument in a simpler form. Like language, cooking is universal since there is no known society that does not process at least some of its food in a culturally patterned manner. Next, we find in the study of speech sounds that there exist both a "vowel triangle" and a "consonant triangle" in which acute and grave sounds are contrasted with compact and diffuse sounds, and these latter are contrasted with each other. Levi-Strauss proposes that similar triangles of contrast may be found in other areas, including cooking. The basis for the contrast in cooking is that between "elaborated" food and "unelaborated" food; also in contrast, and more important, are foods that represent "nature," like roasted foods, or "culture," like boiled foods. Roasting represents nature inasmuch as food is exposed directly to flame; boiling represents culture since the contact between the food and the fire is doubly mediated, first by water, then by the pot. Levi-Strauss then suggests that cooking methods articulate with social structure in that roasted food, representing nature, is served to guests and visitors—relative strangers—while boiled food, representing culture, is associated with intimate and solidary groups, such as the family. Applying this reasoning to cannibalism, he draws a distinction between "endocannibalism," meaning the consuming of kinsmen, and "exocannibalism," the eating of strangers or enemies. Endocannibalism, in which the body is served to small, domestic groups, should be characterized by the boiling of the corpse, whereas exocannibalism, associated with feasts and a general loosening of small-group ties, should be characterized by the roasting of the corpse. However, since cannibalism is an endocuisine from the perspective of human beings as a whole, boiling should be the most frequently used method of preparing the body, whether the corpse is an enemy or a friend. In other words, if one were to examine the distribution of different forms of cannibalism in a sample of societies, one should find boiling the most common method; and where roasting was used, it should be used for enemies rather than friends. In a rare mood, Levi-Strauss observes that these ideas might profit from statistical scrutiny.

Shankman (1969) has put the idea to cross-cultural test. Dealing with frequently difficult data, Shankman defined cannibalism as the regular institutionalized consumption of human flesh, ruling out emergency procedures and private pathology. Beginning with a survey of about 360 societies in which cannibalism had been reported, he eliminated all but 60 of the most reliable, in this case a relative term, considering the arguable nature of much of the evidence. Two criteria besides reliability were involved in choosing the final 60 societies. First, the identity of the victim had to be specified: relative, enemy, or both. Second, the method of preparing the body had to be specified, the definitions of these methods following Levi-Strauss wherever possible. The modes of cooking were: boiling, roasting, baking, smoking, raw, and other (the last being an unordered set to include decomposition, drying, powdering, preserving, cooking in bamboo tubes, and the bone ash method). An examination of the modes of cooking used in societies practicing only exocannibalism, only endocannibalism, and in societies that practice both exocannibalism and endocannibalism indicates, first, that the emphasis on roasting versus boiling may be misplaced, in that corpses seem to be prepared by a great variety of methods, with roasting and/or boiling occurring in little more than half the societies examined. Second, many societies prepare the same class of victim in different ways, further confusing the picture. And within societies, different subcommunities may prepare the same class of body differently. Finally, there is evidently a slight geographical bias, with baking occurring more often in the Pacific, boiling in Africa, and roasting in Central and South America, where "other" categories are also more commonly encountered.

As Shankman summarized the results of the study, "the data do not support either of Levi-Strauss's predictions. The first prediction—that boiling would be the most frequent mode of cooking people—was not confirmed since only 17 of the 60 societies boiled anybody and only 6 of these boiled exclusively" (Shankman, 1969: 63). Shankman admitted that a technological bias was involved here, since cannibalism was sometimes practiced in areas where boiling was unknown. He pointed out however, that this simply indicated that the connection between cooking and social structure was not necessarily determined by the properties of mind; i.e., there were ecological contingencies to be taken into account. The second prediction— that roasting would be associated with exocannibalism—also was not supported. "There does not seem to be any significant difference in frequency except when societies that *exclusively* roast (or exclusively roast and boil) are examined" (Shankman, 1969: 63). The results are opposite in direction to that predicted by the hypothesis.

Levi-Strauss would no doubt have counterarguments. One of them is built into the original presentation of the hypothesis; namely that "the cooking of a society is a language in which it unconsciously translates its structure—or else resigns itself, still unconsciously, to revealing its contradictions" (1966a: 595; quoted in Shankman, 1969: 64). In other words, if the results of the study do not support Levi-Strauss's contentions, it may be because the societies in the sample, or some unknown portion of them, are "contradicting themselves" unconsciously. This is what Marvin Harris has referred to as "showing the bottle instead of the genie" (Harris 1968: 497-8). Despite this built-in defense:

> In his article on the culinary triangle, Levi-Strauss makes predictions and asks that they be tested. It seems that, in this case, he intends to have his predictions verified, but Levi-Strauss's intentions should not be confused with the validity of his predictions. This is because an understanding of Levi-Strauss's intentions does not necessarily contribute to our understanding of cannibalism, although it may contribute to our understanding of Levi-Strauss. [Shankman 1969: 65]

Shankman says that his findings do not prove that there is no relationship between cooking and social structure, only that the particular relationships proposed in the culinary triangle have not been demonstrated. We need to be cautious in our search for such relationships.

For example, even if there were a demonstrable relationship between roasting and the feeding of guests and visitors, on the one hand, and boiling and the feeding of the small domestic group on the other, some possible interpretations have nothing to do with linguistics. For one thing, guests and visitors mean a relatively large group, one which might efficiently be fed by means of the killing of a large animal, like a cow. Large animals, in turn, are most dramatically displayed when they are roasted on a spit over an open fire. In a sense, a double function is served: effort is saved by butchering a large animal, rather than numerous small ones; and the importance of the occasion is marked by the public display of the whole carcass. For everyday domestic purposes, small animals prepared without display will serve. The difference might best be pictured in terms of the contrast between a roast side of beef at a Texas barbecue and the humble meal of boiled chicken at home.

*Geophagy.* The Yurok Indians of California live in the rainy forests along that state's northern coast, near the mouths of the Trinity and Klamath rivers. They are best known in ethnographic circles for their version of the Protestant Ethic, an overriding desire not so much for material goods and certainly not for sensible pleasures but for possession of *tsik*, the razor clam shells that serve as a kind of combination currency and talisman. They go about thinking of *tsik*. But another of their more distinguishing characteristics is their taste for a dish prepared in the following fashion.

> A pit in the earth, several feet deep, lined with stones
> Seagull carcasses
> Seal oil
> Boards and earth
> After lining the pit with stones, fill it with seagull carcasses. Add enough seal oil to cover the carcasses. Cover the pit with boards and earth. Let the preparation sit for several months until the seal oil ferments and the carcasses partly decompose. Serve at room temperature.

Aside from the question of taste, one feels that a man who partakes of such a meal must at least owe his wife or roommates an explanation. But even this appetite for decomposed seagull is comprehensible when considered next to the periodic eating of dirt that occurs here and there around the globe. Geophagy is rather common in some parts of West Africa, including Ghana and Togo. The Ewe (pronounced Eh-veh), who live in southeastern Ghana regularly mine at least 200 tons of edible shale annually from a single site, and much of this is commercially marketed in the form of dry discs. In a recent report by Donald Vermeer (1971), 13.9 percent of adult males among the Ewe admitted to the regular consumption of clay, and 46.4 percent of the females did so. These figures are conservative since both sexes were somewhat reluctant to admit eating clay, particularly the males, who frequently claimed ignorance of the trait or attributed it solely to females. Nevertheless, Vermeer estimates that of those adults who admitted to the regular consumption of clay, males ate approximately 13 grams per day and women about 30 grams, with a range from 1 gram to about 300 grams per day. Although males may purchase small amounts of the clay for their own use or act as middlemen in commercial transactions, it is primarily women who show interest in the discs in the public markets.

> They openly purchase clays in the market, and equally openly consume them. Before buying a number of pieces of [clay] at the market, a woman carefully evaluates the product; where a number of baskets of [clay] are available for sale, she will survey the lot, considering the size, price, shape and color. After selecting one basket of clays from the lot, she commonly takes a sample, bites off a piece of the [clay], and mouths it to evaluate flavor and texture; at the same time she will smell the remaining portion and closely scrutinize it for impurities and texture. Only after being satisfied about the quality of the product will she purchase a number of pieces; if she is not

satisfied with the lot originally chosen, she will sample another in similar fashion. [Vermeer, 1971: 67]

The consumption of these clays is directly associated with pregnancy, particularly the early months, and this is openly acknowledged by both men and women. It might be thought that this is one of those instances in which an apparently useless, perhaps even dangerous, custom has some underlying function, such as providing nutrients that are especially important in pregnancy and that might otherwise be unavailable in the diet, but an analysis of the shales from which the clay is derived revealed no obvious connection between the mineral content of the clay and dietary deficiencies. Nor is the consumption of clay related in any manifest fashion to the establishment or retardation of diseases caused by intestinal worms. *De gustibus non est disputandum.* Those Ewe who partake of clay praise the sensory delights of the discs, particularly their aroma on wet and rainy days.

The habit of living off the land is not confined to West Africa. Laufer (1933) has reviewed the literature and the eating of dirt, in one form or another, seems to be fairly widespread. It occurred among the ancient Greeks and Romans, appeared at an early date in China, in Spain, Bolivia, and Brazil, and in India, where statuettes of edible clay were commercially marketed, something like gingerbread men. In the United States, the practice has occurred most commonly among black women in the rural South, where it is known medically as pica—a term derived from the Latin word for magpie, whose eating habits were held to be nondiscriminatory—or, popularly, as dirt eating.

Cross-culturally, the link between geophagy and pregnancy is strong. John Gillin (1944) has suggested a psychological explanation for the practice. Gianna Hochstein (1968) observes that geophagy is likely to be multidetermined: it may be one way in which a pregnant woman can call attention to her discomfort; it may be a means of symbolizing female solidarity; it may help suppress the pain and nausea caused by uterine cramping during pregnancy; it may supply the body with minerals otherwise lacking in the diet, although what evidence there is suggests that it may do more harm than good; it may maintain intestinal acid balance which promotes the growth of disease-counteracting microorganisms; it may assuage the excess secretion of saliva sometimes associated with pregnancy.

In other words, no one really knows why the practice occurs; it seems to be just another unassimilable fragment in the human jigsaw puzzle. In these circumstances one is tempted to fall back on relatively simple explanations, such as response generalization: perhaps a particular kind of dirt tastes like something else in the diet that *is* nutritious, but again, it is difficult to imagine what in the diet of rural southern black women (or anybody else for that matter) tastes anything like nonorganic clay. The problem clearly needs more research, especially since the consequences appear as likely to be deleterious as otherwise.

*The Dynamics of Food-getting Techniques.* All attempts to extract nourishment from the natural environment are dynamic in the sense that they involve effort and consequent changes in the environment. They are also dynamic in the sense that they are subject to change over time. This section will describe three examples of nourishment-getting techniques. One situation is passive in that it results in no change; it involves the means by which people have adapted to a given distribution of wells. A second example involves another relatively stable set of techniques, but a much more lively one in which camels, a principal source of food and milk in the Near East, are exchanged and redistributed through institutionalized raids. Finally, the third example suggests the profound and often unexpected ramifications of technological attempts to increase efficiency in food getting.

Joan Mencher's article, "Kerala and Madras: A Comparative Study of Ecology and Social Structure" (1966), represents an attempt to apply methods of ecological analysis to complex societies. She compares two neighboring sections of southern India, Kerala and Madras. The two are similar in many respects, showing the same technology, similar patterns of food preferences (the dominant crop is rice), similar linguistic and religious histories, and the same sort of highly developed caste system.

Disclaiming any argument for ecological determinism, Mencher states that "in this paper I hope to indicate the refractive effect of ecology in the two areas on the caste system, on the development of concepts of ritual purity, on the patterning of authority relations, and on the development of machinery to deal with large-scale irrigation practices" (Mencher, 1966: 136).

Kerala is hilly, and settlements tend to be dispersed throughout the area because water is abundant and no cooperative effort is needed for cultivation. Kerala villages have no central districts or downtown areas. Houses are separated from one another, and even temples, tea shops, and courts are scattered. Such a dispersed settlement pattern has prevailed for centuries, mostly due to the easy availability of water in Kerala. "The relatively high water table, coupled with the greater ease in boring through lateritic soils for wells, is another factor making dispersed settlements feasible. Digging a well in Kerala which can provide potable water is not the problem that it is in other parts of India" (Mencher, 1966: 141).

Because water is readily available, the household compound, rather than the village, is the unit of settlement. Inhabitants are identified according to the households to which they belong. The land itself is always owned by individuals or by families, and there is little communally owned area. Even paths are owned by the person holding the land on which the paths are located. No irrigation works are necessary, and no roads needed. Until the eighteenth century, no revenue was collected; so there was no need for a tax collector, village accountant, or any other of the usual village officials.

The picture in Kerala today is one of loosely organized and dispersed villages, with households largely self-sufficient and with little village solidarity. Households are spacious, and they have their own facilities such as bathing pools, shrines, cropland, water tanks, and even burial grounds.

In contrast, Madras, to the east, is characterized by nucleated villages distributed across a flat plain. Residents are drawn together by the need to cooperate in clearing farmland and to locate near places where water will be available year round. Furthermore, cooperative effort is needed in building the irrigation works required for rice cultivation. Traditional villages in Madras have various kinds of land set apart as communally owned property, including paths, roads, threshing grounds, burial grounds, and corrals, in addition to residential land. A number of officials are present in most villages, including accountants and craftsmen such as blacksmiths and barbers. Councils of elders play important roles in the common affairs of the villagers, and there is a strong sense of identification with the community itself, sometimes even overriding differences between castes.

The concept of ritual pollution through contact with members of lower castes is especially pronounced in southern India. In Madras, castes form geographic subcommunities; members of low castes are not permitted to use streets that are located in high-caste neighborhoods. Low-caste members may not use the village wells or the bathing pools used by the high castes. However, the layout of the community makes it difficult to strictly enforce these rules of caste behavior.

In contrast, the dispersed compounds in Kerala permit the rules of ritual pollution to become even more elaborate. Since most household compounds have their own wells and bathing pools, there is no need to share such facilities with members of other castes. The presence of water in each compound makes it easier to remove pollution as well as to avoid it in the first place. Mencher suggests that "a particular principle of social organization or culture, here that of ritual purity, tends to achieve maximal expression if there is no ecological barrier to its doing so." The relative scarcity of water in Madras is such a barrier; no such barrier exists in Kerala.

Another ecologically linked difference between the two areas has to do with patterns of authority. In Kerala, authority resides in individuals or families. Some particular authority figures, landlords, usually control other individuals or families, such as tenants or workers, in a structure resembling that of feudal Europe. In Madras, on the other hand, authority is largely in the hands of caste groups rather than individuals or family landowners, and it is mediated by village officials or village groups like the council of elders. In fact the power of particular castes covers a number of communities. "The Kerala village roughly resembles a pyramid with the large landlord family at the apex... whereas the Madras village situation can be likened to a ranked series of rectangles, each representing a different caste group" (Mencher, 1966: 158).

Mencher also draws connections among dispersed settlement patterns, matrilineal castes, and subcaste differentiation. Inhabitants of Kerala are freer to manipulate their caste status than the villagers in Madras, members of whose castes live next door to one another and gossip about each other.

Finally, irrigation and roads also seem related to social structure. In Madras, where rainfall and drainage patterns encourage irrigation on a large scale, great centralization and bureaucratization have occurred; while in Kerala, efforts to modify the land have largely been limited to family-owned plots and small-scale works. The decentralized nature of political authority in Kerala is further enhanced by the rugged terrain of the area, which inhibits the construction of roads and thereby impedes the development of communications and political organizations with extensive geographic influence.

The Mencher study is a good example of the usefulness of a comparative design contrasting two groups that are very similar except for one major antecedent condition. In this case, the major difference has to do with the nature of the terrain and especially the availability of water, both conditions being essential ecological considerations.

Some pastoral societies are colorful indeed, and the North Arabian Bedouins are among them, a people usually described as fierce and proud. Societies such as the Rwala Bedouin figured prominently in World War I under the intermittent leadership of T.E. Lawrence. According to Louise E. Sweet (1970), one of the core integrating mechanisms of the nomadic Bedouins is institutionalized camel raiding.

North Arab Bedouins live in the northern third of the Arabian peninsula, in a climate that varies from true desert in the south, with virtually no rain, to semidesert in the north, which receives most of its scant rainfall during the winter months, while the summers remain hot and dry. Vegetation is sparse and consists mainly of scrub, with an occasional oasis. Politically, the societies consist of tribal chiefdoms that only rarely come together for communal movements; most of the time they remain organized at some smaller-size level, sometimes as small as family units, depending on the circumstances. The "noble" Bedouins encountered by Sweet keep relatively elaborate and thorough genealogies; they know to whom they are related, and these relationships are extremely important to them. Occasionally they come into contact with non-Bedouin tribes of shepherds, hunters, or other "ignoble" people who live on the periphery of the Bedouin territory or near oases. Beyond this periphery lies the capital of the nation-state which, until relatively recently, did not have a great deal of impact upon the Bedouin.

Bedouins' lives are centered on the camel. It provides them with food, milk, transportation of both freight and people, and products such as wool and hides. No other domestic animal approaches it in importance to them. All means are therefore likely to be used to maximize the herd strength of any particular chiefdom or camp. Unfortunately, camels are slow to reproduce, and there are other obstacles to increasing the size of the herd. As in many areas where rainfall is low, there are great fluctuations between years of drought and years of adequate grazing, and these vary from place to place. One camp may be losing many of its camels to drought and disease, while a neighboring camp or one that is more distant may be doing fairly well. Now, although camels may be exchanged with non-Bedouins, the only established mechanisms for circulating camels *within* Bedouin society is by means of kinship—for example, as a bridal gift or an inheritance. Camels may not be sold to other Bedouins.

Sweet interprets the organized camel raid as a mechanism for redistributing the animals in a more equitable way. According to custom, these raids are conducted only between chiefdoms or tribes of relatively equal status. The Bedouin do raid the settled populations also, but these raids tend to be more deadly and thorough, and the settled populations do not raid back. Between Bedouins, thievery and raiding have become highly conventionalized activities, bound by etiquette and rules that render these activities somewhat less disastrous than they might be. Raids occur after the formal declaration of hostilities. At a given moment, a specific chiefdom may be on hostile terms with some of its neighbors and in a state of peace with others. The peaceful relationship is a relative one, since there are usually parties of petty thieves active against all neighbors. In a "proper" sequence of events—which is not always followed—the incidence of thievery is stepped up; the victims of the thieves begin to complain; finally, hostilities are declared. Small raiding parties take place, and then larger raids are carried out, culminating in an annual ceremonialized raid led by the chief. Like anything else, raiding takes up time and energy, and eventually a point is reached at which major raids against all possible enemies cannot be conducted and a truce is negotiated in which both sides are careful to preserve their honor.

These raids apparently accomplish much and have certain noneconomic consequences. The prestige that accrues to the successful raider, for example, may net him a chief's daughter for a wife. In addition, reciprocal raiding means an exchange of animals, which offsets local losses to fluctuations in the availability of pasturage or water and also "maintains a circulation of camels and camel husbandry over the maximum physical range for camels and the societies which specialize in their breeding" (Sweet, 1970: 278). Further, the practice contributes to the stability of this rather flexibly organized set of tribes and chiefdoms at a level that most efficiently promotes the breeding of camels in this particular ecological setting. Finally, raiding or the threat of raiding enables the chiefdoms to subjugate lesser communities, from whom they exact tribute. Sweet states that the institution of camel raiding "adds its weight to previous studies which suggest that some predatory activities of human societies may be more fully understood as ecological adaptations supporting particular subsistence patterns at their widest range, and at the maximum advantage for the human societies dependent on them" (Sweet, 1970: 288). We are left with the impression that the institutionalized camel raid is an important activity indeed to the Bedouin of North Arabia.

This study follows the functionalist tradition proposed by A.R. Radcliffe-Brown and others, which involves finding adaptive consequences for certain practices or sets of practices. Sweet has demonstrated that these raids have multiple linkages with other institutions, both ecological and nonecological. But here, as in other functionalist works, one might ask if there are not alternative means of accomplishing the same ends. For example, although camels reproduce slowly, are local losses so severe that camps would be wiped out before the losses could be made up by natural means? The raids are so frequent that it would seem that not all of them are prompted by dire threats to survival. If some corrective mechanism must be activated, could not kinsmen camped elsewhere supply the victims of drought and disease with enough additional animals to partly make up for their losses? The distribution of camels among kinsmen as gifts is mentioned; why isn't it sufficient to accomplish much of what raiding accomplishes? If additional mechanisms for transfer of camels between unrelated chiefdoms are necessary, why do the Bedouins not sell them to each other as they do to non-Bedouins? Perhaps camel raiding has consequences that are essential to the survival of camel-breeding desert nomads, but the overall question remains: What would happen if there were no institutionalized raids? Is there no other way to achieve the same ends? Would Bedouin society lose its integral character, not to mention its camels? Some of these questions are intriguing and are liable to solution by inquiry. It is unfortunate that the system Sweet describes is now undergoing significant changes associated with the introduction of fences, industry, gasoline engines, and the other accoutrements of progress.

One of the more interesting studies on the dependency of human upon beast and beast upon nature is Pelto's *The Snowmobile Revolution* (1973), which focuses on the impact of introduced technology upon that set of relationships.

Until recently, only "traditional" methods of transportation were commonly used in circumpolar regions. These included dogsleds, snowshoes, and toboggans in North America, and in the Old World, reindeer sleds and skis. Automobiles and trucks depend upon roads, which are costly to build and to maintain; airplanes, though an important means of contact with the rest of the world, are too expensive for use by most travelers in the arctic. Until the early 1960s, sleds and skis were the only forms of transportation in everyday use among the Skollt Lapps, a reindeer-herding population who live in the northeastern part of Finnish Lapland near Lake Inari and the community of Sevettijarvi.

Such ecological factors as weather, available grazing land, and the prevalence of insects imposed a rather rigid set of constraints upon Skollt Lapp adaptation, resulting in a seminomadic life-style based upon the needs of the partly domesticated reindeer and the desires of the people who herded them. Reindeer that had been loose in the grazing area during the summer were rounded up in the fall, separated into family-owned smaller groups, and brought to the family dwellings to spend the winter. Calves born in the spring were clearly marked to indicate ownership.

During his first fieldwork in the mid-1950s, Pelto found a relatively stable and well-balanced ecological system. During the fall roundups, men on skis or leading tame geldings or sledding behind them spent a great deal of time slowly gathering the scattered groups of rather wary reindeer, bringing them together in a staging area, then leading them in three successive groups to the corral. These were large groups of animals, and they were in contact with men for several weeks, so that to some extent they became accustomed to the company of human beings. Moreover, large groups of animals tend to stick together, attracting free-wandering animals into their orbits.

A great number of families took part in reindeer herding, and during the winter, after the herd had been divided into smaller family groups, the men of the family spent their time around their winter dwellings tending their animals. There were always tasks to be performed in caring for them.

The introduction of the snowmobile in the early 1960s had effects so pervasive and irreversible as to disrupt the stable set of adaptive techniques the Lapps had developed.

Instead of men on skis and on horseback quietly and matter-of-factly rounding up the herd during the fall, men began to travel on noisy, fast-moving machines. The racket produced by the engines frightened and disconcerted the animals, making them harder to herd into large groups. Further, since machine operations were quicker, men spent less time with the animals, and the reindeer remained suspicious. They had to be rounded up in small, wary groups and driven into the roundup enclosures. The drawing power of these groups diminished with their size: not only did stray reindeer avoid them, but many animals that had already been rounded up managed to escape. One of the results of this confusion was that the animals were brought together in slapdash fashion, and the smaller, family-owned groups were mixed together. There were other, unanticipated side effects. The stress of being rounded up under these circumstances interfered with normal reproductive processes and reduced the number of offspring. Being driven rather than led reduced the weight of the animals and induced lung damage in some. The owners marked their animals, then released them after the fall roundup; since most of the reindeer were from neighboring herds, they dispersed and spring calving could not be observed. Instead, the Skollts drove reindeer into enclosures in mid-summer, noted which calves followed which mothers, and marked the calves accordingly, so that identification of owners was still possible.

There were still other economic and social consequences of the use of snowmobiles. The mean number of family-owned animals and calves dropped rapidly. Not only was fertility reduced, but many families sold their animals to finance snowmobiles. Moreover, in the general confusion of the roundup some calves were separated from their mothers, and these unidentifiable animals were auctioned off.

Under previous conditions, ski men and men with geldings worked for low pay, and the roundups tended to be slow but thorough. Now, however, the snowmobilers conducting the roundup work for wages on a per diem basis; so the work is performed more hastily.

With the increased dependency on snowmobiles has come a greater dependency on cash, since snowmobiles cost money to buy and to maintain. Some of the smaller or less lucky reindeer-owning families have had to sell off so many of their animals that they have, in a sense, left the business altogether. The families that started out owning large herds, on the other hand, not only absorbed the expenses incurred by the use of snowmobiles but were able to buy up animals from the smaller and poorer families, with the result that the wealthy families are becoming even wealthier while the herds of the poorer families continue to decrease. With small herders being driven out of the business, more men have been turning to other kinds of jobs, mostly menial, and this further increases stratification. There is thus an overall increase in social inequality.

Finally, with no winter herds to tend at home, the families still involved in reindeer herding have little to do, so they are technically unemployed. The consequences are unfortunate psychologically as well as financially. Pelto presented clear evidence supporting these generalizations. He discussed briefly the impact of the snowmobile on other arctic populations, including some Eskimo communities, in terms of the ecological structure and the social characteristics of the region. Snowmobiles apparently have a less disturbing effect on societies subsisting mainly on fish and sea mammals, not only because extended travel is necessary but also because such hunting requires movement over rugged chunks of sea ice, something for which the snowmobile is unsuited. Where people make a living by wage work, hunting, or trapping, however, the snowmobile tends to be quickly adopted, along with the concomitant dependence upon cash and supplies of fuel and spare parts from the "outside." Pelto ends with some recommendations for restoring the value and the dignity of reindeer herding as a way of life, although he expects it to be a secondary source of income. Specifically, he makes suggestions concerning the demechanization of herding.

Pelto's thorough study of the disruptive effects of introduced technology is reminiscent of, but more comprehensive than, Lauriston Sharp's earlier and much-reprinted classic, "Steel Axes for Stone Age Australians" (Sharp, 1952).

## Sex and Genital Mutilation

Climate may influence our behavior in unexpected ways. We tend to think of the natural environment as one thing, and attention directed towards our sex organs as quite another, but there are connections between them. The first study to be reviewed demonstrates how climate influences architecture, which in turn affects premarital sex norms. The second demonstrates that conditions in the natural environment affect the incidence of genital mutilation, which provides the focal point for much of aboriginal Australian religious ritual.

Anthropologists have written enough about sexual behavior from a pan-human perspective to indicate a considerable range in the restrictions placed upon premarital coitus, from almost complete freedom at one end of the spectrum to the blanket restriction of premarital sex at the other. Highly restrictive societies often promote a sort of virginity mystique, complete with public tests designed to demonstrate the chastity of a bride.

Some of the people of Polynesia—the Tahitians and the Samoans, for example—are among the best known of the permissive societies. They were probably not as permissive as they are usually pictured in such films as *Mutiny on the Bounty,* which should come as no surprise to anyone familiar with the discrepancy between the way some groups are presented in the mass media and the way those groups really are. In any case, the Muria, a tribal people of India, may be taken as an example of a permissive society, although their sexual permissiveness has a rather coercive character. The Muria were studied by Verrier Elwin, a former Anglican monk, and his book about them describes the village dormitory, the *Ghotul,* which the young people enter when they are six or seven and where they live until they are married, in their early twenties (Elwin, 1947). Systems of trial marriage are not at all uncommon in some of the remoter parts of India, but what is remarkable about the Muria *ghotul* is that here, where adolescents of both sexes slept together, a system of promiscuity was imposed upon the young people. The usual kinds of relationships that adolescents are likely to establish among themselves were prohibited within the *ghotul.* A strict rotation of partners was imposed; no couple was permitted to sleep together for more than three nights in succession. The *ghotul* functioned as the center of the adolescent's world, and all members took the rules seriously lest they be expelled. One way of ensuring maximum cohesion among the members was through the prevention of jealousy and the assurance of some satisfaction to even its least desirable members. Through this system of enforced rotation, the *ghotul* was said to cure people of love, which may have been just as well since the Muria eventually married someone to whom they had been betrothed since childhood.

No extended description of an especially restrictive society is necessary for mature American readers, or for anyone who has had contact with Mediterranean societies, where virginity of young women is so important a concern that it is apparently linked not only to family honor but also to economic resources and the problems of organizing labor. (See Pitt-Rivers's *The People of the Sierra* [1961] for an excellent study of a Mediterranean community, and Jane Schneider's article [1971] for a theoretical discussion of the function of family honor in the Mediterranean value system.)

The question, of course, is why such cross-cultural variation should exist. Undoubtedly there are multiple determinants, but what forces in a restrictive society are strong enough to discourage young people from finding ways to satisfy such an urgent, biologically based propensity as the desire to find a mate? Conversely, what prevents people in permissive societies from being particularly anxious about the sexual behavior of unmarried adolescents?

One possible determinant was suggested in a passage by Erving Goffman, a sociologist at the University of Pennsylvania, when he noted that "restrictions placed upon contact, the maintenance of social distance, provide a way in which awe can be generated and sustained in the audience" (Goffman, 1959: 70). Goffman was saying, in other words, that if you want to keep people mystified, then don't let them know what is going on behind the scenes. The notion not only applies to the performance of magicians but may be an important feature of the regulation of sexual behavior as well. Sex, in many societies, is a more profound mystery than its simple mechanical function would suggest. It seems possible that the kind of awe that surrounds sex in restrictive societies might be partly explained by the provision of a special, private place where coitus takes place between properly married couples, and from which children and others are systematically excluded. What better way to "generate awe" in an audience of children than to let them discover from their peers, gradually and imperfectly, that something is going on in the adult world that they will never be able to witness and about which they will never be permitted to ask?

A few years ago I attempted to test the hypothesis that the presence of private settings for sexual behavior was conducive to, and would be associated with, the development of a more restrictive code of premarital sexual behavior (1967). No method of regulating contact between persons seems so effective as an impenetrable physical barrier, and by far the most common impenetrable barriers found around the world are house walls. The assumption then was that, to the extent that house walls provided residents with visual and acoustical privacy, they provided behind-the-scene settings for behavior of whatever kind, and therefore the exposure of children to the sexual behavior of adults was less likely. Where such private places were absent, sex could not be kept secret from children, and their attitude towards it would therefore be more casual.

Like codes for premarital sex, the characteristics of house walls vary widely from one society to another. Some societies have no walls at all. Indeed, as we have seen, some have no houses. The central tribes of Austrialia, when they construct a shelter at all, merely improvise a lean-to from bunches of grass. Other people build houses of stone, as we see in some of the stone cottages of rural Ireland and Scotland.

A sample of ninety-three societies was drawn from the "Ethnographic Atlas" (Murdock et al., 1963), which is a compilation of cultural data on several hundred societies from all geographic regions. The "Ethnographic Atlas" gives information on both wall material and sexual behavior. The wall materials were coded into three types, depending on what seemed to be the degree of penetrability. *Impenetrable* walls were those made of (1) stone, stucco, concrete, or fired brick; and (2) adobe, clay, or dried brick. *Intermediate* walls were made of (1) hides or skin; (2) felt, cloth, or other fabrics; and (3) bark. *Penetrable* walls were made of (1) mats, latticework, or wattle; (2) grass, leaves, or thatch; or (3) nothing at all. These types of walls then provided us with three dimensions of penetrability.

Similarly, the information in the "Ethnographic Atlas" on norms of premarital sexual behavior for females was reviewed. It was possible to classify them into three types. First, premarital sex was considered *unsanctioned* if coitus was freely permitted and not punished, even if pregnancy resulted. Coitus was *conditionally sanctioned* if (1) it was allowed and not sanctioned unless pregnancy resulted; (2) trial marriage occurred, in which monogamous premarital sex was allowed with the expectation of marriage if pregnancy resulted, promiscuous relations being prohibited and sanctioned. And it was classified as *invariably sanctioned* if there was an insistence on virginity, and premarital sex was prohibited, strongly sanctioned, and rare.

When each society was classified as having one type of material for house walls and one type of norm for premarital sex, it was possible to construct a table and examine the relationship between the penetrability of house walls and the restrictiveness or permissiveness of the code for premarital sex. Table 1 shows that, in fact, the relationship is so strong that this distribution is extremely unlikely to have occurred purely by chance.[3]

It is possible to argue that the causality in this argument is the other way around. That is, people don't have restrictive sex norms because they have impenetrable walls, but rather they build houses with impenetrable

### SEX NORMS

| Wall material | | unsanctioned | Conditionally sanctioned | Invariably sanctioned |
|---|---|---|---|---|
| | Penetrable | 18 | 16 | 6 |
| | Intermediate | 3 | 2 | 4 |
| | Impenetrable | 3 | 15 | 26 |

TABLE 1. PREMARITAL SEX NORMS AND THICKNESS OF HOUSE WALLS.

---

3. $X^2 = 11.1$; $P < .001$

walls because they have restrictive sex norms. To establish the direction of causality, it is necessary to turn from architecture to broader ecological considerations.

First, every society has access to a number of different kinds of materials for use in wall construction. Desert dwellers may ordinarily build no houses at all, as in central Australia; so they would be classified as penetrable; or they may build heavy earth houses with impenetrable walls, as the Navaho do. In the arctic tundra, impenetrable houses of snow or stone are found among the Eskimo, while on the other side of the Bering Strait intermediate tents are the usual dwelling forms. So it is not possible to argue that people use a given material for walls because it is the only material available to them.

What seems the most likely determinant of the variation in wall materials is external temperature. One way to maintain an optimal temperature around the body in cold climates is to build stout walls that keep out the chill and keep in the heat. And in hot climates, the best way to stay comfortable is to build houses with thin or open walls in order to take advantage of whatever breeze exists.

Indeed, an examination of the relationships between wall material and distance from the equator revealed that societies with penetrable walls had a mean latitude of 14.9 degrees, while the mean latitude of those with impenetrable walls was 32.1 degrees. Again, the likelihood of obtaining such a distribution by chance is extremely low.[4] The direction of causality in the argument now seems established. People who live in cold climates tend to build houses with thick walls in order to survive. Those who live in the tropics tend to build houses with thin walls or no walls at all (Maxwell, 1967: 79).

Interestingly enough, many of the cases in which societies were relatively close to the equator but nevertheless had strict premarital sex norms were those located in desert areas, particularly the Middle East and northern Africa. Here are people living in a hot climate who nevertheless are jealous of their women's honor. But again, careful examination reveals that architectural influences are at work in the hypothesized manner. In a climate that is hot and damp, a thick-walled dwelling would be uncomfortably muggy, but in a hot, dry climate, where atmospheric vapor pressure is low, the situation is quite different. As Huntington described it:

> In a desert oasis...the most available building material is dry mud (adobe). Large, sun-dried bricks can easily be piled up to form walls. In the

---

4. $t = 9.1$; $P < .001$.

hot, dry air, the most comfortable place during the heat of the day is inside a thick-walled adobe house with a stout roof of the same material. [Huntington, 1959: 303]

In other words, desert architecture still conforms to the demands of climate, and premarital sex norms conform to the influence of architecture.

There are still other considerations in the ecology of premarital coitus. Not all sexual behavior takes place inside the house. Some societies show a preference for the outdoors, where such settings are pleasant and comfortable, just as in our society outdoor copulation probably occurs more often during the summer than during the winter, and more in the countryside than in the city. However, here too, the kind of dwelling seems to be an important determinant in the location of coitus. The Sirionó are a tribe of seminomadic people of Eastern Bolivia who live more by simple hunting and gathering than by farming. They were studied by Allan R. Holmberg in the early 1940s. They live in large, roughly constructed dwellings, surrounded by tropical forest, and their premarital sex norms are permissive. Holmberg describes the way in which the Sirionó choose a site for intercourse:

> During the day, when there are people around, the couple steals off into the forest. If a man is out in the forest alone with a woman, however, he may take his prize without so much as saying a word. During the night, when the Sirionó do not venture out of their hut and when all sex activity takes place in the hammock, a man with desire simply waits until the house quiets down and then wakes up the woman with whom he wishes to have intercourse. At this time, of course, extramarital relations almost never occur.
>
> Much more intercourse takes place in the bush than in the house. The principal reason for this is that privacy is almost impossible to obtain within the hut, where as many as fifty hammocks may be hung in the confined space of five hundred square feet. Moreover, the hammock of a man and his wife hangs not three feet from that of the former's mother-in-law. Furthermore, young children commonly sleep with the father and mother, so that there may be as many as four or five people crowded together in a single hammock. In addition to these frustrating circumstances, people are up and down most of the night, quieting children, cooking, eating, urinating, and defecating. All in all, therefore, the conditions for sexual behavior in the house are most unfavorable. Consequently intercourse is indulged in more often in some secluded nook in the forest. [Holmberg, 1969: 163]

As a matter of fact, Holmberg's study suggests that there are material reasons other than strictly architectural ones for choosing an outdoor location for coitus.

> When intercourse takes place in the hammock the positions are essentially
> the same [as in the forest], but it is more difficult to maneuver because of the
> added movement of the hammock. Sometimes during the height of the act a
> man's knees slip through the strings of the hammock and his whole emotional
> set is disturbed. Informants frequently made jokes about their fellows in this
> respect. [Holmberg, 1969: 165]

On the basis of these statements, one might venture to guess that there is
a perfect correlation between sleeping arrangements involving hammocks
and a preference for making love outdoors. But as far as such preferences
go, the Sirionó are not an isolated case. In a large-scale cross-cultural study
of sexual behavior, Ford and Beach observe:

> It seems clear that possibility of seclusion generally determines whether
> human intercourse takes place within the dwelling or out of doors.... A par-
> ticularly interesting society in this connection is the Kiwai. Formerly, these
> people lived in long, unpartitioned houses which contained several families.
> In those days intercourse regularly took place in the bush. Today they live in
> small one-family dwellings, and marital intercourse within the house is
> becoming the customary pattern. [Ford and Beach, 1951: 80]

It seems likely that in all societies like the Sirionó, where most sexual
contacts are made outdoors, the likelihood of the couple being stumbled
upon or deliberately spied upon by children is greater than in societies in
which seclusion is provided in the house. The effect of preferences for the
outdoors would therefore be similar to that of penetrable walls. Both
would influence premarital sex norms in such a way as to make it difficult
to maintain a sense of awe in young people.

In 1966, I was engaged in a study of temperament of American Samoans, a relatively permissive people. The majority of the houses in the
village I lived in were traditional in style, having a beehive-shaped roof of
coconut or sugarcane thatch supported by a dozen or so poles around the
perimeter of the wooden platform that served as a floor. All houses were
equipped with woven mats that were kept folded along the edge of the
roof, but these mats were lowered only during inclement weather, never
for privacy. The floors themselves were about as large as a medium-sized
room in a modern American house, and the average number of people living in each house was about ten. Since there were neither internal nor external walls, the floors were rather crowded with sleeping bodies at night,
and there was a distinct lack of settings where coitus could take place
without discovery or interruption.

I had intended to collect as much data as I could on sexual behavior in
Samoa, but this proved extremely difficult, since Samoan men tend either
to be too embarrassed to talk about their sexual experiences or inclined to

fabricate them in accordance with what they think the investigator would like to hear. My impression was that Samoan men are adept at effecting intercourse beneath the sleeping sheets with an absolute minimum of movement, but that nevertheless more intercourse, especially between unmarried couples, takes place in the forest at prearranged times and places, usually coinciding with garden tending. I finally came to trust one young man who was employed in Pago Pago. Since he lived in a crowded house and had no opportunity to arrange rendezvous at a garden patch, I was curious about the location of his sexual encounters and asked him to tell me the settings in which he had intercourse over the last year. The female participants and the settings for each act of coitus are given below. In all cases, the time was after dark.

| Partner | Circumstances |
| --- | --- |
| A | On the beach near the airport. |
| A | On the platform of a pick-up truck on the same beach. |
| A | On a woven mat, on the lawn in front of the general store in a neighboring village. |
| B | On soft grass, near the beach of a distant village. |
| C | In the cab of a truck, parked on the grounds of a government-sponsored demonstration farm in a nearby village. |
| D | In the cab of a truck, parked near a powerhouse in Pago Pago. |
| E | In the back seat of a taxi, parked in a remote swamp. |
| F | Same. |
| G | Same. |
| G | In an empty private suite of the hospital at Pago Pago, on partner's duty night. Partner was a nurse. |
| G | New Year's Eve, inside his mother's otherwise empty house in Pago Pago. |
| H | In the space under the floor of a house in Pago Pago. |
| I | On sand, under palm trees, on a small island about sixty miles from American Samoa. |
| J | Inside partner's apartment in Pago Pago. |

It is impossible to know how representative this young man's experience is, but his list illustrates the variety of sites available in a tropical setting. It is also instructive to note that only three of his last fifteen sexual encounters took place inside buildings.

The ecology of premarital coitus is a too-little investigated aspect of human sexual behavior. Not nearly enough data exist for an accurate assessment of the roles of architectural and social variables in determining sex norms; so any general propositions expressed here must be considered tentative. At the same time, available evidence suggests that variations in climate lead people to build houses with walls of differing thicknesses and that premarital intercourse takes place more frequently among people with thin-walled dwellings than among people with thick-walled dwellings, where couples may find seclusion during intercourse. From a global perspective, premarital sex is more common in societies located near the equator and less common in societies in colder climates. Furthermore, it seems that where dwellings are crowded—whether or not they have external walls—people prefer the outdoors as a setting for sex. There is probably a relationship between these two propositions; where no private space is available within dwellings, people in cold climates are not likely to use the outdoors, whereas no similar inhibitions need exist in tropical settings.

These generalizations remain statistical at this point and may not be applicable in any individual instance. That there is no direct and invariable relationship between climate, housing, and sex norms becomes immediately apparent when one component of the formula changes and the others do not. American adolescents, for example, seem to have undergone something in the nature of a sexual revolution over the last decade without the development of any substantial changes in architectural form. And yet, one may suspect that, while the popularity of picture windows in the 1950s may have been coincidental, such things as the simultaneous burgeoning of drive-in movie theaters and automobile ownership among adolescents might not have been so coincidental. The discussion has been limited to the influence of house form on premarital sex, but it is in fact possible to view a sedan as a small, mobile, two-room house, so that automobiles, too, may have an impact on premarital sex norms. The act of intercourse, like any other human act, is bound to be multidetermined.

Some of the correspondences that exist between the environment and human behavior are fairly obvious, while others are not. Genital mutilation seems to be one of those variables whose link with the environment is not readily apparent but operates nonetheless. The best-known treatment of the topic is probably Whiting's article "Effects of Climate on Certain Cultural Practices," which appeared in a *Festschrift* honoring George P. Murdock (Whiting, 1964). Here Whiting noted that there was "a biased geographical distribution of societies in which boys are circumcised. They occur more commonly in tropical than temperate regions and more commonly in the Old World than in the New World" (Whiting, 1964: 511). In fact, as it turns out, circumcision was virtually restricted to Africa and the

Pacific islands, meaning that it was absent in areas where winters were cold and present in most tropical areas except South America. Whiting's earlier work had shown that male circumcision is associated with exclusive mother-infant sleeping arrangements. The hypothesis — or rather, one of the hypotheses, there being more than one candidate — is that such sleeping arrangements lead the male infant to identify too closely with the "wrong" sex, necessitating some sort of dramatic corrective process such as circumcision. Whiting found that there was a biased distribution of sleeping arrangement; in cold-winter regions, mother and father tended to sleep together and the infant to sleep elsewhere, presumably promoting warmth somehow, while in tropical regions, mother and infant tended to sleep together and the father slept elsewhere. Thus, we gain some greater understanding of one way in which the environment can influence our social behavior. At the same time, climatic considerations do not help us to explain the absence of male genital mutilation in South America, where conditions are, so to speak, ripe for their occurrence.

Whiting investigated the incidence of genital mutilation more indirectly, looking at two other customs he had previously found to be linked with circumcision: patrilocal residence and a long postpartum taboo on intercourse between the mother and father (up to several years in some cases). It was quickly found that a high frequency of polygynous marriage is part of this same complex. Whiting then asked if there were some indirect correspondence between polygyny and the environment.

Taking his lead from indigenous theory, Whiting reasoned that polygyny was functional in societies in which there was also a long postpartum sex taboo. He quotes a Yoruba informant on this point: "When we abstain from having sexual intercourse with our husband for the two years that we nurse our babies, we know that he will seek some other woman. We would rather have her under our control as a co-wife so that he is not spending money outside the family" (Whiting, 1964: 516-17). Thus, a long postpartum taboo makes polygyny functional. And, at the same time, it is reasonable that polygyny should be associated with patrilocal residence, since this is by far the most efficient means of organizing polygynous households. Under matrilocal rules of residence, the groom would need to move to the household of his bride's parents, and how does he do that if he marries five wives? The disruption would be excessive. So Whiting's causal sequence links a long postpartum sex taboo with a high frequency of polygynous marriages, and that, in turn, with patrilocal residence, which we already know to be associated with male initiation rites.

So far, so good. But what, then, explains the long postpartum taboo on intercourse? How can this be linked with the environment? Again,

Whiting takes his lead from certain indigenous theories that claim that, if intercourse were carried on during the period of nursing, and the intercourse resulted in pregnancy, the mother's milk would somehow be "spoiled." Suppose the theory were correct, that mother's milk were somehow adversely affected by a new pregnancy. The most likely condition would be an inadequate amount of protein in the milk. Whiting could find no laboratory evidence of such an effect, but neither could he find evidence that would contradict the hypothesis.

When Whiting examined the distribution of kwashiorkor, a disease affecting children at about the age of weaning, the primary cause of which is likely to be protein deficiency, he found that it only infrequently occurred outside the hot, humid tropics. The proposition then to be tested became: "If a prolonged postpartum sex taboo is a cultural means of reducing the frequency of this disease by both prolonging the nursing period and ensuring that the protein content of the lactating mother's milk is not reduced below the danger point, then this taboo should also occur in societies situated in the humid tropics with a food supply low in protein" (Whiting, 1964: 519).

Whiting divided a number of societies into three classes with respect to the protein value of their staple food, and found that low-protein societies are most likely to be located in the rainy tropics, while only a few high-protein societies were found in tropical rain forests, and medium-protein societies were split between tropical rain forests and other climates.

Thus, links have been established between tropical rain forests, low-protein diets, the nursing mother's need to avoid new pregnancies, long postpartum sex taboos, and polygyny and patrilocal residence, which have previously been shown to be associated with circumcision.

Whiting concludes, however, with no demonstrated explanation of the absence of circumcision in South America. He suggests that in fact the causal chain may be broken in that area because postpartum sex taboos are relatively short, there being other cultural means of avoiding pregnancy during the mother's nursing period, such as abortion.

Here, and in his other work as well, Whiting has tended to deal with elaborate causal sequences, which Harris has termed "Rube Goldberg explanations" (Harris, 1968: 452). Harris goes on to suggest that it is less efficient to begin an examination of such a variety of research problems with an inquiry into things like sleeping arrangements, which later turn out to be "a mere appendage to the central causal chain" (Harris, 1968: 461). The important question is not sleeping arrangements but kwashiorkor and other life-threatening conditions. While it is true that Whiting and investigators like him eventually find themselves led to ecological considerations, they "seem to be slowly backing into a position which they might profitably have occupied face-forward from the outset" (Harris, 1968:

461). Harris's judgment may be a bit strong. Whiting's cross-cultural research stands as a model of its kind. Besides, such animadversions seem unwarranted. Why criticize him for not trying to explain something, *per se,* which he did not want to explain? While one may lament another investigator's choice of research problem, the disappointment cannot really be taken as criticism.

Whiting's is not the only study linking genital mutilations with certain characteristics of the environment. Birdsell (1953) studied population density among the aboriginal populations of Australia and found that, the lower the rainfall, and consequently the poorer the food supply, the greater the amount of territory covered by each tribe. Further, he discovered a striking relationship between rainfall and genital mutilations. Along part of the eastern Australian coast, rainfall decreases with increasing distance from the shore. In areas where rain was relatively abundant, no genital mutilations were practiced. Moving inland, however, Birdsell found that circumcision began at about the eight-to-ten-inch rainfall boundary. Farther inland, along the five-inch rainfall line, both circumcision and subincision, a particularly severe form of genital mutilation, were practiced. Although these operations do not affect fertility, they nevertheless seem to function as population control devices in that they eliminate, through infection, some of the more delicate or feeble children. As rainfall decreases, environmental conditions become harsher and fewer people can be supported by their surroundings. Severe genital mutilation is one effective way of limiting the number of people. Mutilation is, moreover, an adaptive device, proving more or less effective over time; in years when food is particularly scarce, it seems likely that pregnancies, impaired by environmentally imposed stresses, produce a greater than average proportion of feeble infants, more of whom will be eliminated through infections. Conversely, when food is relatively abundant, offspring are likely to be healthier and less subject to infection and subsequent death. Thus, such operations appear to be one means of promoting adaptation between the density of a population and its food resources.

Female genital mutilations, such as clitoridectomy, have been relatively neglected in the literature, partly because they occur less commonly than male genital mutilations. Those studies that exist have not established direct relationships between the practice itself and ecological variables (e.g., Brown, 1963; Hewes, in press).

## The Organization and Expression of Environmental Percepts

Having reviewed some of the influences of the natural environment on various human activities—building houses, getting food, having sexual intercourse, and so on—it may be helpful to turn to an examination of the ways in which certain features of the natural environment influence the operation of the human mind. This is a more subtle, and in many ways more difficult, enterprise. I will limit myself here to discussing the relationships that have been proposed between certain aspects of speech and the natural environment (presuming that speech reflects thought in some way). Then I will describe briefly some ideas about cognition that have been advanced by anthropologists interested in componential analysis, and I will conclude with an example of how the inhabitants of New Guinea distinguish between different types of terrain.

About a hundred years ago or more, some people thought that the abiotic (nonliving) environment was itself a direct determinant of many of the properties of a given culture. Arbuthnot (1751) proposed that climate exerted a direct influence on the quality of speech, such that people living in colder climates used more consonants than vowels because they were reluctant to open their mouths and breathe in the frigid air, while people in hot climates used more vowels because they needed the ventilation. Similarly, it was claimed that people living under difficult environmental circumstances developed "harsh" phonetic systems, while inhabitants of more pleasant areas used softer sounds in their speech.

In *The Ten Books on Architecture,* written between 16 and 14 B.C., the retired Roman military engineer Vitruviou Pollio proposed that the differences in pitch between the voices of southern and northern peoples in Europe were determined by climate. The voices of people in the north were heavy because of the cold, damp air, while the voices of people in the south were shrill and high-pitched because the air was warm and dry. One could test the proposition for oneself in model form. Heat two thin cups, cool one of them in water, then strike them both. The warm cup will respond with a higher note. Furthermore, Vitruviou Pollio explained, the differences in the pitch of voices illustrates the harmony of the universe. The heavens are closest to earth in the south and farthest away in the north; so there are differences in the characteristics of northern and southern voices just as there are differences in the pitches of long and short strings on a musical instrument.

It took little effort to demolish such arguments. Edward Sapir, the linguist-anthropologist, pointed out that language might be influenced by the physical environment in three possible ways: through (1) vocabulary; (2) phonetic system; or (3) grammatical form. Sapir went on to show that the vocabulary of a language does reflect the interests of the speakers of that language, a now familiar, low-key generalization. An American Indian might divide into a large number of elaborate categories and subcategories that set of plants that we urbanites might classify simply as "weeds," because American Indians were intimately involved with "weeds" and used plant products for food, medicine, and other needs.

The Eskimo vocabulary identifies three different kinds of snow, and Arabic has several thousand words related to camels and their various conditions.

Nevertheless, as far as grammar and phonemics are concerned, we are "forced to admit that apart from the reflection of environment in the vocabulary of a language, there is nothing in the language itself that can be shown to be directly associated with the environment" (Sapir, 1912: 239).

Sapir was probably on the right track, but his method of exposition leaves one uneasy. In 1912, American anthropology was heavily under the influence of Franz Boas, who carved out a department at Columbia and trained what appears to have been the majority of American anthropologists, Sapir included, who later achieved any sort of prominence. Boas, in reacting to the wild speculations rife among the theorists of the nineteenth century, was given to emphasizing the facts of native life rather than theories concerning them. He sometimes went overboard to avoid making any statement that smacked of speculation. For the most part, he eschewed not only identifiable theorizing but integrative concepts as well. The man's later fieldwork among the Haida consisted primarily of collecting an apparently endless variety of myths, folk tales, recipes, and descriptions of material culture, with few generalizations that might allow readers to grasp generalities within Haida culture. In analyzing the work of others, Boas and his students and followers were wont to "disprove" generalizations by pointing to exceptions. Sapir did the same thing. For example:

> Leaving these general considerations on the lack of correlation between physical environment and a phonetic system as a whole, we may point to several striking instances, on the one hand, of phonetic resemblances between languages spoken by groups living in widely different environments and belonging to widely different cultural strata, on the other hand, of no less striking phonetic differences that obtain between languages spoken in adjoining regions of identical or similar environment and sharing in the same culture. [Sapir, 1912: 235]

Of course there will be exceptions to almost all generalizations made concerning human behavior. The real question is not whether such exceptions occur, but how often they occur. Perhaps in their zeal to denigrate speculation, the Boasians might have missed something. If Sapir were correct in his caution, nevertheless there may have been subtle correspondences between speech and the physical environment that he did not allow for.

More recent methods of analysis make it possible to tease out some of these relationships. A cross-cultural study of Freudian symbols by Leigh Minturn gives us an example. It is well known that certain objects in the environment, such as telephone poles, occur in dreams as male symbols, and other objects, such as vases, occur as female symbols. These objects are represented in languages by nouns. And, in some languages, nouns are classified either as male or female. Minturn's study dealt with some fifty-four unambiguous male symbols and sixty female symbols based on objects, animals, persons or situations, and their gender classification in ten distinct languages—French, German, Russian, Greek, Irish, Maharata (India), Arabic, Tunica (American Indian), Nama (South Africa), and Hausa (West Africa). Minturn describes the results:

> The hypothesis being tested is that nouns representing male or female sex symbols will be classified by the gender appropriate to their symbolic value. The data indicate that such a tendency does exist, particularly for masculine symbols, and, although it is not usually prominent in individual languages, it is consistent across a number of unrelated languages. [Minturn, 1965: 342]

Unfortunately, Minturn's list of symbolic nouns includes things other than objects and animals which are part of the environment, and no separate analysis of naturally occurring things is offered. Moreover, six of the languages are Indo-European and so would be expected to have a high gender-concordance. Still, the study is provocative and is an improvement over the observation that Arabic has several dozen terms to describe the various stages of camel pregnancy.

There are some obvious differences between the native and scientific views of a sociocultural event, sometimes called the "emic" and "etic" approaches. The systematization of the former has led to the development of procedures called folk taxonomics and componential analysis, permitting the relatively precise examination of these events from the "native" point of view. These are the chief procedures underlying a number of related subfields in anthropology, variously referred to as ethnoscience, ethnosemantics, the new ethnography, and cognitive anthropology. It is worthwhile at this point to review some of the characteristics of emic studies, especially insofar as they deal with objects or environmental conditions or processes, which, in fact, many of them do.

Beginning in the last century extensive studies were made in language sounds. Universal alphabets were devised to classify the speech sounds found in all languages. Such alphabets were supposed to be objective but were actually derived primarily from Indo-European languages. The studies emphasized the sounds themselves, regardless of the context in which the sounds occurred. The subdiscipline of linguistics dealing with the strictly auditory properties of speech sounds came to be known as phonetics.

The study of phonetic features of language still remains an important field, but many of the physical variations in these sounds, which were so laboriously recorded, turned out to be insignificant to the speakers of the language. For example, there is always some variation in the way in which a speaker of English produces the sound conventionally written *p*, depending on the place of the sound in the speech stream, the dialect of the speaker, and his or her idiosyncratic speech characteristics. Nevertheless, listeners will interpret the sound as *p*, regardless of much of the variation. The physical properties of the sound are less important than the fact that the sound can be classified as different from other sounds. The study of meaningful classes of speech sounds, called phonemes, was begun around the turn of the century and was known as phonemics.

Phonemics stressed the "inside" view of a language, as opposed to the "objective" view taken by phonetics. At about the same time, an interest was developing in the inside view of whole cultures. Field workers tried to "think like natives." In cultural anthropology, the distinction between the inside view of a culture and the outside view was unclear for many years, with ethnographers shifting back and forth from one viewpoint to another.

The differences are now well recognized. Etic approaches to the study of any group can be characterized as external (although *all* categories, including etic ones, are emically derived). Items of behavior are examined not in the light of the systems in which they occur but rather in that of criteria brought to bear on them by the observer. The observer classifies all comparable data into a system, using criteria that were in existence before the classification began. Sitting behind a one-way mirror and coding the interactions of people in accordance with some a priori system is an example of an etic approach.

In an emic study, the investigator assumes that human behavior is patterned, even though the members of the society being studied may not themselves be aware of many of the relationships between elements of the structure. The goal of an emic approach is to discover the system in its own terms. This point of view, allowing the data to generate their own categories, is more useful for some purposes than an etic one. It is the only valid approach if an investigator is interested in discovering the basis of an indigenous classification scheme.

Analogously, "regularities will appear if one measures continental European manufactured goods with an American or British yardstick, but measuring with a meter stick will much more readily reveal the principles of the system relevant in European culture" (Sturtevant, 1964: 111).

Attempts to impose external criteria on a set of data may lead to grotesque results. Thus, it has been pointed out:

The "ethnopornography" of the Queensland aborigines is what *they* consider pornography—if indeed they have such a category—rather than what was considered pornography by the Victorian ethnologist who entitled the last chapter of his monograph on Queensland aborigine culture "ethnopornography," warned that "the following chapter is not suitable for perusal by the general reader," and described under this heading such topics as marriage, pregnancy, childbirth, menstruation, "foul language," and especially genital mutilations. [Sturtevant, 1964: 100]

Later ethnographers were much more sensitive to the relativity of such concepts, as for example, was Opler in discussing Apache raiding parties in a publication which first appeared in 1941:

> Since it was the socialization of the Chiricahua which was to be examined, I felt that not only the sequences of events but the contexts in which they are placed should be faithful to the Chiricahua view. In order to keep the emphases as the participants feel them, it became necessary to separate items which might have been brought together by some other classification and to unite data which would have been scattered in response to a more conventional topical treatment.... Raid and warfare are subsumed under the maintenance of the household, not because of any notions of my own concerning the nature of these activities, but because, at the period described, the Chiricahua considered the raid a legitimate industry and trained faithfully for its proper fulfillment with this in mind. [Opler, 1965: x]

Finally, to give some example of the flavor with which modern emic analysts approach and execute their tasks, we may quote from an exemplary piece, the introduction to an examination of Mexican weddings. Note the deliberation with which etic "distortions" are avoided and the implicit debt to linguistics (both absent from Opler's statement).

> We present in this paper a preliminary statement of some field procedures directed toward ethnographic descriptions that parallel the categorizations of the people under study. By way of example, we describe wedding ceremonials among the ladino population of Tenejapa, Chiapas, Mexico, in terms of the ways in which they perceive weddings to differ in form.... The description, and the procedures employed in arriving at it, are intended to be free of the distortion introduced by investigators' pre-definition of problem and by the investigators' own implicit perception or assumption of descriptive units. The "units" employed arise from the data through the application of procedures outlined below, and the description is largely an extended definition of these units and their relation to other units. [Metzger and Williams, 1962a: 1076]

Over the last thirty years, a methodology was devised for the study of folk classifications, first applied to kinship terminologies by Ward

Goodenough and Floyd Lounsbury (Goodenough, 1956; Lounsbury, 1956). Both Goodenough and Lounsbury had some previous exposure to mathematics, learning theory, semiotics, and linguistics. Moreover, as students of G.P. Murdock at Yale, they were thoroughly grounded in kinship studies. Goodenough called his method componential analysis, in reference to the fact that the method involves an analysis of the components of a system of folk classification. The complete system itself is called a "domain." All of the simple English words describing kinsmen — *mother, father, cousin,* and so on — constitute a domain, for instance. The analysis of such domains usually involves only a small number of dimensions and at the same time attempts to account for all of the elements within the system. "American English consanguineal core terms," referring to the sort of kinship terms above, are supposed to be adequately defined in terms of only three dimensions: sex, generation, and collaterality (Wallace and Atkins, 1960: 61-62). The overall point of a componential analysis is to discover the way a group of people organizes its percepts of the world, the systems they build out of those percepts, and the discriminating features within the system.

A brief example of what a componential analysis looks like may be helpful at this point. The example comes from an article on laws of land tenure among the Kapauku of New Guinea by Leopold Pospisil (Pospisil, 1965).

In figure 5 we see the Kapauku taxonomy of economically important terrain types. There is a Kapauku term corresponding to each type of terrain. This is the result one gets when one asks an informant *how* he or she divides up any given domain. The procedure is simple, and so is the result. Similar procedures operating within an "etic" framework produce the keys that are familiar to students of biology.

The analysis may stop there, and in some published cases it does. However, a taxonomy can suggest as many questions as it answers. For a fuller understanding of the domain, the next question is usually, Why? That is, the informant is asked in a roundabout way what the criterial attributes of the categories are; for example, What is it that makes a garden different from a yard? (Of course, we are already receiving hints, in a sense, because we are using English words for the terrain types. Pospisil worked only with native terms and provided the translations himself, following the analysis. All he knew was that the Kapauku had a type of terrain called *bugi,* which he named a garden, and another type called *juwu'uda,* which he named a yard.) Pospisil's informants told him the categories represented terrains with different economic properties, which were dependent on their physical features.

Pospisil's analysis of the criteria of economically important terrains in terms of their physical and economic criteria is given in figure 6. As can be

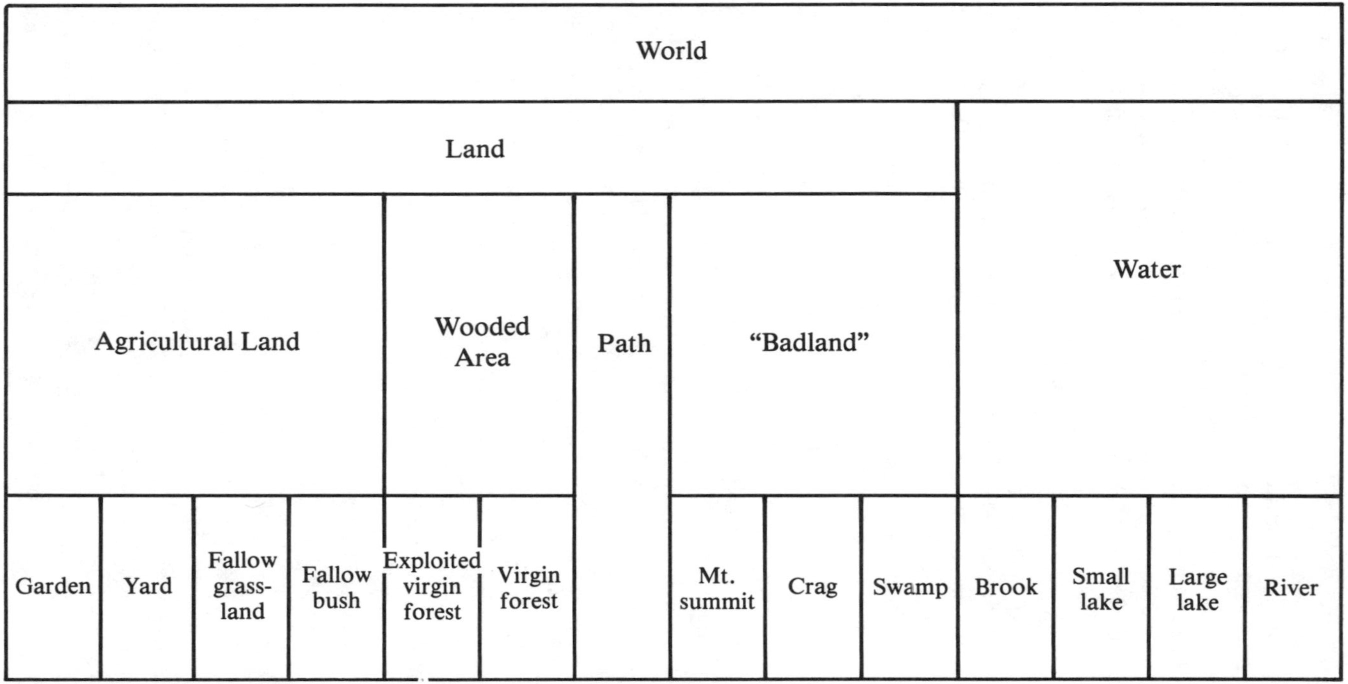

FIG. 5. ECONOMICALLY IMPORTANT KAPAURU TERRAIN TYPES.

Source: Pospisil, 1965: 196. Reproduced by permission of the American Anthropological Association from *American Anthropologist* 67(5): 186-214, 1965.

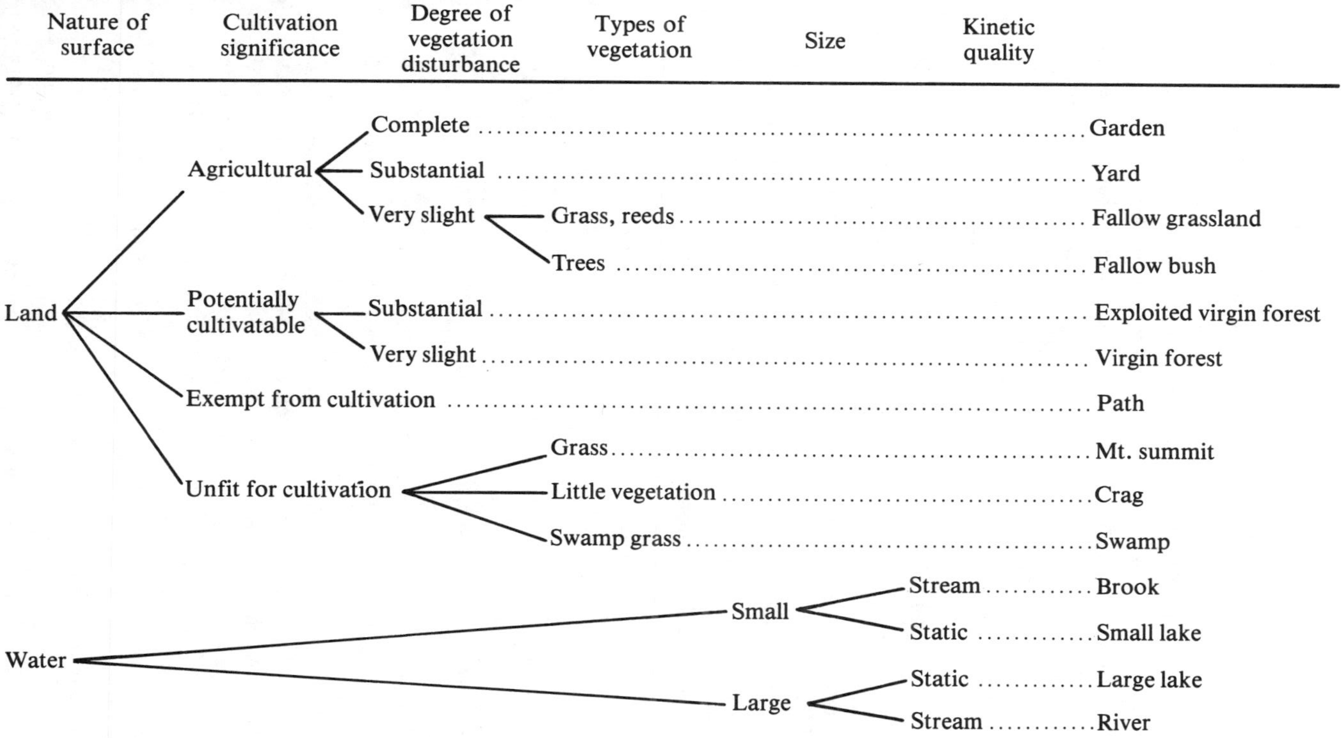

FIG. 6. ANALYSIS OF TERRAIN TYPES.

Source: Pospisil, 1965: 20. Reproduced by permission of the American Anthropological Association from *American Anthropologist* 67(5): 186-214, 1965.

157

seen there are six criteria, each at a different level of specificity: (1) the nature of the surface, (2) cultivation significance, (3) degree of vegetative disturbance, (4) type of vegetation, (5) size, and (6) kinetic quality. The distribution of these components through each level of the taxonomy is not symmetrical. That is, not all the criteria are important for all the types of terrain. Size, for instance, has nothing to do with land. This is acceptable. We find the same thing in many domains. In American kinship terminology, for example, the sex of the relative is important in distinguishing an uncle from an aunt, but sex has nothing to do with identifying cousins. Pospisil writes that these land and water categories were

> designed and labeled by the Kapauku themselves. However, it would be going too far to claim that organizing these folk data into a sequential arrangement and a table is a "folk componential analysis." Although the basic concepts and other interrelationships derive from the natives, the overall organization of the table is mine, for informants certainly did not conceive such a systematically organized total image. Their ideas about contrasts were consistent but were limited to the various unassembled dimensions and levels. Thus, the pieces of the mosaic were there, with the uneven edges of a jigsaw puzzle; it remained only for me to assemble them. [Pospisil, 1965: 199]

A few questions might be raised here, chief among them the epistemology of the criteria. Suppose we elicit a folk taxonomy and suppose we ask the informants why they make the distinctions they do, so that they give us a set of contrasts for each distinction. How do we know that the criteria are actually what the folk *say* they are? To illustrate this problem let us return to Pospisil's analysis. Referring to the paradigm in figure 6, Pospisil reports:

> Kapauku say that the division of their natural habitat is due to the need to distinguish in their legal rules the various land and water environments according to their observable and important physical attributes, but this statement is hardly accurate. My doubts about the sole emphasis upon distinctive physical features in this classification are justified and documented by the fact that many other types of land, conceptualized by the Kapauku and provided with proper terms, have not been incorporated into this legally important folk taxonomy and paradigm. [Many environmental features are thrown into catchall categories] despite...obvious physical and environmental differences. The reason for this is not that there is a striking physical similarity among these features, but that all these terrain types carry the *same economic and legal significance*. In other words, in spite of what the Kapauku *say* they do, this system of terrain classes actually is designed for economic-legal purposes and is used only in a legal context. [Pospisil, 1965: 201; Pospisil's italics]

Bringing this "external" insight to bear on the data, Pospisil develops the paradigm presented in figure 7, which is "culturally more significant than would be a folk taxonomy and an analysis by folk-components" (Pospisil, 1965: 201).

There are additional problems with componential analysis. Too often, the problem of representativeness has been considered of little import. Few analysts have bothered with sampling procedures because it is generally assumed, as in linguistics, that any competent speaker can tell you whether something you say in a given language is correct or incorrect. One informant is as good as another. But is this true in componential analysis? Suppose one elicits a taxonomy from an informant. Would everyone else in his society provide the same information? Further difficulties have been raised (Harris, 1968: 568-604; Burling, 1964).

We may note, however, that the approach has been extremely popular over the last few years, despite the fact that the controversy surrounding it and its practitioners seems to be abating. Outside of linguistics proper, where similar procedures have been matter-of-factly applied to pronouns, cases, affixes, and so on, the emic approach has been used to describe color terminologies, which have received considerable attention recently (Berlin and Kay, 1969; Berlin and Berlin, 1975; Conklin, 1955; Landar et al., 1960; O'Neale and Dolores, 1943; Pollnac, 1975). Other studies have dealt with smells (Aschmann, 1946); musical systems (Bright, 1963); birds (Blumer, 1957); Northern Paiute percepts of things that are eaten, otherwise used, or not used at all (Fowler and Leland, 1967); categories of fish as perceived by people of French origin living on the island of St. Thomas (Morrill, 1967), diseases and drinkables among the Subanun of the Philippines (Frake, 1961, 1964), cuisines (Levi-Strauss, 1967), Tzeltal firewood (Metzger and Williams, 1962b), plants among the Tewa Indians (Robbins et al., 1916), and several other things in several other places. Whatever the strengths and weaknesses of emic studies, it must be admitted that they have been most useful in attracting attention to the problem of the way in which human beings structure the objects and events in their natural environments, a central part of the relationship between people and their surroundings.

### Natural Disasters

All of the material presented so far in this chapter has dealt with regularly occurring natural conditions and people's adaptations to them. The evolution of adaptive mechanisms was naturally a long-term process and could be based on trial-and-error learning. The following section describes

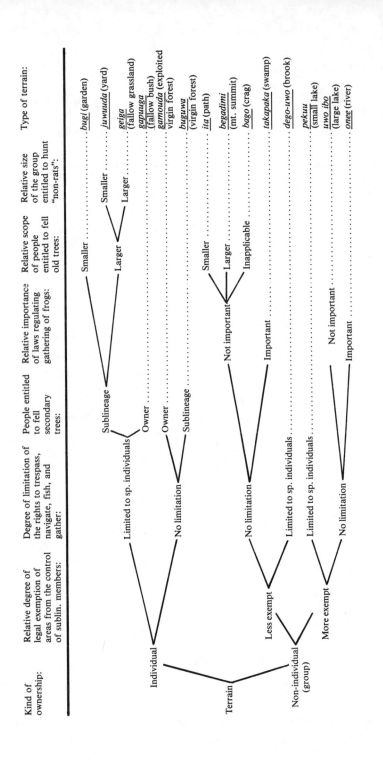

Fig. 7. ANALYSIS OF TERRAIN TYPES IN TERMS OF THEIR CONTRASTIVE LEGAL CORRELATES.

Source: Pospisil, 1965: 205. Reproduced by permission of the American Anthropological Association from *American Anthropologist* 67(5): 186-214, 1965.

temporary sources of extreme environmental stress. If they recur, they do so at irregular intervals, and if preparation for them is made at all, it must take place during the long interims when the stressors themselves are not present. Adaptation is not strictly necessary. One may choose instead to take a chance on dying or being economically ruined, and it may come as a surprise to find how often such risks are taken.

*Geophysical Hazards*

Journalists have described many historical catastrophes, but the scientific study of natural disasters was not very popular until the latter half of the 1940s. There is no need to guess why disaster studies suddenly became of such immediate concern. The first atomic bomb that exploded over Hiroshima raised the specter of multitudes of such bombs raining down on population centers all over the earth at some time in the future. It was not that people, especially members of the Office of Defense Mobilization, became obsessed overnight with the question of how best to organize a town so that, should a tornado blow through it, some coherent and constructive community response might be made. The real concern was not with tornadoes but with the Soviet Union. With the evolution of the international situation—and a shift in intent from one total nuclear war to many smaller limited wars—interest in natural disaster studies has flagged somewhat, which is unfortunate since disasters tend to be dramatic and interesting in themselves and are as instructive as ever on the subject of collective behavior under stress. One might argue, in fact, that disaster studies should be of more relevance than ever. When the earth was sparsely populated, many convulsions of the atmosphere or the earth went unnoticed because fewer people were around to notice or to be immediately affected by them. If this were still the case, most catastrophes would be merely of academic interest. But as population density grows, the number of people likely to be affected by each disaster increases. So, in view of the fact that the world's population shows little tendency to cease growing, we may predict that disasters will involve greater numbers of victims in the future.

Disasters have been described as—

the impinging upon a structured community of an external force capable of destroying human life or its resources for survival, on a scale wide enough to excite public alarm, to disrupt normal patterns of behavior, and to impair or overload any of the central services necessary to the conduct of normal affairs or to the prevention or alleviation of suffering and loss. Usually, the term disaster refers to an episode with tragic consequences to a substantial portion of the population. [Berkner, 1952, quoted in Lemons, 1957: 2]

In the following abbreviated survey of various types of disasters, classified according to their apparent physical causes, we will not consider manmade catastrophes such as airplane crashes, collapsed buildings, urban fires, or nuclear explosions. We will focus primarily on the natural disasters that have always affected people: avalanches, earthquakes, floods, hurricanes, tornadoes, and volcanic eruptions.

*Avalanches.* An avalanche is the sudden descent of large masses of ice, snow, or rock down a mountainside. The word is from French, *aval,* "downward," and *labi,* "to slip or glide." An avalanche may occur anywhere in the world where steep mountain slopes are present. One of the most important recent avalanches occurred in Ranrahirca, Peru, on January 10, 1962, in which more than three thousand people died. Earlier, in 1941, an avalanche in Huaras, Peru, killed about five thousand people. Probably the greatest avalanches in the world take place in the Himalayas, but they are seldom observed or reported. Dwellers on steep, snow-laden mountainsides generally are aware of the dangers of avalanches and can recognize signs of growing danger. However, they seem seldom to take adequate precautions. Perhaps one of the reasons is that the initial warning, the accumulation of snow and ice, signals only a possible event at some indeterminate time in the future. The next warning, the roaring of the mass of material as it slides down the slope, signals that the event is actually taking place, and by that time it is generally too late for escape. Rarely are great numbers of people injured in an avalanche. The slide either kills them or leaves them unharmed.

*Earthquakes.* It is now clear that the lithosphere, the surface of the earth, is a mosaic of rigid plates, constantly shifting, rubbing against one another, breaking apart, or diving under one another. The rate of movement of these vast plates may be between two and eighteen centimeters per year (Dewey, 1972). It has long been recognized that earthquakes do not occur at random but rather are concentrated in certain zones, and it is now believed that these earthquake zones represent lines of contact between two or more plates. The earthquakes indicate the release of tension built up between plates moving in different directions. (It is such shifting, incidentally, that accounts for the fact that the west coast of Africa and the east coast of South America almost match each other's contours, like pieces in a jigsaw puzzle.)

One of the areas most wracked by earthquakes is the rim of the Pacific basin, including the east coasts of Asia and Japan, and the west coasts of North and South America. The greatest loss of life has occurred along the Asian coast since that is where the population is most dense. It has been suggested that some portion of the ritual component of Japanese culture is associated with the anxiety caused by living in a seismically unstable area. Masao Watanabe states that despite this concern, "the Japanese did not initiate the scientific study of earthquakes. This can be explained largely by their attitude of coexisting with nature" (Watanabe, 1974: 279). Whether or not they initiated the scientific study of the phenomenon, a great deal of early interest was expressed by both the Japanese and the Chinese in the causes and measurement of earthquake tremors. Irene Bloom (1974: 850) quotes Forke's (1925: 19-20) description of an early Chinese seismograph, built by Chang Heng in A.D. 132:

> Cast from fine copper...eight feet [in] diameter, which, with its cover, stood up like a wine amphora. It was adorned with seal characters, mountains, turtles, birds, and animals, had a main prop in the centre and eight grooves at the side.... Outside, there were eight dragon heads with copper balls in their mouths and, below, toads which could receive these balls in their open mouths. The cogged wheels were very elaborate, but all concealed in the amphora, the lid of which was tightly closed, leaving no fissure. When there was an earthquake, the amphora shook the dragons, the mechanism became stirred, and they vomited the balls, which were caught by the toads. The sound of the concussion was the signal to rouse the observer. Even if only one dragon was set in motion and seven heads were not stirred, upon investigating the environs the place of the earthquake was discovered. There was the most wonderful agreement with facts, and nothing similar had happened since records were kept. Once the mechanism of one dragon moved, but no earthquake was felt. All the scholars in the capital were surprised at this inaccuracy, but several days later a courier brought the news that in fact there had been an earthquake in Shensi. Then all believed in this wonderful invention, and an astronomer was ordered to record all the places from where earthquakes started.

Each time an earthquake occurs, the distance of slippage involved may actually be less than imagined, perhaps only a few feet, but the sudden release of tension sends out vibrations like ripples in a pool, and these may cause major destruction. Earthquakes occur every day somewhere on the earth's surface, but most are too small to be noticed except on seismographs.

Major earthquakes in the United States have been severe—some 450 people were killed in the San Francisco earthquake of 1906, which was the most disastrous—but our earthquakes pale in comparison to those occurring in other countries. The three greatest earthquakes ever reported (magnitudes of 8.9 on the Gutenberg-Richter scale) were: (1) a submarine quake near the border of Colombia and Ecuador, in 1908; (2) a submarine quake about a hundred miles from the coast of northern Japan in 1933; and (3) at Lebu, south of Concepción, Chile, in 1960. The energy released in each of these quakes was equivalent to an explosion of 140 million long tons of TNT. The greatest loss of life in earthquakes has occurred in the crowded East: 70,000 in Kansu, China (1932); 140,000 in Tokyo (1923); 300,000 in Calcutta (1737); and an estimated 830,000 in China (1556).

Most lives lost during an earthquake are due to collapsing buildings which either kill people outright or bury them in rubble. Only rarely do fissures open in the earth, and they are always shallow. Sometimes as many lives are lost after the earthquake as during the quake itself, because of the fires that ordinarily follow. The fires caused by the San Francisco earthquake of 1906 did twenty times the damage of the quake.

There are no warning signals associated with earthquakes and no effective preventive measures, although attempts are being made to force water into major fault lines and thereby cause a series of minor tremors rather than a single major one. Buildings can be designed to be earthquake-resistant without much additional cost, but few such efforts are being made in the United States. As in the case of avalanches, most people in earthquake zones seem to take the danger for granted. For instance, new structures in San Francisco must conform to a recently instituted building code designed to render them more resistant to earthquake damage. However, proposals to strengthen or replace old and vulnerable buildings such as schools and hospitals have consistently been voted down. Of course, taxes are high enough. But more than that, as Mayor Joseph Alioto said in a televised interview on "Sixty Minutes" (January 14, 1973), "We are not going to live in fear and hysteria. Most of us would rather live one day in San Francisco than one thousand years in Whittier, California." One can only admire such fatalism, while deploring its inevitable consequences.

Similarly, Managua, Nicaragua, was leveled by an earthquake in 1885. Managuans rebuilt their houses, buried their dead, and went ahead with their lives. Again, in 1931, an earthquake and fire killed about two thousand people, but the city was rebuilt and life went on. Another earthquake occurred in 1967, and a fourth on December 23, 1972. This time, 95 percent of the buildings either were destroyed or left unfit for use, and perhaps five thousand people died.

> What some geologists had been saying about Managua became all too apparent: that the city was built over a fault.... Managua has remained on the same site because it was the capital, so decreed by the constitution, and because of inertia of the people created by poverty and custom. There is no powerful overriding economic reason for Managua to be rebuilt where it is. [*New York Times,* Dec. 31, 1972]

On January 12, 1973, the government decided to rebuild Managua six miles from its previous location.

In view of the fact that the primary cause of death in earthquakes is from falling buildings and subsequent fires, for most of human existence, people might have been frightened by earthquakes but were not necessarily in mortal danger from them unless the quakes generated landslides or tidal waves. Until relatively recently, humans were exclusively hunters and gatherers and rarely lived in stable settlements. Lighter dwellings meant less danger in an earthquake. A person standing in the center of an open field could probably survive a major cataclysm.

*Floods.* Along coastlines, floods may result from unusually high tides, from submarine earthquakes, or from storms at sea. Inland, floods may be caused by dam failure, heavy rains, or melting snow. Floods occur regularly in some places in the world, such as along the lower Nile, and the neighboring populations have adapted to them. But at irregular intervals flooding of much greater than ordinary intensity occurs. This may happen anywhere in the world. These unexpectedly severe floods cause most of the flood-related damage and loss of life. The difference between disastrous floods and the sorts of catastrophes we have previously discussed is that, while we don't need avalanches or earthquakes, we do need water. Water provides us not only with drink but also with sources of power, means of transportation and recreation, and, where necessary, irrigation. Floods are not the unmitigated nuisance that previously discussed natural events are; they are instances of a vital resource going out of control.

Some researchers have been puzzled by the fact that people continue to live in areas regularly prone to disastrous flooding and, when driven out, frequently return despite the fact that no new protective measures have been taken. Investigations have dealt with the occupants of flood plains within the moderate frequency range (Craik, 1970; Kates, 1962, 1967; Roder, 1961; Burton, 1961). Briefly, these studies reveal some relationships between the adjustment to flood hazard and such variables as education (though not socioeconomic status), but no startling findings have emerged to explain why people in general, and some people in particular, seem so unconcerned about the possibility of disastrous floods. Kates (1967) could find no relationship between the adoption of flood damage reduction measures and past experience with flooding!

The primary cause of death in floods is drowning, but many people also die as a result of injury associated with collapsing buildings or debris swept along by the current. Rather surprisingly, fire may also play a part in the disaster. A flood may destroy many wooden buildings in a few moments but, if the water subsides quickly, may not thoroughly soak the timbers, which in effect leaves a lot of combustible debris lying about. At the same time, the flood may not extinguish fires contained in stoves, boilers, and ovens. Of course, any destruction of petroleum storage tanks adds to the risk of fire. Finally, epidemics sometimes follow in the wake of large-scale floods.

*Hurricanes.* Hurricanes are named after the Arawak god of storms, Huracan, a figure in native Caribbean mythology. In the Pacific they are called typhoons, from the Beijing dialect *dà fēng,* "big wind."

Regardless of the name, they are the same type of storm: great rotary vortices of air swirling in a counterclockwise direction (in the northern hemisphere) about a center, or eye, where winds may be light and fitful. The entire disturbance may cover an area of thousands of square miles, and the overall shape of the storm resembles that of a huge phonograph record, the eye of the storm forming a hole in or near the center. The whole system moves forward at about twenty miles per hour.

The winds at the outer edges of the storm are relatively light but their force increases as they swirl faster towards the center of the storm. By definition, the speed of the hurricane winds is greater than 72 miles per hour—though not all winds of this speed need be associated with hurricanes—and in the most violent storms, wind speeds of 250 miles per hour may be approached. Winds of such force are liable to lift seas greatly above high-tide levels along coastlines and, under certain conditions, may drive exceedingly high waves, called storm surges, before them. Collapsing buildings and flying debris kill and injure many of the victims, but the majority of deaths occur in association with the heavy rains, high tides, and storm surges that accompany the storms.

These are tropical storms, the majority of them forming in the humid atmosphere of the southwest Atlantic, the Caribbean, or the subtropical Pacific, particularly its western reaches. The causes of hurricanes are unknown, though it seems likely that they have something to do with the circulation of air in the global atmosphere. There are no known preventive measures. Even if we did know how to prevent the development of hurricanes, we would be uncertain of the overall effect of these measures—another instance in which the cure might possibly be worse than the disease. (See "Seeding Hurricanes," *Science,* 1973: 744.)

In the United States most hurricanes occur during the late summer and fall. Between 1887 and 1955, 63 hurricanes appeared in August, 114 during September, and 59 during October, far more than the total for all other months combined. The average lifetime of a hurricane is nine days, although those of August average twelve days and those of July and November about eight days (Lemons, 1957). Over the years, the damage caused by hurricanes has increased enormously—the first billion-dollar hurricane in American history occurred in 1955—largely because there are now so many more artifacts to be destroyed in hurricane-prone areas.

Paradoxically, the number of lives lost has dropped as a result of improvements in the hurricane-warning system.

These storms should not be underestimated in terms of the damage they can do to lives and property. The most destructive typhoons in history have occurred in the Bay of Bengal, especially in the Hooghly River region. Communities along the coastline have repeatedly been destroyed. In 1737, a typhoon killed 300,000 people; another disaster occurred in 1864; in 1942, a storm surge flooded more than 5,000 square miles. "One of the few men who came through the Bengal floods alive said that he saw the sea recede for a dozen miles and then come hurtling back as a solid wall of water thirty feet high, driven by a 120 m.p.h. wind" (Lane, 1965: 30). And of course the newly formed nation of Bangladesh on the Bay of Bengal was stricken by a typhoon in 1970, leaving more than 200,000 dead.

The most destructive hurricane to reach the United States was the Galveston Island hurricane of 1900 which destroyed 3,600 houses and killed 6,000 people. One of the most destructive in recent years was the hurricane of 1938 which inundated and destroyed much of Long Island and New England, killing about 600, injuring almost 2,000, and causing property damage estimated at 250 million 1938 dollars. The storm had been spotted in the South Atlantic approaching the Florida coast but had subsequently arced back to seaward. The *New York Times* forecast for September 21 was for "rain, probably heavy today and tomorrow, cooler, fresh southerly winds" (quoted in McCarthy 1969: 11). The *Times* praised the "admirably organized meteorological service" which had kept "New York and the rest of the world...so well informed about the [Florida] cyclone" (McCarthy, 1969: 11). The hurricane swept across central Long Island at about four o'clock in the afternoon of the twenty-first, traveling northward at an unusual sixty miles per hour, catching the weather bureau and everyone else by surprise. The storm surge struck Long Island and the exposed eastern coast of Connecticut, including New Haven, with a shock strong enough to register on far distant seismographs. Describing the surge, one observer said, "It looked like a thick and high bank of fog rolling in fast from the ocean.... When it came closer, we saw that it wasn't fog. It was water" (McCarthy, 1969: 102). The storm continued north through the valley of the Connecticut River, into Massachusetts, Vermont, and New Hampshire, and into Canada, dropping salty rain more than one hundred miles from the sea.

*Tornadoes.* Tornadoes are small rotary storms with extremely high winds. They usually appear during severe thunderstorms as black, funnel-shaped or ropelike clouds, descending from the base of the parent cloud to the ground. The width of the funnel varies from about fifty feet to two miles. The funnel moves along the ground at an average speed of about forty miles per hour. The usual duration of a tornado is about five minutes, although funnels have been known to dip down and touch the ground only momentarily before lifting again, and at the other extreme, the most disastrous tornado in American history formed in Missouri in 1925 and ended several hours later inside Indiana, having traveled about two hundred miles across three states and killed or injured about two hundred sixty people.

Tornadoes have occurred in Great Britain, the Soviet Union, India, and elsewhere, but they appear with the greatest frequency by far in the United States, particularly in the Mississippi valley, where they accompany intense frontal systems caused by the collision of tropical maritime air masses from the Gulf of Mexico and either polar continental air masses from the Canadian interior or polar maritime air masses from the northwest coast. In late winter, they are most common in the gulf states, but as spring progresses, the areas of greatest frequency move northward until by early summer they are found in the northerly reaches of the central states. Between June and January, their frequency declines. They may occur at any time of the day or night but they usually strike in late afternoon. Ordinarily they track in a zigzag pattern, sometimes in whole loops, from the southwest to the northeast. They frequently occur in groups. It should be emphasized that these statements are statistical generalizations, not rules. Tornadoes have been sighted in all of the continental United States, including Alaska, and may strike from any direction at any time.

The exact causes of tornadoes are still unknown. It may be that in strong cold fronts, the cold air mass may not only bulge under the warm air, thrusting it violently upward, but may in fact bulge out over the top of the warm air mass, forming a wedge of cold air aloft, and this may somehow be associated with the sort of severe hail-bearing thunderstorms that seem to generate tornadoes. Some theorists suggest that tornadoes are caused by atmospheric electricity, others that tornadoes actually represent a sort of spontaneous combustion which burns off an excess of the volatile terpenes that plants exude into warm air, but no one knows.

There are three main mechanisms by which tornadoes cause damage: (1) winds, (2) pressure, and (3) suction. The force of winds in the margins of the tornado funnel is difficult to believe. Their speed has never been measured adequately but is undoubtedly greater than 200 miles per hour, perhaps as great as 500 miles per hour, and some theoretical estimates place it at about 2,000 miles per hour. The force a wind exerts against an object is increased approximately by the square of the velocity, up to the speed of sound. A wind of 50 miles per hour is a considerable inconvenience and may cause some structural damage to buildings, and a wind of 500 miles per hour, which is likely to occur in a major tornado, is a hundred times as powerful as a wind of 50 miles per hour! The actual effect of the wind varies with the shape of the object, but a force of 250 pounds per square foot would not be unthinkable in a tornado. There is nothing necessarily *light* about air. This is the sort of wind that can drive gravel through one's body like shotgun pellets, two-by-fours through cattle, or lengths of straw into tree trunks like arrows.

Equally destructive to buildings or other containers is pressure. In some respects a tornado resembles a small, concentrated low-pressure system. Standard pressure at sea level is 14.7 pounds per square inch. In the funnel of a tornado this may drop as much as 2 pounds within a few seconds. Even in a small shelter, of, say, ten feet by ten feet by ten feet, this is equivalent to a pressure differential of about 1.4 tons between the ceiling and the atmosphere. Or, to put it another way, the air inside this building will suddenly begin pushing against the internal walls and ceiling with a pressure of about seven tons. The pressure differentials are vastly greater for larger structures. The effect of all this is to cause buildings to explode outward as the funnel passes over them. According to many observers, the buildings frequently do so in a sort of slow motion: the roof is lifted off, the walls slowly collapse outward, and the inhabitants are left sitting or standing on the bare floor.

The third destructive force is updraft of suction. Objects, which may be as large as automobiles or freight trains, are lifted into the sky, sometimes whirled around and destroyed, sometimes set down undamaged some miles away. "Updraft" and "suction" would both appear to be misnomers for this phenomenon since they imply a forceful wind. This lifting of objects can occur in the absence of wind and may be fairly gentle. Observers have reported that, as the funnel passed over them, small objects slowly rose into the air. One mother reported her child rising away from her like a helium-filled balloon. Anthony Wallace suggests that the expansion of residual air pockets of normal pressure under such objects as eggs in their cartons cause the objects to pop out of their containers, but this does not seem to fit the above observations. The truth is that no one can give an adequate explanation of tornado updrafts at this point.

The impact of a tornado occurs in three phases as the funnel passes over its victims. First, a wall of high-intensity wind damages structures. Second, as the interior of the funnel reaches the impact point, the drop in atmospheric pressure causes the already weakened buildings to explode, and the updraft agitates the debris and pulls objects and people into the air.

Finally, the rear edge of the funnel reaches the impact point and blows the debris about, causing further damage and killing and injuring more victims, who may be sitting dazed amid the wreckage.

Tornadoes may be detected by radar as well as by sight. The Severe Local Storm Warning Center in Kansas City, Missouri, issues tornado warnings when advisable. The sighting of a funnel-shaped cloud is fair warning, but unfortunately the funnel may be invisible in unusually dry air or absent if the parent cloud is itself in contact with the earth. The storms always seem to cause a great racket, frequently likened to the passing of a multitude of freight trains or, more recently, the roar of jet airplanes. But by the time the noise of the funnel can be heard over the general uproar of the storm, the observer is likely to have only a few seconds to find shelter.

We may close these general observations with what is probably the most widely quoted and certainly one of the most remarkable reports of a personal encounter with a tornado, from a Mr. Will Keller, a farmer in Kansas who dashed to his storm cellar when he saw a tornado approaching him in June 1927:

As I paused to look I saw that the lower end which had been sweeping the ground was beginning to rise. I knew what that meant, so I kept my position. I knew that I was comparatively safe and I knew that if the tornado again dipped I could drop down and close the door before any harm could be done.

Steadily the tornado came on, the end gradually rising above the ground. I could have stood there only a few seconds but so impressed was I with what was going on that it seemed a long time. At last the great shaggy end of the funnel hung directly overhead. Everything was as still as death. There was a strong gassy odor and it seemed that I could not breathe. There was a screaming, hissing sound coming directly from the end of the funnel. I looked up and to my astonishment I saw right up into the heart of the tornado. There was a circular opening in the center of the funnel, about 50 or 100 feet in diameter, and extending straight upward for a distance of at least one half mile, as best I could judge under the circumstances. The walls of this opening were of rotating clouds and the whole was made brilliantly visible by constant flashes of lightning which zigzagged from side to side. Had it not been for the lightning I could not have seen the opening, not any distance up into it anyway.

Around the lower rim of the great vortex small tornadoes were constantly forming and breaking away. These looked like tails as they writhed their way around the end of the funnel. It was these that made the hissing noise.

I noticed that the direction of rotation of the great whirl was anticlockwise, but the small twisters rotated both ways — some one way and some another.

The opening was entirely hollow except for something which I could not exactly make out, but suppose that it was a detached wind cloud. This thing was in the center and was moving up and down. [Quoted in Lane, 1965: 55-57]

One can only admire farmer Keller, who must have been demonically phlegmatic!

*Volcanic Eruptions.* A volcano is an opening in the crust of the earth through which molten lava flows, sometimes accompanied by gases, dust, and rocks. The eruption may be slow or it may occur with explosive force. Volcanoes are classified as active, dormant, or extinct. They may change their status at any time. They are not scattered at random around the earth's surface but are concentrated in zones roughly congruent with the earthquake zones described earlier. Volcanoes are probably formed by the same mechanism as earthquakes: the movement of plates about the earth's surface. Two plates pulling away from each other allow conduits from magma pockets to reach the earth's surface, and a volcano appears. Spewing lava, ash, and gas, the volcano builds up debris around its crater and a mountainous volcanic cone gradually forms. Thereafter, most of the material erupts from fissures in the sides of the cone rather than from the crater itself.

Preventing volcanic eruption is still impossible. There are many warning signs for a coming eruption, but such evidence is often ignored. The heightened eruption of dust and gas from an already active volcano, or any sudden activity in a volcano that has been dormant or extinct, ought to prompt nearby residents to take notice. The most disastrous volcanic eruption of the twentieth century occurred in the spring of 1902 at Mt. Pelee on the Caribbean island of Martinique. Mt. Pelee had been dormant for years but began discharging fine dust and ash in April. The residents of St. Pierre, five miles away, took notice but did nothing except for trying to clear away some of the fine ash that had dusted the streets. In early May, after a series of explosions, a slide of boiling mud rolled down the mountain and killed 30 men working at a sugar mill. The people of St. Pierre were alarmed. Some left the area; others intended leaving but either yielded to the soothing editorials of the local newspaper and the reassurances of the governor of Martinique, who pleaded with them to be "brave" and remain, or were prevented outright from leaving by soldiers posted along the roads. On the night of May 7, Mt. Pelee provided the townsmen with a brilliant display of pyrotechnics and then subsided. Early the next morning, the only sign of volcanic activity was an extremely high column of vapor, but at 7:50 a stunning explosion shook Mt. Pelee, the side facing St. Pierre opened, and a blast of superheated, dust-laden air rushed across St. Pierre at about 300 miles per hour. The town was quickly destroyed by air heated to about 450 degrees Celsius, carrying fragments at a temperature of perhaps 1,000 degrees. The blast then swept over the harbor and out to sea and was heard as far away as Maracaibo, a distance of 800 miles. Dust rained down on ships hundreds of miles away, and about 2 million tons of dust fell on Barbados, 150 miles south of Mt. Pelee. More than 30,000 people were killed, one of the few survivors being a prisoner who survived the blast in the town dungeon. Fourteen ships were sunk, and an estimated 10 miles of land burned black.

*Reactions*

Having described the most significant naturally occurring sources of death and destruction, we may now ask ourselves: What do people do about them—how do they respond before, during, and after the event? What meaning, if any, do they attribute to them? Is it the hand of God or just an excess of wind? These questions are more than merely rhetorical; they have implications for life and death. Probably almost everyone in the United States was prepared for Mt. St. Helens to explode in 1980, yet about eighty people chose to perish in the final eruption, including a man who in effect told interviewers that he knew that he was committing suicide, but that no power on earth could force him to leave the home he had built.

I will deal with some of these issues in this section and will conclude with some observations on how to survive if isolated in a hostile, natural environment, even in the absence of an agent of disaster. In a sense this is a regression to an earlier topic, but the emphasis is on an impromptu, non-cultural response to environmental stress.

*The Time-Space Model of Disaster.* John W. Powell et al. (1953) have developed a model of the time dimension in disasters, dividing each disaster into seven stages with differing behavior correlates.

In the first stage, predisaster conditions exist. The nature of these conditions has some effect on subsequent events. This stage represents, in a general way, the steady state of the social system.

The next stage is one of warning, in which there are indications that something may be up. Frequently these take the form of announcements in the mass media. The most suitable behavior during the warning stage is to take precautionary measures. Whether or not such measures are taken depends to some extent on the nature of the predisaster conditions. If people have little prior experience with the type of disaster to which the warning refers, the warning itself may not be taken seriously. Thus, during the Worcester, Massachusetts, tornado of June 9, 1953, the telephone company and a military air base nearby may have been warned of the tornado more than an hour before it struck, but no warnings were issued to the surrounding communities. Even when proper warnings were issued, their import was not understood by some local residents, most of whom thought of tornadoes as something that happened in Oklahoma or the Midwest. "Within minutes after impact at Worcester...a radio warning *did* go over a police network which was picked up by a patrolman in Fayville, where the impact occurred at about 5:30. The patrolman drove home to protect his two sisters and their four children, but impact caught them sitting in the living room and they never reached the cellar!" (Wallace, 1956: 32).

The third stage is one of threat. Unambiguous cues are presented to residents of the disaster region, and if these cues are interpreted correctly, residents take immediate survival action. Threat time is usually shorter than warning time. There are usually direct physical signs — the roaring of the landslide in an avalanche or the sight of an approaching funnel-shaped cloud in a tornado — and the threat is followed either by disaster itself or a knowledge that the threat has passed.

During the next stage, impact, physical destruction takes place. The period may be relatively short, as in an earthquake or avalanche, or relatively long, as in a hurricane or flood. This immediate destruction is considered primary impact. Very little can be done about it. But frequently, following the period of primary impact, chains of destruction initiated by the disaster may lead to further property damage or loss of life, as in the case of wounds that may prove to be lethal, or fires that frequently follow earthquakes. This is called secondary impact and is subject to human control to some extent. The appropriate course of action during impact is "holding on."

During the stage of isolation, which varies greatly with the location of the disaster area, the type of disaster, and the nature of the rescue facilities available, the disaster area finds itself cut off from outside support. The most appropriate action that can be taken by the disaster population involves taking inventory and then attempting to stop further damage or loss of life through secondary impact. Taking inventory may follow a common pattern. As persons emerge from the wreckage, they may initially feel that this disaster has happened to them alone, or at least that the damage is confined to the limits of their own perception. As they discover the true extent of the disaster, they may become more or less passive sightseers or engage in vigorous but somewhat random efforts to stem secondary impact.

In rescue, aid arrives from surrounding areas, and efforts to combat secondary impact come largely from three groups of people: the survivors themselves, organized units such as hospital emergency teams, and unorganized volunteers from the circumjacent neighborhoods.

When some sort of normality is restored, rehabilitation begins. Extensive reconstructive activities are initiated and implemented; the stage of rehabilitation lasts for a long period of time, involves a great number of workers, and requires much financing. The agencies carrying out rehabilitation tend to be well-established organizations like the Red Cross. As time passes, rehabilitative efforts become less intense.

Finally, the system achieves a state of irreversible change. This refers to changes, not in individuals, but in the structure of the community. Warning systems are improved, relief agencies reorganized, employment patterns affected, and so forth. A new steady state is achieved, but its characteristics differ from those of the predisaster conditions.

In *Tornado in Worcester* (1956), Anthony F.C. Wallace attempted to expand the temporal model of disaster by developing a framework for the analysis of spatial relationships with respect to the involvement of different geographic areas in the disaster. He distinguished five zones. The impact area itself could conveniently be divided into areas of total impact (e.g., that area over which the vortex of the tornado itself had passed) and fringe impact (e.g., those areas subject to the high winds around the edge of the vortex). Surrounding the area of impact was a filter area, whose residents were neighbors of those living in the impact area and who were ordinarily aware of the disaster during or shortly after the period of impact. These people supplied the disaster population with volunteers for rescue work. Beyond this was the area of the organized community, where local rescue teams such as ambulance units were activated and dispatched to the impact area. Finally, there was the area of regional aid, where organizations such as the Red Cross were located. Each of these areas played a part in the various temporal stages of the disaster.

*The Disaster Syndrome.* Wallace (1956: 109-41) suggests that where impact is sudden, unexpected, and destructive, and the population is ill-trained to cope with it, a common pattern of reaction emerges among the survivors, which Wallace refers to as the disaster syndrome. At first, survivors are described as dazed, stunned, or apathetic. They ignore or deny serious damage to the community. In the second stage, survivors become grateful for any help they receive and eager to establish the safety of their family and the rest of the community. In the next stage, there is a mildly euphoric identification with the community, and the population shares goods and pitches in enthusiastically to repair damages to the community. Finally, the euphoria dissipates, and the survivors more or less return to normal.

Wallace also proposes the existence of a counter-disaster syndrome, in which neighbors of the disaster population pour in to give immediate aid, but their behavior, generated largely by a sense of guilt over their own survival, tends to be hyperactive, inefficient, and somewhat irrational. This behavior pattern, akin to what has elsewhere been described as convergence behavior (Fritz and Mathewson, 1956), is not so clearly defined as the disaster syndrome. Furthermore, it may be an overly optimistic interpretation of what goes on following a disaster. No doubt some neighbors and friends feel guilty, and no doubt some portion of the crowds who seem to throng to the disaster area are motivated by a desire to help. But much of the literature too infrequently mentions looters and sightseers, who are not uncommon. Even so small a disaster as an automobile accident on an expressway can be relied upon to cause a certain number of drivers to slow down for a better look at the damage and the bodies.

*Dealing with Hurricanes.* A hurricane is one of the few types of disasters for which people seem, in some instances, to prepare. Residents of the equatorial Atlantic and Caribbean regions may not stay away from hurricane-prone coasts, but they keep track of all hurricanes or potential hurricanes. Some cities, such as Galveston, have taken what appear to be adequate protective measures.

Descriptions of the effects of hurricanes on less-developed communities may be found in Lessa's article "The Social Effects of Typhoon Ophelia (1960) on Ulithi," in A. Vayda's *Peoples and Cultures of the Pacific* (1968) and in Schneider's article in *Human Organization* (1957). Moore's report (1964) provides an excellent case study of hurricane Carla, which struck the gulf coast of Texas in 1961, killing forty-five and causing more than $400 million in damages.

It is curious to note that, in his study of four typhoons on Yap, Schneider states that one of the reactions of the Yapese that puzzled him considerably was their fear that the typhoons had destroyed most of the island's food supply. "The literal content of the concern over food supply was demonstrably unrealistic and grossly out of proportion to the real extent of the damage and deprivation. I was very puzzled when people told me on all sides, 'Alas, alas, no food,' and I spent a good deal of time after each typhoon, and particularly the last one, surveying the extent of damage and destruction both to housing and food resources. I am thus in a position to say that for all practical purposes, there was *some* destruction of food resources, but there was no danger that anyone would go hungry" (Schneider, 1957: 12).

Schneider's explanation for this unrealistic worry is that on Yap typhoons are regarded as supernatural events that take place because someone—someone on Yap—used magic to produce them. The typhoon is, so to speak, a symbol of disordered relationships.

Where the *exchange* of food is the symbol of good relations, it is the absence of food which symbolizes disturbed or broken relations. And when someone has sent a typhoon, relations are not too good. Therefore, the typhoon is seen as expressing a situation of broken relations, symbolized as "no food." It is at this level that the lament, "Ah piri e gafago, dari e thamunamun" ("Ah, alas, no food"), is meant literally. It is not at the level of concrete food at all, for they will voice this lament with food in their hands. [Schneider, 1957: 13]

Samoa suffered a severe hurricane during the period of my field work there—winds were measured at more than 120 miles per hour, and much of the housing was destroyed or damaged. Although there was some crop damage, particularly to breadfruit trees and banana plants, there was no significant shortage of food at any time following the storm. Yet, as on Yap, there was the constantly expressed fear, amounting at times to conviction, that the island would be in a state of famine. Many events only slightly out of the ordinary were interpreted in terms of the famine. A somewhat crowded bus on its way to outlying villages would provoke the comment that it must be full of townspeople leaving Pago Pago to look for food, and so on. In other words, there was an overall similarity between the response of the Yapese and the response of the Samoans to the same sort of storm and to its effects on a similar ecosystem (high volcanic islands). The single noticeable difference was that the Samoans did not attribute the coming of the hurricane to supernatural forces or the machinations of a magician; so their constant fear of famine could have nothing to do with the symbolic breaking up of social relations.

Perhaps the intervention of a magician is not required. Perhaps there need not be a symbol of disordered relationships. The exchange of food in Samoa is extremely important on ceremonial occasions, not for its nutrient value but for its ability to serve as the index of the importance of an event and as an index of any particular family's generosity. In short, there is a sense in which family dignity depends on giving away great amounts of food at ceremonial exchanges like funerals and marriages. Perhaps the social order need not be disrupted by a magician; perhaps even the possibility of famine may be quite enough to worry people.

*Regional Differences in Coping Styles.* Eyewitness accounts of pre-tornado conditions seem frequently to stress certain common points. The air is usually described as sultry, still, and oppressively hot and humid. Then the sky blackens or turns green, and large hailstones fall, accompanied by an intense display of lightning. As common as some of these signs may be, tornadoes occur in their absence. During the afternoon and evening of Wednesday, April 3, 1974, dozens of tornadoes swept through the American Midwest, causing more damage than any other series of storms in the history of the country and killing hundreds of people, the greatest loss of life since the famous tri-state tornado of 1925, described above in the discussion of tornadoes. It affected particularly Kentucky, Ohio, and Indiana.

I had the misfortune to be driving through central Indiana early on the afternoon of April 3 when the first tornado watch was set for that area. I took shelter in the town of Martinsville when the watch was changed to a tornado warning because a funnel cloud had been seen in the vicinity. This tornado missed Martinsville but struck another small town about ten miles away. I again took to the road, hoping to travel far enough north to be out of the area in which most of the trouble was expected. Soon after my somewhat hasty departure from Martinsville, however, the watch was expanded to include almost all of Indiana, and reports of tornadoes were being broadcast from the states on both sides, Illinois and Ohio. I still hoped to reach Chicago, which, with its sturdy reinforced concrete structures, represented a haven, but such was not to be the case. Approaching Lafayette on an interstate highway, I noticed the sky to the west and southwest darkening. A relatively isolated thunderstorm developed, pale green but punctuated only by occasional strokes of lightning. The storm was moving towards the northeast. Along its leading edge were numerous formations of large, globular, udderlike protrusions from the cloud base, forming a configuration resembling a photograph of a cobblestone street viewed upside down. Although I was unaware of any tornado warnings having been issued for the area—and I listened to the radio continuously, now that the station had given up music and simply broadcast reports concerning the waves of tornadoes sweeping across the state—I considered it prudent to move off the highway. The storm was moving in such a way as to cross the highway at about the same time I would reach that section of road.

The nearest town was Frankfort, Indiana. The tornado watch that had been set for Indiana now was changed to a warning, in effect for several communities, including Frankfort. I was faced with the problem of seeking some kind of shelter in a structure sturdy enough to withstand the fierce winds of a tornado funnel. However, I was a stranger in town. Although I presumed that there were basements in many of the residential buildings, I could hardly knock on someone's door and ask to use the cellar! The few public buildings in town to which I might have had access impressed me as flimsy affairs. I might eventually have found a suitable refuge, but I had already driven around the streets of Frankfort too long, for the sky was growing gloomier, and so was I. After trying the door of a sturdy Baptist church—which was locked—I took refuge in an Italian restaurant across the street. As I discovered shortly, the frame building was not as substantial as it appeared to be from outside, and there was no basement. Still, the windows were small, there were several internal walls, and the building itself provided some shelter. About thirty minutes later, as I sat in a booth regarding my dinner with a certain melancholy, a tornado funnel was damaging a schoolhouse in a town two miles away, and another storm—possibly the one I had left the highway to avoid—was virtually destroying the small village of Monticello, an hour's drive away. Curiously enough, in this same brief period, central Indiana experienced a rare earthquake, not very severe—4.4 on the Richter scale—but enough to jiggle the furniture in some houses and cause the residents to fear that they were being swept up in one of the storms. By ten in the evening, the danger to Frankfort was obviously past, and the warnings and watches were dropped.

The experience was interesting. Although I had avoided the funnels and had not, in fact, even seen any of them, I felt I had been close enough to observe some of the surrounding conditions. I was most impressed with the fact that, to the nonmeteorological eye, there were few features to distinguish the storms I had witnessed in Indiana from many such thunderstorms I had experienced in parts of the East and Midwest. First, although the weather was warm and steamy, it was not oppressively hot. Many people wore raincoats; some wore light sweaters. Next, there was never a continuous squall line, nor was the sky uniformly overcast; rather, there were separate bundles of cumulonimbus built up into turret after turret (which later proved to have "topped out" at an altitude greater than ten miles) with intermittent patches of hazy sunshine. These clouds, with the exception noted, were gray instead of green, and the overcast at Frankfort was gray, even when a funnel cloud was only a few miles away. I noticed only two bursts of hail, each lasting only a few seconds, and the hailstones themselves were so small as to be hardly noticeable. The frequency and intensity of the lightning did not seem unusual. Finally, the atmosphere itself was never still. Instead, there was always a breeze, and usually a rather stiff one, even in the absence of an immediate overcast.

I offer these observations only because it seems to be so often assumed that infallible signs are associated with the approach of a tornado. Although I have interviewed people concerning these signs and have often read about them, few of them were in evidence in central Indiana on April 3, 1974. One's own ability to sense "tornado weather" is not exceptionally reliable. The number of additional lives that would have been lost in the absence of the mass media is impossible to calculate.

Finally, it may be worthwhile to mention an impression I have gained in talking to people on the streets in Pennsylvania, on the one hand, and Indiana, on the other, during periods when tornado watches were in effect: Indianans take the threat of a tornado quite seriously, while people living near Philadelphia are likely to dismiss the threat of a tornado because "it can't happen here." During a tornado watch in Lansdale, Pennsylvania, a few miles from Philadelphia, I overheard a conversation between two men and a woman concerning the warning. One of the men shrugged the warning off as an impossibility; the other mentioned that when a warning was in effect one should be ready to move to a cellar; the woman, listening to the conversation uncomprehendingly, commented, "As bad as *that,* huh?" One sensed that for these people, such a disaster seemed as remote a possibility as an invasion by men from Mars. Yet the storms are by no means rare in Pennsylvania. The first tornado recorded in that state occurred in August, 1854. Since then, 235 *verified* tornadoes have occurred; many more were undoubtedly never reported. The southeastern piedmont area of Pennsylvania, which includes Philadelphia, has most often been struck by tornadoes, with a total of 63 since 1854. The city of Philadelphia itself has been struck at least 9 times in the same period, the last time in 1958 (Daily, 1970).

In connection with this sort of denial, it might also be pointed out that *within* tornado-ridden areas, in situations where communities cannot ignore the danger, there is frequently some local legend concerning the invulnerability of the community; other areas may be damaged but a ring of hills to the south of the town always protects it from tornadoes (Wichita, which was struck in 1965); or there is an old Indian myth that "no severe storm will ever hit this town" (Waco, which was struck in May 1953 [Flora, 1953: 125]). Needless to say, whatever comfort is provided to residents by such beliefs can be abruptly terminated when disaster strikes. That is to say, the belief that a tornado — or any other kind of disaster — "never happens here" is always true, until the moment when it is no longer true. (The same generalization applies in areas outside California with reference to earthquakes, a particularly severe example of which, occurring near New Madrid, Missouri, in 1811, was felt over a region of 301,656 square miles.) Furthermore, it seems possible that tornadoes are *more* likely to strike large communities such as Wichita and Waco, due to the added force of the "heat island" effect of urban areas on convection and subsequent severe weather development (Daily, 1970: 23; Chagnon, 1969).

Observers have remarked again and again on the disinclination of people in disaster-prone areas to take measures to protect themselves against possible calamity. People continue to move into flood plains, although they have been flooded out in the past and will be flooded out in the future. People build and rebuild cities atop major structural faults in the earth. This sort of fatalism is a well-recognized fact. Not so well known are the reasons for it.

In one of the very few studies attempting to explain this phenomenon, John H. Sims, a psychiatrist, and Duane D. Baumann, a geographer (Sims and Baumann, 1972), investigated human responses to tornado threats in several states in the northeastern and southeastern United States.

Beginning with the observation that the incidence of tornado deaths seemed to be much higher in the South than elsewhere in the nation, Sims and Baumann systematically examined the distribution of tornado-death days, county by county, and found that this was indeed so. (A tornado-death day was defined as a twenty-four-hour period, from midnight to midnight, during which one or more persons died as a result of tornadoes.) By far the highest number of tornado-death days occurred in the South, clustering around the borders between east Texas, Arkansas, and Louisiana.

One obvious explanation for this finding would be that the South has more tornadoes than other areas of the country, or has a higher population, or both. However, a national map of potential tornado casualties—using an index that takes into account the number of tornadoes an area has experienced as well as the population and size of the area—showed little perceptible agreement with the map of tornado-death days. The highest number of potential casualties has, in general, a more northerly distribution and is particularly high in the northern Midwest (Wisconsin, Illinois, Indiana, Ohio, and Michigan) and in the Middle Atlantic and Northeast. Thus, the most ready explanation is wrong.

Another possible explanation is that the South experiences a greater number of nocturnal tornadoes than the rest of the nation. Nighttime would catch many people asleep and would, in any case, obscure the approaching funnel so that fewer people would have any warning. But a comparison of the diurnal distribution of storms in southern and northern states showed no significant difference. In fact, Sims and Baumann found it interesting that Indiana and Louisiana had almost identical percentages of nocturnal tornadoes but Louisiana had a much higher number of death-days, despite the fact that Indiana had a greater casualty potential.

A third explanation involves the assumption that the tornadoes of the South are fiercer than elsewhere. Using length of path as a measure of a storm's strength, Sims and Baumann compared the tornadoes that occurred in Illinois and Alabama in the decade 1959 to 1968. Alabama, it turned out, experienced 143 tornadoes with an average path of 8.2 miles. Illinois reported 219 tornadoes with an average path of 9.3 miles. It would seem that Alabama not only experiences fewer tornadoes than Illinois, but that, in addition, they are not so fierce.

Sims and Baumann then proceeded to cast doubt on another assumption by simply asking if it were true that housing in the South is flimsier than elsewhere and that flimsy buildings offer less protection from high winds.

Going on to examine the possibility of differences in the efficacy of tornado-warning systems, they pointed out that prior to 1952 no community had access to a nationwide warning system, but the South had many more tornado-related deaths. Since 1953, information from the

Severe Local Storm Center has been serving all areas, but the tornado-death rate remains highest in the South.

The answer seems not to lie entirely in the environment; therefore, the authors reason, perhaps it lies partly in people themselves—in their personalities and cultures. Sims and Baumann began to think in terms of "coping style"—whether one takes an active or passive attitude towards environmental forces, something related to a sense of control over one's own fate, as opposed to, say, God's control over it or luck's control over it. This feeling that the source of control is "internal" rather than "external" seems to vary between individuals as well as between cultures. In many cases, the "internals" inevitably appear, at least to the scientific mind, as more progressive, realistic, intelligent, or healthy. To test the proposition that Northerners are predominantly "internal" while Southerners are more likely to be "external," the authors developed a brief scale of fifteen sentence completion items, designed to cover, first, the ways in which people respond to the threat of a tornado and, second, to measure the locus of control, internal versus external. Their sampling procedures are worth quoting.

> The sentence completion test was administered to a total of 57 respondents, 33 from four counties in Illinois, 24 from four counties in Alabama. All are white females, between the ages of 31 and 60, with at least an elementary school education, and from households with incomes ranging between $5,000 and $10,000. Within each state, the four counties were selected for comparability in respect to past occurrences of tornadoes, potential casualties, and occurrence of tornado-caused deaths. [Sims and Baumann, 1972: 1389]

Of the fifteen items, eight yielded significant differences between the Illinois and Alabama respondents. Three of these items dealt with the locus of control; five dealt primarily with responses to tornadoes.

The first sentence stem was: "As far as my own life is concerned, God..." The Alabamians tended to see God as playing an active role in their lives (e.g., "controls it"), while the Illinoisans more often tended to see God as a benevolent figure who makes one feel more secure but who does not interfere with one's life. "These data suggest that Southerners place more weight than Northerners on a force external to themselves—God—as a causal agent in their lives. They consequently feel themselves to have relatively less power in the determination of their own futures" (Sims and Baumann, 1972: 1389).

The next stem was, "I believe that luck..." Here, most respondents from both states came up with idiosyncratic responses, but nevertheless, more Southerners tended to attribute a great deal of importance to luck, while Northerners either played down its importance or denied its existence. These responses again suggested differences in the locus of control.

In completing the sentence, "Getting ahead in the world results from..."

> the Alabamians again emphasize their belief in a future controlled by an external force; 46 percent see success as coming either directly from God, or indirectly from God via moral behavior. Less than a third of the Alabamians see success as resulting from their own efforts. In direct contrast are the respondents from Illinois, two-thirds of whom are believers in the Protestant Ethic—success results from hard work, one form of the more abstract conviction that one's future results from what one does himself. [Sims and Baumann, 1972: 1390]

Of the five sentence stems dealing with the tornado experience, three refer to the tornado threat itself. "During the time when a tornado watch is out, I..." elicits responses that differ in a number of ways from North to South. Alabamians tend to depend on themselves. They "watch the sky" or "look at the clouds," while Illinoisans tend more often to depend on mass media—television or radio—or to use some other form of technology such as barometers. Illinoisans also take direct action, like alerting others or seeking shelter, with far greater frequency than Alabamians. The Illinoisans have "trust in technological expertise, in the authority of science, and, indeed, in man's organized, social power to confront and cope with (if not conquer) nature. But each Alabamian is on his own and faces the whirlwind alone with his God" (Sims and Baumann, 1972: 1390).

The same difference is reflected in responses to the stem, "The best way of identifying 'tornado weather' is..." The Illinoisans more often use technology; the Alabamians more often use their own senses. According to their responses to the next stem, "The job done by the weather bureau in forecasting tornadoes...", more Illinoisans than Alabamians see the weather bureau as trustworthy.

"The survivors of a tornado..." elicits more "active" responses from Illinoisans (e.g., "need to be helped") and more emotion-oriented responses from Alabamians (e.g., "feel terrible"). The final stem, "A community's response to the disaster of a tornado...", elicits a curious set of responses. The majority of respondents from both states indicate that the community gives assistance to the survivors (e.g., "is to help the needy") but many more Alabamians do so than Illinoisans (79 percent versus 55 percent). On the other hand, 21 percent of the Illinoisans commented on the psychological effects of the disaster, noting that it "brings people together" or "brings out the curious," whereas no Alabamians made such a response. Sims and Baumann comment that these Illinoisans are "sufficiently removed from the shock experience to give responses that comment objectively on psychological phenomena." It seems to me that it also requires removal from the shock to think about giving assistance to the survivors. The relative lack of personal involvement on the part of the Illinois respondents may be related to their dependence on the mass media for information about storm developments: reliance on community-organized communications facilities such as TV stations may imply reliance on community-organized rescue facilities such as the Red Cross or the National Guard. This lack of direct involvement in the business of others has its less healthy aspect, but let us not make too much of what seven Illinos women say in response to an abstract query.

All in all, say Sims and Baumann, the sentence stems dealing with locus of control

> reveal Illinoisans to be more autonomous, more prone to see themselves as responsible for directing their own lives, and more confident in their efficaciousness. On the other hand, Alabamians are seen to be more heteronomous, feeling themselves to be moved by external forces—fate, luck, and particularly God. They are consequently less confident in themselves as causal agents, less convinced of their ability to engage in effective action. [Sims and Baumann, 1972: 1391]

Responses to the items dealing with the tornado experience show that the Illinoisans are generally more active and display more objectivity and rationality in reacting to a tornado and more acceptance of technology and authority. The Alabamians are passive, and they tend to ignore technological aids.

These differences in coping styles are surely not the only factors involved but, the authors argue, "may be relevant to the disproportionately higher death rate from tornadoes in the South. Fatalism, passivity, and perhaps most important, lack of trust in and inattention to society's organized systems of warning constitute a weak defense against the terrible strike of the tornado" (Sims and Baumann, 1972: 1391).

This article appeared in *Science,* the official journal of the American Association for the Advancement of Science. The brouhaha following its publication was remarkable to observe. Such a slur on Southern character could not pass without strenuous objection—"emotional," "irrational," "passive," "superstitious" indeed! The objections ranged from the obvious (the sample was too small to warrant the generalizations) to the curious (one respondent claimed that *his* family handled tornado threats differently, thereby arguing from a sample of one household). Other letters to the editor pointed out, accurately enough, that differences in housing styles could not be so easily dismissed, that we knew little about the distribution of basements, root cellars, and other suitable storm shelters.

Well, what do Sims and Baumann really have? They apparently have a real difference between Alabama and Illinois in terms of the proportion of observed deaths from tornadoes as against the expected number. Taking the number of reported tornadoes into account, the Illinois counties seem to experience fewer deaths despite a greater casualty potential. Then too, the authors have noted real differences in sentence-stem responses which seem to indicate that the Alabamians place their fate in the hands of God, that they depend on their own senses to warn them of approaching danger, and that they are somewhat more emotional or empathic. Assuming these differences are real, the question becomes one of how these differences are related to one another (if in fact they are).

The question is important, and the answer given by Sims and Baumann is suggestive but not conclusive. The roots of their difficulties are largely methodological.

To begin with, a "tornado-death day" may not really be the best way to measure fatalities caused by tornadoes since it depends on type frequency rather than token frequency. In other words, a tornado-death day is a twenty-four-hour period during which "one or more" tornado-related fatalities occurs. Suppose that between 1916 and 1953, a given county in Alabama experienced five separate 24-hour periods during which tornadoes killed one or more people. That county would be rated as having five tornado-death days. And suppose an Illinois county experienced only one twenty-four-hour period during which a tornado killed one or more people. That county would have only one tornado-death day. Yet, if each of the Alabama tornadoes killed only one person, and if the single Illinois tornado managed to kill one hundred people, it would be misleading to argue that Alabamians cope less effectively with tornadoes than Illinoisans do. To be fair, however, we need to note that the concept of death days prevents a region's score from being unnaturally high when an unusual number of storms happen to strike major cities in that region.

Similar objections could be raised against the means of measuring potential casualties from tornadoes. The heavy band of potential casualties running through the Midwest, Middle Atlantic, and New England states may be, as much as anything else, an artifact of population density. A high population density itself would boost the number of potential casualties and, more than that, it would imply that any given tornado is more likely to be reported there than in areas of low population density.

One might even argue that in densely populated areas, single tornadoes are more likely to be reported as two or more separate storms. Since tornadoes frequently change shape, skip from place to place, and occur in groups, the possibility of overreporting is real enough. All of this would add — without justification — to the potential casualty rating an area receives, and would increase the apparent danger in the densely populated areas of the North and lessen the apparent danger in the less populated parts of the South.

The question that really renders the relationship between tornado deaths and sentence-stem responses problematic is that of sampling and control. The reader is given no idea of how the fifty-seven respondents were chosen. Moreover, all of the variables that were presumably controlled for were stated in terms of the range of their values, rather than their mean values. This is unfortunate indeed, especially since the mean values for the Alabama and Illinois groups must have been available to the investigators. As it now stands, the respondents from Alabama could all have been white females who are sixty years old, high school dropouts, living in isolated rural communities or on small farms, with an income of $5,000; respondents from Illinois could all have been white females, thirty-one years old, college educated, living in suburbs or cities, with incomes of $10,000. That is to suggest that what Sims and Baumann got were socially desirable responses from elderly ladies in the rural South, and tough-minded responses from liberated urban housewives in Illinois. This may not be true at all — but who can tell? Further, aside from the size, selection, and nature of the female sample, what about the men? One wonders whether Alabama men would be so passive and pious.

The Sims and Baumann study, for all its methodological weaknesses, is infinitely better than no study at all, however, for some of the facts concerning human responses to the threat of disaster are undeniable. One of these facts is that many people seem to care very little that they live under conditions of imminent doom. We most often take it for granted that under dangerous conditions people experience fear and take protective action. But when it comes to natural disasters, this commonsense assumption seems not to hold true; Sims and Baumann are among the few investigators who have paid any attention to this rather startling fact (but see also Burton, 1972, Burton et al., 1968).

*Survival in Hostile Environments.* Many of the areas we have described sound hostile to man but they need not be lethal, even in the absence of other human beings. Although an isolated individual might perish in a strange environment, human beings, once organized into cultures, are highly adaptable creatures. Some groups of Eskimos live along the shores of the Arctic Ocean where no vegetation exists beyond lichens and occasional pieces of driftwood. Others, such as the Kalahari Bushmen or the central tribes of Australia, seem to exist in equally harsh circumstances, and as far as it is possible to tell, they are as content as any of the rest of us.

We tend to think of people such as Eskimos and Bushmen as living a hand-to-mouth existence, surviving from one moment to the next, barely keeping ahead of starvation or dehydration, not to mention sunburn, frostbite, or punctured feet. Yet, as we have seen, some recent ecological studies of the !Kung Bushmen have demonstrated that most of their time is spent sitting around and chatting with one another (R.B. Lee, 1969). Let us emphasize the fact that the Bushmen live in an extreme environment — a hot, dry desert, no doubt one of the most inhospitable places on earth. How easy it must have been for hunters and gatherers to have made a living where Miami now stands.

The ability to survive hostile environments depends to a great extent on one's capacity for utilizing what food sources exist, rather than what one might prefer. *Escalope de Veau Chanticleer* might not be easy to come by, and one might need to learn to eat like the Shoshoni of the Great Basin, running down an antelope on foot, disemboweling it, and eating its intestines as one long tube, squeezing the contents out the other end. Read Dougal Robertson's *Survive the Savage Sea* (1973) for a case study in making the most of what you have.

This matter of gastronomy is an interesting subject but, for the moment, let us note that probably the best guide to survival in hostile or extreme environments is to be found in Nesbitt, Pond, and Allen's *The Survival Book* (1968). Should you be shipwrecked, or should your plane light in an uninhabited area, land or sea, you would want a copy at hand. All climatic areas are covered. Unfortunately, Nesbitt et al. are rather weak on the identification of poisonous plants:

> If you are not sure of your identification of a plant, test it before you eat it in any quantity. First take a mouthful, chew it and hold it in your mouth for a few minutes. If it has a bitter taste or is disagreeable in any other way, spit it out. Obviously a bitter taste is not always an indication of poison — for example, olives and lemons are bitter. But even a nonpoisonous plant with a disagreeable taste can make you ill, so don't take unnecessary chances. [Nesbitt et al., 1968: 54]

Here is an observer of a somewhat different mind, quoting a knowledgeable survivor of the Australian desert:

> My bush-culture friend, H.A. Lindsay, insists *witjuti* grubs (plump ugly insect larvae) are not only the perfect nutritional food, but delicious as well. I

will listen to him on other things, but not on this. He has for the other things an encyclopedic knowledge of what is edible and what is not among the thousands of wild vegetables in Australia. Few flowers here are innocent. Our literature's subsistence means in the wilderness is eating "berries." One of the popular natural food nuts the other day declared there were no inedible plants that tasted good; nature does not deceive, he said. Well, as a teacher of American jungle fighters in northern Australia and the islands in the second World War Lindsay propounded his Four-Hour test for edibility: "First crush it and smell it; if it has the characteristic smell of peach leaves and bitter almonds, this reveals the presence of prussic acid, a very deadly and swift poison. If it smells all right, crush some of it and rub it on the skin inside your elbow. If it doesn't raise blisters or make the skin red and sore, try a bit on your tongue. If it doesn't sting or burn and the flavor seems all right, chew a little, gargle the juice in the back of your throat, and spit it out. Now wait to see if your throat becomes sore. If it doesn't, eat a *little* of it and wait for four hours, to see if any ill effects in the way of vomiting, giddiness, internal pains, or purging follow. If there are no ill effects, it may be safe to eat a quantity of it." [Greenway, 1972: 192]

# CHAPTER FOUR

# Constructed Environments

Initially I described three main types of ecosystems characterized by different environments: the natural environment, the man-made environment, and the interpersonal environment. Having dealt at some length with the interactions between people and their naturally occurring environments, we are now in a position to deal with people and the other two kinds of environments, which may collectively be called constructed environments since both are functions of human convention, one consisting of artifacts and the other of normative behavior.

## Manipulation of Interpersonal Space

This section will examine some ways of describing the spatial aspects of interpersonal relationships, the rules governing such relationships, and some of the conceptual mechanisms behind them.

### Proxemics

There is no widely accepted name for the study of interpersonal space and the management of space-related relationships. Proxemics seems as good a candidate as any, though it has not been used much outside of the discipline of anthropology.

*Dimensions of Approach.* Edward Hall has coined the term proxemics to refer to the ways in which people structure space in their relationships with other human beings (Hall, 1963, 1969, 1974; Delong, 1971). Hall thinks that proxemic behavior is manifested on three levels.

The first level, the "infracultural," is concerned with spatial behavior that goes beyond culture and has its base in the evolutionary past. Research at this level is concerned with human territoriality and the effects of crowding.

The "precultural" level is concerned with how people use their senses in the perception of space—this is the physiological level of human experience to which culture lends structure and meaning. Hall's precultural level seems to involve certain common but variable properties of perception, such as the sense of one's movement through space and the perception of distance. That these perceptions are culturally modifiable, even in their most rudimentary form, has been demonstrated in recent studies that show that people are differentially susceptible to optical illusions, depending on the kind of environment they grew up in. People who spent their childhood in "carpentered" environments, in which artifacts are dominated by right angles—ordinary crates and rectangular houses, for example—rather than round contours, are predisposed towards the perception of certain illusory effects, as are people who grew up in areas where landscape is dominated by distant vistas, such as plains, rather than complicated proximate textures, such as forests (Segall et al., 1966).

Hall's third level, the "microcultural," deals with the structuring of space as it is modified by the effects of culture. This level is further broken down into three aspects: fixed-feature, semifixed-feature, and informal space.

Fixed-feature space consists simply of those spatial features that are materially fixed in the environment of a particular culture. They are the features of space that individuals cannot do very much about, and they include the layout of cities and the arrangement of interior spaces such as rooms.

The semifixed characteristics of space involve furniture arrangements, screens, movable partitions, and the provision of involvement shields of one sort or another as influences on human interaction.

The third aspect of proxemics, informal space, is concerned with how people actively use the fixed and semifixed features of their surroundings to structure small amounts of space in face-to-face encounters with each other: how close one gets to others, whether one faces them while talking to them or looks away, and so forth. Evans (1973) provides a summary of some relevant research, emphasizing the relationship between personality characteristics and variations in the management of informal space. Another important research summary is in Lett et al. (1969), "A Proposition Inventory of Research on Interpersonal Distance."

As a result of Hall's cross-cultural experiences—he was a government employee associated with a postwar program of redevelopment—he became aware that several systems were involved in interactional distance, or informal space. Eventually he was able to reduce proxemic behavior to eight different systems or dimensions (Hall, 1963). The whole field of the management of spatial relationships in encounters is extremely complex, but if these relationships are viewed in terms of Hall's eight dimensions they become more comprehensible.

The eight dimensions identified by Hall are: (1) postural-sex identifiers; (2) sociofugal-sociopetal orientation, referring to mutual orientation; (3) kinesthetic factors, based on what two people need to do in order to touch each other; (4) the touch code, involving the major ways in which people touch each other; (5) retinal combination, which refers to eye contact; (6) thermal factors, or the degree of heat flow between people; (7) olfaction, or smelling; and (8) voice loudness.

One of the major problems Hall encountered in studying proxemic behavior was recording it. He wanted to be able to record what was going on in a given interaction accurately enough so that someone else, reading one's notes, could know about it too. Hall was concerned with developing a technique for recording proxemic behavior according to his system of eight dimensions in the same way that a composer writes out a musical score on a sheet of paper so that someone else can later read the notes and reproduce the music the composer had in mind.

For the first of his proxemic dimensions, Hall proposed three ways of recording behavior. The first method uses abbreviated descriptive phrases, the second uses pictographic symbols, and the third has a number code. Other dimensions are noted either pictographically or numerically. In actual research, of course, the number code is the easiest to use as it takes only a few minutes to memorize.

1. Postural-sex identifiers. In trying to reduce all the possible positions that people can assume into some manageable number, Hall identified three major postures, any of which can of course be assumed by either sex. The subject could be (1) lying down, (2) sitting or squatting, or (3) standing. In the postural-sex identifiers, there are six possibilities, which could be recorded as shown in figure 8.

Here and elsewhere in this notation system, Hall intends that the more active subject in the encounter be noted first. For example, if a standing man is talking to a more relaxed woman, the encounter at that point in time is noted as 56. Since the man is active, his posture is noted first.

2. The sociofugal-sociopetal axis. These are terms coined by Humphry Osmond (1957) to describe spatial arrangements that keep people apart or

|  | Abbrev. descriptive phrase | Picto- graphic symbol | Number code |
|---|---|---|---|
| Man prone | m/pr | | 1 |
| Man sitting | m/si | | 3 |
| Man standing | m/stg | | 5 |
| Female prone | f/pr | | 2 |
| Female sitting | f/si | | 4 |
| Female standing | f/stg | | 6 |

FIG. 8. SEX AND BASIC POSTURES.

Reproduced by permission of the American Anthropological Association from *American Anthropologist* 65(5): 1003-26, 1963.

draw them together. Sociopetal arrangements tend to increase interaction and sociofugal ones to decrease it. Hall defines this axis according to the orientation of bodies to one another, and any of nine major positions can be identified, as shown in figure 9.

Interpretation of these codes is relatively straightforward if it is understood that the pictographs represent people viewed from above, their orientation represented by the dark circle. In 0, for example, two people face one another. This orientation is used when people want to talk to each other with some intensity. Position 2 is more casual. Position 4 is used when two people are viewing something, such as a parade. Subsequent positions are increasingly sociofugal until, with position 8, we reach a point at which communication becomes positively difficult. It should be noted that a person wishing to disengage from an encounter with another can indicate and accomplish this by assuming, gradually, increasingly sociofugal orientations. Also, such sociofugal positions are a means of defending one's personal space under crowded conditions.

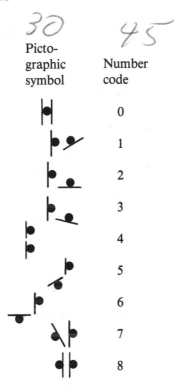

FIG. 9. SOCIOFUGAL-SOCIOPETAL AXIS.

Reproduced by permission of the American Anthropological Association from *American Anthropologist* 65(5): 1003-26, 1963.

3. Kinesthetic factors describe interpersonal distances and are based on what people can do to each other with their arms, legs, and bodies. Another person may be perceived as close to us, not only because we *see* the person nearby, but because he or she can grab us, caress us, or punch us if so inclined. There is thus an inner circle, so to speak, within which kinesthetic factors must be accounted for. Basically, Hall proposes that one person can touch another in four different ways: with the head or body; with the elbows or knees extended; with the arms fully extended; or with the arm and leg extended and the body leaning towards the other person. These distances are designated by the numbers 1 through 4. Because one person may assume one position while the second person in the encounter may assume a different position, at least two numbers will be

needed to describe a given encounter, one for each person. Moreover, there are intermediate positions. For example, there may be more space between the persons than is suggested by position 11 (which is very close indeed) but less than in position 12 (in which the two participants are one elbow's length away from one another). Hall proposes that the insertion of a zero between the two numbers can indicate such an intermediate position. The example described above would be designated by number 102. Eliminating redundancies, Hall states that eleven possible combinations can account for all of the positions that one is likely to observe. The pictographs and their numerical codes are shown in figure 10.

Code

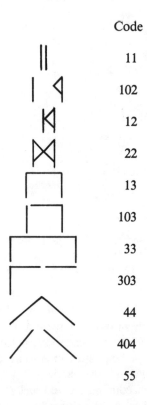

| | 11

102

12

22

13

103

33

303

44

404

55

Fig. 10. Kinesthetic Codes. Touch can occur through extensions of the body, such as projectiles.

Reproduced by permission of the American Anthropological Association from *American Anthropologist* 65(5): 1003-26, 1963.

The symbols should be clear enough. In position 102, for example, the participants in the encounter are less than one elbow's length away from one another, but rather more distant than is indicated in position 11, where touching is imminent. In position 33, the distance is such that participants can touch one another only if they both fully extend their arms. In the final category, 55, which has no pictograph, are distances at which people can reach each other only by throwing stones, shooting arrows or bullets, and so forth. Since modern nuclear weapons are projectiles that can trigger the movement of other projectiles, it is apparent that we all occupy the category of 55 with respect to one another, but in practice the category is restricted to face-to-face meetings.

4. The touch code describes the characteristics of the touch, once it occurs, including duration and quality. It is delineated on a seven-point scale for each participant in the encounter, generating a matrix in which the designations vary from 00 — mutual caressing — to 66 — no contact at all. The seven points of the scale are: (0) holding and caressing, (1) feeling or caressing, (2) extended or prolonged holding, (3) holding, (4) spot touching, as in tapping someone on the shoulder, (5) accidental touching, as in brushing against somebody in a crowd, and (6) no contact.

5. Retinal combination refers to the amount of eye contact that each person maintains with the other. There are four points on the scale, which are named according to the part of the retina that the other's image falls on, as shown in figure 11.

Hall outlines four major possibilities for eye contact: (1) foveal (sharp), (2) macular (clear), (3) peripheral (fuzzy), and (8) no eye contact at all. Because each person can fix the other's image in any of these ways, there are several possible combinations. Hall admits that determining the degree of eye contact is difficult in practice but maintains that it is not impossible with training. Eye contact has been linked to some very elementary behavioral forms. Infants are more aroused when they are shown two circles placed side by side — like eyes — than when they see circles one above the other. They are even more aroused if solid black circles, like pupils, are placed within the "eyes" (Coss, 1965). Eye contact is important in establishing a willingness to communicate with others, in signalling threat or a desire for intimacy, in indicating dominance or submission. In European or American conversations, the person who "has the floor" breaks off eye contact and looks away from the listener (although he or she may glance up periodically at grammatical breaks to make certain that the listener is paying attention) and restores eye contact when he or she has finished speaking and is willing to give the floor to the other (Kendon, 1967).

6. Thermal factors have not received much attention in the behavioral sciences, but Hall suggests that they are important enough to warrant

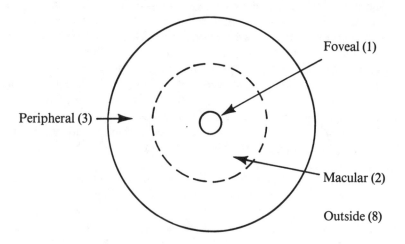

FIG. 11. RETINAL SCHEMA.

Reproduced by permission of the American Anthropological Association from *American Anthropologist* 65(5): 1003-26, 1963.

much more research. He tells a story about sitting next to another person at a dinner table and suddenly feeling he had to draw his hand away, without knowing why. When he experimented and put his hand back where it had been, he noticed that he could feel the heat radiating from the other's hand, which was close to his on top of the table. One can feel this effect by holding the palm of the hand close to one's face, an inch or two away.

Since so little is known about heat zones, Hall is willing to map out only four possibilities, expecting that others will be added in the future. These are (1) conducted heat detected, through touching; (2) radiant heat detected; (3) heat probably detected; and (4) heat not detected.

7. Olfaction is another proxemic dimension with which too little work has been done, although it receives considerable attention from the general public. We constantly witness advertisements that tell us we should not offend other people with the odor of our breath or our bodies. Perhaps advertising in some ways is ahead of the behavioral sciences in determining what is important to people in their daily lives.

The sociological approach to odors might ask:

What effects do differences in culture and life-style have upon the perception and generation of odors? What social meanings are attributed to such perceived and generated odors? What social functions do such meanings fulfill? More specifically: Why are Negroes and lower-class persons often stereotyped as being "foul smelling"? To what extent are alleged malodors used as grounds for avoiding interaction? What is the significance of the fart taboo? What are the dynamics of odor manipulation? Why, for instance, do people perfume? And does the use of incense during religious services have a sociological relevance? [Largey and Watson, 1972: 1021]

The above approach takes the quality of an odor for granted and focuses instead upon the meaning bestowed upon a given smell by the people doing the smelling—the meaning of course having been learned from others. A different approach is adopted in Turk et al.'s *Human Responses to Environmental Odors* (1974), which deals, in part, with the physical properties of odors as well as the assessment of individual and group responses to smells.

Since so little is known of this proxemic dimension, Hall has simplified the recording as much as possible. He uses five categories: (1) differentiated body odor detectable, including foot odor, sexual odors, and armpit odor; (2) undifferentiated body odor detectable: one can smell heat and moisture from another but cannot locate any particular source; (3) breath detectable; (4) olfaction probably present; and (5) olfaction not present.

8. Voice loudness, the last of Hall's proxemic dimensions, is modified to conform to the established conventions regarding distance, relationship between participants, and the situation or subject being discussed. In other words, one regulates the volume of one's voice so as to talk more loudly at a distance, when angry, or at a New Year's Eve party. Moderate voice levels are normal in encounters in which the participants don't know each other well.

Standards of correct voice volume vary greatly from one society to another, but since no universal standards have been developed, the investigator has to use his or her own culturally calibrated judgment. Hall thinks that seven steps are sufficient to cover most transactions: (0) silent, (1) very soft, (2) soft, (3) normal, (4) normal +, (5) loud, and (6) very loud.

A few years ago, in concert with other researchers at the New Jersey Bureau of Research in Neurology and Psychiatry, I attempted to develop a workable proxemics notation form. The sample form (figure 12) was serviceable enough to cover most transactions, although it took a minimum of several seconds to record each event.

Age _____     Diagnostic category _____          Residence _____          Date _____

Age _____     Diagnostic category _____          Residence _____          Test site _____

Observations

|          | A | B | C | D | E | F |
|----------|---|---|---|---|---|---|
| 1) S-P      |   |   |   |   |   |   |
| 2) SFP      |   |   |   |   |   |   |
| 3) Kin.     |   |   |   |   |   |   |
| 4) Touch    |   |   |   |   |   |   |
| 5) Visual   |   |   |   |   |   |   |
| 6) Thermal  |   |   |   |   |   |   |
| 7) Olfactory|   |   |   |   |   |   |
| 8) V. vol.  |   |   |   |   |   |   |

FIG. 12. PROXEMICS NOTATION FORM.

Hall does not argue that he has invented the definitive means for recording the dimensions of proxemic interaction. He anticipates that many changes must be made in the future if the scheme is to prove valuable. Many of these changes will depend upon research into such subjects as eye contact, and many of the scale steps will ultimately depend upon how the "natives" themselves differentiate such dimensions as eye contact, rather than upon categories developed a priori by the investigator.

Hall has done an excellent job of outlining the sensory modalities by means of which communication, sometimes of the most subtle sort, takes place. The world about us, human and nonhuman, is perceived in terms of these sensory experiences. But with the exception of visual impressions, we only infrequently talk about them, and then only when our thresholds of pleasantness and unpleasantness are exceeded. Few people comment on the external temperature, for example, unless it is unusually high or low. It seems that when the temperature is within normal limits there is no comfortable way to say so in everyday discourse. There are standardized phrases in American English to deal with extreme temperatures—"Hot enough for you?" and so on—but about the best we can do with optimal thermal conditions is something like, "Nice day, isn't it?" in which there is no mention of temperature.

In other words, we may discuss objects, persons, or events as they appear, while ordinarily taking their nonvisual sensory impact for granted. The city dweller may return from a summer visit to Yosemite and Yellowstone national parks and assemble a group of friends in order to bore them with slides (after having previously bored them with redundant postcards). But the traveler does not bring back a sample of the odor of Yosemite's pines or the sulfurous stink of Yellowstone's geyser basins. Usually the odors are not even mentioned, although they may be as unique in the traveler's experience as the visual aspects of the parks. If a person were even to attempt a description of the olfactory spaces through which he or she had moved—beyond the most elementary level, as in, "You ought to smell the trees"—if a person were to be more articulate and precise, he or she might be thought odd unless the gathering were a heavily intellectual one. Only poets devote much attention to odors and textures. But on those occasions when they try, even military heroes can succeed in being vivid. In *The Seven Pillars of Wisdom,* T.E. Lawrence describes his meeting with regular British troops for the first time in months, after sojourning with Arab irregulars:

> The intruding contrast mixed with longing for home, to sharpen my faculties and make fertile my distaste, till not merely did I see the unlikeliness of race, and hear the unlikeliness of language, but I learned to pick between

their smells: the heavy standing, curdled sourness of dried sweat in cotton, over the Arab crowds; and the feral smell of English soldiers; that hot pissy aura of thronged men in woollen clothes: a tart pungency, breath-catching, ammoniacal; a fervent fermenting naphtha-smell. [Lawrence, 1935: 642]

*Zones of Distance.* Driving one morning along the streets of a city, I stopped behind a string of other cars waiting for a red light. The driver in front of me had stopped some distance from the car in front of him, and while everyone was waiting for the light to change, he slowly crept up to close the distance. I felt obliged to shift into first gear and keep a close distance behind him. Then I noticed in the rearview mirror that two or three cars behind me were also creeping along, maintaining a close distance. Everyone in line felt the same compulsion to stay only a few feet behind the next car while waiting for the light to change.

This urge to maintain an agreed-upon distance between cars waiting for a light — even when there is no necessity for it, no threat of other cars cutting into the line, and even while it involves the inconvenience of creeping along behind another driver — illustrates what Edward Hall means by the term *hidden dimension.* The rules are unspoken but are followed implicitly. An almost moral force seems to operate here. Maintaining a given distance between waiting cars is the "right" thing to do, and people will work to do so. Similar considerations hold true in the maintenance of "proper distances" between animals, including people, in other situations.

Two concepts concerned with distance between individual animals of different species have been developed by H. Hediger, a Swiss animal psychologist (Hediger, 1968: 39-50). One of these is "flight distance." A wild animal in the field will permit a human being to get only so close before it flees. Unless the animal takes cover, it may stop after it puts a certain amount of distance between itself and the intruder, while continuing to keep an eye on the intruder. Hediger's term for this interspecies spacing mechanism is flight distance. In general, an animal's flight distance varies directly with the size of the animal. Larger animals, like elephants, may have a flight distance of half a mile; smaller animals, like lizards, have a flight distance of only a few feet. Flight distances have been found to be so precise and consistent that they can sometimes be measured in inches. Animals in captivity may become accustomed to the presence of people to the extent that they will permit an intruder to approach more closely than in the wild. Thus, they may develop a "secondary" flight distance in zoos, circuses, or homes.

In many predatory and aggressive animals, flight distance is maintained until the animal is cornered. When it is unable to retreat further, the animal turns and begins to stalk the intruder or openly attack him. The name given to this narrow zone separating flight from attack is "critical distance." Flight distance is radial, in that the animal may attempt to escape from the intruder in any direction; critical distance, however, is always linear, in that the animal approaches the intruder directly.

Hediger makes the point that lion trainers use these concepts to place lions where they want them within the cage (Hediger, 1968: 123-24). The trainer approaches the lion until the animal flees; that is, until its flight distance has been penetrated. The lion eventually finds itself in a location in which all avenues of escape are closed. As the trainer continues to approach, penetrating the animal's critical distance, the lion turns and stalks the man. This stalking is always direct, so that an animal will deliberately surmount intervening objects, such as short platforms, to reach the trainer. In order to get the lion to remain on the platform, the trainer quickly steps out of the critical zone, at which point the lion stops stalking and remains on the platform. By the careful manipulation of these distances and reactions—for which they have no name—trainers can get beasts of prey to perform on tables, chairs, pyramids, and seesaws. The various props that trainers use, the chairs and whips, come to be seen by animals as an extension of the trainer himself. These and other props, such as whistles and pistols, also add to the audience's enjoyment by lending an air of drama to the situation. No doubt bullfighters have an equally precise knowledge of distancing mechanisms.

"Individual distance" is Hediger's term for the minimum distance within which animals of the same species may approach one another (Hediger, 1968: 83). It is analogous to the term "personal space" as used by behavioral scientists in that both terms denote a kind of conceptual bubble that the animal carries around. The radius of that bubble represents the distance at which conspecifics keep each other. The distance varies with circumstances: smaller during rutting seasons, for example, and larger for dominant animals than for animals that occupy lower positions in the hierarchy of status. It also seems true in many human societies that the more exalted one's position is, the less closely he or she may be approached by outsiders. Hall (1969: 124) quotes Theodore F. White's description of how John F. Kennedy's individual distance suddenly increased when his nomination became a sure thing.

Social distance (Hediger, 1961: 54) is to a group of animals what individual distance is to an individual animal; it is a zone that contains the group and, in a sense, belongs to it.

Social distance in animals reminds me of an elastic rubber band, which invisibly connects all members of a group. This social distance is specific and can be measured exactly in meters and centimeters. If this band is stretched over and above its specific value, the result will be an unhealthy reaction. [Hediger, 1961: 54]

When animals exceed the customary distance between themselves and other members of the group, they lose communication with the other members and are exposed to various dangers, such as predation. Among some animals, an unusual extension of social distance is a sign of severe illness.

Hall points out that social distance is not always rigidly fixed but is partly determined by environment.

> When the young of apes and humans are mobile but not yet under control of the mother's voice, social distance may be the length of her reach. This is readily observed among the baboons in a zoo. When the baby approaches a certain point, the mother reaches out to seize the end of its tail and pull it back to her. When added control is needed because of danger, social distance shrinks. To document this in man, one has only to watch a family with a number of small children holding hands as they cross a busy street. [Hall, 1969: 15]

Hall has himself elaborated on Hediger's discussion of distancing. He has done a sort of global coding of interactional distances. He classifies distance zones into four types—intimate, personal, social, and public—in order of increasing distance. Each has what he calls a close phase and a far phase. These may be described very briefly.

Intimate distance, close phase, is the distance at which physical contact is imminent; wrestlers, lovers, and subway riders are likely to spend some time at the close phase of intimate distance from one another. One can feel the heat from another's body, or smell the odor of his or her hair or breath.

Intimate distance, far phase, involves a separation of bodies by about six to eighteen inches. Touching another is easily accomplished; heat and smell may still be detected. This is the customary conversational distance in some societies, but Americans find it too short for comfort.

Personal distance, close phase, is found at a distance of one and a half to two and a half feet. One's perception of the other is clear and sharp and he can be physically reached without difficulty. It is seen during conversations in America, particularly in crowded settings like parties, or in other settings where the background noise level is likely to be high. Under quieter circumstances, "a wife can stay inside the circle of her husband's close personal zone with impunity. For another woman to do so is an entirely different story" (Hall, 1969: 120).

The personal distance, far phase, constitutes a zone about two and a half to four feet away from a person. The maintenance of the far phase of personal distance is sometimes described as "keeping somebody at arm's length." The other can be reached by stretching out one's arm. Subjects of personal interest can be discussed at this distance, at a voice level somewhat above that customarily used in previous phases. Body heat and odor are usually not detectable.

Social distance, close phase, occurs at four to seven feet. Interactants are too far away from one another to touch easily. This is the distance at which impersonal business is dealt with. People who work in the same place tend to interact with one another at this distance; it is frequently used at casual gatherings as well.

Social distance, far phase, occurs at seven to twelve feet. At this distance, some of the details of another's appearance are lost, such as the capillaries in the eyes. Transactions taking place in this zone are likely to be not only impersonal but formal. Important people may use desks or other props to keep visitors at this distance. The voice level is necessarily raised somewhat. It is often the distance to which people retreat from a group of others when they don't want to be involved in what is going on.

Public distance, close phase, occurs at twelve to fifteen feet. Here the voice must be relatively loud in order for communication to occur, and interactants tend to use a formal style of dialogue, being careful of grammar and word usage. Involvement with other interactants is quite limited. Speakers addressing small groups operate at this distance.

Public distance, far phase, occurs at twenty-five feet or more. This distance is characteristic of public address. So many details of perception are lost that speech and gestures must be exaggerated or amplified to be effective.

Hall has proposed that customs regarding the maintenance of distance vary from one society to another. Arabs, for example, seem to get along comfortably with strangers at much shorter distances than Americans do. Hall describes an experience he had while he was seated in a deserted hotel lobby in Washington, waiting for a friend.

> A stranger walked up to where I was sitting and stood close enough so that not only could I easily touch him but I could even hear him breathing. In addition, the dark mass of his body filled the peripheral field of vision on my left side. If the lobby had been crowded with people, I would have understood his behavior, but in an empty lobby his presence made me exceedingly uncomfortable. Feeling annoyed by this intrusion, I moved my body in such a way as to communicate annoyance. Strangely enough, instead of moving away, my actions seemed only to encourage him, because he moved even closer. In spite of the temptation to escape the annoyance, I put aside thoughts of abandoning my post, thinking, "To hell with it. Why should I move? I was here first and I'm not going to let this fellow drive me out even if he is a boor." Fortunately, a group of people soon arrived whom my

tormentor immediately joined. Their mannerisms explained his behavior, for
I knew from both speech and gestures that they were Arabs. [Hall, 1969:
155-56]

*Systematic Variations in Proxemic Behavior.* Variations in proxemic
behavior in different societies have long been noticed and commented
upon, usually in anecdotal form as in T.E. Lawrence's account of meeting
British troops again after a long absence:

> In the night my colour was unseen. I could walk as I pleased, an uncon-
> sidered Arab: and this finding myself among, but cut off from, my own kin
> made me strangely alone.... The English fellows were not instinctive, nor
> negligent like the Australians, but held themselves, with a slow-eyed, almost
> sheepish care. They were prim in dress, and quiet; going shyly in pairs. The
> Australians stood in groups and walked singly: the British clung two and
> two, in a celibate friendliness which expressed the level of the ranks: the com-
> monness of their Army clothes. "Holding together" they called it: a war-time
> yearning to keep within four ears such thoughts as are deep enough to hurt.
> [Lawrence, 1935: 641]

These sorts of impressionistic observations are frequently worthless, but
sometimes they may also hit the mark. In this case, given the common
stereotype of the "staid" English and the "brash" Australians, we might
point to some experimental findings, such as the tendency for extraverts to
approach another person more closely in conversations (Leipold, 1963;
Williams, 1963), to speak more than introverts (Carment et al., 1965), and
to sit directly opposite another person in a variety of face-to-face situations
(such as standing around in a circle and talking), while introverts more
often choose a more oblique angle (such as might occur when two people
walk side by side).

E.T. Hall has generalized from impressions such as Lawrence's and proposed that whole human groups can be designated as contact or noncontact groups, terms borrowed from ethology. Contact groups tend to
engage more often in a wide variety of expressive behaviors: they stand
closer to one another, maintain eye contact for longer periods, speak
louder, and otherwise maintain a higher level of sociosensory input (Hall,
1964; 1969: 57-58).

It is clear that Hall categorizes the English as a noncontact group and
the French as a contact group. He even mentions the small size of the
typical French automobile as an expression of a desire for sensory input:
the crowding of its occupants, the bouncing along the road, the noise of
the engine, and so on (Hall, 1969: 144-45). Critics have pointed out that
the English drive equally small automobiles; so, increasingly, do
Americans. Indeed, some of Hall's statements sound like those of the

fellow at a party who has just returned from his first round-the-world cruise: "The Englishman is fastidious about his clothes and expects to spend a great deal of time and attention in their purchase" (Hall, 1969: 142).

Generalizations about what used to be called national character—that is, cultural and personality attributes of whole nation-states—are bound to be expressed in oversimple terms, like any other generalization in the behavioral sciences. Finding exceptions is too easy. The issue that ought to be addressed is, not whether there are exceptions to the generalization, but the extent to which the generalization holds true.

In any case, such propositions are much more likely to be criticized or ridiculed when they concern nation-states such as England and France, whose characteristics are likely to be somewhat familiar to most readers. Similar generalizations about less well-known societies, including the kind generally dealt with by anthropologists, undoubtedly go undisputed because few people know enough about the behavior of the members of the group to argue about it. In some cases, virtually nobody but the ethnographer knows anything about them.

Somewhat more systematic empirical research has been conducted by a number of investigators. Probably one of the more visible names in the cross-cultural investigation of proxemic behavior is that of O. Michael Watson, who has studied the proxemic behavior of Arab and American students under controlled conditions and found the differences hypothesized by Hall (Watson and Graves, 1966; Watson, 1968a). He has also added greater clarity to concepts of proxemic subsystems, suggesting that some features of proxemic behavior can be organized into larger analytic units. "Laboratory research has suggested the possibility that *sub*systems are operable within a system of proxemic behavior. Eye contact and directness of facing...for instance, seem to make up one such subsystem, one which might serve to classify a certain group along a direct/indirect dimension" (Watson 1969: 223). He has also emphasized the distinction between proxemics and proxetics—the latter being the study of behavior and the former the study of the *meaning* of that behavior—and has suggested lines for future research (Watson, 1968b).

A useful review of findings on interpersonal distance through 1969, found in Lett et al.'s "A Propositional Inventory of Research on Interpersonal Distance" (1969), organizes the many relevant hypotheses into tabular form and discusses each briefly.

Like all such research, studies of cross-cultural variations in proxemic behavior involve certain assumptions concerning the nature of the relationship between given environments and the activities that occur in them. Although the cultural background of the interactants may be of great importance, the dynamics of the relationships are probably not simple. Some illuminating assumptions about these dynamics, usually taken for granted, are made explicit by Proshansky et al. The authors point out that "most, if not all, of the assumptions point to the need for investigations that are willing to discard the relatively simple cause-and-effect paradigm that typifies some of the more laboratory-oriented behavioral science research" (Proshansky et al., 1970: 37).

Certain studies exemplify the need to take several variables into account. It is a well-accepted assumption in architecture and design that certain settings are conducive to certain kinds of behaviors and that users of settings are drawn from a homogeneous population. But the assumption is sometimes unjustified. One might be ill-advised to study the behavior of public library patrons in a New England Yankee town in order to design a more efficient and usable library for the benefit of a largely Latin American population in a New Mexican border town. The introduction of variability to the design of public institutions allows for a self-selective process to take place; for instance, Latin Americans might choose to study in groups at small tables, while others might use individual carrels. Similarly, "when assuming a homogeneous group, we expect the preferences of the current user group to match with those of the larger population from which they are drawn. But this is not likely. Consider the case where all graduate students now use the library because of their need to read the technical journals kept on reserve there. An expansion of the library that responds to their needs in the same proportion as the existing use will overdesign for the graduate students" (Eastman and Harper, 1971). Cross-cultural as well as intracultural differences should be taken into account in the design of buildings and spaces for the use of multiple occupants.

Architects and designers have begun to realize that buildings are something more than "hollow sculpture," whose most glorious function is personal expression. Buildings are settings for behavior, and it is deceiving to work on the planner's scale of 1 inch to 100 feet since, on such a map, "decisions affecting 68-inch people are made from an altitude of 3,500 feet" (Fitch, 1974). The dialogue between designers and behavioral scientists is increasing (Gutman, 1975); designers are turning more often to behavioral scientists for advice, and the latter are ready more frequently with relevant advice to give (e.g., Gutman, 1972; Sommer, 1969, 1974). In some cases, the designers have themselves become de facto social scientists (e.g., Alexander, 1964; Studer, 1969).

Designers will undoubtedly find that variations in cultural and personal standards of proxemic behavior will provide them with challenging problems. Investigations have begun to reveal possible differences of varying degrees of significance in the interpersonal behavior of groups such as

American blacks (Willis, 1966), Mexicans (Baxter, 1970), Greeks, Americans, Italians, Swedes, and Scots (Little, 1968), some of which data is summarized in Mehrabian (1972:2-30).

Of course there is a paradox involved here. If we find clear-cut differences in proxemic behavior among all cultural groups, the problem is really simplified rather than complicated, since we will know that we invariably need to take such differences into account in the design of public places. In order to keep the problem complicated, we will mention that these differences are not uniformly reported; it appears, for example, that there is an overall similarity in the structuring of interpersonal distance by Caucasian Americans, native Japanese, and Hawaiian Japanese (Engebretson and Fullmer, 1970).

## Territoriality

Territoriality is a powerful concept in the understanding of spatial behavior. We have already seen its usefulness in studies of animals, and it can be equally valuable in the analysis of human behavior.

*Types of Territories.* This section and adjacent ones are intended as reviews of some ideas that have emerged from the relatively recent increase of interest in the study of the organization of spatial behavior—behavior that isn't the result of the experimenter's manipulations. The concepts and studies treated by no means constitute an exhaustive list.

Some of the earliest contributions to the study of spatial behavior have come from ethologists, people who are primarily interested in observing and measuring naturally occurring animal behavior in field situations. The term *territoriality* refers to behavior by which an organism characteristically lays claim to an area and defends it against members of its own species. Here we may sometimes use it in a looser sense. A number of functions of territoriality have been delineated (Carpenter, 1958). Territoriality offers protection from predators since it enables an animal to know where convenient hiding places may be found, and it facilitates breeding by providing a home base that is relatively safe. Territoriality also exposes to predation the unfit who are too weak to establish and defend a territory of their own, thus enhancing the strength of the species through natural selection. However, animals who might otherwise be subordinate may become more aggressive in their own territories, and so territoriality may enable genetic variants to survive. As we have noted, it is sometimes the less adapted individuals who make possible the survival of the population under changing environmental circumstances. In certain species territoriality localizes waste disposal and inhibits parasites. It also leads to proper spacing, which helps to prevent a too-intensive exploitation of the resources on which the animal depends.

Similar behavior in human populations has been expressed in sayings like "A man's home is his castle." Lawyers may refer to the right to privacy, or gang members may talk about preserving their "turf" from intrusions by rival gangs. Territorial behavior seems to serve some of the same functions in human beings as in animals. If animals avoid intraspecies aggression through spatial segregation, so do people. This is presumably one of the results of the relatively sharp boundaries between ethnic groups in urban settings — black ghettoes, Little Italys, and Chinatowns inhibit interaction between members of different ethnic groups and thus discourage clashes between representatives of conflicting value sets. These invisible borders can sometimes be as effective as barbed wire fences. In 1966, the two sides of Ashland Avenue in Chicago offered an illustration.

> Sixty-third from Justine to Ashland is any ghetto block in America. Sammy's Lounge, three doors from Ashland, screams the presence of a three-piece rhythm and blues group; across the street an unnamed overheated restaurant sells links and ribs. There is a store front church, a liquor store with more wine than whiskey in the window, a beauty salon with a heavy traffic in wigs. On a humid late afternoon in August, people — black people — stroll aimlessly or stand idly in little knots.
> 
> The next block, from Ashland to Marshfield, is equally typical. Three bars all bear the proud names of Irishmen. Teen-age blond girls pore avidly over an enormous selection of rock-and-roll and hairdo magazines in the drugstore. A brightly lit, air conditioned coffee shop offers ham and eggs at a bargain price until 11 A.M. In that block, too, people — white people — stand or stroll. [Marine, 1966, quoted in Sommer, 1969: 15]

On one side of the street, there were no black people. On the other side of the street, there were no white people. Neither, for that matter, was there any conflict.

The concept of territoriality occupies a central place in any discussion of spatial behavior. It is so general a concept that it is related to most other concepts developed in the field. It is a basic behavioral system characteristic of living primates, including people, and of many subprimate zoological forms.

Lately, sociologists have devoted more attention to the regulation of the use of space. This line of interest developed largely independently of the earlier, Chicago-based school of social ecology, perhaps under the influence of work done in ethology, which by the 1960s had become too popular and too stimulating to ignore. Also, by this time psychiatrists and others concerned with the design of psychiatric hospitals had done some work in the area.

Aside from Goffman's essays (Goffman, 1971: 28-61) and the reports of his fieldwork, some of which has relevance in a consideration of territories (Goffman, 1961: 227-62), probably one of the most influential articles to appear recently is Lyman and Scott's "Territoriality: A Neglected Sociological Dimension" (Lyman and Scott, 1970). Lyman and Scott suggest that there is a general human need for "free territories," places where one can get away from others and engage in behavior that is idiosyncratic or in some way "peculiar" but is nevertheless necessary to one's identity. Since all people need free territories, regulating access to territories—that is, setting up some sort of boundaries around a space and controlling who goes in or comes out—is an extremely important consideration in the study of organized social life. Moreover, territorial control varies from group to group, with certain kinds of people, such as blacks and inmates, particularly deprived of such power. Lyman and Scott also claim that women and youths are relatively deprived of territorial control.

Actually, free territories is a term borrowed from Goffman (1961: 230), who used the term "free places" to describe certain locations within a mental hospital where surveillance of patients by staff was tacitly reduced, so that patients could break the rules a bit and do the things one needs to do as a human being. In the case of Goffman's hospitals, patients used a patch of woods for some secret drinking, other places for poker games, and still others simply to get away from the noise and bustle of the ward, to "get out from under" for a few moments.

Lyman and Scott propose that a typology of four kinds of territories can be distinguished: public, home, interactional, and body territories. Public territories are those places that a person can enter or leave at will because he or she belongs to a group that, in a sense, "owns" the area. Of course, one cannot *do* whatever one likes, but there is freedom of access. Public territories are open to everyone, but behavior there is limited for a number of reasons. First, illegal or openly objectionable behavior is not permitted; such control agents as policemen are usually present, and they monitor the goings-on and prevent or terminate objectionable behavior. Second, access to public territories varies somewhat according to the character of the population. Thus, children are not permitted to use playgrounds after dark; blacks are not supposed to stroll through affluent white suburbs unless their appearance is such that they can be assumed to be servants on their way to or from work.

Public territories are essentially ambiguous places, and there is frequently some underlying feeling that certain kinds of people don't belong there. Thus there may be conflict between the citizen's right to use these places and the informal restrictions placed on their use; this sometimes takes the form of dramatic sit-ins, wade-ins, and so on.

"Home territories" are areas where people feel some sense of control. Examples are hobo jungles, gay bars, the turf of adolescent gangs, the club cars of train commuters, the park benches of old people in small towns, and so forth. Home territories may overlap with public ones, so that the same street might be public territory for adults and a home territory for gang members. These places are frequently indicated by special "identity pegs" or territorial markers, such as graffiti or unusual dress or behavior. Some home territories are places reserved by the management of restaurants and taverns for regular neighborhood patrons. I recall particularly a small restaurant in New York's Little Italy that always kept empty a table that was fully set—no matter how crowded the establishment might otherwise be—for the exclusive use of certain locally important businessmen and their families who were likely to drop in on a regular basis. Ruesch and Kees (1972: 89-148) discuss ways in which home territories may be tagged by means of the presence or arrangement of artifacts.

Home territories may be established through colonization, in the way that most ethnic groups ordinarily settle in a selected neighborhood when they first arrive in a country. Not only do immigrants in America do this, but Americans who live overseas are likely to colonize an area; for example, Kifisia, near Athens, is recognized as an American enclave. Similarly, students from a certain school, or even from a certain class cohort, may "discover" a bar and patronize it regularly.

Public areas are easily converted into home areas for specialized groups. Beggars may stake out mutually exclusive home territories on some city blocks. Idle residents may loiter on street corners, monopolizing the space and jeering at passersby. Ethnic neighborhoods are colonized portions of a city where the territorial stakes are often openly visible and easily interpreted, as by store signs in a foreign language or the consistent ethnic character of the names of the stores' proprietors. These home territories may be open to display for groups of transients. Some decades ago, well-to-do New Yorkers went "slumming" in Harlem; more recently, certain commercial lines in San Francisco have conducted bus tours of Chinatown and, for a briefer period, of the Haight-Ashbury district.

Home territory is a relative concept in that, from the point of view of the traveler, any given area whose inhabitants differ in language or interactional rules from the traveler's own social group is a home territory of that group. Thus, from a global perspective, each society represents a population who have carved out a home territory from what must previously have been public territory, in however remote a past. Pan-globally, purely public territories are now found only on the high seas and in remote, largely uninhabited areas like Antarctica. Foreign travelers are very much aware of the fact that they are "guests" in someone else's home territory and, like tourists through Chinatown, they frequently engage guides who interpret exotic artifacts and events for them. In Samoa I was sometimes asked to assist a friend who operated a tourist bus, usually for the service of passengers from Australia and New Zealand on transient liners. I was carefully instructed to point out the features of the land that were rich in local connotations, such as a place where a certain event was supposed to have taken place in Samoan mythology, rather than such humdrum features as plantations where important crops were grown.

Interactional territories is a concept related in some ways to Hediger's idea of social distance. Lyman and Scott use the term to refer to any area where a social gathering may occur. "Surrounding any interaction is an invisible boundary, a kind of social membrane....Every interactional territory implicitly makes a claim of boundary maintenance for the duration of the interaction" (Lyman and Scott, 1970: 95). Rules govern access to interactional territories, though the rules are not easily articulated by the people who follow them. These territories are movable and are easily disrupted or reconstituted. For example, a cluster of people may move along the sidewalk talking to one another, split up for a few moments, then get back together and resume their conversation. The boundaries may often be under challenge by nonparticipants. When someone new appears, the boundaries may break down and a new subject of conversation be introduced. Of course, certain kinds of strangers may be ignored, the way a panhandler may be treated as if he were not there. Others may be granted "temporary visas" that permit them to enter an interactional territory for a limited period of time, as when a student attempts to join a group of faculty members in conversation.

Body territories include the space occupied by the body, including internal space. This is the most private of all the territories belonging to a person. Even one's right to access to one's own body territory is restricted, and the right to touch others' is universally subject to sanction. Another's body territory can be converted into one's home territory, however, as in exclusive sexual access in monogamy.

Body territories also have to do with decoration and grooming. Certain changes in the appearance of the body may be signs of status—for example, dueling scars for members of German fraternities—or signs of stigma. In cases of patricide in traditional China, not only was the murderer subject to a long and lingering death, but the criminal's mother's face was tattooed with four characters indicating that she was guilty of parental neglect (Gray, 1878: 238).

One important variant of body territory is "inner space," or mental territory which may be violated in a number of ways, as by figuring out someone's thoughts or identity despite the fact that he or she is trying to prevent such discovery. Means of violation may include physical coercion, hypnosis, detection of signs of arousal in the person being questioned (as with a polygraph), or the application of methods of detection like those used by Sherlock Holmes. The violation of inner space is a rather common notion in certain psychoses, in which the victim believes his obscene or unrespectable thoughts are being monitored by someone else. The idea of inner space is obviously related to Goffman's informational preserve (Goffman, 1971: 38-40) and to Calhoun's concept of conceptual space (Calhoun, 1966), and the idea of body territory to Goffman's body sheath (Goffman, 1971: 38). This sort of definitional overlap is frequently encountered in the study of spatial behavior.

In any case, we shall find that wherever there are territories, these territories are vulnerable, by definition, to encroachment by others.

*Territorial Encroachment.* Lyman and Scott (1970) distinguish between three kinds of territorial encroachment: violation, invasion, and contamination. Violations occur when someone uses a territory when he or she has no right to do so. These moves may be deliberate or voluntary. An example of a deliberate violation would be a desperate man using the ladies' room of some public facility; unintentional violations would include a situation in which hunters trespass unknowingly on private property.

Invasion takes place when someone who is not a member of a group crosses the group's boundaries and disrupts events or changes their implications. Perhaps the clearest example is an actual military invasion of one country by another and the subsequent change in government.

Contamination of a territory occurs when the territory is rendered somehow "impure." The prototypical example is the touching of an upper-caste Indian by a member of the *harijan,* the so-called untouchables, but similar contamination of body territories is a fairly salient concern among all peoples. The rules governing touching are strict ones, and they apply even to contact between friends and lovers. Ashley Montagu has written a fairly comprehensive paperback on the subject, including its biological aspects (1972).

Contamination can be transmitted by objects. Thermal contamination takes place, for example, when one sits in a chair whose surface is still warm from the body of the previous occupant, a consideration that goes double for toilet seats. The notion that some sort of underlying germ theory may account for part of the belief system concerning contamination has been suggested by Mary Douglas (1966).

If you care to, you may reconstitute some of these primitive feelings the next time you eat fried chicken by thinking of all the other things you've done with your right hand lately.

Again, however, it is important to note that these conventional beliefs about contamination vary considerably among peoples. The other members of my household in Samoa were always, it seemed to me, disturbingly casual about using my toothbrush if their own were unavailable. A rather interesting pattern of behavior occurs in some parts of rural Japan at the end of a hard working day, when the members of a family line up to use the bathtub. There is ordinarily only a single large Japanese tub and enough hot water to fill it once. The senior men bathe first, and the others follow in order of seniority and sex, all of them using the same water (Beardsley et al., 1959: 88-89).

Interactional territories are rather easily contaminated. Contamination occurs, for instance, when one of the group members renders the space impure by passing gas, removing shoes from unclean feet, or using obscene words when such language has not been established as customary. The subject of territorial offenses and the modalities through which these offenses can occur is discussed by Goffman in *Relations in Public* (1971: 44-58).

It is a tribute to the complexity of the human nervous system that these sometimes subtle proprieties concerning the conventional use of space, conventional behavior generally, have been so ingrained in people that their observation is implicit. It needs to be mentioned that part of the subtlety of the above rules stems from the fact that they vary from one situation to another. Thus, for example, the use of obscenity in a classroom may be considered a deliberate act of befoulment, but the same event may be considered a playful joke among adolescent boys or a sign of madness in a psychiatric patient.

Lyman and Scott (1970) state that the definition of territorial violations differs according to circumstances. That is, in some settings behavior that would otherwise be regarded as a threat is permitted to occur. This may depend upon the social characteristics of the violator—adolescent gangs generally do not defend their territories from adults and children, but only from other adolescents. In other cases, location may be the most important factor. Men may ordinarily do no more than shake hands in public, but one man may give another a massage in an athletic club. However, such activities may be defined as territorial violations if they threaten to change the meaning of the territory. Reactions to threatening behavior may take several forms.

When the intruder is of a sort that cannot be tolerated, he or she may be physically expelled. Warfare may occur between nations, and physical fights between individuals. The choice of weapons may be escalated in accordance with the social distance between the combatants. In northern Ireland, for instance, fistfights between young men who are brothers are probably not uncommon, but violence between members of groups of differing political and religious loyalties takes more serious forms. Usually, however, territorial defense takes forms more subtle than physical violence.

The occupants of a territory may insulate themselves by placing some sort of barrier between themselves and potential invaders. Lyman and Scott (1970: 103-4) suggest that "the narrow streets, steep staircases, and regularized use of Cantonese dialects in Chinatowns serve notice on tourists that they may look over the external trappings of Chinese life in the Occidental city but not easily penetrate its inner workings." Certain kinds of uniforms or other symbols of status may discourage unwarranted use of another's territory, and so may facial expressions and the use of gestures and postures.

The Chinese would seem to be adept at the use of such barriers. In Occidental Chinatowns, the barriers are set up in such a way as to insulate a relatively small number of Chinese-Americans from a relatively large number of non-Chinese Americans. In China itself, however, similar barriers protect the vast number of native Chinese from the relatively minute number of Westerners:

> In the last quarter of the seventh century, the Emperor Kang Hsi decided that foreign businessmen had certain technological secrets that China might use, but that they were essentially Barbarians and should be segregated in a small area outside the walls of the great South China port of Canton.
>
> In the last quarter of the twentieth century, the men who rule China have basically the same opinion. Although foreign devils travel more widely in China now than then, the thousands of businessmen who come here every year for China's spring and autumn export-commodity fairs are mostly segregated together in the vast twelve-hundred-room Tung Fang Hotel on the northern edge of the city. [*San Francisco Examiner and Chronicle,* November 30, 1975]

In a different set of processes called linguistic collusion, the violator is defined as an unknowing outsider. That is, "the defending interactants may engage one another in conversation and gestures designed to so confuse the invader that he responds in a manner automatically labeling him eligible for either exclusion from the group or shameful status diminution"(Lyman and Scott, 1970: 104).

Linguistic collusion occurs when storekeepers in ethnic enclaves use a foreign language in talking to other customers. Professors may increase their use of jargon in the presence of students, and doctors may adopt an especially dignified manner around patients. Gay people may speak in a more flagrantly homosexual manner in the presence of straights.

A rather elaborate means of repelling another was in fairly common use by members of the counterculture a decade ago, when they considered themselves sharply differentiated from members of the establishment. This form of linguistic collusion, called the "put on," is exemplified in the following *Playboy* interview with rock singer Bob Dylan (quoted in Argyle, 1969: 200-201).

PLAYBOY: How do you get your kicks these days?
DYLAN: I hire people to look into my eyes, and then I have them kick me.
PLAYBOY: And that's the way you get your kicks?
DYLAN: No. Then I forgive them, that's where my kicks come in.
PLAYBOY: Did you ever have the standard boyhood dream of growing up to be President?
DYLAN: No. When I was a boy, Harry Truman was President; who'd want to be Harry Truman?
PLAYBOY: Well, let's suppose that you were the President. What would you accomplish during your first thousand days?
DYLAN: Well, just for laughs so long as you insist, the first thing I'd do is probably move the White House. Instead of being in Texas, it'd be on the East Side of New York. McGeorge Bundy would definitely have to change his name, and General McNamara would be forced to wear a coonskin cap and shades.

As Argyle comments, this technique consists "of refusing to accept normal role-relationships by adopting deliberately nonmeshing responses, which prevent any proper interaction taking place, and make the other person look like an idiot" (Argyle, 1969: 200). This sort of linguistic collusion belongs to a class of procedures that Watzlawick et al. (1967: 75-78) call "disqualification of communication," which invalidates whatever messages are sent or received.

*The Absence of Free Space.* It will be recalled that Lyman and Scott use the term *free territory* to refer to places to which people may retreat and engage in idiosyncratic behavior essential to their identity. The writers add that some segments of society are systematically denied access to free territories. Many black urban youths, for example, live in crowded homes and patronize crowded public facilities, reached by means of crowded streets. They or their families may be under surveillance by the police or by social workers. They may try to carve home territories out of public places, but these are subject to constant intrusion by others.

Lyman and Scott hypothesize that, as other forms of free space are perceived by some groups within the sociocultural system to be denied them, these groups, whenever possible, will more frequently and intensively use the area of body space as a free territory.

This substitutive use of body space can take three forms. The first, "manipulation," is based upon the fact that there is considerable freedom in bodily movements and postures in public places, so that identities can be established and conventions flouted without fear of punishment. Thus, for example, children who are forced to sit quietly at adult gatherings may make faces at one another, movie actors who are otherwise unrecognized can adopt certain idiosyncratic mannerisms, and teenagers who are denied approval for sexual activities and denied territories for that purpose can develop dances that involve little body contact but nevertheless suggest forbidden erotic activities.

The second form, "adornment," consists of uncovering or marking the body in unusual ways. Distinctive ornamentation or dress, public nudity, or idiosyncratic grooming can all serve as identity markers.

The final form, "penetration," involves the exploitation and modification of inner space in the search for free territories. This is the ultimate in the exercise of body freedom: musing, daydreaming, drugs. It may be one component of institutionalization among hospitalized schizophrenics—a well-known process in which an active psychotic admitted to a psychiatric ward loses rather quickly whatever residual social skills he or she had when admitted and becomes like the other long-term residents. Under ordinary ward conditions, of course, there is no free space whatever: a number of people sleep in the same big room, toilets are out in the open rather than in stalls, and so on. In these circumstances, all idiosyncratic behavior is public, and institutionalization may be merely an extension of a perfectly normal process.

Some comments might be made on Lyman and Scott's interesting article. Some of them apply as well to many other conceptual analyses of environment-related behavior. In the delineation of particular types of territories, public, home, interactional, and body territories are apt to strike a reader as somewhat unordered. What are their common dimensions, and how do they differ from one another? The same questions may be asked about types of encroachment. Who can operationally distinguish between a violation and a contamination? (One possibility would be to delete the category of violation entirely, and define invasion as a violation of rights of access, and contamination as a violation of environmental usage.)

The hypothesis that, as free territories decline, the use of body territories increases has a certain plausibility, but is it really true that such spaces have declined over the last decade? How does the hypothesis explain the radical changes that have occurred recently in the use of body territories? These changes would seem to have occurred at the same time that access to free spaces has actually increased.

Similarly, have young people really developed suggestive dances as they have been denied the opportunity to engage in direct sex in private? Or have increased sexual opportunities, erotic dances, and suggestive body adornment all developed at roughly the same time? If memory serves, the young people of a generation ago were both more sexually frustrated and more "conventional" in appearance and behavior. Are "thong" swimsuits really the result of sexual deprivation?

Lyman and Scott state that "the occupants of a territory may extend its use to others whose presence is not regarded as a threat" (Lyman and Scott, 1970: 102). This notion of threat—which goes relatively unelaborated in the article—may be a key to understanding the concept of territorial behavior. What, specifically, is the nature of that threat? At least three kinds of threat may be distinguished. One has to do with the violation of norms, and this is rather thoroughly covered by Lyman and Scott under one or another title. A second has to do with competition for scarce resources. Where social and physical resources are widespread and readily available, less territorial behavior occurs; but where they are scarce, the likelihood of territorial behavior increases. This is certainly true of many infrahuman animals. And even among people, we have mineral rights in land purchases, but no air rights, air being an essential resource but a readily available one.

Finally, physical safety can be an extremely important consideration. That is, the threat may have less to do with the properties of the mind than with the security of one's body. *Homo sapiens* having proved to be a populous and aggressive animal, boundary maintenance reduces contact and enhances safety. The more effective the available weaponry, the greater the distance maintained. When we established the "high seas," the limit from the coast was three miles, the distance that a cannon shell could travel at that time. But twenty years ago, the United States found the installation of missiles in Cuba, more than ninety miles away, to be intolerable. Finally, of course, a concern for physical safety is largely responsible for prohibited air zones over the capitol and other important federal buildings, as well as crowded airports, nuclear plants, and the like. This relationship between safety and distance has been investigated by Kinzel (1970) in a prison population. His finding that the size of the body buffer zone—that is, the most comfortable distance from others—is much greater in prisoners with a history of violent behavior suggests that the above notion relating distance to the effectiveness of available weaponry should be modified. Perhaps what is significant is not only the effectiveness of the weaponry but the likelihood of its use.

*Preserves.* In *Relations in Public* (1971: 28-40), Goffman explores other sorts of territories, which vary from "fixed" (geographically identified, such as houses or fields) through "situational" (artifacts and spaces that may be used temporarily, such as restaurant tables), to "egocentric" (those that move around with the individual and of which he or she is the center).

Goffman calls these areas preserves rather than territories, a more apt term since some of them are not spatial in character.

The first of Goffman's preserves is "personal space," defined as "the space surrounding an individual, anywhere within which an entering other causes the individual to feel encroached upon, leading him to show displeasure and sometimes to withdraw" (Goffman, 1971: 29-31). Goffman conceives of personal space as a variable contour. There is very little of it behind a person but a great deal around the face, limbs, and genitals. Generally speaking, in crowded places where contact must occur, people allow "ritually neutral" parts of the body to touch—elbows, for example, rather than such "profane" parts as the buttocks or such "sacred" parts as faces and lips. Of course, personal space is audience specific in that some people are allowed to approach us in ways that other people are not.

The "stall," according to Goffman, is a "well-bounded space to which individuals can lay temporary claim, possession being on an all-or-none basis" (Goffman, 1971: 32). Stalls usually involve some sort of scarce good, such as a comfortable chair, a table with a view, an empty bed, a telephone booth, or a tennis court. Stalls may be occupied by parties, whereas personal space is exclusively individual. Furthermore, stalls may be temporarily vacated and later reclaimed. The boundaries may sometimes be problematic; personal space may be assured in movie theater seats, but who gets the common arm rest?

A third kind of preserve is "use space," referring to a space around or immediately in front of a person, whose claim to that space is limited to instrumental consideration. We try not to walk in front of a person viewing a painting in a museum, for example, and we try to keep out of the way of a custodian mopping the floor or a golfer wielding a club.

The "turn" refers to one's preserve in a sequential order, according to category—"upper classmen first"—or on an individual basis—"first come, first served." Examples include passing around a bottle or a joint, waiting for an available prostitute, using the family bathroom in the morning, or taking the next empty table in a crowded restaurant.

The "body sheath" refers to the skin and whatever happens to be covering it, as well as the interior of the body. This is somewhat different from personal space in that it concerns the regulation of contact. Possibly one of the more disturbing features of a visit to the dentist is that we are permitting him to examine a part of the body that hardly anyone else has seen, not even ourselves. There is something disconcerting about the notion that someone who may be a complete stranger has the right to view all that fleshy, vascular membrane and stained enamel. And, then too, there are circumstances under which we might be embarrassed to touch our own bodies, as in masturbation.

A "possessional territory" is "any set of objects that can be identified with the self and arrayed around the body wherever it is" (Goffman, 1971: 38). Primary examples are those artifacts usually called personal effects, but objects we use temporarily, such as ashtrays and eating utensils, are also included.

Some objects are more vulnerable to contamination than others. If we discover that, in our absence, another person has made use of a particular dollar bill of ours, then returned it to its place, no contamination has occurred. If we find that this person has made use of our comb, we might feel somewhat uneasy. If he or she has used our toothbrush, we are seriously disturbed.

"Information preserves" are those "facts about himself to which an individual expects to control access while in the presence of others" (Goffman, 1971: 38-39). Simply put, there are things about ourselves that we do not want others to know, and we do not expect or desire most people to ask about them. But, as with the other preserves, the informational preserve is audience specific. For example, we might be offended if a casual acquaintance inquired about the quality of our sex lives, but we might be willing to pay for the privilege of divulging this information to a psychotherapist.

Finally, a "conversational preserve" refers to the right of an individual to exert some control over who can summon him into talk and when he can be summoned; and the right of a set of individuals once engaged in talk to have their circle protected. Goffman also discusses territorial violations and remedial moves, which we will examine later in this chapter.

One characteristic of Goffman's approach to the use of space—and of Lyman and Scott's and of Barker and Wright's as well—is that they deal almost not at all with the physical characteristics of the settings, beyond such assumptions as the fact that a setting must be surrounded by barriers to perception. Rather, Goffman defines each preserve almost entirely in terms of the kinds of activities that take place there.

*Shields.* What does one do if he or she is visiting with a couple of friends in their living room, and the couple gets into an argument? The conflict concerns some trivial disagreement over an event or over the interpretation of an event that holds no personal interest for the visitor. The visitor knows that the argument will shortly be resolved or at least will end, but meanwhile the argument is moving inexorably towards an apparently high, though still decorous, level of passion. The visitor has nothing to contribute, no solution to offer, and would prefer not to participate. However, there is an increasing likelihood that one of the arguers may appeal to this third party, putting his or her case before the visitor and requesting that it be validated.

Put more broadly, when three people are in proximity, and two of them are doing something with each other from which the third would prefer to be excluded, how does the third person decrease his or her chances of being drawn into the activity?

The observer could stand up and withdraw, but this might be an excessive reaction. The threat to withdraw might even be interpreted as a sign of interest, of willingness to be involved. A more reasonable response, in the above example, would be to look somewhat bored and pick up a magazine from the living room table and begin to look through it. In effect, the two people arguing have established around them an interactional territory, in Lyman and Scott's terms, and in effect the visitor is trying to preserve the present boundaries and prevent their being extended to include him.

One of Goffman's spatial concepts concerns involvement shields (Goffman, 1963: 38-42), portable "barriers" that allow a person to engage in some sort of side involvement, some minor bit of business involving withdrawal from what he or she should be attending to. An example might be schoolchildren in class, hiding an open comic book inside the notebook in front of them. Involvement shields are conventional gestures, used by everyone, and if they are obvious enough they can be interpreted for what they are by the people against whom they are used. Thus, a man with an overcoat carefully folded over his lap in a pornographic movie theater is something more than just a man with an overcoat folded over his lap. The other viewers know it, and he knows they know it. Similarly, if a person observing an argument picks up a magazine and begins reading it, more is involved than a person reading a magazine.

These barriers are ordinarily used to mask small expressions of unsuitable or out-of-role behavior. Years ago, European ladies used fans to hide their blushes of embarrassment or self-consciousness. Today we may cover a yawn with our hand in order to give the impression that we are interested in what is going on. Or we may cover our face with a propped-up newspaper in public settings in order to lessen the possibility that we will be drawn into an unwanted conversation with a neighbor. Involvement shields are also used to mask behavior more suitable to another area: television performers, discouraged from smoking while on camera, may keep a lighted cigarette in an ashtray out of camera range or hidden behind another object such as a desk and puff on the cigarette only when the camera is elsewhere.

*Regions.* Goffman's contributions to our understanding of spatial behavior have been rather incidental to his concern with interactional processes, but there has been some spinoff. In this section I will discuss his distinction between front and back regions, and I will also deal with two other sets of his ideas that appear to be related: staged authenticity and the relative nature of regions.

Goffman's primary contribution to spatial concepts of behavior may be his demarcation of regions as part of a dramaturgical interpretation of social life. Our social life consists of routines that we perform — sometimes as individuals, sometimes as members of a team — for the benefit of an audience. Goffman calls the place where performances are staged a *front region,* defining a region as a place that is bounded to some degree by barriers to perception. Examples of front regions might include classrooms, doctors' offices, churches, one's living room when visitors are present, and almost any bounded public setting such as a bus. The behavior performed in front regions is highly structured so as to preserve the actor's decorum and present the audience with a suitable overall image.

The performers usually have a number of environmental props to help them manage the impressions they make on their audience. The clinical psychologist hangs a degree on the wall; the physician in his consulting room is surrounded by technological paraphernalia; the military officer slaps a swagger stick against his thigh, and administrators carry briefcases. The particular routines in which actors engage depend upon the setting. A performer is never in complete control of the behavior of the audience; rather, audience and performer cooperate in forming a definition of the situation. For example, in some classrooms there is an unspoken agreement between the professor and the students that he or she will go through the motions of attempting to teach them something, while their responsibility is to attempt to fool the professor into believing that they have learned something of consequence. The professor seems to care, they act as if they are interested, and the index of a successful performance is a passing grade. Similarly, a nightclub comic cannot simply step onstage and run through a routine as if on videotape. The comic adapts to the audience's responses, waiting for the laughter to subside, or waiting for it to appear, becoming more happily expressive with an enthusiastic audience or more manifestly desperate with a poor one. In the same way, a doctor might tell a weak-willed bronchitic patient not to stop smoking entirely but to cut down as much as possible. The professor and the students cooperate to define the situation as one in which an unpleasant task must be performed with as few disruptions as possible; the comedian and the audience cooperate to define a performance as a poor one or a good one; and the doctor and the patient cooperate to define an acceptable response in terms of the difference between what the doctor wants and what the patient can do.

Such machinations go on in front regions. In back regions, a performer may engage in the profane behavior necessary to continued human existence—things he or she prefers to keep hidden from the audience. In most American homes, the bedroom and the bathroom serve as back regions. Audiences are excluded from these bounded areas, and it is here that the personal or team image projected by a performance is deliberately contradicted. The team may store its props in the back region; clothing may be checked and examined for flaws. This is where the wife used to ask, "Are my seams straight?" Performances may be practiced. A stock situation in filmed comedies has the shy and inept hero making an aggressive, out-of-character speech to his boss, while the camera dollies back to reveal that he is speaking to a mirror. Finally, back regions provide places where the poorer performers may be sequestered, in the way that the idiot grandsons of European kings could be hidden in the cellars.

It is a common observation that the higher one's status, the more necessary the presence of a back region where one may "break role." One who commands a great deal of respect from the audience has more to lose if caught out of role than a person of lower status. It would be one thing to pass a man urinating in the gutter of an otherwise empty street if he were an obvious derelict, quite another thing if he were an august political personage.

Institutions have back regions and front regions, and the distinction between the two is often sharp because of clear-cut divisions between various statuses and activities in institutions that deal with the public. In other words, the audience must be kept out of the back region. If we, the audience sitting in the front region of a restaurant, being entertained and served by a team of appropriately costumed performers behaving like waiters and waitresses, were privy to what was going on in the back regions—the kitchen and scullery—not only might we be offended, we might lose our appetites.

A third requirement of the dramaturgical setting is that not only must audience and performers in the front region and the supporting cast and tools in the back region be shielded from one another, but both of them must be shielded from the outside as well. Audiences are a select group, and what goes on between the audience and the performer in the front region is often something very special, an activity from which hostile or ignorant outsiders must be excluded. So a third region must be added: the outside region. All of these areas—front, back, and outside—must be bounded in one way or another. The notion of an outside region corresponds to the physical structure of buildings, in which the individual rooms used as back regions and front regions are shielded from the rest of the world by outer walls.

Goffman's rhetoric may make the dramaturgical model sound like a playful or at least superficial game, but the empirical realities represented by his concepts are critically important. One may remember when, some years ago, Walter Jenkins, a presidential aide, engaged in a homosexual act in what he thought was a back region, namely a booth in a public rest room where gay men habitually met. Outsiders—FBI agents—had deliberately penetrated the boundary surrounding this back region, and their observation of this prestigious individual's behavior led to his dismissal.

One of the difficulties frequently pointed out with respect to the spatial layout of commercial buildings is that a disproportionate amount of floor area is given over to the front region. The roles of performers are relatively structured in front regions. Rules, written or not, prohibit smoking, drinking coffee, gossiping, or "goofing off." Therefore, in the absence of a suitable back region in which to change roles, staff members are continuously concerned with impression management. They must look busy or engage in "make work" and clandestinely smoke in bathrooms or out-of-the-way niches. If suitable back regions were provided, more effort might actually be devoted to goal realization, and the institution itself might become more effective in a general way.

The fact that certain kinds of establishments are likely to be divided into front and back regions is well known to many patrons of those establishments. The management may actually assume that patrons are interested in seeing what goes on "behind the scenes," especially if there is reason for curiosity. Pizzerias may be arranged so that the sinks, ovens, and other paraphernalia of the chef are not only visible from the customers' tables but may be situated in front of a sort of display window facing the sidewalk, to allow passersby to see the chef rolling out the dough and twirling it in the air. Similarly, some Chinese restaurants, such as Sam Woh's in San Francisco, require that the visitor enter the establishment through the kitchen. As the Chinese cooks glance up from their work, seeming to appraise each new arrival, some customers may feel as if they are out of place, seeing something one shouldn't see, while other customers feel that this is the "real thing"—no tourist trap here!

The feeling that one is seeing the "real thing" when glimpsing some part of what is ordinarily presumed to be a back region has undoubtedly led some establishments to create a number of spaces between the front and back regions that are designed to make visitors feel that they have been admitted to the back region, when in fact they have only been admitted to a front region that *appears* to be a back region. These are "staged" back regions, somewhere between front and back, and MacCannell has proposed that these sorts of spaces constitute a continuum, involving six points or stages (MacCannell, 1973).

Stage 1 is equivalent to Goffman's front region. It is recognized for what it is by visitors and is the kind of space beyond which visitors try to penetrate.

Stage 2 is a front region that has perfunctorily been decorated to resemble a back region: fishnets on the wall of a seafood restaurant or plastic salamis and cheeses on the wall of a supermarket delicatessen, the kinds of displays that add to atmosphere.

Stage 3 consists of front regions totally organized to look like back regions, such as on-stage sex shows that take place in a mock bedroom.

Stage 4 is closely related to stage 3 and is a back region open to outsiders. Essentially this stage appears to consist of the revelation of activities that originally took place in settings from which visitors were excluded. The revelation may be deliberate, as when the signing of a peace treaty, itself the result of secret negotiations, is made public, or it may be inadvertent or reluctant, as when the private, tape-recorded conversations of political figures are, by order of a high federal court, turned over to the public.

Stage 5 is a back region that is altered somewhat because the visitor is allowed to look at it. Sam Woh's kitchen is probably a reasonable example.

Stage 6 corresponds to Goffman's back region, and it is the kind of setting visitors want to see but from which they are generally excluded.

The concept of staged authenticity extends, of course, to events as well as to spaces. Tourists know this so well that they often assume that any particularly exotic event has been deliberately staged by the participants for the purpose of impressing tourists. Thus Vladimir Nabokov, a Russian literateur on a butterfly-collecting trip through the American West, speaks through his creation, Humbert Humbert, of "Indian ceremonial dances, strictly commercial" (Nabokov, 1970: 159), an undeservedly offhand dismissal. The presence of outsiders may be neither a necessary nor a sufficient condition for such a performance. I was much impressed with the overall similarity in the form of the ceremonial dances performed by the Red Lake Chippewa in the course of an afternoon powwow performed in a plaza before hundreds of other Indians and tourists, and dances performed before only a handful of witnesses, myself the only non-Indian among them, very early on a misty morning, at a burial ground in the remote woodlands. Though the motives may have been different, the *behavior* was nearly identical. The assumption that an activity is somehow contaminated by the presence of tourists may prove invalid.

Front region and back region are relative concepts. That is, the "frontness" or "backness" of a space can only be determined with reference to the properties of adjacent spaces, in much the same way that electrical potential can only be measured with reference to the potential of another specific point. There is therefore a constant "chain of perception" (Ruesch and Kees, 1972: 82), in which people watch other people watching other people. Ruesch and Kees include an interesting photograph of spectators watching people playing a game, and passersby watching the spectators. The chain of perception establishes a relativity in the properties of spaces, depending on the perspective of the viewer. From the point of view of the municipality, for example, construction work should ideally take place in a back region, shielded from public view, in order that the image of the city not be marred by open holes in the earth. The construction site itself is a back region where unsightly activities may be carried out. However, from the point of view of the pedestrian who has stopped to peek through the holes in the fence, the site is a front region where performers do interesting things. The performers are aware of their observers, and they doubtless try to find back regions, such as trailers or sheds, in which to escape the scrutiny of the public and of their supervisors. Moreover, there are likely to be further back regions, such as toilets, in relation to which such shelters as trailers are front regions where certain kinds of activities cannot be performed for fear of censure by the other participants.

Thus, there are few settings in which the frontness or the backness of the region is undiluted. In most instances, spaces can be placed on a continuum in terms of their accessibility to a more and more limited audience, becoming more "back" and less "front" in the process. It might finally be suggested that there is no space in which complete freedom from disclosure is guaranteed, particularly in these sophisticated days. And if no one else is present, there is the concept of a "generalized other," the animal to which we refer when we ask, "What would people say if they knew I was doing this?" and which lends a certain queasy quality to our most furtive acts.

*Markers of Distinctive Space.* Most of the territorial defense mechanisms we have discussed depend upon the presence of the defender. That is, they are mechanisms for the defense of personal space. But there are obviously times when people want to signal that a given territory "belongs" to them, whether or not the territory happens to be occupied at the moment. People do not want to return home to find strangers, or even friends, sitting uninvited in the living room. Nor do they ordinarily want to return from the stacks to find their seat in the library occupied.

Ethologists call the signals of territorial ownership "markers." These mechanisms identify a territory as already occupied by a conspecific. In animals, as we have seen, territorial defense may involve actual fighting; but markers are particularly useful in that they enable animals to avoid each other, eliminating the need for combat. These markers frequently affect the sense of smell. Wolves, for example, leave their scent by urinating around the perimeter of their territory. A similar mechanism is found in some plants, particularly desert plants. A visitor to the deserts of California is likely to be impressed by the regular spacing of the shrubs, so uniform that it seems they must have been deliberately planted. Many of these shrubs, such as creosote bush and brittle bush, exude certain toxic substances that discourage the growth of other plants nearby. However, we must be wary of drawing too fine a parallel between human behavior and the adaptive processes of other organisms.

In animals, the maintenance of distance is directly linked to competition for scarce resources, and in many cases the space defended appears to shrink when resources are plentiful and to grow when they are not. Undoubtedly, competition for scarce resources is one component of human territoriality, but many other factors may be equally important.

Goffman (1971: 41-44) discusses the kinds of markers that are generally available for use. "Central markers" are objects that are placed at the center of an area, with the claimed territory radiating outward from the marker. Examples might include a drink at a bar, a purse on an airplane seat, or a notebook on a library table.

"Boundary markers" distinguish the interface between two claimed areas. The rubber or plastic bars on supermarket checkout counters, fences around one's home, and warning signs along the perimeter of privately owned land are included in this category.

Goffman uses the term "ear markers" to refer to signs of ownership embedded in an object to indicate possession. Such ear markers as engraved signatures on household items help to increase the recovery rate of stolen goods, but the urge to personalize items seems at times to go beyond utilitarian needs. People spend extra money for the privilege of owning engraved items that are sentimentally charged, such as wedding rings, or even distinctive license plates in states where they are available.

Goffman points out that personal possessions are frequently used as markers. A book lying on a library table is an ambiguous symbol, but a purse is not. A place that is "owned" is best signified by an object that is clearly owned, though the danger arises that the object, rather than the space, will then be appropriated.

It also seems likely that, when territorial violations become commonplace, markers may become more pronounced. Thus, for example, the privately owned land along the Coast Highway a few hours' drive north of San Francisco looks ideal for hiking or picnicking, but it is clearly marked by large, hand-painted signs proclaiming KEEP OUT. POISON. In less inviting places, where violations are unlikely, territorial markers become less important for the purpose of protecting encroachments.

Sommer (1969: 54-57) describes some of the problems associated with the use of markers, most of them arising from the fact that the rules governing reserved territories in public places are implicit. What happens, for example, when someone sits down in a theater and drapes coat, hat, packages, and program over the adjacent six seats? Other patrons will reluctantly accommodate themselves to this claim, although there is no law stating that they must.

Sommer describes an experiment by Becker and Requa that dealt with the effectiveness of markers in library rooms of moderate density. In each test, an unsuspecting male student was seated at a six-chair table—three chairs to a side—occupying an end chair on one side. The experimenter approached the table and seated himself on the same side but at the opposite end, so that subject and experimenter were separated by a single empty chair. After a quiet interval of five or fifteen minutes, the experimenter left a pile of paperback books at his seat and walked away. After another interval—either twenty minutes or an hour—another experimenter approached the subject and asked if the marked seat were occupied.

The first finding was that the territorial marker, all by itself, was effective, since none of the marked chairs were occupied by others. Second, the first experimenter's claim to the chair was supported by a majority of the subjects. Finally, the response of the subject varied with the length of time the first experimenter had been away. Eighty percent of the subjects supported the claim after a twenty-minute interval; but only 54 percent did so after an hour.

The arrangement of objects within a space may be studied from a number of perspectives, aside from their use as territorial markers. One of the most obvious approaches involves an assumption that such arrangements reflect some of the attributes of the arranger. Another perspective treats the arrangement of people with respect to objects as an independent variable that is associated with certain kinds of social behavior.

Ruesch and Kees (1972) examine some of the characteristics of grouped artifacts. They point out, for example, that spaces between groups of objects, or frames inserted between them, serve as a kind of material punctuation to separate groups into configurational entities. The whole that is formed by groups of more or less different objects provides a kind of object syntax, analogous to the arrangement of words in a sentence.

Object syntax follows inevitably from the accumulation of possessions, since some method of filing them away for future retrieval must be concocted. The objects may be lined up horizontally (books on a shelf), piled one on top of the other (papers on a desk), spread out on a flat surface (the dummy's bridge hand), or dumped (children's toys in a closet).

Regardless of the method of storage, some system must be devised for categorizing objects as similar or different. Ruesch and Kees suggest that objects of similar function may be arranged so as to be readily available, a procedure that reflects "subject thinking," and an example of which is the storage of bread and rolls together in the breadbox. Alternatively, objects may be coded and filed in terms of their qualifying adjectives, as when books are shelved together because they are blue or falling apart. This is called predicate thinking and in its most extreme form is characteristic of schizophrenic behavior, since schizophrenics often ignore the essential characteristics of things and mistake them for one another on the basis of superficial attributes. Thus, for instance, one young man "became increasingly preoccupied with certain thoughts. On hearing the word 'home,' he understood 'homo'; if he heard the word 'fair,' he felt 'fairy' was the word really meant" (Arieti, 1959: 461). Some years ago I entered a restaurant with a friend, and we sat at an empty table. He glanced at his seat, stared silently at me for a moment, then asked, "Why is mine the only chair at this table with black and white stripes?" I thought his question was odd and asked why he was concerned. He replied, "Well, you have to admit they do look like prison stripes." Though I failed to recognize it, he was in the initial phase of acute schizophrenia and was hospitalized a few days later. Fortunately he recovered in a few months.

Ruesch and Kees also comment on the function of furniture arrangements in facilitating interaction. Facilitative arrangements include face-to-face chairs, large sofas, open uncluttered lounge spaces, and a casual appearance. Furniture may also retard interaction, as when coffee-table hurdles are inserted between chairs, chairs face in the same direction, chairs and sofas are small and far apart, or an apparently rigid and stringent arrangement of chairs seems to discourage rearrangement.

The treatment of objects provides us with a stable and important record of their owner's behavior: "Every interior betrays the nonverbal skills of its inhabitants. The choice of materials, the distribution of space, the kinds of objects that command attention or demand to be touched, have much to say about the preferred sensory modalities of their owners. Their sense of organization, the degree of freedom left to imagination, their esthetic rigidity, all are revealed in their houses. Psychiatrists working with adults need only examine the environment with which individuals surround themselves to gain insights into their relationships to objects, people, and places" (Ruesch and Kees, 1972: 135).

In some cases, objects are arranged by people other than those for whose use they are primarily intended, and disjunctions may occur. For example, it seems that because of their sensory impairment, elderly people may require a much more cluttered environment in order to maintain spatial orientation than their custodians are likely to think necessary or suitable (DeLong, 1970).

There is evidence that the arrangement of objects may influence social behavior. When a group of people are seated at rectangular or square tables, having a discussion, the people with whom an individual is likely to talk differ according to the degree of dominance exercised by the leader of the discussion. When leadership is weak, people are likely to talk to others sitting across the table from them. When leadership is strong, they tend to address others sitting next to them (Steinzor, 1950; Hearn, 1957). There is also evidence that different arrangements of people at a table indicate different degrees of psychological closeness to people from different cultural backgrounds (Sommer, 1968, 1969: 63-64). It seems possible, then, that the long-enduring argument concerning the shape of the table and the arrangement of discussants at the Paris peace talks among Americans and Vietnamese in 1969 had more than symbolic value.

An example of the interaction between the characteristics of objects arranged in the home and the behavior of occupants may be found in Laumann and House's (1970) study of the living rooms of 897 white men living in the Detroit area. Traditional furnishings were found principally in the homes of white, Anglo-Saxon Protestants who had been well-to-do for some time; modern furnishings were more often found in the homes of upwardly mobile Catholics. Properties of living room furniture were also related to political attitudes. People whose furniture was characterized by a consistent style were more likely to have a relatively extreme view of political issues than those with furnishings in mixed styles. Traditional living rooms were also associated with traditional views of marriage and family life. These findings, striking as they are, should be accepted with caution, since the particular items of furniture checked in each household were selected before the study was carried out and might not have been representative; further, some of the researchers had difficulty making sophisticated judgments concerning the styles of the furnishings.

*Privacy as an Interpersonal Boundary Process.* Some few words are in order concerning Irwin Altman's (1975) conception of the relationship between environment and social behavior. In a discussion of the concepts of privacy, personal space, territoriality, and crowding, Altman proposes that *"the concept of privacy is central to understanding environment and behavior relationships; it provides a key link among the concepts of crowding, territorial behavior, and personal space"* (Altman, 1975: 6, Altman's italics).

Privacy is a dynamic process by means of which an individual or a group of people make themselves more or less available for interaction with others. Altman suggests that, at any given time, an individual or group may be characterized by a desired level of privacy that may or may not match the level of privacy actually achieved. Crowding is an important consideration when the achieved level is less than the desired level; similarly, social isolation indicates that the achieved level is greater than the desired one. Personal space, territory, verbal and nonverbal behavior serve as interpersonal control mechanisms, that is, the means by which one tries to change the achieved level of privacy in such a way as to match the desired level.

The system is dynamic in that the desired level changes over time, with a person or group needing more or less social stimulation depending upon recent experiences and current circumstances, a correspondence that echoes Calhoun's mythematical pool game discussed in chapter 1. To the extent that a discrepancy between desired and achieved levels of privacy is perceived, the individual has recourse to various interpersonal control mechanisms.

Let us take an example. A man comes home from work. It has been a bad day; he has been harassed; people have pestered him with demands on his time and energy; he has discovered that he is soon to receive an extended visit from a relative he dislikes; he has just ridden on the subway during rush hour; trembling and perspiring, he approaches his door, only to find an insurance salesman outside ringing the bell. An agonizing hour later he is alone at last and he wants to keep it that way for a while.

He may maintain a rough state of congruence between his desired and achieved levels of privacy by means of interpersonal control mechanisms. He may, for instance, simply tell casual visitors that he wants to be alone, which is verbal behavior; he may defend his territory by standing squarely in the doorway, blocking their entrance; if the visitors *must* be admitted, our host may signal his displeasure by sitting farther away from them than he normally would, or by angling his body away from them, which represents a manipulation of personal space; finally, he may use nonverbal behavior, throwing up an involvement shield by watching television instead of listening attentively to his guests or, even more directly, by yawning conspicuously.

Altman's is, I believe, the most cogent and persuasive model yet proposed for understanding relationships among the concepts of crowding, personal space, territory, and privacy. It is certainly not the definitive explanation (see also Johnson [1974] and other explorations of the concept in Margulis [1974]), but Altman has been able to marshal a great deal of empirical evidence to substantiate his argument. It is a good, systematic beginning.

In fact, if we add to his model the notion that, not only do individuals and groups vary over time in their desired level of privacy, but that there are relatively consistent differences between people over time, then the model becomes even more heuristic. We might similarly agree to the commonsense observation that some people tend habitually to eat more than others, although at any given time an individual may be hungry or satisfied. If such differences do appear consistently in subsequent studies, however, then the need for privacy may be treated as a personality trait or a group trait that may be increased or lessened under certain experimental conditions, the way certain psychologists have treated other needs, notably affiliation, power, and achievement. One need only glance through McClelland's *The Achieving Society* (1961) to gain some idea of how far such an approach might be taken, and there are dozens of other directions in which the model might lead investigators.

Altman (1975: 10-31) summarizes some of the recent work on privacy done by anthropologists and other investigators, including Murphy's exemplary article, "Social Distance and the Veil," which appeared in *American Anthropologist* in 1964. Here Murphy discusses the use of the veil by men among the Tuareg, nomadic pastoralists in north central Africa, and describes the cloth as a mechanism for regulating the amount of information to be gained by someone from the face of the wearer, as a means of maintaining or lessening social distance. The veil is worn highest, concealing the greatest part of one's face, in the presence of peers and superiors, and is lowered when dealing with persons of humbler status. The position of the veil is related to the vulnerability of the wearer, to how much he has to lose in the course of a given transaction. What the wearer has to lose is dignity, by showing anxiety in the presence of others whose opinion he values. The face is an extremely expressive part of the body, and the Tuareg, like the rest of us, are subject to undesirable loss of emotional control.

The ultimate roots of masking, Murphy suggests, lie in role conflict and alienation, which are universal attributes of social organizations. In our own society, similar devices can be observed. As in Victorian society decorous ladies used to avert their eyes or cover parts of their faces with fans, in today's society sunglasses may serve a similar purpose, and so may facial hair. When material masks are normally inserted between interactants, this is shielding with a vengeance, designed not to deceive but to preclude the possibility of communication.

Murphy admits that such shielding does not work perfectly; although the veil covers all of the face except a slit around the eyes, the Tuareg have become adept at interpreting subtle cues such as skin wrinkles and the set of the body. Personal identification is seldom a problem, since there are always slight variations in the kinds of clothing worn or ways of wearing it. Further, the Tuareg use a series of other cues from the body parts left open to public view.

*Purdah,* a Hindi word, originally Persian, has come to refer to a mode of female dress occasionally encountered in Moslem communities in the Near East and India, in which women wear in public a garment resembling a tent, with only the narrowest of slits for vision, behind which, at any distance, the most expressive eyes must go unremarked. Even in cases of such extreme masking, it was reported to me that young men on crowded city streets could recognize particular young women by their *feet*.

## Adapting to the Built Environment

We have seen that the interpersonal environment, constructed according to conventions governing spatial relationships between people, is a highly structured and influential factor in social life. Such conventions are no less powerful because few of the people subscribing to these rules would be able to articulate them well.

Like the interpersonal environment, the built environment is the result of human conventions, and it too exerts a powerful influence over our behavior. This influence sometimes has negative results, which is ironic since we are responsible for the nature of the built environment in the first place.

In this section I will examine some of the better-known studies of the interaction between architecture and human life, as well as some lesser-known but quite interesting ones; then I will deal with spatial needs, particularly as expressed in the desire for privacy; and finally I will discuss the way in which the design of buildings can be considered a means of regulating human behavior.

### Introduction

We have already remarked upon the increasing rapport between designers and architects on the one hand, and behavioral scientists on the other. (See Jensen [1974] for an architect's reaction to such collaboration.) Within this interface, there is a widespread tendency for sociologists to deal with problems related to city planning (e.g., Gans, 1961, 1962), and for psychologists to concentrate more on environmental perception and the perception or influence of interior design (e.g., Canter, 1968a, 1968b, 1974), although this disciplinary division of labor is by no means uniform. Apart from this, anthropologists and designers share a more general interest in the area, exemplified by the eclectic methods they use. Edward T. Hall is the most visible figure in this area of anthropology, but a number of others may be noted, including John Gulick.

In some ways, the study of behavior as it is related to one's home provides a common meeting ground for these various perspectives (e.g., Esber, 1971).

In Terence R. Lee's "Psychology and Living Space" (1963-64; also see Lee 1968), the essential proposition is that neighborhoods are geographic areas that grow out of social interaction, and they are organized to the extent that interactions are shared. Lee suggests that neighborhoods tend to be of a size that can be meaningfully grasped by people, namely about seventy-five acres, which might have as many as 2,500 residents or more. This is the sort of area that residents are likely to perceptually organize into something they call "their" neighborhood.

In Lee's study, children who lived closer to a school performed better in the classroom than did children living farther away, presumably because the commuting children needed to pass without transition from one perceptual area into another. If, in fact, it is fatiguing for a child to operate in two spatially segregated areas, is this equally true for commuting adults? Is the passage from one area to another eased, in some sense, if it is associated by one or another ritual to mark the transition? Lee's study has obvious implications for the card games and martini drinking that go on in the cars of the Long Island Railroad.

Similarly, Lewis Mumford's (1960-61, 1961) concept of the garden city involves housing and work spaces that are close together. This type of environment may already be observed in the suburbanization of industries and the subsequent reduction of commuting distances.

In *Slums and Social Insecurity,* an important work in the interface between architecture and behavior (Schorr, 1966), Alvin Schorr suggests that the negative effects of environment may sometimes be best studied under extreme conditions. As an example, a number of subsistence techniques may be developed in mild, pleasant climates producing abundant food, but adaptive choices may be very narrow in the arctic. Likewise, in slums one may find compelling evidence of the negative effects of housing; poor housing may lead to poor physical health through the influence of inadequate hygiene, and it may also lead to a deterioration of psychological well-being because of the effect of ugly surroundings on emotions. An experimental demonstration of this link occurs in Maslow and Mintz (1956). Of course, the most applicable causal model here may not be the relatively simple linear one, in which poor housing yields devalued behavior. Instead, a circular model of causality may be more appropriate, in which the results of behavior feed back to housing. It is essential to realize here, and in all other discussions of design and behavior, that environment and behavior are interdependent parts of a more general system. In a sense, we are all trapped in this circle, but for the poor the circle is vicious.

Another approach to the area views buildings as organic wholes, subject to certain laws and principles governing their growth and decay. This is the perspective assumed by Cowan (1962-63, 1965) and others. They seek general laws, largely ignoring the evaluative aspect of architecture. Cowan suggests that buildings may have movable walls and other design features that, in effect, convert what is usually fixed-feature space into semifixed-feature space. Externally, buildings may be constructed so as to allow easy expansion (Weeks, 1963-64).

Thus, for example, office buildings may be designed to grow and change with the evolving needs of the company. Of course, planners must take into account the effects of such changes on personnel.

Cowan's interest in the space-user relationship grows out of a design interest, rather than what is usually called basic research. He has noted that functional obsolescence precedes deterioration, and that therefore it would be most efficient to build throwaway buildings or to introduce adaptability into the design. The problem is conceived as a strictly practical one. In addition, it might be possible to determine a "natural size" for rooms, in which case we might build as many rooms of this size as practicable in a large organization. Such a design would correspond to biological generalization in evolution and would presumably enhance the building's likelihood of survival.

In another influential work, *Community and Privacy,* relating household design to neighborhood activities, Chermayeff and Alexander (1963) present a typology of physical areas, both public and private. Jurisdiction over public and private areas may be held by an individual, a family, or some larger group, such as a neighborhood. The thrust of the book is to relate family-private spaces, namely houses, to group-private spaces, namely those under the control of the larger neighborhood.

One of the questions addressed is how group-private spaces are indicated as such. That is, how do you keep unwanted outsiders from entering the area? This can be accomplished by a number of means. First, it is possible to do this formally, by fencing the neighborhood off or posting "keep out" signs, designating internal road systems as private. But residents can achieve the same end informally by putting up signs stating "No trucks over 5 tons" or "No peddlers allowed"; by varying the street width so that through traffic is hindered; by keeping the speed limit low to discourage through traffic; by establishing zoning regulations, or by building cul-de-sacs. All of these methods limit the accessibility of the neighborhood for the public at large, and they have obvious implications for the people who live in the area.

There is the additional problem of moving people and things from vehicles and from the sidewalk into the house and back, the issue here being the maintenance of family-private spaces.

Here again there are certain obvious means of blocking unwanted traffic. Houses may be set far from the roads. There may be private driveways, gates, locks on doors, and vestibules in which deliverymen, salesmen, and other agents of commercial enterprise may wait.

It may be worth pointing out that structural attempts to increase privacy may fail, and that when they do the results may be distressing. Houses that are physically isolated are probably more likely than others to attract burglars, and safety rests entirely on their internal security systems, which are fallible. The sort of protective layout suggested by Chermayeff and Alexander may paradoxically increase the risk of invasion. The single example of the Polanski-Tate residence in the hills near Los Angeles, which was chosen for a murderous visit by the Manson "family" partly because of its isolation, should suffice. The slightly paranoid tenor of *Community and Privacy,* which alienated some earlier readers, has perhaps come to seem a little more realistic in recent years.

Nevertheless, emphasis on the maintenance of privacy within the family and the exclusion of outsiders remains a weakness in the book. As Altman (1975: 10-31) has observed, privacy is a dialectic process. "Social interaction is a continuing interplay or dialectic between forces, driving people to come together and to move apart. There are times when people want to be alone and out of contact with others and there are times when others are sought out, to be heard and to hear, to talk and to listen" (Altman, 1975: 22). Privacy suggests, not so much exclusion of others, but rather a means of regulating their access. Or, as Proshansky et al. put it, "the specific circumstances under which [the] sense of privacy is experienced vary widely, but in all cases psychological privacy serves to maximize freedom of choice, to permit the individual to feel free to behave in a particular manner, or to increase his range of options by removing certain classes of physical constraints" (Proshansky et al., 1972: 33).

Gans's (1962) *Urban Villagers* gives instances in which the ability to conduct certain sorts of "personal" activities under the scrutiny of one's neighbors provides real satisfaction. For example, it is easy to imagine a young man who has just bought a shiny new automobile and who deliberately parks it at the curb of his working-class residential neighborhood and lovingly washes it in front of whatever witnesses present themselves.

Like everyone else, social scientists and architects tend to project their own states of mind onto other segments of the population. They sense in others an urgent need for privacy, meditation, solitude, and reflection — perhaps long uninterrupted periods of time in which to write books — to an extent that may well be unjustified. Certainly, anyone moving into a Samoan community and building a dwelling along the lines suggested in Chermayeff and Alexander would be an actuarial oddity. Of course, the resident would have more opportunity to "think things over," but what a price to pay! Similar cautions must be exercised in applying the characteristic needs of middle-class professionals to members of exotic working-class populations. The same point is made in Fried and Gleicher's (1961) criticism of "urban renewal" programs, and in Yancey's (1971) case study of a spectacular failure in public housing.

We may also add that some of the interplay of behavior in homes and neighborhoods is difficult to discern and interpret. That is, the job of mapping out these complex influences is not an easy one. For example, as one drives through congested residential areas of cities, it is common to see old people sitting at open windows, apparently enjoying the stream of pedestrians and slow-moving automobiles below. In rural areas, the elderly may observe slightly thinner streams from their front porches. In unwalled societies like Samoa, they need not move from their sleeping areas—sometimes they are unable to—but they *still* sit and watch the stream of pedestrians, joining their scrutiny to that of the argus-eyed children. The overall impression gained is that, in many communities, relatively immobile elderly people serve as a constant monitoring system during the most important hours of social activity.

As the previous passages suggest, the ways in which we adapt to the built environment may be obvious or they may be subtle and indirect. Sometimes the link between our behavior and the world we have constructed around us may be so obscure as to escape all but the most careful statistical analysis.

The study made by Segall, Campbell, and Herskovits (1966) has already been mentioned. The authors demonstrated that susceptibility to particular optical illusions is influenced by residence in "carpentered" environments—that is, environments characterized by a preponderance of right angles. Another study reports that, where the built environment is largely circular, as among the Zulu, individuals with less exposure to European life-styles prefer circles to squares in designs, while more Europeanized individuals do not (L.C. Doob, quoted in Allport and Pettigrew, 1957: 106).

Robbins (1966b) hypothesized that the shape of a society's domicile would be congruent with its art style. Specifically, a society with circular houses would prefer curved lines in its art style; a society with rectangular houses would prefer straight lines.

Robbins systematically compared straight and curved lines in the graphic art styles of thirty societies with judgments from the "Ethnographic Atlas" on house shapes in the societies.

The specific prediction turned out to be wrong, and not merely wrong, but opposite in direction. "In societies where the primary house type is circular, there appears to be a preference for or predominance of straight lines in art style; and in those societies in which the house type is rectangular, there is a preference for or predominance of *curved* lines in the cultural art style" (Robbins, 1966b: 746).

Robbins interpreted his results in terms of Daniel E. Berlyne's article (1962) relating optimal levels of arousal to exploratory behavior. Briefly, when novelty is too low, one is bored; when it is too high, one is confused. Despite Doob's earlier findings, there seems to be a general tendency for exploratory behavior such as art to serve as a way to introduce novelty into an otherwise predictable life.

## Spatial Needs

The following three sections will explore several aspects of privacy. First, I will discuss the ways in which stress may be generated in families by a lack of living space and privacy. Next I will present some information on the issue of privacy in the lives of Samoan villagers in a community where there is literally no place that is absolutely private. Finally I will describe a cross-cultural study of privacy that, among other things, speculates on likely historical roots for the concept of privacy.

*Households, Space, and Stress.* American families have undergone a curious change over the past one or two generations. It used to be observed that middle-class families were strict with their children, while working-class parents were permissive, but the tide has shifted. Recently, it seems that working-class parents are becoming restrictive, while middle-class parents are more permissive (summarized in Miller, 1958, 1960).

The shift in child-rearing behavior has been attributed to everything from fallout to Dr. Spock, but it may have as much to do with the management of space as anything else. Simply put, middle-class families have had more space available per family member than poorer families. Children could play inside the house, under the parents' scrutiny without being underfoot. Close parental supervision encouraged restrictive child-training practices. Working-class families, with presumably equally large numbers of children, had less space available inside the house, so their children were sent to play outside where a state of relative anarchy prevailed. Lack of space necessitated permissive child-training practices.

With recent shifts in the standard of living and in birth-control practices, families have prospered and grown smaller. There is now enough space within the working-class household to shelter the younger children, and working-class parents are as strict as they ever were—thus, they now seem restrictive. Increasing prosperity has made it possible for middle-class children to escape the constant scrutiny of their elders.

Of course some poorer families, notably urban minority groups, still lack the space needed to keep their younger children in the house without their getting underfoot. For black families, especially, the street remains the child's most important playground, the place where he or she feels at home. Moreover, even when the children of poorer families are at home, they suffer. Scheflin's work with space management in black and Puerto Rican ghetto households reveals that in many families, several children must sleep in the same bed, sometimes so many that they can fit in the bed together only if they lie across it. At any given time, there may not be enough space for the entire family to sit down together. In this way, the children of families living in poverty are forced to spend most of their time outdoors. Away from the scrutiny of parents, they develop their own rules of deportment, which are suitable for children but frequently disastrous when followed by adults.

Here is Scheflin's description of a typical response to the typical crowded household.

> A black father has certain problems about living space in his home. His wife may keep him out of the kitchen. He probably has a favorite seat in the living room and he owns half the bed, but these spots are often occupied until late at night. He can chase the kids from his favorite seat or off of the bed, but for some reason he often seems reluctant to do so. We have often observed a father enter a room, glance at the children in his seat and then pace the apartment. He goes to the bedroom for a few minutes, but there are kids there. He walks around the kitchen. Then he re-enters the living room, glances again at his seat and maybe hollers at the kids for messing up the living room, but he does not demand his seat.
>
> ...He paces the hall and kitchen for a while. Then he goes out to have a beer. Someone will say he does not take responsibility for his family. He might say there is no place for him in that house and no one pays attention to him. Maybe it is a vicious circle. [Scheflin, 1971: 440-41]

John Zeisel has proposed that, given the conditions of such households, designers should build public spaces in such a way as to accommodate some of the overflow while at the same time minimizing the damaging and defacing of public structures (Zeisel, 1974, 1975). Sommer's book *Tight Spaces* (1974) provides a critique of current attempts to achieve these goals.

A paper by Robinson (1969) reports on spatial arrangements of the households of Taos Pueblo, characterized by a small number of rooms, high density, and compact settlement patterns. Conditions are such that continuous personal contact with other persons is almost unavoidable. Robinson suggests that the stress imposed by this crowding of household members results in a compensatory attempt to maintain highly structured standards regarding personal space, an idea advanced elsewhere by Calhoun (1966). Restraint, moderation, and cooperation become primary virtues in the pueblo. Nevertheless, the high density of the living arrangements leads to stimulus overload and subsequent suspicion and factionalism. Robinson also discusses other reactions to the crowded arrangements, such as frequent travel over large distances. She points out that, curiously enough, Taos has no linguistic equivalents for our words *crowded* or *privacy*. A similar analysis of spatial management in crowded low-income housing in Peru appears in Alexander (1969).

It is necessary to point out, however, that some of the empirical research dealing with the effects of crowding on family relationships has produced contradictory findings. The effects of crowding may be more subtle than suggested above. A study by Booth and Edwards on crowding in Toronto households, for example, revealed that household congestion had "a small positive influence on the incidence of sibling quarrels and on the incidence with which parents struck their children. In general, however, crowding [was] found to have little or no effect on family relations" (Booth and Edwards, 1976: 308). In this study, family adjustment was measured by responses to a questionnaire rather than by systematic behavioral observations. There may be a difference between the frequencies of real and reported events, such as arguments, but there is no way of knowing. Such studies at least cast doubt on simple generalizations concerning the relationship between space and stress within the household.

Jonathan Freedman's (1976) hypothesis concerning the relationship between crowding and social interaction may explain some of these contradictory findings. He feels that crowding intensifies one's response to *all* social situations, so that good experiences become even more enjoyable as crowding increases, and bad experiences become worse. Freedman feels that inasmuch as crowding is likely to be inevitable, we may as well learn to live with it. The difficulty with this attitude, however, is that our responses are likely to affect others as well as ourselves. Freedman's own work reveals that crowded courtrooms are likely to influence the jury, and certainly we would all prefer situations in which potential murderers who are depressed and angry are able to avoid crowds.

The literature on ecological aspects of housing is enormous. We won't be able to cover it adequately here, but interested readers should turn to Pastalan's (1971) useful bibliography, which includes sources dealing with the ecological approach to housing problems, the perception of architectural space, the neighborhood scale, territoriality, the perception of the environment from paths and roads, the scale of the city, childhood and the environment, housing legislation, minority group and low-income housing, design and standards, government and family housing, spatial and density effects on human behavior, social aspects of housing, and housing and territoriality. Altman (1975) also reviews much of the recent literature.

*Privacy in Samoa.* Samoans often give their newborn children evocative or commemorative names. Along with more traditional names such as Seunga, one encounters names such as Mulinu'u ("the rear end of the village"), who might be glad that he recently acquired a chief's title and is now called Asepaolo; Vaimatangi ("water-wind"); Venikempi, who was born during the construction of Van Camp's tuna-processing plant; and Sonoma, who was born while the Matson freighter of that name was in port. During the moon flights, Apollo II was born. But if the referent of his name is clear enough, the circumstances surrounding his conception remain cloudy, to judge from this report in the *Samoan Times:*

> Jake King, 47, who hit the news two months ago when he obtained a court order stopping the Government of American Samoa from deporting him, was in court for trial last week on a criminal charge of failing to support a one-year-old boy purported to be his son.
>
> After a two-day hearing the case was completed and Associate Justice Joseph Goss is expected to deliver his verdict this week.
>
> The prosecution...alleged that Apollo II is the natural son of King.
>
> King pleaded not guilty to the charge and denied that the boy is his son.
>
> Prosecution witness Miss Teva Vai, 19, of Olosega Island, testified that during the period October 26 to November 5, 1968, she met King at Olosega and went for walks along the beach with him from nine to twelve o'clock on several occasions.
>
> She alleged that during this period there were relations between her and King, and that as a result Apollo II was born in July, 1969.
>
> King, though admitting that he had gone for lengthy walks with Teva, denied relations and said their association was platonic. He said it could not have been otherwise, because wherever he and Teva went they were being followed by at least 15 inquisitive children.

One may be forgiven if he sympathizes with both Teva and Mr. King; it won't make very much difference to Apollo II, since Samoan society has a gentle way of assimilating the most unlikely aliens, and Apollo II by no means represents as unique a phenomenon as his name does, despite the effect on privacy of those fifteen inquisitive children.

Generally speaking, there are four kinds of houses in Samoa: the guest house, the living house, the half-caste house, and the European house, along with an array of auxiliary buildings, some of them no more than sheds thrown together in a few hours.

The guest house is an open, thatched-roof structure, built usually on a platform of coral pebbles, the roof shaped something like a beehive. The living house is a similar structure, but oblong in shape. In both kinds of houses, the roof thatching may be replaced with corrugated tin. The half-caste house looks like an oblong dwelling house except that it has a shed built into one side; the major part of the half-caste house is open, but the shed is enclosed by planks or fiberboard. The European house is a simple dwelling of obvious European derivation; it has walls, its roof is usually of tin, and it may or may not have doors. The last three types of houses are likely to be built on short stilts. The first two traditional types provide nothing that we would recognize as privacy; the half-caste house at least has a shed that screens occupants and their activities from passersby. The European house clearly provides the most privacy, but even here the advantage is relative. In all cases where the house is unwalled, woven mats about the size of doormats are tied to one another and secured under most conditions under the eaves of the house. These mats can be lowered at will, of course, but in fact they are *never* lowered for privacy, only for protection against occasional raw weather.

Like most Samoan villages, the one in which I lived consisted mainly of unwalled houses scattered around an open field called a *malae,* corresponding roughly to the *zocalo* of some parts of Latin America, where civic functions were held. Although it was surrounded by forest, there were few trees in the village itself, and one could see for a considerable distance. As a result, one was always pretty much aware of the everyday activities of the neighbors, and supplementary information was supplied by the children of the community, who seemed eagle-eyed and ubiquitous. One man found his sister-in-law in the embrace of a visitor from Honolulu and said to the fellow: "Look, you're a good friend of mine. Don't misunderstand. But why you go into my house when my kids are there when you do that? You got your own place. I don't care. But these kids see everything. They look like they're sleeping but they're really watching everything."

Jake King may have put it more succinctly, but Margaret Mead's point is made more vividly:

> All of an individual's acts are public property. An occasional love affair may slip through the fingers of gossip,...but there is a very general cognizance on the part of the whole village of the activity of every single inhabitant....The oppressive atmosphere of the small town is all about them; in an hour children will have made a dancing song of their most secret acts. This glaring publicity is compensated for by a violent gloomy secretiveness. Where a Westerner would say, "Yes, I love him but you'll never know how far it went," a Samoan would say, "Yes, of course I lived with him, but you'll never know whether I love him or hate him." [Mead, 1968: 100]

Grattan makes a similar point in advising European visitors to Samoan villages that "they should remember that little actual privacy is prescribed in Samoan custom itself, and it is not unlikely that they are being watched, probably by children, even if they think they are unobserved. This should never be forgotten, and hence every care should be taken to ensure that conduct in a Samoan village is not such as will give rise later to unfavourable or disrespectful comment" (Grattan, 1948: 66).

It may be worth mentioning that Margaret Mead was describing the situation as it existed during her fieldwork in the mid-1920s, when the population of American Samoa was something like 8,000. By the time of my fieldwork forty years later, the population was closer to 20,000 — an increase of 12,000 observers, many of them youngsters, in an area limited to about seventy-five square miles. When sociologists talk about agents of social control, they usually mean the police, but perhaps, from the perspective of the entire population of human beings, children should be one of the first topics of consideration.

The point here may be made most emphatically by stating that, in the village in which I did my fieldwork, a village that was typical by most ordinary standards, *there was no such thing as absolute privacy.* By that, I mean that, within the confines of the village, there was no location in which one could shut oneself away so that an observer could not rather easily peek in on him. There was, for example, nothing resembling a modern bathroom, with frosted windows and lockable doors. Perhaps the greatest degree of privacy is afforded by the bush — the forest surrounding the village — within which there are certain cleared areas belonging to extended families, where gardens are tended by family members working within sight of one another. Perhaps secrets are discussed here and assignations occur, but the forest is threaded through with paths, and one never knows when an intruder will stumble upon the scene.

An example will perhaps crystallize some of these points. The chief in whose house I lived owned one of the few television sets in the village, and as a result he usually had evening visitors, mostly children from neighboring families. (Some of these viewers, incidentally, young and old, believed that the action portrayed on such fictional programs as "Adventures in Paradise" was really happening to real people, and that somehow the activities were showing up on the screen at the very time they were occurring. Some of the women made remarks in Samoan to the effect that, if that Captain Troy ever showed up in *this* village, they would give him a big feast, he was such a good fellow.)

On a Saturday night, three visitors appeared from a dwelling at the opposite end of the village, about a half mile's distance away. Two of them were young children, and the third was a girl of about twenty, Vaivai, who happened to be visiting for a few days. By nine thirty in the evening, the two children were dozing on the floor and mumbling that they wanted to go home. They asked me to walk them home because they were uncomfortable wandering about in the darkness, and I accompanied them and Vaivai home.

The next morning, as I approached one of the chief's granddaughters to help her start the Primus stove, she looked up from the floor and said "Vaivai," with the kind of mocking, expectant smile I had come to recognize as being associated with ridicule. My inquiries drew no response.

At about noon, the chief returned from Pago Pago, where he spent most of his mornings shopping, visiting, and drinking beer with chiefs from the other villages, and he approached me expansively and accused me of having designs on that girl last night. This happened to be in Samoan, and I missed a few of the expressions he used and asked a young man sitting nearby to translate them. The young man refused. "I don't know," he told me, "that chief is an old man but he still says all the bad words."

Again, later that afternoon, the chief made some remark to me about how I liked to go walking with girls in the dark. About three o'clock in the afternoon, I met another woman, a member of my adopted extended family, and she asked: "How is Vaivai? You have a good time last night?" She remarked that she hardly ever saw me during the day, I was always roaming around, here and there, at night. Somewhat later, I encountered another older woman who was also a member of my family, who inquired after Vaivai's health. During the entire day, on an irregular basis, two of the younger girls of neighboring families were conspicuously evident around the house, standing and staring at the windows of my room for a few minutes at a time, silently and independently.

My reaction to all this ribbing was one of real embarrassment. When the subject was brought up in conversation, I always tried to dismiss the incident as nothing and to change the subject by asking a question about some unrelated topic. When a teenage boy of my extended family made up a child's song about me and Vaivai, I found myself blushing—at the age of twenty-eight.

I cite this instance as common, not singular in any important respect, since I saw a number of other people suffer the same sort of ridicule.

One would be justified in asking if there were no means of compensating for the public nature of most acts. That is, how does one do something that one prefers to keep from the other villagers?

First, I must say that I found no evidence of the "gloomy secretiveness" described by Margaret Mead. At least among young men, a great deal of bonding occurs, strong enough in some cases to be insulated by jealousy against disruption, and an unmarried man is likely to be fairly candid with his few close friends. Invariably, this candor is rudimentary in that, while one may admit bluntly that he "likes" a woman, or that he has done something rather shameful, he is not likely to sit back and coolly analyze his personal feelings; these are, in any case, never subjects for extended discussion. However, I would characterize this less as gloomy secretiveness than as a genuine disinclination to introspect. Actions, including the exercise of social skills, are more important than insight. In other words, the topics discussed in gossip sessions are circumscribed and do not penetrate deeply into the subject's character. Much more so than in Western society, each possible infraction tends to be treated as an independent event rather than the repetitive expression of a central "problem." Thus, each time an individual appears drunk in public, the neighbors will say, "So-and-so is drunk." In between instances, they do not call the person a drunkard. With certain exceptions, such as homosexuality, which tends to be flamboyantly expressed, Samoans are loathe to speculate about motives, and they do not apply labels to people. This circumscription has the effect of mitigating the impact of public exposure.

A second compensating mechanism is something related to what psychologists call extinction, by which I mean that the novelty of seeing people engaged in activities ordinarily considered private soon wears off. The vast majority of acts — public or private — are mundane and essentially uninteresting. How long does one watch another person eating at home before tiring of it? How many times must one observe another person discretely urinating before urination becomes "ground" instead of "figure"? Unless an act has social significance, there is soon no particular reason for remarking upon it.

For acts that *do* have social significance, of course, there are always locations or circumstances that provide some relative degree of privacy. Lovers are, after all, less likely to be discovered in the forest than on the *malae,* and less in the dark than during daylight.

It is curious to note, though, that during the period of my fieldwork, there were several instances of couples being caught on the *malae* in the dark, *in flagrante delicto.* It is difficult to emphasize too strongly how embarrassing such an incident is for a young man and especially for a young woman, and yet these couples had not *bothered* to retreat to a location affording greater privacy than the town square.

This points up another compensating mechanism, mentioned by Grattan: lowered standards. To a certain extent, Samoans have learned to take the lack of privacy for granted, and they expect to be discovered occasionally. Following the numerous instances of public disclosure of activities intended as private, I never heard the culprit (or victim) grumble about the absence of places where seclusion could be guaranteed. I use the absolute *never* deliberately. No villager ever confessed to me, or to anyone else, so far as I could determine, a desire to get away from all those prying eyes for a while.

A final set of compensatory acts that may be mentioned is fabrication. Many Samoans, including those from Western Samoa, are adept at falsifying their identities and confabulating events. This may, in part, be a result of the Samoan's having learned well how to adjust to external circumstances rather than to any kind of internal gyroscope. In large measure, their success depends upon that ability. Again, we may quote Margaret Mead:

> No individual plays continuously a fixed role, except the high chief, whose role is so hedged about with etiquette, procedure, and lack of any real executive authority that he is not likely to overstep his bounds. But most individuals play a series of parts of differing importance in a series of differently organized activities; a man's attention is focused upon his behavior in relation to a situation, as host, as guest, as chief, as a member of the council, as a member of a chief's working group, as a fisherman beneath the leader, as a member of a war party in which his role is determined by his division membership in the village,...as the heir in his patrilineal line, as...the cross-cousin with a veto, in his mother's family, as the ranking member of one group, as the man of lowest rank in the next group he enters, as the chief to whom a young man kneels as he gives a message at noon time, and as the father of a daughter upon whom the same young man, who must now be received courteously, calls in the evening. Such a man does not develop a fixed response to others which is definitely either dominance or submission, leadership or discipleship, authoritarian insistence or meek compliance, exhibitionism or refusal to play any public part; the multiplicity and contrast between his roles prevent any commitment to one personality type from developing. *Whereas in a different type of society, it is possible to predict what a given individual A will do as compared with a given individual B, in Samoa it is much more possible to predict what a series of men, A, B, and C, will do in a given situation.* [Mead, 1937: 296; emphasis added]

As I have described the situation earlier, Samoans tend to learn, as part of this adaptation to circumstances, that there are times when lying is not totally unexpected. The sort of honesty so valued in the West has little absolute meaning in Samoa. A party visiting another village is required to recite the genealogical history of the host village, praising the virtues of its important figures, even if those figures don't deserve to be so praised. And in small groups, fabrication can be a rather common activity.

> There are unilateral lies, told by the liar for his own benefit, and designed to really deceive the listener ("Lend me ten dollars and I will pay you back

next payday"). Some unilateral lies are designed to deceive the listener, but for the listener's benefit ("I heard about that fight you got into with X and I think you were entirely justified"). There are also reciprocal lies, in which two or more people indulge in verbal fantasies, sometimes protracted, neither of the participants believing what they are saying but nevertheless enjoying the tales simply for their entertainment value. [Maxwell, 1969: 179-80]

Of course, unilateral and reciprocal lies are frequently encountered in our own society, perhaps in most societies, and there are slang expressions to describe them, but I mean to emphasize here the difference in the degree to which fabrications are employed and the variant nature of the circumstances surrounding their occurrence. I have, for instance, been approached by a middle-aged man in a public place, who introduced himself to me, formally and politely, giving a false name and identity. Young men frequently are known by completely different names in separate villages.

As Roberts and Gregor (1971: 214) have pointed out, lying often blunts the impact of village gossip. To the extent that fabrication occurs, the listener can seldom be quite certain about the epistemological status of the event. "Maybe it happened and maybe it didn't; since so many people around here lie, it's hard to be sure."

These, at least in one society, are some of the ways in which the lack of privacy and the resulting compensatory mechanisms operate. These topics, surprisingly, have not been of much interest to ethnographers, and it is only recently that anything systematic has been done with them. Customs regulating access to the activities of one's neighbors certainly deserve more attention than they have received so far.

*A Cross-cultural Study of Privacy.* In an initial attempt to examine degrees of variation in domestic privacy from a cross-cultural perspective, Roberts and Gregor (1971) found that societies that were high in political integration—that is, characterized by complex political organizations— were also high in domestic privacy. To better illuminate the dynamics of the relationship, Roberts and Gregor chose a small sample of societies that were low in political integration—that is, characterized by small, autonomous settlements, or lacking in political organization even at the community level. Subsequently, each of these forty-two societies was grouped into one of five categories of privacy, on the basis of permeability of houses to sight and sound, closable windows and doors, partitions within dwellings, and the number of people ordinarily residing together. The societies and their categories are given below:

*Very high:*        Chukchee, Kikuyu, Lapps, Lolo, Luo, Tallensi, Tara-
                    humara.

| *High:* | Fang, Ila, Koryak. |
|---|---|
| *Intermediate:* | Dorobo, Iban, Jivaro, Papago, Seri, Tehuelche, Tikopia, Tubatulabal. |
| *Low:* | Andamanese, Chippewa, Gilyak, Mundurucu, Nambicuara, Tapirape, Toda, Trukese, Vedda, Wogeo, Yaruro, Yahgan. |
| *Very low:* | Delaware, Goajiro, Ifaluk, Manus, Mataco, Murngin, Senara, Sirionó, Tiwi, Tucuna, Tupinamba, Yokuts |

Roberts and Gregor then explored some of the associations between degrees of privacy and variables selected from the "Ethnographic Atlas." Some of the associations "suggest that even among these societies with little political integration, those with domesticated plants and animals are more likely to be higher in privacy than those dependent upon gathering, hunting, and fishing. Perhaps privacy as we know it is a neolithic development" (Roberts and Gregor, 1971: 202). Privacy is also associated with certain social structural variables, including unilineal descent systems and modes of marriage, and certain characteristics of expressive culture, such as kinds of games played and the presence of high gods. The latter correspondence "shows that the higher the privacy the more likely the presence of strong high gods.... Perhaps when human surveillance diminishes, supernatural surveillance increases" (Roberts and Gregor, 1971: 202).

The authors suggest that "it would appear that privacy, as we know it, is largely a neolithic invention occurring primarily in the Old World and associated with the Near Eastern cultural complex which later diffused to all the centers of high culture in the Old World" (Roberts and Gregor, 1971: 203). They also speculate upon the possible psychological determinants of privacy and the psychological results of different levels of privacy.

Roberts and Gregor next examined privacy patterns among the Zuni in the American Southwest, where Roberts had conducted fieldwork, and among the Mehinacu of Brazil, where Gregor had worked.

> The Mehinacu turn out to be an extreme example of a society whose privacy pattern is radically different from the one we know. Here spatial and physical barriers to penetration and surveillance are minimal. Institutionalized privacy among the Mehinacu largely relies instead on rules of kinship and religious taboos. Among the Zuni there is a quite different pattern of privacy, but even here the restrictions on the flow of information are primarily a function of the religious system. In fact... Zuni religion, among other things, defines a set of rules for establishing hidden regions and maintaining secret knowledge within the society. [Roberts and Gregor, 1971: 200]

By this last statement, Roberts and Gregor mean that privacy and the persistence of the religious cults that form the very foundation of Zuni life were inextricably mixed. In the course of a house-to-house survey of material goods, Roberts found that "the most private of all the settings were to be found in the storage areas within the bedrooms or in the main storeroom, for it was here that objects of religious importance were kept" (Roberts and Gregor, 1971: 218).

The authors argue that in this case, the religious system may have been able to persist in the face of outside pressure because it was grounded in complex patterns of private places and private behaviors, all designed to protect "classified information" from discovery by outsiders or deviants.

The description of Mehinacu patterns of privacy focuses both on the relative paucity of private behavior settings and on compensatory mechanisms, including seclusion barriers, affinal avoidance patterns, patterns of etiquette concerning intruding on others, concealed paths through the surrounding forests, discretion, civil inattention, and prevarication. Indeed, in some respects the overall behavioral configuration is similar to that prevailing in Samoa (see also Gregor, 1974).

The tentative conclusion drawn in this study is that our own conception of privacy is the result of a particular evolutionary track, beginning perhaps at about the time of the domestication of large animals and of cereal grains during the Neolithic period some seven thousand years ago, and diffusing outward from the Near East as part of a much larger complex of behaviors and ideas. The notion of privacy as a set of prohibitions against seeing or hearing the activities of a nuclear family residing within a given dwelling belongs to that larger complex and is not found in all societies. Societies that are part of different cultural traditions also have rules concerning the flow of information, but the functions of these rules and their provenience are likely to be different from our own.

*Regulating Movement*

The remaining sections of this book will examine the consequences of varying degrees of fit between aspects of the built environment and the requirements of human behavior, particularly movement through space.

*Introduction.* Every institution has to establish a system for assigning places to people. Users must be funneled into areas suitable for their purposes; environmental signals concerning spaces must be clear enough to be correctly interpreted by the users. When these signals are "crossed," something like the following may result:

> I found the usual entrance to the public library locked and the sign in the window "Use West Door." Though I am mentally alert generally, I have

never known directions. As a boy I imagined that north was up and south was down but I was never sure whether east was to my right or left. The library sign made no sense to me so I entered the first door available, which turned out to be the "south" door. It led through a dim corridor into a brightly lit office area. Clerks on both sides who were busy typing library cards and purchase orders paid no attention to my presence. Further on I found a large storeroom containing unopened crates of books and several shelf areas filled with books that I can only assume were for the use of the library staff. To this day I regret not having examined more this librarian's library. The corridor continued past a gray-green elevator and a stairway out of *The Hunchback of Notre Dame.* Rather than stray too far from my familiar world, I returned to the main office and asked how to find the stacks. The girl assumed I was library staff and my question had no meaning for her. Suddenly a glint of recognition came into her eyes—I was a user rather than staff! Apparently she hadn't seen a user for years. Because there was no way to pass from the staff area into the user area except by a secret panel in one of the stacks, I returned to the outside the way I entered. I've used the library many times since then but I have never seen another trace of that strange "staff" world. [Sommer, 1974: 103]

Certain kinds of institutions, namely those serving impaired populations, face acute problems in this area. A few years ago, Jeanne Bader, Wilbur Watson, and I proposed a typology of restraint systems in common use in an institution housing elderly residents, more or less impaired (Maxwell et al., 1972). Among the relatively competent residents who could interpret not only the explicit signs but the interactional and architectural nuances concerning the proper use of space on the ward, the most important form of regulation was consensual control. By this term, we referred to the joint recognition of territorial rights between staff and residents and the ability of each to respond mutually and adaptively to the demands of the other. This, of course, is the primary means by which all social behavior is regulated.

But we also found several other restraint systems in use, most of them applied to the more impaired residents in the institution. Physical-object constraints were those that involved material artifacts. They might be fixed features such as walls or semifixed features such as furniture or doors. Fixed features involved decisions about architecture and design that, once made, were difficult to change. They were, moreover, extremely important in determining the routes of passage to internal and external spaces, and these in turn influenced the flow of people within and around the building. Semifixed features, on the other hand, were generally designed in such a way as to be easily changed, as doors may be opened or closed.

Another set of physical constraints involved pharmaceutical substances rather than objects. Drugs such as tranquilizers, and others that induce drowsiness as a side effect, tend to retard the movement of individuals through space, although that may not be their stated purpose.

We also found instances of the application of physical devices, such as straps, to keep residents seated in their chairs. In other institutions, the devices may be only partial, as in handcuffs or casts on fractured limbs.

It should be mentioned that there is nothing wrong with restraint systems per se. Where consensual restraint is impossible, the use of some other form of restraint is mandatory at times, both for the safety of the resident and for the efficiency of the institution. One would hardly care to have disoriented residents shuffling about in the kitchen, the infirmary, or the morgue. What we found disturbing was the fact that decisions about the imposition of restraints were most often left in the hands of lower-level staff members whose primary task was to keep the unit orderly. The routine application of restraints seems likely to accelerate the deterioration of marginally impaired residents who are thus deprived of opportunities to practice interactional skills.

Of course, no such rules applied to staff members themselves. On the contrary, staff had easy access to all of the ward areas assigned to residents and, moreover, staff could use certain areas that were denied to residents, such as the nurses' station and the staff lounge and bathroom. This is a standard arrangement in many institutions dealing with residents who are in some way defined as impaired. Barry Schwartz (1968) points out that in some establishments exclusive jurisdiction over a private place may be paid for — pay toilets, for instance — and the rules governing access to restricted areas reflect and affirm status divisions within the institution.

*Behavior-contingent Physical Design.* It has been pointed out frequently that there are times when architects and designers do not fit the built environment to human needs. Indeed, there are some notorious examples of misguided or badly thought-out buildings. Boston's John Hancock Tower, the tallest building in New England and the most visible structure in the city's skyline, has had more than ten thousand of its windows replaced because of their poor design. Many of the replacement windows themselves were blown out to shatter on the streets below, and they were finally replaced with plywood. The same architects designed a research center at Massachusetts Institute of Technology with doors that, it developed, could not be opened because of building-generated wind currents. Shnohomen, Sweden, is another example of a complex of apartment buildings characterized by a great deal of resident dissatisfaction and anomie. A satellite of Stockholm in which no cars are permitted, Shnohomen consists of huge, undifferentiated buildings within walking distance of a wide mall that seems to be used primarily by young people who desire to get far enough away from authority figures to smoke illegal substances in comfort. No doubt one of the least functional of design features in large buildings is the installation of permanently sealed windows that require that the heating and air conditioning be in operation all the time. The University of California San Diego campus, which is in La Jolla, is apparently designed not to take advantage of the characteristics of its natural setting, built as it is in a geographic location characterized by one of the most comfortable, equable climates in the world. Its Mediterranean climate provides mild winters and warm summers, with summer heat alleviated by the layer of sometimes fog-bearing marine air that sweeps onto the California coast. Some architects estimate that sealed windows can add as much as 20 percent to the energy cost of a building (Metzger, 1975).

Built-in flexibility, as proposed by Cowan and others, is of course a good idea. But how does one get from an existing structure to a modified one by means of this flexibility? That is, how does one know when to change a building, and in what direction?

In speaking of psychiatric hospitals, Humphry Osmond has observed that we need "architectural autopsies," systematic studies of the ways human beings use their buildings. We need, in other words, to overcome the "hollow sculpture" approach to architecture.

> We must learn to think much more like plane designers who have, I believe, as their motto "Draw 'em, build 'em, test 'em, fly 'em, scrap 'em." The human and material organization of a ward in a mental hospital is as complicated as a modern jet plane and about as expensive. Yet our ways of attacking the problems involved are very different. The aircraft designers pay the very greatest attention to their prototype. After they have built a machine of the most up-to-date design, it is tested by a team of the most skilled experts. From what they learn, the production model is built. This is finally handed over to pilots who are specially trained to understand the ways of the new plane. [Osmond, 1957: 29]

One of the more sophisticated analysts of the problems facing the designer who wants to integrate his plans for a building with the behavior of the potential residents is Raymond G. Studer. An architect himself, Studer became a psychologist de facto when he turned to the study of environmental psychology, only to find that *all* psychology was environmental psychology.

In a series of publications Studer has explored this problem and related ones (e.g., Studer, 1966a, 1966b, 1967, 1969, 1970, 1971; Studer and Stea, 1966). One of his most significant arguments is that it is impossible to "solve" the "problem." This is partly because of the complicated,

time-related nature of human behavior and human needs, which continue
to shift even as we attempt to deal with them, and partly because no problem is solved without the creation of other problems. Studer is convinced
that

> We do not, as has so often been mentioned, know enough about what must
> be done environmentally to precisely realize our human goals. Because of this
> ignorance and some of the complex conceptual issues which grow out of it, we
> can only view the environmental design act (i.e., the self-conscious effort to
> structure our environment) in a different way than is traditional in the design
> community. There can be no "solution" per se, only an environmental
> *hypothesis* regarding what might be the human effect. [Studer, 1971: 327]

In sum, what designers need now is not so much additional data, but

> a new epistemology of environmental design, one which recognizes the uncer-
> tainty and state-changing requirements for man-environment equilibrium.
> We would do well to realize that we are simply involved in an *experiment,* an
> experiment in which the various actors are making decisions...to manipulate
> the man-made environment toward some equilibrium state with respect to
> our individual and collective goals. We are involved in an on-going experi-
> ment to better our environmental lot. [Studer, 1971: 327]

In another paper, Studer (1969) proposes that the most commonly used
unit for solving many of the problems associated with design is the human
"need," but that needs are not themselves observable. What *is* observable is
the behavior of users, and behavior is what ought to provide relevant,
verifiable guidelines for design. Studer discusses several ways of discovering dissonances between behavior and physical design, and he attempts to
pin down empirically the stages that characterize these methods: first, the
designer compares the requisite behavior system with the existing behavior
system and tries to identify dysfunctions due to the existing physical
system; next, he or she compares the simulated behavior system with the
requisite behavior system, and finally the designer compares elements of
the realized behavior system with the requisite behavior system and tries to
identify dysfunctions due to the realized physical system. If the
dissonances so identified are within defined levels of tolerance, the
physical solution is partially confirmed. For example, if a newly built
prison is expected to reduce the frequency of violent acts, eighty of which
ordinarily occur during a year, and their frequency is in fact reduced to
five, then it may be assumed that the physical plant "works." As Studer
sums it up, a planning effort committed to well-being is one that is constantly being modified and improved, moving towards a state of equilibrium. The ongoing experiment, in other words, is the solution.

Of course, other students of design have addressed the problem of behavior-environment congruence in broad terms (e.g., Alexander, 1964; Sommer, 1974; Holland, 1966; Wicker, 1974; Design Innovations, 1970; Broadbent, 1970: 2). Occasionally there is a focus on designing certain environmental features to fit specific aspects of human behavior, such as climbing stairs (Fitch et al., 1974) or elimination and grooming (Kira, 1976). At this end of the broad-focus/narrow-focus spectrum, we find a concern with highly specific design problems in which the ultimate aim is not the accommodation of the physical system to emitted, naturally occurring human behavior, but the enhancement of worker productivity and increased efficiency in the performance of technical tasks such as flying an airplane, at which point we enter the realm of human engineering and ergonomics, which are mentioned briefly in the following section. At the broad-focus end of the spectrum, Studer and the others mentioned in this section are concerned primarily with the interface between physical characteristics of the built environment and the everyday aspects of human behavior—with what one architect called "architecture [as] the three-dimensional expression of human behavior" (Vriend, 1963; quoted in Lipman, 1969: 192).

Applying the data and ideas generated by behavioral scientists and designers to the interface between architecture and behavior has been most extensive in the area of institutions; that is, buildings occupied part-time or full-time by a relatively large number of users for specific purposes. Most influential have been studies of institutions built to house elderly, impaired residents or psychiatric patients. In some instances experimental buildings have been constructed in accordance with researchers' recommendations.

*Design and Use of Institutional Space.* There is a more voluminous social science literature in the area of institutional design and use than that in any other facet of the architecture-behavior interface. Therefore, this discussion will necessarily be brief in comparison with existing literature on the subject, more of a broad guide to the more important work than a description of specific findings. Most of the work to be reviewed consists of case studies or general essays, with little systematic theory linking the two.

The significance of institutional design may be illustrated by an anecdote of Humphry Osmond, a British psychiatrist who has been awarded the American Psychiatric Association Silver Plaque Merit Award.

> I had a lucky experience in San Francisco when I had a slight but unpleasant attack of influenza in a strange hotel. Feeling extremely unwell, I got out of my room in order to post a letter, and I then started walking around this building, which is a hollow square. After a time, I realized that something very strange was happening, for I seemed to have walked round several

times. This particular hollow square happened to be absolutely identical all the way round. To add to the sport, the numbers of the rooms are the same on each side. True, on one side there is a letter G placed next to the room number, but if you are not feeling well, you don't notice such refinements. After I had walked around for a bit, I realized that I either had to go down and get a bell hop to show me where I was, and they would think I was drunk, or else there must be some meaning in this mystery. I couldn't believe this particular hotel could have put the same numbers on two rooms. It's immoral, apart from anything else. [Osmond, 1967]

Osmond has also described his experience in a hotel characterized by long corridors with floor-to-ceiling mirrors at either end, enabling one to watch one's own image approaching from many yards away along the narrow hallway, past door after identical door, step by measured step, an effect to unsettle even the most stable among us.

Schools and dormitories have provided a fertile field for the study of adaptive spatial behavior. Among many such studies may be mentioned the crowding studies of Valins and Baum (1973) and Baum and Valins (1973), delineating a "stress-coping" sequence in which it is reported that students living under crowded dormitory conditions are more likely to maintain greater distances from others in nondormitory situations. They also appear less likely to help others in minor tasks such as mailing stamped and addressed envelopes found on the floor (Bickman et al., 1973).

Hoag and Johnson (1975) have conducted a comparison between "open" and "traditional" classrooms; that is, between classrooms that are large and in which tables and chairs are arranged in an apparently informal manner, and classrooms that are small, with the furniture arranged in the traditional manner. The behavior of children in the classrooms is systematically observed and analyzed. Flexible furniture arrangements have been designed (Beckman, 1968), and the effects of fixed-feature space and other environmental factors on classroom participation and performance are examined in Sommer (1967; 1969: 98-119; 1974: 81-101).

Preiser has studied the means by which evaluation of student housing may be standardized (Preiser, 1969). Harris and Paluck's (1971) study of crowding at Hunter College, a branch of the City University of New York, suggests that high-density situations in which personal space is frequently violated need not lead to aggressive behavior. The investigators noted an increase of behavior, such as the use of involvement shields, that shut out the perception of others. What little aggression occurred was more frequent between front-line staff, such as cafeteria workers, and students, during transactions in which others could not be shut out.

Certainly one of the earliest studies relating school environments to behavior was Barker and Wright's *The Midwest and Its Children* (1954), using a technique they called psychological ecology. This is a comprehensive study, although its methodology has been roundly criticized (Harris, 1964: 144-48).

Perhaps the most important study of dormitory behavior in recent years has been that of Dutch-born Sim Van der Ryn, formerly California's state architect, and his colleagues at the University of California, Berkeley (Van der Ryn, 1967; Van der Ryn and Silverstein, 1967). Van der Ryn and Silverstein's monograph, *Dorms at Berkeley: An Environmental Analysis,* presents a case study of the high-rise student housing there. The study was prompted by the high vacancy rate that began in 1964. Student attitudes towards the dorms were measured by means of observation, interviews, questionnaires, and activity logs. Three major sources of dissatisfaction were uncovered: a lack of personal determination in the design and modification of the standardized rooms, too much space devoted to lounges and other public spaces and too little devoted to private study areas, and the fact that the dorms seemed designed for occupancy by idealized types of students rather than ordinary ones. The authors end with practical suggestions for improving student living spaces.

Another investigation of student satisfaction with conventional dormitories, apartments, suites, and irregular or unconventionally designed residence halls suggests that the overall definition of the residence hall is also an important variable, quite aside from particular architectural features. Least satisfaction was registered with conventional dorms and most satisfaction with housing complexes that were considered irregular or unconventional by students (Davis and Roizen, 1970).

The work of the School Environments Research Project of Ann Arbor (1965) may serve as a useful introduction to the literature, especially that dealing with the impact of physical rather than social variables upon efficiency and comfort. It is probably reasonably representative up to the date of publication.

A great deal has been written about the design and use of medical settings and quasi-medical settings such as psychiatric units and homes for the aged. Many of the more important studies have come from the team of Edwin P. Willems, Shalom E. Vineberg, William F. LeCompte, and Anson J. Levine, then at the University of Houston. Their papers (e.g., Willems and Vineberg, 1969; Vineberg and Levine, 1969; LeCompte, 1969) follow Barker and Wright's earlier leads in focusing upon the measurement of observed behavior and relating kinds of behavior to kinds of physical settings. Observations were made at the Texas Institute of Rehabilitation and Research in Houston. Rosengren and DeVault (1970) have studied scheduling in an obstetrics ward, investigating the integration of spatial and temporal demands. Earickson (1970) has studied the delivery system of medical services in terms of the location of the hospital in surrounding urban space.

As far as the design of psychiatric hospitals is concerned, Osmond (1967) has pointed out that some of the earliest and best were built in the middle of the last century by Thomas Kirkbride of Philadelphia. The Kirkbride hospitals demonstrate a laudable balance between cheerful, sunny alcoves where patients may have relative privacy, and larger central areas where they may engage others if they care to. In Kirkbride's words:

> A hospital for the insane should have a cheerful and comfortable appearance; everything repulsive and prison-like should be carefully avoided. No one can tell how important this may prove in the treatment of patients nor what good effects may result from first impressions thus made upon an invalid on reaching a hospital. Nor is the influence of these things on the friends and relatives of the patients unimportant. [Kirkbride, 1880: 52]

We have unfortunately not absorbed Kirkbride's lessons, the prevailing atmosphere of most psychiatric institutions, particularly public ones, remaining prisonlike.

Some observers have given firsthand accounts of what it is like to stay in such a unit (e.g., Deane, 1961). Probably the best-earned set of impressions comes from Kiyo Izumi, an architect who took LSD under medical supervision — sympathetic medical supervision — before visiting the University Hospital in Saskatoon, Saskatchewan, and Saskatchewan Hospital in Weyburn, and who subsequently recorded his experiences.

> I began to comprehend many of the patients' remarks and concerns. For example, how a room "leaked" and a patient saw himself flowing away. To be "startled" by the monotony of one color, such as beige throughout the institution, may sound contradictory, but there was such a phenomenon, which could immobilize a patient. Similarly, the ubiquitous terrazzo floor, suspended ceiling, and similar "uniformity" added to the patient's confusion in relating himself to time and space.... The hard, glaring, and highly reflective surfaces of polished terrazzo floors, glazed-tile walls, and white ceiling tiles created spaces of unusually intimidating qualities, particularly if other people were also in this space. The acoustical qualities of such enclosed space heightened the effect of "tautness," and this quality became indistinguishable from psychic and physical tensions. [Izumi, 1970: 387-88]

After his experiences, and following discussions with patients and professionals, Izumi recommended that certain principles of design be followed in the construction of psychiatric facilities: (1) provide as much privacy as possible; (2) minimize ambiguity in architectural design and detail; (3) create an environment without intimidating qualities; and (4) create spatial relationships that reduce the frequency and intensity of undesirable confrontations. These recommendations were closely followed in the design of the Yorktown Psychiatric Centre in Saskatchewan.

Concerning Izumi's second recommendation, Mayer Spivak has called for "sensory honesty" in the design of psychiatric facilities, including the elimination of sensory paradoxes, such as long tunnels that distort the perception of distance and of other people, creating interrelated cross-sensory illusions involving space and time (Spivak, 1967). More generally he has observed that buildings, and the rooms within them, are transmitters of messages. A bed "says" lie down and go to sleep. Some rooms "say" we expect you to be crazy and destroy things. It has often been argued that we draw our identities from the behavior of others, but little attention has been given to the cues we receive from the built environment in which we are forced to live (Spivak, 1966). It may well be that such architectural cues become more important as our ability to accurately sense and organize social cues diminishes. This is a hypothesis that M. Powell Lawton has formulated with respect to brain-damaged elderly, and which he calls the "environmental docility hypothesis" (Lawton, 1970, 1972, among other works).

Another discussion of related issues can be found in Good et al. (1965), the results of a conference for designers and mental health professionals in Kansas, antedating much of the more recent work in the field.

Concerning Izumi's first recommendation, providing for the privacy of psychiatric patients, Ittelson et al. (1970) offer some experimental support for the idea that privacy enhances patients' "confidence" or, at least, the tendency to interact with others. In this study, it was reported that patients in single rooms were more likely to keep active when they were alone, and that they were more interested in seeking the companionship of others, while patients in more populated wards were relatively passive and apathetic. Mostly, they sat around doing nothing.

Also directly related to Izumi's first recommendation is the work of Humphry Osmond, a collaborator and a former colleague of Izumi's. His numerous publications (e.g., 1957, 1959a, 1959b, 1966) are models of enlightened inquiry. In his article "Function as the Basis of Psychiatric Ward Design" (Osmond, 1957), he has suggested that the design of the facility be suited to the needs of the patients. Certain assumptions underlie his argument. Acute schizophrenics, for instance, are likely to be disoriented, frightened, and overwhelmed by the presence of others, particularly strangers who have an unknown degree of control over their behavior. Buildings designed to house them should take this into account. "It would be heartless to house legless men in a building which could only be entered by ladders or very steep gradients. But so little thought has been given to the care of the mentally ill that buildings far more detrimental have been foisted upon them" (Osmond, 1957: 23).

Osmond believes that buildings have certain general qualities that may be referred to as "sociofugality" and "sociopetality." The former is an aspect of design that discourages interaction and drives people apart, a familiar example being the waiting room of a railway station or airport, where seats are lined up side by side in a large, acoustically active room, brightly lighted. Sociopetality is an aspect of design that encourages inter-action and tends to bring people together in stable relationships, a good ex-ample being the small seminar room with round table and comfortable chairs or, indeed, the average middle-class living room. Osmond has sug-gested that psychiatric hospitals should provide both sociofugal and sociopetal spaces, and intermediate spaces as well, in an attempt to accom-modate the needs of patients who are likely to be in varying states of withdrawal. Specifically, hospitals ought to be round instead of square and, along the periphery, provide small private rooms for patients in acute withdrawal, who are least able to handle social relationships. Four private rooms should open up onto a smaller, intermediate space, with comfort-able chairs and a central table, so that, as he or she emerges from a state of withdrawal, the patient may gradually get to know a few neighbors. Final-ly, a larger central area should be provided for patients who wish to prac-tice interactional skills in larger social settings. The interior design should be as homelike as possible with perhaps less attention paid to luxury than to comfort.

A number of buildings have been designed along the lines suggested by Osmond. The implementation of these ideas, however, is not always easy. Round buildings cost more than square or rectangular buildings. One organization planning such a building had what has probably become a commonplace experience over the past decade; although the building had been adequately funded, estimates of cost overrun increased so rapidly, even before construction, that the planners had to revert to a more conven-tional design.

Additionally, small variations in the design of the building seem to make a difference, and so do the kinds of users. At one such institution I have visited, Haverford State Hospital near Philadelphia, the design did not work as planned. For one thing, the four-person spaces had been equipped with large folding doors opening onto the central space, fixtures that were a nuisance to open and close. Consequently, the doors were left open all the time, converting the four-person space from an intimate set-ting into what patients and staff referred to as an alcove, hardly more than an entranceway into the private rooms. Then, too, few of the patients were in states of acute withdrawal. Many, already very deteriorated and thoroughly institutionalized, had been moved in from more traditional wards; others were severely retarded; and some had behavior disorders. Finally, the buildings themselves were rectangular, although the effect this had on general patterns of use is impossible to determine. Suffice it to say that the buildings did not provide a fair test of the hypothesis. However, both staff and patients preferred the Osmond design to conventional designs. Accessible patients appreciated the privacy afforded by the individual rooms; and staff felt that their duties were more comfortably discharged in such a setting.

A great number of other studies of mental hospitals have been conducted (see, for example, Jules Henry's article on the relationship between the use of space and the characteristics of users in a psychiatric unit [Henry 1964]). For reviews of these, and references, the reader should consult such general sources as Proshansky et al. (1970); Altman (1975); *Milieu,* the newsletter of the Environmental Research Foundation in Topeka; the periodical *MES,* published by the Association for the Study of Man–Environment Relations, Inc., Orangeburg, New York; Moos and Insel (1974); and *Man Environmental Reference* 1 (1974). Lack of space precludes a recounting of all the relevant literature here.

Geriatric settings have lately been receiving almost as much attention as psychiatric ones. Gerontology is probably one of the fastest growing disciplines in the behavioral sciences. The above-mentioned general works also contain reviews of literature dealing with homes for the aged and with the broad relationship between old people and their environments. In addition, Pastalan and Carson's (1970) reader is essential, and the Gerontology Project Group's *Research in Environmental Analysis and Design for the Aging* (1971) is a valuable source of references and reviews. This report is published by the Department of Design and Environmental Analysis at the College of Human Ecology, Cornell University. Also useful are Kent, Kastenbaum, and Sherwood's *Research, Planning, and Action for the Elderly* (1972), and Bell's (1976) reader in social gerontology. Not a review, but a report of an important, relevant study is Lawton's (1975) *Management of Housing for the Elderly.* One could almost gain an overview of the field from a perusal of Lawton's works alone. This field is expanding, and justifiably so, since the age structure of industrialized countries is shifting in the direction of fewer children and a greater number of old people, who constitute a minority group to which most of us will someday belong.

*High Rises.* High-rise apartment buildings make it possible for a great number of people to live on a small amount of valuable urban land. However, the resulting high population density would seem in many cases to exacerbate some of the forms of human behavior that middle-class Americans define as noxious — drug use, violence, theft, public drunkenness, and apathy.

Urban Chinese in America and Hong Kong have been able to manage an economically precarious existence rather well under crowded conditions. Public order is somehow maintained in San Francisco's Chinatown despite a population density of 880 persons per acre, and in Hong Kong despite a density of as much as 2,000 per acre (Schmitt, 1963).

In the United States, the acid test for high-rise apartment buildings has been in public housing, and the most spectacular example received considerable coverage in the mass media. This, of course, is Pruitt-Igoe, a series of high-rise apartment buildings in St. Louis, occupied by relocated (or perhaps dislocated) black families.

Edward T. Hall has observed that territoriality in black neighborhoods is a multifamily function and that

> if housing projects are to be designed in terms of black culture, they should be congruent with the informal, social, and territorial realities of that culture. Public housing for blacks should be planned to organize and not disrupt or separate functions. Overall distances should be held to a minimum and massive scale should be avoided, for there is something about the intimacy of black culture that is antithetical to large anonymous masses. In addition, there should be functions for the group to perform, alleys to be paved, yards to be kept up, children to correct and be involved with. Otherwise, group cohesiveness does not emerge. In the absence of group support and involvement of the type indicated, marginal individuals seem to lead extraordinarily fragmented, precarious lives in which the territorial alternatives may not include even venturing across the street. In their present form, high-rise apartments enhance fragmentation of social relationships and, therefore, they can be said to be dysfunctional for many blacks. [1971: 247-48]

Something like this apparently happened at Pruitt-Igoe, a $36 million complex of forty-three eleven-story buildings, constructed in the early 1950s. Within a decade, the incidence of rape, robbery, and aggravated assault in Pruitt-Igoe was more than twice that of the city as a whole. The buildings were defaced, the elevators became inoperative and were used as public bathrooms, visitors were sniped at and bombarded with objects from the windows above the entrances. Individual families were terrorized by teenage gangs, and insurance collectors were robbed and killed. The result has been the destruction of Pruitt-Igoe; the last of the original buildings was razed a few years ago. Of added significance is the fact that Pruitt-Igoe was designed by Minoru Yamasaki, a glamour architect of immense talent and great popularity, and that in itself would have made the project famous.

Conflict between tenants and maintenance personnel added to disillusionment with the project, but perhaps the largest share of responsibility belongs with Yamasaki and his collaborators, who must have had in mind a population of users different from the ones who were to become the actual tenants. In effect, they atomized the cohesive neighborhood group and disrupted the informal social networks that Hall considered so important. It would seem to take the sort of public spaces that are absent in places like Pruitt-Igoe to generate the neighborhood-based solidarity necessary to the maintenance of social order. In many areas of America, at least, nothing seems to challenge that order more than urban anonymity, and the overwhelming majority of high-rise apartment buildings multiply that anonymity to an unknown power (Yancey, 1971). In the alien spaces of typical high-rise apartment buildings, there is no sense of community control. In Lyman and Scott's terms (1970), public areas such as laundry rooms, stairways, elevators, and corridors become home territories for exploiters, some of them from neighboring slums, when the tenants themselves relinquish control of them.

This view is supported by Oscar Newman's work (1972), a study of public housing projects that found a clear relationship between the structure of the building and the amount of crime and vandalism there. The most striking finding was a direct relationship between the number of stories in a building and the amount of crime. It might be concluded that high-rise buildings, under certain circumstances, foster behavior that threatens the welfare of tenants, and the higher the building the greater the threat.

It might be mentioned that due track was kept of the deterioration of Pruitt-Igoe over the course of its existence, for reasons already mentioned. The larger share of this effort came from journalists. We have, therefore, learned a great deal more about the evolution of behavior in this setting than we would have if we had limited ourselves to one or two quick, static studies. In the field of spatial behavior, too little use has been made of time-oriented or "process" approaches (Golledge, 1970).

*The Interiors of Rooms.* We all know from personal experience that certain rooms make us feel comfortable and others seem to offend our senses. A number of investigators have tried to operationalize these subjective feelings, primarily through the use of long lists of adjectives. The users of a room are given a chance to say whether or not each adjective accurately describes a given room, or to specify the extent to which the adjective describes the room. Joyce Vielhauer's dissertation (1965) was an early attempt to assess the environment in this way. Similarly, Collins (1968) was able to extract eight cluster dimensions from an adjective checklist: (1) disorderly, gloomy; (2) cheerful, joyful; (3) different, dramatic; (4) deep, elongated; (5) amusing, active; (6) conservative, colorful; (7) knotted, jagged; and (8) festive, elegant. Canter (1968a) used the semantic differential technique to establish underlying dimensions in an architectural context and was able to identify two factors rather clearly: an evaluative one and something approximating "comfort." Kasmar et al. (1968) used the self-ratings of psychiatric subjects and a psychiatrist to assess the effects of two rooms, one beautiful and one ugly, on mood and the perception of the environment. Canter (1970) has used rating scales for space and equipment in schoolrooms, and Kasmar (1970) has developed a sixty-six-item list of bipolar adjectives, called the Environmental Description Scale, which has been used to measure certain features of three campus settings. Many of these studies, of course, are intended for use in widely varied architectural settings. However, as Lawton (1973) has pointed out, there is little basis for comparing the studies because of the different adjective pools used. As far as adjective checklists are concerned, there should be a greater overlap in content.

On the other hand, it seems unarguable that the interior design of rooms and the arrangement of objects within them are important variables in the understanding of interpersonal behavior. As Osmond (1967: 23) has observed, "powerful men have long recognized the advantage of having their underlings traverse long corridors and advance down great halls to meet them. At the end of this, great men often prefer to greet their guests from a raised throne." Or, to take a single example, we may refer to the experience that Phil Karlson, a movie director, had when he was called to meet the famous mogul, Samuel Goldwyn, for a job interview.

> I went over there. He had an office a mile long and it was the last mile walk.... You walked all the way over to his desk, so by the time you got there, you didn't know what the hell you were going to say or what was going on. He had an overstuffed chair for whoever his guests would be in the office, and you sat in it, and I swear to God, it went down... and he raised! You were way down here looking up at Sam Goldwyn. [Quoted in McCarthy and Flynn, 1974: 329]

It must, of course, be recognized that relations between people and their surroundings take place in a larger sociological context. No part of the environment is evaluated or responded to in a social vacuum. A funeral parlor remains a funeral parlor, for instance, no matter how elegant the decor or how comfortable the seating arrangements.

Cheek et al. (1971) attempted to delineate certain social process variables involved in the interrelationship between the environment of the psychiatric ward and the responses of users. Specifically, the study investigated the introduction of carpeting into roughly similar chronic wards at two state psychiatric hospitals in the mid-Atlantic states. At the first hospital, the introduction of the carpets was perceived as a qualified success by the administration, and as a qualified failure by the ward staff. The staff had not been consulted ahead of time about the carpet, and they resented it as a fait accompli of the administration. Partly because they had never had any instruction concerning the means by which institutional carpets are cleaned, and probably also as an expression of their original resentment at having been left out of the decision, they feared that an inordinate amount of their time would be taken up with maintenance. When delivery of the proper cleaning equipment was delayed, their fears were confirmed. As one staff member put it, "We hated it more." There was also a common feeling among staff that priority should have been given to supplies that were frequently difficult to obtain, such as toilet paper and toothpaste. Staff did agree, however, that the appearance of the ward had been improved, however high the price may have been.

At the second hospital, reactions to the carpet were as good as they were bad at the first hospital. No staff members were assigned to the carpeted ward until after it had been completely furnished. There was no question of consultation with ward staff, with the exception of the head housekeeper, who had had previous experience with commercial carpets and who had pretested samples of the carpets to be installed. She was instrumental in persuading other ward staff that the carpet was a good idea. Although most of the staff members, arriving at the unit after the carpet had been installed, felt that it was not a good idea, their feelings grew more positive over time. Although some inconveniences were experienced — patients needed to be watched more closely during smoking periods, for example — morale was high, and satisfaction with the carpet was widespread.

The study suggested that two major classes of social process variables were relevant to the relationship between the physical environment of the ward and people's responses to it: "definitions of the environment" and "social organizational variables."

In the first hospital, where the carpeting was a failure, "from the point of view of the people actually working and living in the ward, some needs are more immediate than others, and they are thus organized into a rough hierarchy of importance.... The carpeting of the ward was seen as a response to a dysfunction or need occurring too far down in the hierarchy" (Cheek et al., 1971: 117). Similarly, communications between administration and staff were insufficient. No one had consulted the ward staff before installing the carpet. Even following the installation, no figure emerged who could mediate between administration and staff.

In the case of the second ward, neither of these problems was important.

> These two defects in the innovating process—failure to recognize residents' important needs, and absence of adequate feedback—are of critical significance in any study of environmental change. Alexander [1964], for example, describes a developmental sequence in which dysfunctions and irritations in the environment are permitted to accumulate until they pass a certain threshold, at which point an architect or designer, whose status is legitimated by some external authority, attempts a global and often inappropriate restructuring of the physical environment. Then, after the job is finished, the innovator seeks no feedback, and the resident is left to cope with a new set of dysfunctions between what he or she needs and what the physical environment offers. A similar sequence of events seems to have contributed to the failure of the carpeting at [the first ward]. [Cheek et al., 1971: 117–18]

In 1966, Alexander Kira, professor of architecture at Cornell University, published an important study concerning the design of bathroom facilities. The study reported the results of a thorough search of the literature on the subject, a field survey of attitudes toward and problems with traditional bathroom facilities, and a laboratory investigation of the chief difficulties and needs connected with the use of traditional bathrooms. The original report covered the historical and cultural background of the bathroom, the psychological, physiological, and behavioral sides of hygiene activities, and the major design problems of hygiene facilities. Kira observed that:

> Little attention has been paid, even by the manufacturers of basic equipment, to the underlying problems of human accommodation, comfort, and safety. The reasons for this neglect are complex, and involve, among other things, the societal and psychological taboos which surround the subject and which seem almost to have built up into a culture-wide embarrassment. The simple and inevitable body functions have largely come to be regarded as unmentionable and vulgar. At the same time, however, the sexual functions and aspects of the body are almost a staple of modern conversation. [Kira, 1966: vi]

Of course it was not always so. Kira proposed that during historical periods characterized by a pragmatic conception of human beings, high standards of personal hygiene prevailed, while during periods of preoccupation with sin, sex, guilt, and salvation, standards of cleanliness have tended to be neglected. During the more relaxed periods, public bathing, whether in man-made facilities or in supposedly curative spas, was common, as it is today in Japan and to a lesser extent in Scandinavia. Even elimination has sometimes become part of a public performance in Europe. Kira quotes Wright in describing the use of such facilities:

> Kings, princes, and even generals treated it as a throne at which audiences could be granted. Lord Portland, when Ambassador to the Court of Louis XIV, was deemed highly honoured to be so received, and it was from this throne that Louis announced *ex cathedra* his coming marriage to Mme. de Maintenon. [1960: 39]

The larger portion of the book was concerned with an analysis of the degree of fit between existing facilities and human anatomy and posture, with full consideration given to culturally determined interferences (e.g., the difficulty imposed on our assuming the "best" posture for defecation by the fact that we tend to wear tailored clothing and restrictive undergarments) and individual sensibilities (e.g., the avoidance of recognizable noise during urination).

The report was, in many respects, rather dry and technical. For instance, in describing the dispersion of the male urinary stream, Kira states that:

> The behavior of a simulated stream was studied, assuming a point of origin of 29 inches above the floor, relative first, to an intercepting plane at a height of 16 inches (standard water closet), and then to an intercepting plane at a height of 9 inches (point of assumed interception of a floor mounted urinal and of the proposed squat closet)....When we consider that the stream assumes the form of a warped conical solid with a shifting base, it is obvious, as indicated in Figure 43, that the size and shape of the necessary container or enclosure is directly related to its distance from the point of origin in order to completely contain the stream. [Kira, 1966: 145]

The analysis is straightforward, blunt, and useful, and concludes with recommended design criteria for various facilities, but it is by no means written for the mass market, and it is surprising that the original report sold more than 100,000 copies.

In 1976, Kira published an expanded and revised version of the book, with better illustrations of people and products, and dealing also with hygienic problems posed by public facilities and by the special needs of the disabled and elderly.

Kira's work, on the whole, is exemplary. The problem that it addresses is typical of many problems associated with the built environment. We tend to take for granted a set of facilities that falls far short of our needs, simply because it has been handed down to us. But consider how inadequate the bathroom really is, and how easily it might be modified to better suit our needs. Consider, for example, what contortions one needs to perform in the conventional bathroom in order to wash the hair without washing the rest of the body and without splashing water and lather over the rest of the room. One needs to fit one's head into the small space between the faucet of the bathroom sink and the basin itself, which usually involves immersing the face in soapy water. Or consider the everyday act of taking a bath. Few containers are less suited to the accommodation of the human frame than the traditional bathtub, with its deep, nearly vertical ends, one of which ordinarily has a faucet sticking out of it. It would seem an inexpensive and commonsense innovation to design a tub in which the user is able to lie back and stretch out comfortably, with a shape contoured in such a way as to provide an integral back rest, something like a reclining chair, with additional provisions for getting into and out of the tub (Kira, 1976: 50–71).

Similar design criteria should also be applied to other spaces in the home, particularly functional rooms like the kitchen, where space is often sacrificed in order to provide more space for the less frequently used living room. The results might ease the minor irritations of ordinary living. Wouldn't it be a relief not to have to stand on a stool in order to reach kitchen shelves? Wouldn't it be even more of a relief for those over age sixty-five?

Perhaps the greatest obstacle to the introduction of these innovations lies not in the processes of design and manufacturing but in overcoming certain widespread, stereotyped notions concerning "normal" arrangements in households.

> The likelihood of fully realizing the substantive improvements described and suggested in [these] pages depends very much on the consumer's level of concern and willingness to demand and pay for more rational, more convenient, and safer solutions. As has been amply demonstrated time and time again, a society can have anything it cares enough about and is willing to pay for. [Kira, 1976: viii]

Kira's observation, needless to say, applies to many of the problems discussed in this book, not only to bathrooms and kitchens.

# Epilogue

The theme of this book has been that the world can be conceptually separated into three parts: (1) the natural environment consisting of weather, terrain, animals, plants, and water; (2) the interpersonal environment consisting of other people; and (3) the built environment consisting of buildings and related artifacts. These environments influence our thoughts and behavior, which, in turn, influence our environments. In fact, as the first chapter illustrates, the same generalization applies to our morphology and physiology as well as to our thoughts and behavior.

Needless to say, we do not think of our surroundings as being divided in this trinary fashion, if we think of our surroundings at all. Instead, our experience of the world around us is characterized by a transcendental unity of apperception, to lease one of philosophy's more dazzling phrases. The three types of environments are of course very much enmeshed in one another.

This work has been organized around the concept that culture—which, to borrow an expression, is "that complex whole which includes knowledge, belief, art, morals, laws, customs"—can be, but is ultimately best understood as something other than, a thing unto itself.

It is true that particular cultures and culture as a whole move in accordance with certain principles, probabilistic tendencies, the way water running downhill follows certain well-worn grooves. Of course, developmental accidents may occur—a strange pathogen lands on earth, a madman takes over as head of state—but on the whole people live and die trying to cope with a set of customs that provide more or less satisfaction, are more or less familiar, and are more or less challenging.

These customs are in a constant state of change; the debate has centered around the impetus of these changes. Indeed, why should behavior change diachronically? Why don't people settle down and live as their grandparents did and like it?

Some psychologists, including David McClelland, hold that cultures change because of variations in childhood training practices. Some sociologists believe with Emile Durkheim that the world is undergoing a shift from mechanical solidarity, in which individuals identify with a group because they feel themselves similar to the other members, to organic solidarity, in which they are linked together by their dependence on one another through the division of labor. Others, as Marx did, see the impetus for change as rooted in the struggle between the classes. Some anthropologists, such as Leslie White, state that culture evolves according to its own rules; it is autogenic, determined by nothing outside of itself. Hegel and other philosophers have proposed that what is called progress is nothing more than the expression of a mystical *Zeitgeist,* a world mind, which is in the process of unfolding.

I would argue for the significance of environment as an impetus for change. I hope that I have made it clear that there is a relationship between people and the particular climate in which they find themselves. This relationship is complex and many-threaded. Climate influences people in three major ways. First, it may influence their psychomotor behavior or moods directly, whether or not the mediating mechanisms are obvious. For example, it would appear that air with a preponderance of negative ionization tends to allay pain, exert a tranquilizing effect, and promote a sense of alertness, well-being, and relaxation in human beings (Kornblueh, 1960, 1962). Second, climate is involved to some extent in the material inventory of a culture and is especially important in those artifacts that act as buffers between the body and its micro-environment. We have seen, for example, that there is a tendency for people living in certain climates to build houses with thin walls or with no walls at all, and for these people to show permissive rather than restrictive sexual codes for their unmarried females. In other ways, too, architecture and design have important consequences for human behavior, whether or not such consequences are intended. Finally, we know that climate is a primary determinant of the kind of habitat in which people live. People in low-latitude arid areas are going to differ in significant ways from people living in tropical rainy climates, because climate influences soil and vegetation, which in turn influence the local fauna, and all of these have some effect on the exploitative techniques and artifacts developed by people living in a particular culture.

In these ways, climate influences the manner in which people behave and in which they relate to one another. These influences are particularly important because the ways in which people subsist are, within certain circumscribed limits, the most important "entry points" for the introduction of extrasocietal influences into the social system.

At the same time, however, I cannot believe that environmental influences act upon human beings who are genetic blanks. Aside from obvious contrasts between the internal milieu of the two sexes, there are some reasonably well-recognized differences between people in the size and appearance of certain internal organs, including some of the endocrine glands. And from studies within our own culture, the autonomic nervous system, which affects the endocrine glands and the secretion of hormones, has been shown to have a significant genetic component. It thus seems likely that an individual's hormonal balance has a hereditary basis that is independent of learning and therefore independent of society.

The importance of endocrine secretions to the understanding of human behavior cannot be minimized, since they are related to the following forms of activity: overall level of psychomotor behavior, overall energy level, insomnia, general motivation, sexual drive, emotion, intellectual ability, masculinity and femininity, aggressiveness, enthusiasm, normality of growth and reproductive functions, and ability to respond to emergency situations and to withstand prolonged stress.

It has become traditional in the social sciences to consider biology a constant. This does not necessarily mean that biology may actually be discounted. As Wenger, Jones, and Jones observe:

> The extent to which individual differences in endocrine excretions [*sic*] contribute to personality differences in individuals who show no frank endocrine disorder remains a question. Some investigations suggest that they play an important role, and many authors in the past have written as though all personality differences are due to our endocrine glands. Such an extreme position is certainly in error. But slight differences in hormonal blood levels may well account for differences in temperament, which often is defined as the biological basis of personality. [Wenger, Jones, and Jones, 1956: 240]

Thus, for instance, Robertson (1976) reports a number of studies demonstrating relationships between prior aggression in young men and rates of testosterone production and plasma concentration (Persky et al., 1971). Testosterone levels seem also to be higher in prisoners convicted of violent crimes than in prisoners convicted of other kinds of crimes (Kreuz and Rose, 1972). Testosterone level has also been linked to dominance and aggression within prison populations (Ehrenkranz et al., 1974). The results of these and other investigations suggest phenomena that behavioral scientists ignore only at their own peril. As important as learning and situational factors may be in the understanding of human behavior, the constitutional substrate is likely at times to exert an independent influence on behavior and at times to confound results. Unless these individual differences are taken into account, they may mask the very real influence of social factors. Wearing conceptual blinders will not make the problem go away.

I have outlined some of the ways in which somatic evolution seems to have produced human bodies more or less adapted to certain kinds of environments. Here I mean to propose that human constitutions act as a sort of stage upon which environmental influences enact a culture. That complex whole is determined jointly by the imposition of environmental influences upon a constitutional substrate with, at any given time, an arrangement of elements partly dependent upon what has gone on before.

A part of what has gone on before—and what has been going on for some time—is that the natural environment is receding as an *immediate* influence upon our behavior. We have not substantially changed our climate, but we have developed particularly effective buffers against its direct effects. Assume for the moment that on hot and muggy days, people are likely to feel sluggish and irritable, or alert and jovial, or anything else that they tend not to feel on cool, dry days. What happens when the air conditioner is introduced?

In simpler societies, people's welfare is closely tied to naturally occurring local conditions. The more extreme the environment, the more ingenuity is required for survival. In contrast, in Boston or Seattle there are still macroenvironmental effects, but they are not so immediately powerful, nor do they demand such constant attention. Winter nights may be a little gloomy, but one simply flicks on the electric lights. Even if it is raining outside when there is work to be done, one probably will only be outside between the house and the car and between the car and the work place. The point is not that the macroenvironment demands no changes in behavior, but that the buffering mechanisms are so effective in vitiating its immediate effects that it tends to be taken for granted, and one really need not be exposed to it much of the time. In New York City, people travel miles to see the *trees* in Central Park. People may sometimes emerge from their work places to find to their surprise that the day has changed from sunny to stormy while they have been secluded in their shelters. A city dweller may grow up without seeing any unconfined birds or mammals other than dogs, cats, squirrels, rats, English sparrows, and pigeons.

The receding natural environment is an apparent fact. As it recedes from our everyday awareness, it is replaced in turn by the impact of the built environment—the houses, public buildings, institutions, and vehicles in which we spend an increasing amount of time. The natural landscape too is replaced by urban vistas, and the predominant American visual array may be typified by the neon-lighted suburban boulevard. Architecture and design now have an immediate and profound impact upon the behavior of an unprecedented number of people. Since it is people who build this environment in the first place, this impact constitutes feedback. The irony is that, although this feedback is of enormous importance to us in our daily concerns, few of us are able to assess accurately its significance. The external aspects of buildings and their interior layouts, as well as their orientation to each other and to public facilities, have been determined in a most offhand manner, and we, who have been both the perpetrators and the victims of the process, are in most cases unable to say more than that we like or dislike a built place. There have been signs of change in the growing collaboration between architects, planners, and behavioral scientists, although the gap between the planners and analysts still exists.

Furthermore, the natural habitat is receding only as a direct perceptual effect; its influence is changing from particular to general. If we now need to respond less immediately to the proximate weather and proximate resources, we need more often to take global considerations into account. A drought no longer means starvation and death in our Midwestern states, as it currently does in the Sahel, but it does mean higher prices in our supermarkets. Similarly, a shift in the nature and sources of energy may lead to an enormous change in gasoline prices, which affects the kind and amount of driving Americans do and thus the kinds of places in which they are willing to live, the kinds of jobs they are willing to take, and the way they spend their free time.

The environment as frontier is gone. There are very few surprises in store for us. The prerequisites of existence within the limits of our circumstances are now fairly clear.

> From the viewpoint of the social sciences, man's social and psychological environment is largely a product of his own creation, and he, in turn, is fundamentally influenced by this product. Indeed, the social effect on man of the environment he himself has created may prove to be the most important aspect of this relationship. For in the long run of history, the product becomes the master. Man has produced modifications in his environment that have set irreversible evolutionary trends in motion. [Proshansky et al., 1970: 2]

The present question is whether we can organize and govern ourselves in such a way as to exert some influence over the direction of those trends and so preclude the imposition of those natural checks on development and well-being to which *Homo sapiens*, like all other animals, is subject. That is the next frontier.

# References

Adams, Robert McC. "Early Civilizations, Subsistence, and Environment." In *City Invincible,* edited by C.H. Kraeling and R. McC. Adams. Chicago: University of Chicago Press, 1960.

Adams, Robert McC. *The Evolution of Urban Society.* Chicago: Aldine, 1966.

Adams, T., and Covino, B., "Racial Variations to a Standardized Cold Stress." *Journal of Applied Physiology* 12 (1957): 9-12.

Alexander, Christopher. *Notes on the Synthesis of Form.* Cambridge: Harvard University Press, 1964.

Alexander, Christopher, et al. *Houses Generated by Patterns.* Berkeley, Calif. Center for Environmental Studies, 1969.

Alihan, Millov A. *Social Ecology.* New York: Columbia University Press, 1938.

Alihan, Millov A. "Community and Ecological Studies." In *Studies in Human Ecology,* edited by G.A. Theodorson. New York: Harper and Row, 1961

Allport, Gordon W., and Pettigrew, T.F. "Cultural Influence on the Perception of Movement: The Trapezoidal Illusion among Zulu. *Journal of Abnormal and Social Psychology* 55 (1957): 104-13.

Altman, Irwin. "Territorial Behavior in Humans: An Analysis of the Concept." In *Spatial Behavior of Older People,* edited by L.A. Pastalan and D.H. Carson. Ann Arbor: University of Michigan-Wayne State University, Institute of Gerontology, 1970.

Altman, Irwin. *The Environment and Social Behavior: Privacy, Personal Space, Territory, Crowding.* Monterey, Calif.: Brooks/Cole Pub. Co., 1975.

Anderson, James N. "Ecological Anthropology and Anthropological Ecology." In *Handbook of Social and Cultural Anthropology,* edited by J.J. Honigmann. Chicago: Rand McNally, 1974.

273

Anderson, W.J.R.; Baird, D.; and Thompson, A.M. "Epidemiology of Still-births and Infant Deaths Due to Congenital Malformations." *Lancet* 21 (1958): 1304-6.

Arbuthnot, John. *An Essay Concerning the Effects of the Air on Human Bodies.* London: J. and R. Tonson, and S. Drap., 1751.

Ardrey, Robert. *The Territorial Imperative.* New York: Atheneum, 1966.

Argyle, Michael. *Social Interaction.* Chicago: Aldine, 1969.

Arieti, Silvano. "Schizophrenia: Symptomatology and Mechanisms." In *American Handbook of Psychiatry,* vol. 1, edited by S. Arieti. New York: Basic Books, 1959.

Aschmann, H. "Totonac Categories of Smell." *Tlalocan* 2 (1946): 187-89.

Ashby, W. Ross. *An Introduction to Cybernetics.* London: Chapman and Hall, 1956.

Ashdown, Charles H. *British and Continental Arms and Armour.* New York: Dover, 1970.

Baker, Paul T. "Racial Differences in Heat Tolerance." *American Journal of Physical Anthropology* 16 (1958): 287-305. (a)

Baker, Paul T. "American Negro-White Differences in Thermal Insulative Aspects of Body Fat." *Human Biology* 31 (1958): 287-305. (b)

Baker, Paul T., and Weiner, Joan S., eds. *The Biology of Human Adaptation.* Oxford: Clarendon Press, 1966.

Balikci, Asen. "The Netsilik Eskimos: Adaptive Processes." In *Man the Hunter,* edited by Richard B. Lee and Irven Devore. Chicago: Aldine, 1968.

Barker, Roger G., and Wright, Herbert F. *The Midwest and Its Children.* Evanston, Ill.: Row, Peterson, 1954.

Baum, Andrew, and Valins, S. "Residential Environments, Group Size, and Crowding." *Proceedings of the Annual Convention of the American Psychological Association,* 8 (1973): 211-12.

Baxter, J.C. "Interpersonal Spacing in Natural Settings." *Sociometry* 33 (1970): 444-56.

Beardsley, Richard K.; Hall, John W.; and Ward, Robert E. *Village Japan.* Chicago: University of Chicago Press, 1969.

Beckman, R. "Motivating Space: A Report on the School Landscape." *Interiors,* Dec. 1968.

Bell, Bill D., ed. *Contemporary Social Gerontology.* Springfield, Ill.: Charles C. Thomas, 1976.

Berkner, L.V. "The Common Aspects of Disasters." Address given at the American Association for the Advancement of Science (AAAS) Symposium on Disaster Recovery, St. Louis, Mo., December 27, 1952.

Berlin, Brent, and Berlin, Eloise Ann. "Aguaruna Color Categories." *American Ethnologist* 2 (1975): 61-88.

Berlin, Brent, and Kay, Paul. *Basic Color Terms.* Berkeley: University of California Press, 1969.

Berlyne, Daniel E. "New Directions in Motivation Theory." In *Anthropology and Human Behavior,* edited by T. Gladwin and W.C. Sturtevant. Washington, D.C.: Anthropological Society of Washington, 1962.

Best, Jay Boyd, and Rubenstein, I. "Environmental Familiarity and Feeding in the Planarian." *Science* 135 (1962): 916-18.

Bickman, L.; Teger, A.; Gabriele, T.; McLaughlin, C.; Berger, M.; and Sunaday, E. "Dormitory Density and Helping Behavior." *Environment and Behavior* 5 (1973): 465-80.

Bierstedt, Robert. *The Social Order.* New York: McGraw-Hill, 1970.

Birdsell, Joseph B. "Some Environmental and Cultural Factors Influencing the Structure of Australian Aboriginal Populations." *American Naturalist* 87 (1953): 169-207.

Blair, F. "Population Structure, Social Behavior, and Environmental Relations in a Natural Population of the Beach Mouse (*Peromyscus polionotus leucocephalus*)." *Contributions of the Laboratory of Vertebrate Biology,* no. 48 (1951).

Bloom, Irene. Letter to the editor. *Science* 184 (1974): 850.

Blumer, R. "A Primitive Ornithology." *Australian Museum Magazine* 12 (1957): 224-29.

Booth, A., and Edwards, J.N. "Crowding and Family Relations." *American Sociological Review* 41 (1976): 308-21.

Boulding, Kenneth E. Introduction to *An Essay on the Principle of Population* by T.R. Malthus. Ann Arbor; University of Michigan Press, 1959.

Boulding, Kenneth E. *The Image.* Ann Arbor: University of Michigan Press, 1965.

Bright, W. "Language and Music: Areas for Cooperation." *Ethnomusicology* 7 (1963): 26-32.

Broadbent, G. "Systems and Environmental Design." Paper presented at the Environmental Design Research Association Conference, Pittsburgh, Pa., October 1970.

Brooke, Iris. *Dress and Undress.* Westport, Conn.: Greenwood Press, 1954.

Brown, G.M., and Page, J. "The Effect of Chronic Exposure to Cold on Temperature and Blood Flow of the Hand." *Journal of Applied Physiology* 5 (1953): 221-27.

Brown, Judith K. "A Cross-cultural Study of Female Initiation Rites." *American Anthropologist* 65 (1963): 837.

Brues, Alice M. "The Spearman and the Archer." *American Anthropology* 61: 458-69, 1959. Reprinted in *Man in Adaptation,* edited by Yehudi Cohen. Chicago: Aldine, 1968.

Buckley, Walter. *Modern Systems Research for the Behavioral Scientist.* Chicago: Aldine, 1968.

Burgess, Ernest W. "The Growth of the City: An Introduction to a Research Project." In *Studies in Human Ecology,* edited by G.A. Theodorson. New York: Harper and Row, 1961.

Burgess, Ernest W., and Bogue, Donald J., eds. *Urban Sociology.* Chicago: University of Chicago Press, 1964.

Burling, Robbins. "Cognition and Componential Analysis: God's Truth or Hocus Pocus?" *American Anthropologist* 66 (1964): 20-28.

Burt, W.H. "Territoriality and Home Range Concepts as Applied to Mammals." *Journal of Mammalogy* 24 (1943): 346-52.

Burton, Ian. "Invasion and Escape on the Little Calumet." University of Chicago Department of Geography Research Paper no. 70, 1961.

Burton, Ian. "Cultural and Personality Variables in the Perception of Natural Hazards." In *Environment and the Social Sciences: Perspectives and Applications,* edited by Joachim F. Wohlwill and Daniel H. Carson. Washington, D.C.: American Psychological Association, 1972.

Burton, Ian; Kates, Robert W.; and White, G.F. *Natural Hazard Working.* Paper No. 1. Toronto: Department of Geography, University of Toronto, 1968.

Calhoun, John B. "Population Density and Social Pathology." In *The Urban Condition,* edited by Leonard Duhl. New York: Basic Books, 1963.

Calhoun, John B. "The Role of Space in Animal Sociology." *Journal of Social Issues* 6 (1966): 46-58.

Calhoun, John B. "Space and the Strategy of Life." *Behavior and Environment,* edited by A.H. Esser. New York: Plenum Pub. Corp., 1971.

Cannon, Walter B. *The Wisdom of the Body.* New York: W.W. Norton, 1939.

Canter, David. "Connotative Dimensions in Architecture." *Architectural Psychology,* no. 2, winter 1968. (a)

Canter, David. "Office Size: An Example of Psychological Research in Architecture." *Architect's Journal,* April 1968, pp. 881-88. (b)

Canter, David. "The Development of Scales for the Evaluation of Buildings." Paper presented at the annual meeting of the British Psychological Society, Southampton, England, April 1970.

Canter, David. *Psychology for Architects.* London: Applied Science Pub., 1974.

Canter, David, and Canter, S. "Close Together in Tokyo." *Design and Environment* 2 (1971): 60-63.

Carment, D.W.; Miles, C.S.; and Cervin, V.B. "Persuasiveness and Persuasibility as Related to Intelligence and Extraversion." *British Journal of Social and Clinical Psychology* 4 (1965): 1-7.

Carneiro, Robert. "Slash and Burn Cultivation among the Kuikuru and Its Implications for Cultural Development in the American Basin." In *The Evolution of Horticultural Systems in Native South America: Causes and Consequences.* Anthropological Supplement no. 2, Caracas, Venezuela, 1961.

Carpenter, C.R. "Behavior of Red Spider Monkeys in Panama." *Journal of Mammalogy* 16 (1935): 171-80.

Carpenter, C.R. "Territoriality: A Review of Concepts and Problems." In *Behavior and Evolution,* edited by A. Roe and G.G. Simpson. New Haven: Yale University Press, 1958.

Chagnon, S.A., Jr. "Urban-Produced Thunderstorms at St. Louis and Chicago." Paper presented at the Sixth Conference on Severe Local Storms, American Meteorological Society, Chicago, 1969.

Cheek, Frances E.; Maxwell, Robert J.; and Weisman, Richard. "Carpeting the Ward: An Exploratory Study in Environmental Psychiatry." *Mental Hygiene* 55 (1971): 109-18.

Chermayeff, Serge, and Alexander, Christopher. *Community and Privacy: Toward a New Architecture of Humanism.* New York: Doubleday, 1963.

Chitty, D. "Morality among Voles (*Microtus agrestis*) at Lake Vyrnwy, Montgomeryshire in 1936-39." *Philosophical Transactions of the Royal Society of London* B., 236 (1952): 505-52.

Christian, John J. "The Adreno-pituitary System and Population Cycles in Mammals." *Journal of Mammalogy* 31 (1950): 247-59.

Clarke, G. *Elements of Ecology.* New York: John Wiley and Sons, 1954.

Clarke, William C. *Place and People: An Ecology of a New Guinean Community.* Berkeley: University of California Press, 1971.

Collins, J.B. "Some Verbal Dimensions of Architectural Space Perception." Doctoral dissertation, University of Utah, 1968.

Conklin, Harold C. "Hanunoo Color Categories." *Southwestern Journal of Anthropology* 11 (1955): 339-44.

Coon, Carleton S. *The Origin of Races.* New York: Alfred A. Knopf, 1962.

Coss, R.G. "Mood-provoking Visual Stimuli, Their Origins and Applications." UCLA Industrial Design Graduate Program, 1965, cited in *Social Interaction,* by Michael Argyle. Chicago: Aldine, 1969.

Cowan, P. "Studies in the Growth, Change and Aging of Buildings." *Transactions of the Bartlett Society* 1 (1962-63): 55-84.

Cowan, P. "Depreciation, Obsolescence, and Aging." *Architect's Journal* 16 (June 1965): 1395-1402.

Craik, Kenneth H. "Environmental Psychology." In *New Directions in Psychology 4.* New York: Holt, Rinehart, and Winston, 1970.

Daily, P.W., Jr. *Tornadoes in Pennsylvania.* Institute for Research on Land and Water Resources. Information Report no. 63. University Park: Pennsylvania State University, 1970.

Darby, H.C. "The Clearing of the Woodland in Europe." In *Man's Role in Changing the Face of the Earth,* vol. 1, edited by William L. Thomas. Chicago: University of Chicago Press, 1956.

Darling, Frank. *A Herd of Red Deer.* London: Oxford University Press, 1937.

Darling, Frank. "Man's Ecological Dominance through Domesticated Animals on Wild Lands." In *Man's Role in Changing the Face of the Earth* vol. 2, edited by William L. Thomas. Chicago: University of Chicago Press, 1956.

Davie, Maurice R. "The Pattern of Urban Growth," In *Studies in Human Ecology,* edited by George A. Theodorson. New York: Harper and Row, 1961.

Deane, W.N. "The Reactions of a Non-Patient to a Stay on a Mental Hospital Ward." *Psychiatry* 24 (1961): 61-68.

DeLong, Alton J. "The Micro-spatial Structure of the Older Person: Some Implications for Planning the Social and Spatial Environment." In *Spatial Behavior of Older People,* edited by L. Pastalan and D. Carson. Ann Arbor: University of Michigan Press, 1970.

DeLong, Alton J. "Content vs. Structure: The Transformation of the Continuous into the Discrete." A review of *Hidden Dimension,* by Edward T. Hall (paperback ed.). *Man-Environment Systems* 1 (1971): R-9.

"Design Innovations." *Hospitals: Journal of the American Hospital Association.* Feb. 1970.

Dewey, J.F. "Plate Tectonics." *Scientific American,* May 1972, pp. 56-68.

Dornstreich, M.D., and Morren, G.E.B. "Does New Guinea Cannibalism Have Nutritional Value?" *Human Ecology* 2 (1974): 1-12.

Douglas, Mary. *Purity and Danger.* London: Routledge and Kegan Paul, 1966.

Downs, Roger M., and Stea, David, eds. *Image and Environment: Cognitive Mapping and Spatial Behavior.* Chicago: Aldine, 1973.

Durkheim, Emile. *The Elementary Forms of the Religious Life.* New York: Free Press, 1965.

Earickson, Robert. "Spatial Behavior of Hospital Patients: A Behavioral Approach to Spatial Interaction in Metropolitan Chicago." University of Chicago Department of Geography Research Paper no. 124, 1970.

Eastman, Charles M., and Harper, J. "A Study of Proxemic Behavior: Toward a Predictive Model." Unpublished manuscript, Carnegie-Mellon University, Pittsburgh, Pa., 1971.

Ehrenkranz, P.; Bliss, J.E.; and Sheard, M.H. "Plasma Testosterone: Correlation with Aggressive Behavior and Social Dominance in Man." *Psychosomatic Medicine* 36 (1974): 469-75.

Elman, Richard. "Bitch." *Oui Magazine,* Dec. 1972, pp. 44-45.

Elsner, R.W.; Andersen, K.L.; and Hermansen, L. "Thermal and Metabolic Responses of Arctic Indians to Moderate Cold Exposure at the End of Winter." *Journal of Applied Physiology* 16 (1960): 659-61.

Elton, Charles S. *Animal Ecology.* London: Methuen, 1966.

Elwin, Verrier. *The Muria Gond and Their Ghotul.* Bombay: Oxford University Press, 1947.

Engebretson, D., and Fullmer, D. "Cross-cultural Differences in Territoriality: Interaction Distances of Native Japanese, Hawaii-Japanese, and American Caucasians." *Journal of Cross-Cultural Psychology* 1 (1970): 261-69.

Engels, Friedrich. *The Part Played by Labor in the Transition from Ape to Man.* New York: International Pub., 1950.

Errington, Paul L. "An Analysis of Mink Predation upon Muskrats in North-Central United States." Research Bulletin, Iowa Agricultural Experimental Station, 320 (1943): 797-924.

Esber, George S. "Indians, Architects, and Anthropologists." Paper presented at the annual meeting of the American Anthropological Association, New York City, Nov. 1971.

Evans, G.W. "Personal Space: Research Review and Bibliography." *Man-Environment Systems* 3 (1973): 203-15.

Eysenck, Hans J. *Fact and Fiction in Psychology.* Harmondsworth, Middlesex, England: Penguin, 1965.

Fairholt, Frederick W., and Dillon, H.A. *Costume in England: A History of Dress,* vol. 1. London: Bell and Sons, 1885.

Faris, Robert E.L. *Chicago Sociology: 1920-1932.* Chicago: University of Chicago Press, 1967.

Fitch, James M. *American Building 2: The Environmental Forces That Shape It.* New York: Houghton Mifflin, 1974.

Fitch, James M.; Templer, J.; and Corcoran, P. "The Dimensions of Stairs." *Scientific American,* June 1974, pp. 82-90.

Flew, Antony. *Introduction to T.R. Malthus: An Essay on the Principle of Population.* Harmondsworth, Middlesex, England: Penguin, 1970.

Flora, Snowden D. *Tornadoes of the United States.* Norman: University of Oklahoma Press, 1953.

Ford, Clellan S., and Beach, Frank A. *Patterns of Sexual Behavior.* New York: Ace Books, 1951.

Forke, Alfred. *The World Conception of the Chinese: Their Astronomical, Cosmological, and Physico-Philosophical Speculations.* London: Probsthain, 1925.

Fowler, Catherine S., and Leland, Joy. "Some Northern Paiute Native Categories." *Ethnology* 6 (1967): 381-404.

Fox, James W., and Cumberland, Kenneth B. *Western Samoa: Land, Life, and Agriculture in Tropical Polynesia.* Christchurch, New Zealand: Whitcombe and Tombs, 1962.

Frake, Charles O. "The Diagnosis of Disease among the Subanun of Mindanao." *American Anthropologist* 63 (1961): 113-32.

Frake, Charles O. "How to Ask for a Drink in Subanun." *American Anthropologist,* special publication, *The Ethnography of Communication* 66 (1964), pt. 2: 127-32.

Franklyn, J. *Heraldry.* New York: Barnes and Noble, 1968.

Freedman, Jonathan. *Crowding and Behavior: The Psychology of High-Density Living.* New York: Viking Press, 1976.

Freedman, R.L. "Wanted: A Journal in Culinary Anthropology." *Current Anthropology* 9 (1968): 62-63.

Fried, Marc, and Gleicher, Peggy. "Some Sources of Residential Satisfaction in an Urban Slum." *Journal of the American Institute of Planners* 27 (1961).

Fritz, C.E., and Mathewson, J.H. *Convergence Behavior in Disasters: A Problem in Social Control.* Washington, D.C.: National Academy of Sciences-National Research Council, 1956.

Gans, Herbert J. "Planning and Social Life: Friendship and Neighbor Relations in Suburban Communities." *Journal of the American Institute of Planners* 28 (1961): 134-40.

Gans, Herbert J. *Urban Villagers.* New York: Free Press, 1962.

Garn, Stanley M., and Block, Walter D. "The Limited Nutritional Value of Cannibalism." *American Anthropologist* 72 (1970): 106.

Gauldie, E. *Cruel Habitations: A History of Working-Class Housing 1780-1918.* New York: Barnes and Noble, 1974.

Geertz, Clifford. *Agricultural Involution.* Berkeley: University of California Press, 1963.

Gerontology Project Group. "Research in Environmental Analysis and Design for the Aging." Department of Design and Environmental Analysis, College of Human Ecology. Cornell University, Ithaca, N.Y., 1971.

Gilliam, Harold. *Weather of the San Francisco Bay Region.* Berkeley and Los Angeles: University of California Press, 1970.

Gillin, John P. "Custom and Range of Human Response." *Character and Personality* 13 (1944): 101-34.

Goffman, Erving. *The Presentation of Self in Everyday Life.* New York: Doubleday-Anchor Press, 1959.

Goffman, Erving. *Asylums.* Garden City, N.Y.: Doubleday-Anchor Press, 1961.

Goffman, Erving. *Behavior in Public Places: Notes on the Social Organization of Gatherings.* New York: Free Press, 1963.

Goffman, Erving. *Relations in Public: Microstudies of the Public Order.* New York: Harper and Row, 1971.

Goffman, Erving. *Frame Analysis: An Essay on the Organization of Experience.* Cambridge: Harvard University Press, 1974.

Golledge, Reginald G. "Process Approaches to the Analysis of Human Spatial Behavior." Paper prepared for National Science Foundation conference, "Form and Process in Geography," Ann Arbor, Michigan, April 1970.

Good, L.R.; Siegel, S.M.; and Bay, A.P. *Therapy by Design: Implications of Architecture for Human Behavior.* Springfield, Ill.: Charles C. Thomas, 1965.

Goodenough, Ward. "Componential Analysis and the Study of Meaning." *Language* 32 (1956): 195-216.

Gould, Peter R. "Man Against His Environment: A Game Theoretic Framework." In *Environment and Cultural Behavior,* edited by A.P. Vayda. Garden City, N.Y.: Natural History Press, 1969.

Grattan, F.J.H. *An Introduction to Samoan Custom.* Apia, Western Samoa: Samoan Printing and Publishing Co., 1948.

Gray, J.H. *China: A History of the Laws, Manners, and Customs of the People,* vol. 1. London: MacMillan, 1878.

Green, R.G., and Evans, C.A. "Studies on a Population Cycle of Snowshoe Hares on Lake Alexander Area," I, II, III. *Journal of Wildlife Management* 4 (1940): 220-38, 267-78; 347-58.

Green, R.G., and Larson, C.L. "A Description of Shock Disease in the Snowshoe Hare." *American Journal of Hygiene* (1938): 28 190-212.

Greenway, John. *Down among the Wild Men.* Boston: Atlantic-Little, Brown, 1972.

Gregor, Thomas A. "Publicity, Privacy and Mehinacu Marriage." *Ethnology* 13 (1974): 333-50.

Gulick, John. "The Lebanese Village: An Introduction." *American Anthropologist* 55 (1953): 367-72.

Gulick, John. "Images of an Arab City." *Journal of the American Institute of Planners* 29 (1963): 179-98.

Gulick, John. *Tripoli: A Modern Arab City.* Cambridge: Harvard University Press, 1967.

Gunda-Debrecen, B. "Die Raumaufteilung der ungarischen Bauernstube, ihre gesellschaftliche Funktion und kultisch Bedeutung." *Deutsches Jahrbuch für Volkskunde* 8 (1962). 368-91.

Gusinde, Martin. *Die Selk'nam.* Die Feuerland-Indianer, vol. 1. Vienna: Modling, 1931.

Gusinde, Martin. *Die Yamana.* Die Feuerland-Indianer, vol. 2. Vienna: Modling, 1937.

Gusinde, Martin. *Anthropologie der Feuerland-Indianer.* Die Feuerland-Indianer, vol. 3. Vienna: Modling, 1939.

Gutman, Robert. *People and Buildings.* New York: Basic Books, 1972.

Gutman, Robert. "Architecture and Sociology." *American Sociologist,* 10 (1975): 219-28.

Hall, Edward T. "A System for the Notation of Proxemic Behavior." *American Anthropologist* 65 (1963): 1003-26.

Hall, Edward T. "Silent Assumptions in Social Communication." *Disorders of Communication* 42 (1964) 41-55.

Hall, Edward T. *Hidden Dimension.* Garden City, N.Y.: Doubleday-Anchor Press, 1969.

Hall, Edward T. "Environmental Communications." In *Behavior and Environment: The Use of Space by Animals and Men,* edited by A. Esser. New York: Pelnum, 1971.

Hall, Edward T. *Handbook for Proxemic Research.* Washington, D.C.: Society for the Anthropology of Visual Communication, 1974.

Hall, K.R.L., and Devore, Irven. "Baboon Social Behavior." In *Primate Behavior,* edited by I. DeVore. New York: Holt, Rinehart, and Winston, 1965.

Hallowell, Irving A. "The Size of Algonkian Hunting Territories: A Function of Ecological Adjustment." *American Anthropologist* 51 (1949): 35-45.

Hammel, H.T. "Thermal and Metabolic Responses of the Alakaluf Indians to Moderate Cold Exposure." Wright Air Development Center Technical Report no. 60-633, 1960. (a)

Hammel, H.T. "Responses to Cold by Alacaluf Indians." *Current Anthropology* 1 (1960): 146. (b)

Hammel, H.T.; Elsner, R.W.; LeMessurier, D.H.; Anderson, K.L.; and Milan, F.A. "Thermal and Metabolic Responses of the Australian Aborigine Exposed to Moderate Cold in Summer." *Journal of Applied Physiology* 14 (1959): 605-15.
Harris, E.G., and Paluck, R.J. "The Effects of Crowding in an Educational Setting." *Man-Environment Systems,* May 1971 p. S55.
Harris, Marvin. *The Nature of Cultural Things.* New York: Random House, 1964.
Harris, Marvin. "The Cultural Ecology of India's Sacred Cattle." *Current Anthropology* 7 (1966): 51-66.
Harris, Marvin. *The Rise of Anthropological Theory: A History of Theories of Culture.* New York: Crowell, 1968.
Harris, Marvin. *Culture, Man, and Nature.* New York: Crowell, 1971.
Haswell, M.R. *Economics of Agriculture in a Savannah Village.* Colonial Research Studies no. 8, H.M.S.O., London, 1953.
Hawley, Amos H. "Ecology and Human Ecology." *Social Forces* 22 (May 1944): 398-405.
Hearn, G. "Leadership and the Spatial Factor in Small Groups." *Journal of Abnormal and Social Psychology* 104 (1957): 269-72.
Hediger, H. "The Evolution of Territorial Behavior." In *Social Life of Early Man,* edited by S.L. Washburn. Chicago: Aldine, 1961.
Hediger, H. *Wild Animals in Captivity.* New York: Dover, 1964.
Hediger, H. *The Psychology and Behavior of Animals in Zoos and Circuses.* New York: Dover, 1968.
Heider, Karl. "Environment, Subsistence, and Society." In *Annual Review of Anthropology,* vol. 1, edited by B.J. Siegel, A.R. Beals, and S.A. Tyler. Palo Alto, Ca.: Annual Reviews, 1972.
Hellstrom, B., and Anderson, K.L. "Heat Output in the Cold from Hands of Arctic Fishermen." *Journal of Applied Physiology* 15 (1960): 771-75.
Henry, Jules. "Space and Power on a Psychiatric Unit." In *The Psychiatric Hospital as a Social System,* edited by A.F. Wessen. Springfield, Ill.: Charles C. Thomas, 1964.
Hewes, Gordon H. "Clitoridectomy: An Anthropological Review of the Strange Custom of Female Circumcision." *Medical Aspects of Human Sexuality,* in press.
Hippocrates. "On the Sacred Disease." In *The Origins of Scientific Thought,* edited by G. de Santillana. New York: New American Library, 1957.
Hoag, R., and Johnson, W. "Open and Traditional Classrooms: A Comparative Study." *Man-Environment Systems* 5 (1975): 263-64.
Hochstein, Gianna. "Pica: A Study in Medical and Anthropological Explanation." *Essays on Medical Anthropology, Southern Anthropological Society Proceedings,* no. 1 edited by T. Weaver, 1968, pp. 88-96.
Hoebel, E. Adamson. *Anthropology: The Study of Man.* New York: McGraw-Hill, 1966.
Holland, L.B. *Who Designs America?* Garden City, N.Y.: Doubleday-Anchor Press, 1966.
Holmberg, Allan. *Nomads of the Long Bow.* New York: Natural History Press, 1969.
Homer. *The Odyssey,* translated by Robert Fitzgerald. Garden City, N.Y.: Doubleday-Anchor Press, 1963.
Huntington, Ellsworth. *The Mainsprings of Civilization.* New York: New American Library, 1959.

Hyams, E. *Animals in the Service of Man*. Philadelphia: J.B. Lippincott, 1972.
Irving, L.; Anderson, K.L.; Bolstad, A.; Elsner, R.; Hildes, J.A.; Nelmes, J.D.;
    Peyton, L.J., and Whaley, R.D. "Metabolism and Temperature of Arctic In-
    dian Men during a Cold Night." *Journal of Applied Physiology* 15 (1960)
    635-44.
Ittelson, William H.; Proshansky, Harold M.; and Rivlin, Leanne G. "A Study
    of Bedroom Use on Two Psychiatric Wards." *Hospital and Community
    Psychiatry* 21 (1970): 177-80.
Izumi, Kiyo. "LSD and Architectural Design." In *Psychedelics*, edited by
    B. Aaronson and H. Osmond. Garden City, N.Y.: Doubleday-Anchor Press,
    1970.
James, William. *Psychology: Briefer Course*. New York: Macmillan, 1962.
Jay, Robert R. *Javanese Villagers*. Cambridge, Mass.: MIT Press, 1969.
Jensen, R. *Cities of Vision*. New York: John Wiley and Sons, 1974.
Johnson, C.A. "Privacy as Personal Control." In *Privacy*, edited by
    S.T. Margulis, Environmental Design Research Association 5, Man-
    Environment Interactions, Evaluations and Applications, no. 6, 1974.
Kalish, Richard A. "Life and Death: Dividing the Indivisible." *Social Science
    and Medicine* 2 (1968): 249-59.
Kasmar, Joyce V. "The Development of a Usable Lexicon of Environmental
    Descriptors." *Environment and Behavior* 2 (1970): 153-69.
Kasmar, Joyce V.; Griffin, W.V.; and Mauritzen, J.H. "The Effect of
    Environmental Surroundings on Outpatients' Mood and Perception of
    Psychiatrists." *Journal of Consulting and Clinical Psychology* 32 (1968):
    223-26.
Kates, Robert W. "Hazard and Choice Perception in Flood Plain Management."
    University of Chicago Department of Geography Research Paper no. 78,
    1962.
Kates, Robert W. "The Perception of Storm Hazard on the Shores of Megalop-
    olis." University of Chicago Department of Geography Research Paper no.
    109, 1967.
Kendon, Adam. "Some Functions of Gaze Direction in Social Interaction."
    *Acta Psychologica* 26 (1967): 1-47.
Kent, Donald; Kastenbaum, Robert; and Sherwood, Sylvia, eds. *Research Plan-
    ning and Action for the Elderly*. New York: Behavioral Pub., 1972.
Kinzel, A.F. "Body-Buffer Zone in Violent Prisoners." *The American Journal
    of Psychiatry* 127 (1970): 59-64. Reprinted in *Issues in Social Ecology*, edited
    by R.H. Moos and P.M. Insel. Palo Alto, Calif.: National Press Books,
    1974.
Kira, Alexander. *The Bathroom: Criteria for Design*. New York: Bantam Books,
    1966.
Kira, Alexander. *The Bathroom*. New York: Viking Press, 1976.
Kirkbride, Thomas S. *On the Construction, Organization and General Arrange-
    ments of Hospitals for the Insane*. Philadelphia, Pa.: J.B. Lippincott, 1880.
Kolansky, H., and Moore, W.T. "Effects of Marijuana on Adolescents and
    Young Adults." *Journal of the American Medical Association* 216 (1971):
    486-92.
Koppen, Wladimir. *Grundriss der Klimatkunde*. Berlin: Mindel Verlag, 1918.
Kormondy, Edward J. *Concepts of Ecology*. Englewood Cliffs, N.J.: Prentice-
    Hall, 1969.

Kornblueh, I.H. "Electric Space Charges and Human Health." *Bulletin of the American Meteorological Society* 41 (July 1960): 361.

Kornblueh, I.H. "Artificial Ionization of the Air and Its Biological Significance." *Clinical Medicine* 69 (Aug. 1962): 1779.

Kreuz, L.E., and Rose, R.M. "Assessment of Aggressive Behavior and Testosterone in a Young Criminal Population." *Psychosomatic Medicine* 34 (1972): 321-32.

Kroeber, Alfred L. "The Superorganic." *American Anthropologist* 19 (1917): 163-213.

Kroeber, Alfred L. *Anthropology.* New York: Harcourt, Brace, 1923.

Kroeber, Alfred L. *Handbook of the Indians of California,* Bulletin of the Bureau of American Ethnology, no. 78. Washington, D.C.; 1925.

Kroeber, Alfred L. *Cultural and Natural Areas of Native North America.* University of California Publications in American Archaeology and Ethnology, vol. 38, 1939.

Kroeber, Alfred L. *Configurations of Culture Growth.* Berkeley: University of California Press, 1944.

Kroeber, Alfred L. *Anthropology.* New York: Harcourt, Brace, 1948.

Kroeber, Alfred L., and Richardson, James. "Three Centuries of Women's Dress Fashions: A Quantitative Analysis." *University of California Anthropological Records* 5 (1940): 111-54.

Krog, J.; Folkow, B.; Fox, R.H.; and Andersen, K.L. "Heat Circulation in the Cold of Lapps and North Norwegian Fishermen." *Journal of Applied Physiology* 15 (1960): 654-58.

Kybelova, L.; Herbenova, O.; and Lamarova, M. *Pictorial Encyclopedia of Fashion.* New York: Crown, 1968.

Landar, Herbert, et al. "Navajo Color Categories." *Language* 36 (1960): 368-82.

Lane, Frank. *The Elements Rage.* Philadelphia: Chilton Books, 1965.

Largey, G.P., and Watson, D.R. "The Sociology of Odors." *American Journal of Sociology* 77 (1972): 1021-34.

Laufer, Berthold. "Geophagy." Field Museum of Natural History publication no. 280:2, Anthropological series 18, Chicago, 1933.

Laumann, E.O., and House, J.S. "Living Room Styles and Social Attributes: The Patterning of Material Artifacts in a Modern Urban Community." *Sociology and Social Research* 54 (1970): 321-42.

Lawrence, T.E. *The Seven Pillars of Wisdom.* Garden City, N.Y.: Doubleday, 1935.

Lawton, M. Powell. "Ecology and Aging." In *The Spatial Behavior of Older People,* edited by L.A. Pastalan and D.H. Carson. Ann Arbor: University of Michigan Institute of Gerontology, 1970.

Lawton, M. Powell. "Some Beginnings of an Ecological Psychology of Old Age." In *Environment and the Social Sciences: Perspectives and Application,* edited by J.F. Wohwill and D.H. Carson. Washington, D.C.: American Psychological Association, 1972.

Lawton, M. Powell. "The View of the Outside from the Inside: Environmental Cognition." Unpublished manuscript, Philadelphia Geriatric Center, 1973.

Lawton, M. Powell. *Planning and Managing Housing for the Elderly.* New York: Wiley-Interscience, 1975.

LeCompte, William F. "The Treatment Environment of a Comprehensive Rehabilitation Facility: The Behavior Setting Survey." Paper presented at the American Psychological Association symposium "Ecological Research in Complex Organizations: The Rehabilitation Center as a Paradigm Case," Washington, D.C., September 2, 1969.

Lee, Richard B. "What Hunters Do for a Living, or, How to Make Out on Scarce Resources." In *Man the Hunter,* edited by R.B. Lee and I. De Vore. Chicago: Aldine, 1968.

Lee, Richard B. "!Kung-Bushman Subsistence: An Input-Output Analysis." In *Environment and Cultural Behavior,* edited by A. Vayda. Garden City, N.Y.: Natural History Press, 1969.

Lee, Richard B. "Population Growth and the Beginnings of Sedentary Life Among the !Kung Bushmen." In *Population Growth: Anthropological Implications,* edited by B. Spooner. Cambridge: MIT Press, 1972.

Lee, Richard B., and DeVore, Iver, eds. *Kalahari Hunter-Gatherers.* Cambridge: Harvard University Press, 1976.

Lee, Terence R. "Psychology and Living Space." *Transactions of the Bartlett Society* 2 (1963-64): 9-36.

Lee, Terence R. "The Urban Neighborhood as a Socio-spatial Schema." *Human Relations* 21 (1968): 241-67.

Leeds, Anthony, and Vayda, Andrew, eds. *Man, Culture, and Animals: The Role of Animals in Human Ecological Adjustments.* Washington, D.C.: American Association for the Advancement of Science, 1965.

Leipold, W.D. "Psychological Distance in a Dyadic Interview as a Function of Introversion-Extroversion, Anxiety, Social Desirability and Stress." Doctoral dissertation, University of North Dakota, 1963.

Lemons, Hoyt. "Physical Characteristics of Disasters; Historical and Statistical Review." *Annals of the American Academy of Political and Social Science* 309 (Jan. 1957).

Leopold, Aldo. *Game Management.* New York: Charles Scribner's Sons, 1939.

Lessa, William A. "The Social Effects of Typhoon Ophelia (1960) on Ulithi." In *People and Cultures of the Pacific: An Anthropological Reader,* edited by A.P. Vayda. Garden City, N.Y.: Natural History Press, 1968.

Lett, E.E.; Clark, W.; and Altman, Irving. "A Proposition Inventory of Research on Interpersonal Distance." Research Report, Naval Medical Research Institute, Bethesda, Md., May 1969. Reprinted in *Man Environment Reference: Environmental Abstracts,* Ann Arbor, University of Michigan Architectural Research Laboratory, 1974.

Levi-Strauss, Claude. "Le triangle culinaire." *L'Arc* 26 (1965): 19-29.

Levi-Strauss, Claude. "The Culinary Triangle." *Partisan Review* 33 (1966): 586-95. (a)

Levi-Strauss, Claude. *The Savage Mind.* Chicago: University of Chicago Press, 1966. (b)

Levi-Strauss, Claude. *Structural Anthropology.* Garden City, N.Y.: Doubleday-Anchor Press, 1967.

Levi-Strauss, Claude. *The Raw and the Cooked: Introduction to a Science of Mythology, I.* New York: Harper and Row, 1969.

Leyhausen, Paul. "The Communal Organization of Solitary Mammals." In *Environmental Psychology,* edited by H. Proshansky, W. Ittelson, and L. Rivlin. New York: Holt, Rinehart, and Winston, 1970.

Leyhausen, Paul. "Dominance and Territoriality as Complemented in Mammalian Social Structure." In *Behavior and Environment,* edited by A.H. Esser. New York: Plenum Pub. Corp., 1971.

Linton, Ralph. "The Tanala of Madagascar." In *The Individual and His Society,* edited by Abram Kardinar. New York: Columbia University Press, 1939.

Lipman, Aron. "The Architectural Belief System and Social Behavior." *British Journal of Sociology* 20 (1969): 190-204.

Little, Kenneth B. "Cultural Variations in Social Schemata." *Journal of Personality and Social Psychology* 10 (1968): 1-7.

Lounsbury, Floyd G. "A Semantic Analysis of the Pawnee Kinship Usage." *Language* 32 (1956): 158-94.

Lyman, Stanford, and Scott, Marvin. "Territoriality: A Neglected Sociological Dimension." In *A Sociology of the Absurd,* by S. Lyman and M. Scott. New York: Appleton-Century-Crofts, 1970.

Lynch, Kevin. *The Image of the City.* Cambridge, Mass.: MIT Press, 1960.

MacCannel, Dean. "Staged Authenticity: Arrangements of Social Space in Tourist Settings." *American Journal of Sociology* 79 (1973): 589-603.

McCarthy, F.D., and McArthur, M. "The Food Quest and the Time Factor in Aboriginal Economic Life." In *Anthropology and Nutrition,* Records of the American-Australian scientific expedition to Arnhem Land, vol. 2, edited by C.P. Mountford. Melbourne, Australia: Melbourne University Press, 1960.

McCarthy, J. "The '38 Hurricane." *American Heritage* 20 (1969).

McCarthy, Todd, and Flynn, Charles. *King of the B's: Working within the Hollywood System.* New York: E.P. Dutton, 1974.

McClelland, David C. *The Achieving Society.* Princeton, N.J.: D. Van Nostrand Co., 1961.

McKenzie, Roderick D. "The Ecological Approach to the Study of the Human Community." In *Roderick D. McKenzie: On Human Ecology,* edited by A.H. Hawley. Chicago: University of Chicago Press, 1968.

MacNeish, S. "Mesoamerican Archaeology." In *Biennial Review of Anthropology,* edited by B. Siegel and A.R. Beals. Stanford, Calif.: Stanford University Press, 1967.

Malthus, Thomas R. *An Essay on the Principle of Population.* Harmondsworth, Middlesex, England: Penguin, 1970.

Man-Environment Reference 1: *Environmental Abstracts.* Ann Arbor: Architectural Research Laboratory, University of Michigan, 1974.

Margulis, S.T., ed. *Privacy.* EDRA 5. Man-Environment Interactions: Evaluations and Applications, no. 6, 1974.

Marine, G. "I've Got Nothing Against the Colored, Understand." *Ramparts,* Nov. 1966.

Marshall, Lorna K. "The !Kung Bushmen of the Kalahari Desert." In *Peoples Of Africa,* edited by J. Gibbs. New York: Holt, Rinehart, and Winston, 1965.

Maslow, Abraham H., and Mintz, N.L. "Effects of Esthetic Surroundings: I. Initial Short-term Effects of Three Esthetic Conditions upon Perceiving 'Energy' and 'Well-being' in Faces." *Journal of Psychology* 14 (1956).

Mason, Otis. "Technogeography, or the Relation of the Earth to the Industries of Mankind." *American Anthropologist* 7 (1894): 137-61.

Mason, Otis. "Influence of Environment upon Human Industries or Arts." *Annual Report of the Smithsonian Institution,* 1895, pp. 639-65.

Maxwell, George. *In Malay Forests.* New York: D. Appleton, 1911.

Maxwell, Robert J. "Onstage and Offstage Sex: Exploring an Hypothesis." Cornell *Journal of Social Relations* 1 (1967) no. 2.

Maxwell, Robert J. "Samoan Temperament." Doctoral dissertation, Cornell University, 1969.

Maxwell, Robert J.; Bader, Jeanne; and Watson, Wilbur H. "Territory and Self in a Geriatric Setting." *Gerontologist* 12 (1972): 413-17.

May, Jacques M. "The Ecology of Human Disease." In *Studies in Human Ecology.* Washington, D.C.: Anthropological Society of Washington, 1957.

Mead, Margaret. *Sex and Temperament in Three Primitive Societies.* New York: William Morrow, 1935.

Mead, Margaret. "The Samoans." In *Cooperation and Competition among Primitive Peoples,* edited by Margaret Mead. Boston: Beacon Press, 1937.

Mead, Margaret. *Coming of Age in Samoa.* New York: Dell Pub. Co., 1968.

Meggers, Betty J. "Environment and Culture in the Amazon Basin: An Appraisal of the Theory of Environmental Determinism." In *Studies in Human Ecology.* Washington, D.C.: The Anthropological Society of Washington and the General Secretariat of the Organization of American States, 1957.

Mehrabian, Albert. *Nonverbal Communication.* Chicago: Atherton/Aldine, 1972.

Mencher, Joan P. "Kerala and Madras: A Comparative Study of Ecology and Social Structure." *Ethnology* 5 (1966): 135-71.

Metzger, Duane, and Williams, Gerald. "A Formal Ethnographic Analysis of Tenejapa Ladino Weddings." *American Anthropologist* 65 (1962): 1076-1101.

Metzger, Duane, and Williams, Gerald. "Procedures and Results in the Study of Native Cognitive Systems: Tzeltal Firewood." Unpublished manuscript, Anthropology Research Projects, Preliminary Reports, Stanford University, 1962.

Metzger, H.P. "Architects: Living with Their Mistakes." *San Francisco Sunday Examiner and Chronicle,* Dec. 28, 1975.

Meyer, David R. *Spatial Variation of Black Urban Households.* University of Chicago Department of Geography Research Paper no. 129, 1970.

Miller, D.R. *The Changing American Parent.* New York: John Wiley and Sons, 1958.

Miller, D.R. *Inner Conflict and Defense.* New York: Holt, Rinehart, and Winston, 1960.

Minturn, Leigh. "A Cross-cultural Linguistic Analysis of Freudian Symbols. *Ethnology* 4 (1965): 336-42.

Mitchell, William P. "The Hydraulic Hypothesis: A Reappraisal." *Current Anthropology* 14 (1973): 532-34.

Monge, Carlos M. "Man, Climate and Changes of Altitude." In *Man in Adaptation,* vol. 1, edited by Y. Cohen. Chicago: Aldine, 1968.

Monkhousen, J.J. *Principles of Physical Geography.* New York: American Elsevier, 1970.

Montagu, M.F. Ashley. *Touching: The Human Significance of the Skin.* New York: Perennial Library, 1972.

Montesquieu, Baron de. *The Spirit of Laws,* translated by T. Nugent. Cincinnati, 1873.

Moore, G.T. "Spatial Relations Ability and Developmental Levels of Urban Cognitive Mapping: A Research Note." *Man-Environment Studies* 5 (1975): 247-48.

Moos, Rudolf H., and Insel, Paul M. *Issues in Social Ecology: Human Milieus.* Palo Alto, Calif.: National Press Books, 1974.

Morgan, Lewis Henry. *Houses and House Life of the American Aborigines.* Chicago: University of Chicago Press, 1968.

Morrill, W.T. "Ethnoichthyology of the Cha-Cha." *Ethnology* 6 (1967): 405-16.

Mowat, Farley. *Never Cry Wolf.* Boston: Atlantic Monthly Press, Little, Brown, 1963.

Mumford, Lewis. "The Social Function of Open Spaces." *Landscape* 10 (1960-61): 1-6.

Mumford, Lewis. "The City in History." New York: Harcourt, Brace, 1961.

Murdock, George P. "Ethnographic Atlas." *Ethnology* 2 (1, 3, and 4), 1963.

Murphy, Robert F. "Social Distance and the Veil." *American Anthropologist* 66 (1964): 1257-74.

Nabokov, Vladimir. *The Annotated Lolita,* edited by A. Appel Jr. New York: McGraw-Hill, 1970.

Napier, John. "The Evolution of the Hand." In *Human Variations and Origins: An Introduction to Human Biology and Evolution.* San Francisco: W.H. Freeman and Co., 1962.

Nesbitt, Paul H.; Pond, A.W.; and Allen, W.H. *The Survival Book.* New York: Funk and Wagnalls, 1968.

Newman, Oscar. *Defensible Space.* New York: Macmillan, 1972.

Odend'hal, S. "Energetics of Indian Cattle in Their Environment." *Human Ecology* 1 (1972): 3-22.

O'Neale, L.M., and Dolores, J. "Notes on Papago Color Designations." *American Anthropologist* 45 (1943): 387-97.

Opler, Morris E. *An Apache Life-Way.* New York: Cooper Square Pub., 1965.

Osmond, Humphry. "Function as the Basis of Psychiatric Ward Design." *Mental Hospital* (April 1957): 23-29.

Osmond, Humphry. "The Relationship between Architect and Psychiatrist." In *Psychiatric Architecture,* edited by C. Goshen. Washington, D.C.: American Psychiatric Association, 1959. (a)

Osmond, Humphry. "The Historical and Sociological Development of Mental Hospitals." In *Psychiatric Architecture*, edited by C. Goshen. Washington, D.C.: American Psychiatric Association, 1959. (b)

Osmond, Humphry. "Some Psychiatric Aspects of Design." In *Who Designs America?* edited by L.B. Holland. New York: Doubleday-Anchor Press, 1966.

Osmond, Humphry. "Man and His Visual Environment." Lecture 2, Harvard University, July 18, 1967.

Pastalan, Leon A. "Bibliography on Ecological Approach to Housing Problems." Unpublished manuscript, Syracuse University, Aug. 1971.

Pastalan, Leon, and Carson, Daniel H., eds. *The Spatial Behavior of Older People.* Ann Arbor: University of Michigan Department of Gerontology, 1970.

Pearson, Ross N. *Physical Geography.* New York: Barnes and Noble, 1968.

Pelto, Pertti J. *The Snowmobile Revolution: Technology and Social Change in the Arctic.* Menlo Park, Calif.: Benjamin-Cummings Pub. Co., 1973.

Pelto, Pertti J., and Pelto, Gretel. *The Human Adventure.* New York: Macmillan, 1976.

Penfield, Wilder, and Rasmussen, T. *The Cerebral Cortex of Man.* New York: Macmillan, 1950.

Penniman, T.K. *A Hundred Years of Anthropology.* New York: International University Press, 1965.

Persky, H.; Smith, K.D.; and Basu, G.K. "Relation of Psychologic Measures of Aggression and Hostility to Testosterone Production in Man." *Psychosomatic Medicine* 33 (1971): 265-77.

Pitt-Rivers, Julian A. *The People of the Sierra.* Chicago: Phoenix, 1961.

Poggie, John J.; Pelto, Pertti J.; and Pelto, Gretel, eds. *The Evolution of Human Adaptations.* New York: Macmillan, 1976.

Pollnac, Richard B. "Intra-cultural Variability in the Structure of the Subjective Color Lexicon in Buganda." *American Ethnologist* 2 (1975): 89-110.

Porteous, A. *Forest Folklore.* London: Allen and Unwin, 1928.

Pospisil, Leopold. "A Formal Analysis of Substantive Law: Kapauku Papuan Laws of Land Tenure." Formal Semantic Analysis, *American Anthropologist* Special Publication 67 (1965) pt. 2: 186-214.

Powell, John W.; Rayner, J.; and Finesinger, J.E. "Responses to Disaster in American Cultural Groups." In *Symposium on Stress.* Washington, D.C.: Army Medical Service Graduate School, 1953.

Preiser, Wolfgang F.E. "Behavioral Design Criteria in Student Housing: The Measurement of Verbalized Response to Physical Environment." *Man-Environment Systems* (May 1969): 19.

Proshansky, Harold M.; Ittelson, William H.; and Rivlin, Leanne G., eds., *Environmental Psychology.* New York: Holt, Rinehart, and Winston, 1970.

Proshansky, Harold M.; Ittelson, William H.; and Rivlin, Leanne G. "Freedom of Choice and Behavior in a Physical Setting. In *Environment and the Social Sciences: Perspectives and Applications,* edited by J.F. Wohlwill and D.H. Carson, Washington, D.C.: American Psychological Association, 1972.

Randall, Mark E. Comment on "The Limited Nutritional Value of Cannibalism." *American Anthropologist* 73 (1971): 269.

Rapoport, Amos. *House Form and Culture.* Englewood Cliffs, N.J.: Prentice-Hall, 1969.

Rappaport, Roy A. *Pigs For the Ancestors.* New Haven: Yale University Press, 1968.

Rappaport, Roy A. "The Flow of Energy in an Agricultural Society." *Scientific American,* March 1971, pp. 116-32.

Reina, Ruben. "Milpas and Miperos: Implications for Prehistoric Times." *American Anthropologist* 69 (1967): 1-20.

Roach, Mary Ellen, and Eicher, Joanne B. *The Visible Self.* Englewood Cliffs, N.J.: Prentice-Hall, 1973.

Robbins, Michael C. "House Type and Settlement Patterns: An Application of Ethnology to Archaeological Interpretation." *Minnesota Archaeologist* 28 (1966): 2-26. (a)

Robbins, Michael C. "Material Culture and Cognition." *American Anthropologist* 68 (1966): 745-48. (b)

Robbins, W.W., et al. "Ethnobotany of the Tewa Indians." Bureau of American Ethnologists, Bulletin 55, 1916.

Roberts, John M., and Gregor, Thomas. "Privacy: A Cultural View." In *Privacy,* edited by J.R. Pennock and J.W. Chapman. New York: Atherton, 1971.

Roberts, John M.; Strand, Richard F.; and Burmeister, E. "Preferential Pattern Analysis." In *Explorations in Mathematical Anthropology,* edited by P. Kay. Cambridge, Mass.: MIT Press, 1971.

Robertson, Douglas. *Survive the Savage Sea.* New York: Bantam Books, 1973.

Robertson, L.S. "A Comment on Biosocial Theories of Aggression." *American Sociological Review* 41 (1976): 170-72.

Robinson, P. "Outer Space and Inner Space in Taos Pueblo." Paper presented at the annual meeting of the American Anthropological Association, New Orleans, Nov. 1969.

Roder, W. "Attitudes and Knowledge on the Topeka Flood Plain." University of Chicago Department of Geography Research Paper no. 70, 1961.

Rosengren, William R., and DeVault, Spencer. "The Sociology of Time and Space in an Obstetrical Hospital." In *Environmental Psychology*, edited by H.M. Proshansky, W.H. Ittelson, and L.G. Rivlin. New York: Holt, Rinehart, and Winston, 1970.

Ruesch, Jurgen, and Kees, Weldon. *Non-Verbal Communication: Notes on the Visual Perception of Human Relations*. Berkeley: University of California Press, 1972.

Sahlins, Marshall D., and Service, Elman R. *Evolution and Culture*. Ann Arbor: University of Michigan Press, 1960.

Sapir, Edward. "Language and Environment." *American Anthropologist* 14 (1912): 226-42.

Schaller, George B. *The Mountain Gorilla*. Chicago: University of Chicago Press, 1963.

Schaller, George B. "The Behavior of the Mountain Gorilla." In *Primate Behavior,* edited by I. DeVore. New York: Holt, Rinehart, and Winston, 1965.

Scheflin, Albert E. "Living Space in an Urban Ghetto." *Family Process* 10 (1971): 429-40.

Schmitt, R.C. "Implications of Density in Hong Kong." *Journal of the American Institute of Planners* 29 (1963): 210-17.

Schneider, David M. "Typhoons on Yap." *Human Organization* 16 (1957): 10-14.

Schneider, Jane. "Of Vigilance and Virgins: Honor, Shame, and Access to Resources in Mediterranean Societies." *Ethnology* 10 (1971): 1-24.

Scholander, P.F.; Hammel, H.T.; Hart, J.S.; LeMessurier, D.H.; and Steen, J. "Cold Adaptation in Australian Aborigines." *Journal of Applied Psychology* 13 (1958): 211-18.

School Environments Research Project. SER 1: Environmental Abstracts. Architectural Research Laboratory, University of Michigan, Ann Arbor, 1965.

Schorr, Alvin L. *Slums and Social Insecurity*. U.S. Department of Health, Education and Welfare, Social Security Administration, Research Report no. 1. Washington, D.C.: U.S. Government Printing Office, 1966.

Schwartz, Barry. "The Social Psychology of Privacy." *American Journal of Sociology* 73 (1968): 741-51.

*The Scottish Clans and Their Tartans*. 41st ed. Edinburgh: Johnston and Bacon, Ltd., 1968

"Seeding Hurricanes." *Science* 179 (Feb. 1973): 744.

Segall, Marshall H.; Campbell, Donald T.; and Herskovitz, Melville J. *The Influence of Culture on Visual Perception*. Indianapolis, Ind.: Bobbs-Merrill, 1966.

Selye, Hans. *The Physiology and Pathology of Exposure to Stress*. Montreal: Acta, 1950.

Shankman, Paul. "Le Roti et le Boulli: Levi-Strauss's Theory of Cannibalism." *American Anthropologist* 71 (1969): 54-69.

Sharp, Lauriston. "Steel Axes for Stone-age Australians." *Human Organization* 11 (1952): 17-22.

Shields, James, and Slater, Eliot. "Heredity and Psychological Abnormality." In *Handbook of Abnormal Psychology*, edited by H.J. Eysenck. New York: Basic Books, 1961.

Silverman, Philip. Review of B. Gunda-Debrecen, "Die Raumaufteilung der ungarischen Bauernstube, ihre gesellschaftlich Funktion und kultische Bedeutung." *Deutsches Jahrbuch für Volkskunde,* Band 8, Jahrgang 1963, Teil, II. Manuscript.

Simmel, Georg. *The Sociology of Georg Simmel,* translated by Kurt H. Wolfe. New York: Free Press, 1964.

Sims, John H., and Baumann, Duane D. "The Tornado Threat: Coping Styles of the North and South." *Science* 176 (June 1972): 1386-92.

Slobodkin, Lawrence B. *Growth and Regulation of Animal Populations.* New York: Holt, Rinehart, and Winston, 1961.

Smith, Hobart M. *Handbook of Lizards.* Ithaca, N.Y.: Comstock Pub. Ass., 1946.

Smith, Robert J. "The Japanese House." Unpublished manuscript, Cornell University Press, Ithaca, N.Y., 1963.

Sobin, S. "Experimental Creation of Cardiac Defects." Congenital Heart Disease, 14th M and R Report of the Pediatric Research Conference, Ohio, 1954.

Sommer, Robert. "Classroom Ecology." *Journal of Applied Behavioral Science* (Oct. 1967): 489-503.

Sommer, Robert. "Intimacy Ratings in Five Countries." *International Journal of Psychology* 3 (1968): 109-14.

Sommer, Robert. *Personal Space: The Behavioral Basis of Design.* Englewood Cliffs, N.J.: Prentice-Hall, 1969.

Sommer, Robert. *Tight Spaces: Hard Architecture and How to Humanize It.* Englewood Cliffs, N.J.: Prentice-Hall, 1974.

Sopher, David E. *Geography of Religions.* Englewood Cliffs, N.J.: Prentice-Hall, 1968.

Southwick, Charles H. "The Population Dynamics of Confined House Mice Supplied with Unlimited Food." *Ecology* 36 (1955): 212-25. (a)

Southwick, Charles H. "Regulatory Mechanisms of House Mice Populations: Social Behavior Affecting Litter Survival." *Ecology* 36 (1955): 627-34. (b)

Southwick, Charles H. *Proceedings of the Zoological Society of London,* 131 (1958): 163-75.

Spencer, Herbert. *Principles of Sociology.* New York: D. Appleton, 1896.

Spivak, Murray. "Some Psychological Implications of Mental Health Center Architecture." Paper presented at the sixth annual meeting of the New England Psychological Association, Boston, Mass., Nov. 1966.

Spivak, Murray. "Sensory Distortion in Tunnels and Corridors." *Hospital and Community Psychiatry* 18 (1967).

Spoehr, Alexander, ed. *Pacific Port Towns and Cities.* Honolulu: Bishop Museum Press, 1963.

Squire, Geoffrey. *Dress and Society.* New York: Viking Press, 1974.

Steinzor, B. "The Spatial Factor in Face-to-Face Discussion Groups." *Journal of Abnormal and Social Psychology* 45 (1950): 552-55.

Steward, Julian H. *The Theory of Culture Change: The Methodology of Multilinear Evolution.* Urbana: University of Illinois Press, 1955.

Steward, Julian H. *Alfred Kroeber.* New York: Columbia University Press, 1973.

Steward, Julian H., and Faron, Leslie C. *Native Peoples of South America.* New York: McGraw-Hill, 1959.

Stott, D.H. "Cultural and Natural Checks on Population Growth." In *Culture and the Evolution of Man,* edited by M.F. Ashley Montagu. New York: Oxford University Press, 1962.

Stricker, R.L., and Emlen, J.T. "Regulatory Mechanisms in House-Mouse Populations: The Effect of Limited Food Supply on a Confined Population." *Ecology* 34 (1953): 375-85.

Studer, Raymond G. "On Environmental Programming." *Architectural Association Journal* 81 (1966): 290-96. (a)

Studer, Raymond G. "Behavior-Contingent Architecture: Some Implications for Experimental Communities." Paper presented at the conference on the Experimental Community, Racine, Wis., 1966. (b)

Studer, Raymond G. "The Dynamics of Behavior-contingent Physical Systems." Paper presented at the Portsmouth College of Technology symposium on Design Methods, Portsmouth, England, 1967. Published in *Design Methods in Architecture,* edited by G. Broadbent and A. Ward. London: Lund Humphries, 1969.

Studer, Raymond G. *Some Aspects of the Man-designed Environment Interface.* Student publication of the School of Design, North Carolina State University, 1969, pp. 77-98.

Studer, Raymond G. "The Organization of Spatial Stimuli." In *Spatial Behavior of Older People,* edited by L. Pastalan and D. Carson. Ann Arbor: University of Michigan Press, 1970.

Studer, Raymond G. "Comment" on Session V: Communal Behavior and the Environment. In *Behavior and Environment: The Use of Space by Animals and Men,* edited by A.H. Esser. New York: Plenum Pub. Corp., 1971.

Studer, Raymond G., and Stea, D. "Environmental Programming and Human Behavior." *Journal of Social Issues* 22 (1966): 127-36.

Sturtevant, William C. "Studies in Ethnoscience: Transcultural Studies in Cognition." *American Anthropologist,* Special Publication 66, 1964, pt. 2, pp. 99-313.

Sweet, Louise E. "Camel Raiding of North Arabian Bedouin: A Mechanism of Ecological Adaptation." In *Death and Diversity.* Peoples and Cultures of the Middle East, vol. 1, edited by L.E. Sweet. Garden City, N.Y.: Natural History Press, 1970.

Theodorson, George A., ed. *Studies in Human Ecology.* New York: Harper and Row, 1961.

Thomas, Franklin. *The Environmental Basis of Society.* New York: Century, 1925.

Thompson, Gladys. *Patterns for Guernseys, Jerseys, and Arans.* New York: Dover, 1969.

Thompson, W.R., Jr. "Influence of Prenatal Maternal Anxiety on Emotionality in Young Rats." *Science* 125 (1957): 698-99.

Thompson, W.R., Jr., and Sontag, L.W. "Behavioral Effects in the Offspring of Rats subjected to Audiogenic Seizure during the Gestational Period." *Journal of Comparative Physiology and Psychology* 49 (1956): 454-56.

Tolman, Edward C. "A Stimulus-expectancy Need-Cathexis Psychology." *Science* 101 (1945): 160-66.

Tromp, Solco W. *Medical Biometeorology: Weather, Climate, and the Living Organism.* New York: Elsevier, 1963.

Turk, Amos; Johnston, James W. Jr.; and Moulton, D.G., eds. *Human Responses to Environmental Odors.* New York: Academic Press, 1974.

Valins, S., and Baum, A. "Residential Group Size, Social Interaction, and Crowding." *Environment and Behavior* 5 (1973): 421-39.

Van der Ryn, Sim. "Berkeley—How Do Students Really Live?" *Architectural Forum,* July-Aug. 1967, pp. 90-97.

Van der Ryn, S., and Silverstein, M. *Dorms at Berkeley: An Environmental Analysis.* Berkeley: Center for Planning and Developmental Research, 1967.

Van Lawick-Goodall, Jane. "Chimpanzees on the Gombe Stream Reserve." In *Primate Behavior,* edited by I. DeVore. New York: Holt, Rinehart, and Winston, 1965.

Van Lawick-Goodall, Jane. *In the Shadow of Man.* New York: Houghton-Mifflin, 1971.

Vayda, Andrew, ed. *Environment and Cultural Behavior.* Garden City, N.Y.: Natural History Press, 1969.

Vayda, Andrew, and Rappaport, Roy. "Ecology: Cultural and Non-Cultural." In *Introduction to Cultural Anthropology,* edited by J.A. Clifton. Boston: Houghton-Mifflin, 1968.

Vermeer, D.E. "Geophagy among the Ewe of Ghana." *Ethnology* 10 (1971): 56-72.

Vielhauer, Joyce. "The Development of a Semantic Scale for the Description of the Physical Environment." Doctoral dissertation, Louisiana State University, 1965.

Vineberg, Shalom E., and Levine, A.J. "The Network of Perceptions and Judgments Regarding Staff Roles." Paper presented at the American Psychological Association symposium "Ecological Research in Complex Organizations: The Rehabilitation Center as a Paradigm Case." Washington, D.C., Sept., 1969.

Von Uxküll, J. "A Stroll through the World of Animals and Men." In *Instinctive Behavior: The Development of a Modern Concept,* edited by C.H. Schiller. New York: International Universities Press, 1957.

Vriend, J.J. "Netherlands." In *Encyclopedia of Modern Architecture,* edited by G. Hatje. London: Thames and Hudson, 1963.

Wagner, Philip. *The Human Use of the Earth.* New York: Free Press, 1960.

Walens, Stanley, and Wagner, Roy. "Pigs, Proteins, and People-Eaters." *American Anthropologist* 73 (1971): 269-70.

Wallace, Anthony F.C. *Tornado in Worcester.* Publication 392. Washington, D.C.: National Academy of Sciences—National Research Council, 1956.

Wallace, Anthony F.C., and Atkins, J. "The Meaning of Kinship Terms." *American Anthropologist* 62 (1960): 58-80.

Ward, J.S.; Bredell, G.A.C.; and Wenzel, H.G. "Responses of Bushmen and Europeans on Exposure to Winter Night Temperatures in the Kalahari." *Journal of Applied Psychology* 15 (1960): 667-70.

Washburn, Sherwood L. "Speculations on the Interrelations of the History of Tools and Biological Evolution." In *The Evolution of Man's Capacity for Culture,* edited by J.N. Spuhler. Detroit: Wayne State University Press, 1959.

Watanabe, Masao. "The Conception of Nature in Japanese Culture." *Science,* Jan. 25, 1974.

Watson, L. *Supernature.* New York: Bantam Books, 1973.

Watson, O. Michael. "Proxemic Behavior: A Cross-cultural Study." Doctoral dissertation, University of Colorado, 1968. (a)

Watson, O. Michael. "Proxemics and Proxetics." Paper presented at the 67th annual meeting of the American Anthropological Association, Seattle, Wash., Nov. 1968. (b)

Watson, O. Michael. "On Proxemic Research." *Current Anthropology* 10 (1969): 221-24.

Watson, O. Michael, and Graves, Theodore D. "Quantitative Research in Proxemic Behavior." *American Anthropologist* 68 (1966): 971-85.

Watzlawick, Paul; Deavin, J.H.; and Jackson, Don D. *Pragmatics of Human Communication: A Study of Interactional Patterns, Pathologies, and Paradoxes.* New York: W.W. Norton, 1967.

Weeks, J. "Indeterminate Architecture." *Transactions of the Bartlett Society* 2 (1963-64): 83-106.

Wenger, M.A.; Jones, F.N.; and Jones, M.H. *Physiological Psychology.* New York: Holt, 1956.

White, Leslie A. *The Science of Culture.* New York: Grove Press, 1949.

White, Leslie A. *The Evolution of Culture.* New York: McGraw-Hill, 1959.

Whiting, John W.M. "Effect of Climate on Certain Cultural Practices." In *Explorations in Cultural Anthropology,* edited by W.H. Goodenough. New York: McGraw-Hill, 1964.

Wicker, Allan W. "Processes Which Mediate Behavior-Environment Congruence." In *Issues in Social Ecology: Human Milieus,* edited by R.H. Moos and P.M. Insel. Palo Alto, Calif.: National Press Books, 1974.

Willems, Edwin P., and Vineberg, Shalom. "Direct Observation of Patients: The Interface of Environment and Behavior." Paper presented at the American Psychological Association symposium "Ecological Research in Complex Organizations: The Rehabilitation Center as a Paradigm Case," Washington, D.C., Sept. 2, 1960.

Williams, J.L. "Personal Space and Its Relation to Extraversion-Introversion." Master's thesis, University of Alberta, 1963.

Willis, F.N., Jr. "Initial Speaking Distance as a Function of the Speakers' Relationship." *Psychonomic Science* 5 (1966): 221-22.

Wissler, Clark. *The American Indian.* New York: McMurtrie, 1917. Reprint. Garden City, N.Y.: Doubleday, 1967.

Wissler, Clark. *The Relation of Nature to Man in Aboriginal America.* New York: Oxford University Press, 1926.

Wittfogel, Karl. "The Theory of Oriental Society." In *Readings in Anthropology,* vol. 2, edited by M.H. Fried. New York: Crowell, 1959.

Wright, Lawrence. *Clean and Decent.* New York: Viking Press, 1960.

Wyndham, C.H., and Morrison, J.F. "Adjustment to Cold of Bushmen in the Kalahari Desert." *Journal of Applied Physiology* 13 (1956): 219-25.

Wynne-Edwards, V.C. *Animal Dispersion in Relation to Social Behavior.* New York: Hafner Press, 1962.

Yancey, William L. "Architecture, Interaction, and Social Control: The Case of a Large-Scale Housing Project." *Environment and Behavior* 3 (1971): 3-22.

Yoshimura, H., and Iida, T. "Studies on the Reactivity of Skin Vessels to Extreme Cold." *Japanese Journal of Physiology* 1 (1950-51): 177-85.

Zeisel, John. "Designing Schools to Minimize Damage from Vandalism and Rough Play." *Schoolhouse* 15, Educational Facilities Laboratories, 1974.

Zeisel, John. *Sociology and Architectural Design.* New York: Russell Sage Foundation, 1975.

Zeuner, F. *A History of Domestic Animals.* London: Hutchinson, 1963.

Zinsser, Hans. *Rats, Lice and History.* New York: Bantam Books, 1971.

Zorbaugh, Harvey. *The Gold Coast and the Slum.* Chicago: University of Chicago Press, 1929.

# Index